TESTIMONY

the text of this book is printed
on 100% recycled paper

At Shostakovich's Moscow apartment: (from the left) the composer's wife Irina, his favorite student, Boris Tishchenko, Dmitri Shostakovich, Solomon Volkov. On the wall, a portrait of Shostakovich as a boy by Boris Kustodiev. The inscription on the photograph reads: "To dear Solomon Moiseyevich Volkov in fond remembrance. D. Shostakovich. 13 XI 1974. A reminder of our conversations about Glazunov, Zoshchenko, Meyerhold. D.S."

TESTIMONY

The Memoirs of
Dmitri Shostakovich

as related to and edited by

Solomon Volkov

Translated from the Russian by Antonina W. Bouis

HARPER COLOPHON BOOKS
HARPER & ROW, PUBLISHERS
NEW YORK, CAMBRIDGE, HAGERSTOWN, PHILADELPHIA, SAN FRANCISCO
LONDON, MEXICO CITY, SÃO PAULO, SYDNEY

All photographs except where otherwise credited are from the personal collection of Solomon Volkov.

A hardcover edition of this book is published by Harper & Row, Publishers.

First HARPER COLOPHON edition published 1980.

ISBN: 0-06-090812-2

80 81 82 83 84 10 9 8 7 6 5 4 3 2 1

Contents

Preface   xi

Introduction   xix

TESTIMONY   3

Major Compositions, Titles, and Awards   277

Index   283

Illustrations

Frontispiece: Irina Shostakovich, Boris Tishchenko, Dmitri
Shostakovich, and Solomon Volkov

Following page 86:

Shostakovich and fellow students at Leningrad Conser-
vatory
The young Shostakovich
Leningrad Conservatory
Alexander Glazunov, composer and longtime director of
the Conservatory
Shostakovich with the great director Meyerhold
With Meyerhold, Mayakovsky, and Rodchenko, 1929
Shostakovich's patron, Marshal Tukhachevsky, and his
wife, Nina
Nikolai Akimov, director of a scandalous production of
Hamlet
Mikhail Zoshchenko, the influential satirical writer
Nina Varzar, Shostakovich's first wife
With musicologist Ivan Sollertinsky, his closest friend
Boris Asafiev, the great Soviet musicologist
Stalin and Zhdanov at the bier of Sergei Kirov
Time cover portraying Shostakovich in a fire fighter's

helmet during World War II

With his favorite student, Veniamin Fleishman

Prokofiev, Shostakovich, and Khachaturian

Playing for bomber pilots during World War II

Khrennikov assailing Shostakovich at the first Composers' Congress, 1948

The Congress in the session that condemned many leading composers

Following page 182:

In New York, 1949, to attend the Cultural and Scientific Congress for World Peace

Shostakovich with his wife, Nina, in a box at Leningrad Philharmonic

With his mother, Sofiya Vasilyevna, 1951

In the dressing room of his son, conductor Maxim Shostakovich

Paul Robeson and actor Solomon Mikhoels in Moscow

Title page of Yiddish song collection edited by Shostakovich, 1970

Accompanying a performance of his cycle, *From Jewish Folk Poetry*

The composer at work

With his third wife, Irina

With the composer Muradeli, listening to folk musicians in the Kirghiz Republic, 1963

The New York Philharmonic, under Leonard Bernstein, on its first visit to Moscow, 1959

Receiving a certificate from Aaron Copland in Moscow, 1960

With Solomon Volkov, 1965

Score of the Thirteenth Symphony inscribed to Volkov, 1972

With conductor Gennady Rozhdestvensky and Volkov, 1975

At a performance of his last quartet, 1974

With his young grandson

Reading one of his many official speeches

The funeral of Shostakovich, August 14, 1975

Preface

My personal acquaintance with Shostakovich began in 1960, when I was the first to review the premiere of his Eighth Quartet in a Leningrad newspaper. Shostakovich was then fifty-four. I was sixteen. I was his fanatic admirer.

It is impossible to study music in Russia and not come across the name Shostakovich in childhood. I remember when, in 1955, my parents returned in great excitement from a chamber concert: Shostakovich and several singers had performed his "Jewish Cycle" for the first time. In a country that had just been lashed by a vicious wave of anti-Semitism, a prominent composer had dared publicly to present a work that spoke of the Jews with pity and compassion. This was both a musical and a public event.

That was how I came to know the name. My acquaintance with the music came several years later. In September 1958, Yevgeny Mravinsky conducted Shostakovich's Eleventh Symphony at the Leningrad Philharmonic. The symphony (written after the 1956 Hungarian uprising) is about the people, and rulers, and their juxtaposition; the second movement harshly depicts the execution of defenseless people with naturalistic authenticity. The poetics of shock. For the first time in my life, I left a concert thinking about others instead of myself. To this day, this is the main strength of Shostakovich's music for me.

I threw myself into studying all scores of Shostakovich that I could get. In the library, furtively, the piano reduction of the opera *Lady Macbeth of Mtsensk District* was taken out from under stacks of books. Special permission was required before I could get the music of the First Piano Sonata. The early, "left" Shostakovich was still officially banned. He was still defamed in music history classes and in textbooks. Young musicians met secretly, in small groups, to study his music.

Every premiere precipitated a struggle—hidden or overt—in the press, in musical circles, in the corridors of power. Shostakovich would rise and make his awkward way to the stage to respond to the loud calls from the audience. My idol would walk past me, his small head with its cowlick held carefully in balance. He looked very helpless, a misleading impression, as I later learned. I burned to help him in any way I could.

The opportunity to speak out came after the first performance of the Eighth Quartet, an extraordinary work and in a sense his musical autobiography. In October 1960, the newspaper printed my ecstatic review. Shostakovich read it—he always read the articles about his premieres closely. I was introduced to him. He said a few polite phrases and I was in heaven. Over the next few years I wrote several other articles about his music. They were all published and they all played their part, great or small, in the contemporary musical process.

I came to know Shostakovich during the years when he was perhaps most dissatisfied with himself. One could get the impression that he was trying to distance himself from his own music. The inner—not the external—tragedy of his situation became clear to me when, in the spring of 1965, I helped to organize a festival of Shostakovich's music. It was the first festival of its kind in Leningrad, the composer's native city; symphonies, choruses, and many chamber works were performed. I spoke with Shostakovich about festival-related activities in his rather elaborate hotel room. He was obviously nervous and avoided questions about his latest works. With a wry grin, he said he was writing the film score for a biography of Karl Marx. Then he stopped talking, and drummed his fingers feverishly on a table.

The only concert of the festival that Shostakovich was willing to approve was the evening devoted to his students' works. He strongly implied that I should agree with him about its importance. It was impossible not to obey. I began studying the music of his students, burrowing deeply into the manuscripts. One of them in particular caught my eye: Veniamin Fleishman's opera, *Rothschild's Violin*.

Fleishman had entered Shostakovich's class before the Second World War. When the front moved up to Leningrad itself, he joined the Volunteer Brigade. These were condemned men and almost none returned. Fleishman left behind no grave and no compositions except for *Rothschild's Violin*.

The story of this opera, based on a Chekhov story, is full of tantalizing loose ends. It is known that Fleishman, at Shostakovich's suggestion, had begun composing an opera of that name. Before he left for the front, he allegedly finished the reduction. But the only thing available to researchers is the score, written from beginning to end in Shostakovich's characteristic nervous handwriting. Shostakovich maintained that he had merely orchestrated the work of his late student. The opera is a marvel, pure and subtle. Chekhov's bittersweet lyricism is presented in a style that could be described thus: mature Shostakovich. I decided that *Rothschild's Violin* had to be staged.

I could not have done it without Shostakovich, of course; he helped in every possible way. He could not come to Leningrad in April 1968 for the premiere; his son, Maxim, the conductor, came in his stead. It was a stormy and rousing success with glorious reviews. A marvelous opera was born onstage, and with it a new opera theater—the Experimental Studio of Chamber Opera. I was the artistic director of the Studio, the first such group in the Soviet Union. A week before the premiere I had turned twenty-four.

Then the official administrators of culture accused all of us of Zionism: poor Chekhov, poor Fleishman. Their resolution read: "The staging of the opera pours water on the enemy's mill"—and it meant an irreversible closing of the production. This was a defeat for Shostakovich as well as for me. He wrote me in despair: "Let's hope that Fleishman's *Violin* will eventually get its due recognition." But the opera was never staged again.

For Shostakovich *Rothschild's Violin* represented unhealed guilt, pity, pride, and anger: neither Fleishman nor his work was to be resurrected. The defeat brought us closer together. When I began work on a book on young Leningrad composers, I wrote to Shostakovich with a request for a preface. He replied at once, "I'll be happy to meet with you," and suggested a time and place. A leading music publisher agreed to do the book.

According to my plan, Shostakovich would write about the ties between the young Leningraders and the Petersburg school of composition. At our meeting I began talking to him about his own youth, and at first met with some resistance. He preferred to talk about his students. I had to resort to trickery: at every convenient point I drew parallels, awakening associations, reminding him of people and events.

Shostakovich met me more than halfway. What he finally told me about the old conservatory days was extraordinary. Everything that I had read and heard previously was like a watercolor faded beyond recognition. Shostakovich's stories were quick, incisive pencil sketches—sharp, clear, and pointed.

Figures familiar to me from textbooks lost their sentimental halos in his tales. I grew very enthusiastic and so, without realizing it, did Shostakovich. I had not expected to hear anything like this. After all, in the Soviet Union the rarest and most valuable thing is memory. It had been trampled down for decades; people knew better than to keep diaries or hold on to letters. When the "great terror" began in the 1930s, frightened citizens destroyed their personal archives, and with them their memory. What was henceforth to be thought of as memory was defined by each day's newspaper. History was being rewritten with dizzying speed.

A man without a memory is a corpse. So many had passed before me, these living corpses, who remembered only officially sanctioned events—and only in the officially sanctioned way.

I used to think that Shostakovich expressed himself frankly only in his music. We had all come across articles in the official press with his name at the bottom.* No musician took these high-flown, empty declarations seriously. People from a more intimate circle could even tell which "literary adviser" of the Composers' Union had stitched together which article. An enormous paper mountain had been erected which almost buried Shostakovich the man. The official mask sat tight on his face.

That's why I was so stunned when his face peered out from behind the mask. Cautiously. Suspiciously. Shostakovich had a characteristic way of speaking—in short sentences, very simply, often repetitiously. But these were living words, living scenes. It was clear that the composer no longer consoled himself with the thought that music could express everything and did not require verbal commentary. His works now spoke with mounting power of only one thing: impending death. In the late 1960s, Shostakovich's articles in the official press were preventing the audience he most cared about from truly listening to his music when it was played. When that final door was to close behind him, would anybody even hear it?

My book on the young Leningrad composers was published in 1971 and was sold out immediately. (Until I left the Soviet Union in 1976, it was used throughout the country in the teaching of contemporary Soviet music.) Shostakovich's preface had been cut severely, and it dealt only with the present—there were no reminiscences.

This was the final powerful impetus for him to give the world his version of the events that had unfolded around him in the course of half a century. We decided to work on his recollections of these events. "I must do this, I must," he would say. He wrote me, in one letter: "You must continue what has been begun." We met and talked more and more frequently.

Why did he choose me? First, I was young, and it was before youth, more than anyone else, that Shostakovich wanted to justify himself. I was devoted to his music and to him, I didn't tell tales, I didn't boast about his kindness to me. Shostakovich liked my work and he liked my

*In many instances Shostakovich had not even been asked to sign, since such a formality was considered unnecessary. After all, how could anyone possibly doubt that Shostakovich, like every other Soviet citizen, adulated the leader and teacher? Thus there appeared exalted praise for the "wonderful works of Comrade Stalin" in *Literaturnaya gazeta* (September 30, 1950) over the signature of D. Shostakovich. He had never even read the passionate panegyric.

book on the young Leningraders; he wrote me about it several times.

His desire to remember, which would arise impulsively, had to be nurtured constantly. When I spoke with him about his dead friends, he was amazed to hear me talk about people and events he had forgotten. "This is the most intelligent man of the new generation" was his final evaluation of me. I repeat these words here not out of vanity, but because I want to explain how this complex man came to a difficult decision. For many years it had seemed to him that the past had disappeared forever. He had to grow accustomed to the idea that an unofficial record of events did still exist. "Do you not think that history is really a whore?" he once asked me. The question reeked of a hopelessness that I could not comprehend; I was convinced of the opposite. And this, too, was important to Shostakovich.

This is how we worked. We sat down at a table in his study, and he offered me a drink (which I always refused). Then I began asking questions, which he answered briefly and, at first, reluctantly. Sometimes I had to keep repeating the same question in different forms. Shostakovich needed time to warm up.

Gradually his pale face would turn pink and he would grow excited. I would go on with the questioning, taking notes in the shorthand that I had developed during my years as a journalist. (We discarded the idea of taping for a variety of reasons, chief among them the fact that Shostakovich would stiffen before a microphone like a rabbit caught in a snake's gaze. It was a reflex reaction to his obligatory official radio speeches.)

I found a successful formula to help Shostakovich speak more freely than he was accustomed to, even with close friends: "Don't reminisce about yourself; talk about others." Of course, Shostakovich reminisced about himself, but he reached himself by talking about others, finding the reflection of himself in them. This "mirrored style" is typical of Petersburg, a city on water, shimmering, spectral. It was also a favorite device of Anna Akhmatova. Shostakovich revered Akhmatova. Her portrait, a gift from me, hung in his apartment.

At first we met in Shostakovich's cottage near Leningrad, where the Composers' Union had a resort. Shostakovich went there to rest. It was not very convenient and dragged out our work, making each resumption difficult emotionally. The work went smoothly once I moved to Moscow in 1972, taking a position with *Sovetskaya muzyka,* the country's leading musical journal.

I became a senior editor of *Sovetskaya muzyka.* The main objective of my move had been to be closer to Shostakovich, who lived in the building that housed the journal's offices. And even though Shostakovich was frequently out of town, we could meet more often.* Work would begin with a phone call from him—usually early in the morning, when the office was still empty—his jangling, hoarse tenor voice asking, "Are you free now? Could you come up here?" And the exhausting hours of cautious exploration would begin.

Shostakovich's manner of responding to questions was highly stylized. Some phrases had apparently been polished over many years. He was obviously imitating his literary idol and friend, the writer Mikhail Zoshchenko, a master of precisely refined ironic narrative (translations cannot transmit the fine, beadwork subtlety of his writing). Phrases from Gogol, Dostoevsky, Bulgakov, and Ilf and Petrov found their way into his conversation. Ironic sentences were spoken without a trace of a smile. Conversely, when an agitated Shostakovich began a deeply felt discussion, a nervous smile twitched across his face.

He often contradicted himself. Then the true meaning of his words had to be guessed, extracted from a box with three false bottoms. My persistence waged battle with his crankiness. I would leave, wrung out. The mound of shorthand notes was growing. I read them over and over, trying to construct from the penciled scribbles the multifigured composition that I knew was there.

I divided up the collected material into sustained sections, combined as seemed appropriate; then I showed these sections to Shostakovich, who approved my work. What had been created in these pages clearly had a profound effect on him. Gradually, I shaped this great array of reminiscence into arbitrary parts and had them typed. Shostakovich read and signed each part.

It was clear to both of us that this final text could not be published

---

*In addition to our main work, I also helped him with many less essential but burdensome affairs. Shostakovich was a member of the editorial board of *Sovetskaya muzyka* and he was expected to give written evaluations of materials submitted for publication. He was often asked for his support when there was a conflict over a musical problem. In such cases I functioned as his assistant, preparing evaluations, replies, and letters at his request. Thus I became something of an intermediary between Shostakovich and the journal's editor in chief.

in the U.S.S.R.; several attempts I made in that direction ended in failure. I took measures to get the manuscript to the West. Shostakovich consented. His only insistent desire was that the book be published posthumously. "After my death, after my death," he said often. Shostakovich was not prepared to undergo new ordeals; he was too weak, too worn out by his illness.

In November 1974, Shostakovich invited me to his home. We talked for a while and then he asked me where the manuscript was. "In the West," I replied. "Our agreement is in force." Shostakovich said, "Good." I told him I would prepare a statement to the effect that his memoirs would appear in print only after his death (and subsequently I sent him this letter of agreement). At the end of our conversation, he said he wanted to inscribe a photograph for me. He wrote: "To dear Solomon Moiseyevich Volkov, in fond remembrance. D. Shostakovich. 13 XI 1974." Then, just as I was about to leave, he said, "Wait. Give me the photo." And he added: "A reminder of our conversations about Glazunov, Zoshchenko, Meyerhold. D.S." And he said, "This will help you."

Soon thereafter, I applied to the Soviet authorities for permission to leave for the West. In August 1975 Shostakovich died. In June 1976 I came to New York, determined to have this book published. My thanks go to the courageous people (some of whose names I do not even know) who helped bring the manuscript here safely and intact. I have been supported since my arrival by the Russian Institute at Columbia University, where I became a Research Associate in 1976; contact with my colleagues there has been both beneficial and rewarding. Ann Harris and Erwin Glikes of Harper & Row were immediately responsive to the manuscript, and I am grateful to them for their advice and attentiveness. Harry Torczyner, my attorney, gave me invaluable help.

And finally, I thank you, my distant friend who must remain nameless—without your constant involvement and encouragement, this book would not exist.

Solomon Volkov

New York, June 1979

Introduction

BY SOLOMON VOLKOV

T HE figure who lay in the open coffin had a smile on his face. Many times I had seen him laughing; sometimes he roared with laughter. Often he had snickered or chuckled sarcastically. But I couldn't remember a smile like this: aloof and peaceful. Quiet, blissful, as though he had returned to childhood. As though he had escaped.

He liked to tell a story about one of his literary idols, Nikolai Gogol: how he had apparently escaped from his grave. When the grave was dug up (in Leningrad in the 1930s) Gogol's coffin was empty. Later, of course, the incident was clarified; Gogol's body was found and returned to its assigned place. But the idea itself—hiding after death—was greatly enticing.

He had escaped and could not be affected by the official obituary printed in all the Soviet newspapers after his death on August 9, 1975: "In his sixty-ninth year, the great composer of our times passed away—Dmitri Dmitrievich Shostakovich, Deputy of the Supreme Soviet of the U.S.S.R., laureate of the Lenin and State prizes of the U.S.S.R. A faithful son of the Communist Party, an eminent public and state figure, citizen artist D. D. Shostakovich devoted his entire life to the development of Soviet music, reaffirming the ideals of socialist humanism and internationalism. . . ."

And so on and so forth, in cast-iron bureaucratese. The first signature under the obituary was that of the Soviet leader Leonid Brezhnev, and then followed, in alphabetical order, the chief of the secret police, the defense minister . . . (The long list of signatures is ended by a truly minor figure: Vladimir Yagodkin, the Moscow propaganda chief, who will be remembered only because he set bulldozers on an outdoor exhibit of dissident art in September 1974.)

At the official funeral, on August 14, the top administrators from the ideological departments crowded around Shostakovich's bier. Many of them had for years made a career of denouncing his sins. "The ravens have gathered," a close musician friend of Shostakovich said, turning his pale face to me.

Shostakovich had known all this ahead of time; he had even written music to a poem that described the "honored" funeral of a Russian genius of another era, Alexander Pushkin: "So much honor that there is no room for his closest friends . . . To the right and the left, huge hands at their sides, the chests and crude faces of the gendarmes . . ."

Now none of this mattered: one more grotesque scene, one more contradiction, could not worry him. Shostakovich had been born in the midst of contradictions, on September 25, 1906, in Petersburg, the capital of the Russian empire, which still reverberated from the revolutionary tremors of 1905. The city would have to change its name twice in a decade—in 1914 it became Petrograd and in 1924, Leningrad. The conflict between the rulers and the people never ceased here; it was just less visible from time to time.

Russian poets and writers had long created an evil image of Petersburg, a place of "doubles" and ruined lives. It was the grandiose project of a tyrant, Peter I, who forced its construction in a swamp at a cost of countless lives, the mad dream of a total autocrat. Dostoevsky, too, thought that "this rotten, slimy city would rise with the fog and disappear like smoke."

This Petersburg was the source, and the framework and the setting, of many of Shostakovich's works. It was the site of the premieres of seven symphonies, two operas, three ballets, and most of his quartets. (They say that Shostakovich had wanted to be buried in Leningrad, but they buried him in Moscow.) In acknowledging Petersburg as his own, Shostakovich doomed himself to an enduring psychological duality.

Another contradiction—between his Polish ancestry and his constant striving to handle in his art, like Dostoevsky or Mussorgsky, the most vital problems of Russian history—came from his heredity. Heritage and history crossed paths. The composer's great-grandfather Pyotr Shostakovich, a young veterinarian, took part in the uprising of 1830, a desperate attempt to gain Polish independence from Russia. After the cruel repression of the uprising and the taking of Warsaw, he was sent with thousands of other rebels into exile in the Russian wilderness—first to Perm, then to Ekaterinburg.

Even though the family became Russified, the admixture of "foreign blood" undoubtedly made itself felt. And Shostakovich was reminded of it himself before his trip to Warsaw for the Chopin Competition in 1927, when the state authorities wondered whether "that Pole" should be permitted to go or not.

Shostakovich's grandfather Boleslav participated in the preparations for another Polish uprising—in 1863—which the Russian Army also routed. Boleslav Shostakovich had close ties to the revolutionary Land and Freedom organization, one of the most radical socialist groups. He was sent to Siberia. In those years in Russia the words "Polish" and "rebel" and "instigator" were almost synonymous.

The fashionable radicalism of the 1860s in Russia was markedly materialistic. Art was rejected as the pastime of the idle and a popular slogan of the times declared that "A pair of boots is worth more than Shakespeare." This attitude endured. The composer's father, Dmitri Boleslavovich Shostakovich, did not involve himself in politics; he worked with the famous chemist Dmitri Mendeleyev and lived a quiet life as a successful engineer in Petersburg. He married a pianist, Sofia Vasilyevna Kokoulina. Music was a serious interest of the family and they no longer scorned Mozart and Beethoven, but their underlying philosophy still held that art had to be useful.

Young Shostakovich—Mitya—was nine, relatively old, when he began piano lessons. His first instructor was his mother, who, when she saw his rapid progress, took him to a piano teacher. The following conversation was a favorite family story:

"I've brought you a marvelous pupil!"

"All mothers have marvelous children. . . ."

Within two years he played all the preludes and fugues in Bach's *Well-Tempered Clavier*. It was clear that he was exceptionally gifted.

He did well in general school subjects too. He always wanted to be best at whatever he did. When he began composing, almost simultaneously with his piano lessons, he worked at it seriously; among his earliest compositions is the piano piece "Funeral March in Memory of the Victims of the Revolution." This was an eleven-year-old's reaction to the revolution of February 1917, which overthrew Nicholas II. Vladimir Lenin, leader of the Bolshevik Party, had returned to Russia from abroad. At the Finland Station in Petrograd, he was greeted by crowds; we would have seen young Mitya among them.

That same year the October Revolution brought the Bolsheviks to power. Civil war broke out soon afterward. Petrograd, no longer the capital (Lenin had moved the government to Moscow), slowly emptied. Shostakovich's family remained loyal to the new regime and did not leave the city as did many of the intelligentsia. The country was in chaos. Money had virtually lost its value. Food was beyond price. Factories closed, transportation stopped. "In glorious poverty Petropol is dying," wrote the poet Osip Mandelstam.

In 1919, in the midst of this tumult, Shostakovich came to the Petrograd Conservatory, which still enjoyed its reputation as the best musical academy in the country. He was thirteen. The building had no heat. When classes were able to meet, the professors and students huddled in coats, hats, and gloves. Shostakovich was among the most persistent of the students. If his piano teacher, the famous Leonid Nikolayev, did not come to the conservatory, Mitya headed for his house.

The family's circumstances grew more and more harrowing. In early 1922 his father died, succumbing to pneumonia as a result of malnutrition. Sofia Vasilyevna was left with three children: Mitya, then sixteen; the elder daughter, Maria, nineteen; and the younger, Zoya, thirteen. They had nothing to live on. They sold the piano, but the rent was still unpaid. The two older children went to work. Mitya found a job playing piano in a cinema, accompanying silent films. Historians like to say that this hack work was "beneficial" to Shostakovich, but the composer thought back on it with revulsion. In addition, he grew ill. The diagnosis was tuberculosis, and the disease ravaged him for almost ten years.

Perhaps a different person would have been broken by this, but not Shostakovich. He was stubborn and tenacious. He had had faith in his genius from early childhood, even though he kept this conviction to himself. His work was primary. At all costs, he was determined to remain a top student.

The earliest portrait we have of Shostakovich (done in charcoal and sanguine by the distinguished Russian artist Boris Kustodiev) communicates this stubbornness and inner concentration. It shows another quality as well. In the portrait Shostakovich's gaze resembles the poetic description made by a friend of his youth: "I love the spring sky just after a storm. That's your eyes." Kustodiev called Shostakovich Florestan. But young though he was, Shostakovich thought the comparison too romantic. Craft was all. He placed his faith in it as a child and he depended on it all his life.*

The gifted young Shostakovich seemed then to be a faithful adherent of the reigning musical traditions of the Rimsky-Korsakov school of composition. Though Rimsky had died in 1908, the key positions at the conservatory continued to be held by his associates and students. Shostakovich's teacher of composition was Maximilian Steinberg, Rimsky's son-in-law. Shostakovich's first musical triumph was a confirmation of his affinity for the "Petersburg School." He was nineteen when he wrote a symphony for his graduation. It was performed that same year (1926) by a leading orchestra under a top conductor at the Leningrad Philharmonic. Its success was instantaneous and wild; everyone liked the work, which was striking, temperamental, and masterfully orchestrated, and at the same time traditional and accessible. Its reputation spread rapidly. In 1927 the symphony had its Berlin premiere under the baton of Bruno Walter, in 1928 it was conducted by Leopold Stokowski and Otto Klemperer, and in 1931 the First be-

*In his mature years he told a student who complained that he couldn't find a theme for the second movement of his symphony: "You shouldn't be looking for a theme; you should be writing the second movement." As late as 1972, in a letter to me, he was still emphasizing the importance of musical craft.

came part of the repertoire of Arturo Toscanini. The reaction was enthusiastic almost everywhere. Shostakovich was alluded to as one of the most talented musicians of the new generation.

Yet at this moment of triumph, Shostakovich shied away from a future as a derivative composer. He decided he did not want to become the "lady pleasing in all respects" of Gogol's *Dead Souls*. He burned many of his manuscripts, including an opera based on a long Pushkin poem and a ballet on a fairy tale by Hans Christian Andersen, thinking them nothing more than scribbling. He was afraid that if he used academic techniques he would lose his "own self" forever.

Despite the conservatory tradition, the 1920s were a time when "left" art predominated in the new Russia's cultural life. There were many reasons for this, and one of the primary ones was the readiness of the avant-garde to cooperate with Soviet power. (The most prominent representatives of traditional culture had left Russia, or were sabotaging the new regime, or were waiting things out.) For a time the leftists seemed to be setting the tone of cultural politics. They were given the opportunity to realize several daring projects.

Outside influences added to this trend. As soon as life had settled a bit after the introduction of the New Economic Policy (NEP) in 1921, new music came in from the West and was eagerly learned and performed. In the mid 1920s in Leningrad there was an interesting premiere almost every week: the compositions of Hindemith, Křenek, *Les Six,* and the "foreign" Russians—Prokofiev and Stravinsky. Prominent avant-garde composers, including Hindemith and Bartók, came to Leningrad, and played their works. Shostakovich was excited by this new music.

The prominent visiting musicians, like many others, were awed by stories of how generously this new progressive state supported the new arts. But, in truth, there are no miracles. It soon proved that the state patrons of the arts were willing to support only those works that contained propaganda. Shostakovich received an important commission: to write a symphony for the tenth anniversary of the Revolution. He fulfilled this commission successfully. "A Symphonic Dedication to October" (his name for the work), with a chorus to the bombastic verses of the Komsomol poet Alexander Bezymensky, marked (with a few other works) Shostakovich's switch to modernist techniques. The score has a part for a factory whistle (though the composer notes that it can be replaced by a unison sounding of French horn, trumpet, and trombone).

Shostakovich wrote several other major commissioned works then. They were all generally well received by the press. Influential figures in musical administration supported the talented young composer. They were obviously preparing the vacant post of official composer for him.

But Shostakovich was in no hurry to fill the vacancy, even though he wanted success and recognition very badly—and financial security as well. By the late 1920s the honeymoon with the Soviet government was over for genuine artists. Power had come to behave as it always must: it demanded submission. In order to be in favor, to receive commissions and live peacefully, one had to get into state harness and plug away. For a while, as a young and aspiring artist, Shostakovich had gone along with the new patrons' preferences, but as he matured in his work, the simple-minded demands of Soviet officialdom became more and more difficult for him to endure.

What was Shostakovich to do? He could not and did not want to enter into open conflict with the authorities. Yet it was clear to him that total submission threatened to become a creative dead end. He chose another path; whether consciously or not, Shostakovich became the second (Mussorgsky was the first) great *yurodivy* composer.

The *yurodivy* is a Russian religious phenomenon, which even the cautious Soviet scholars call a national trait. There is no word in any other language that can precisely convey the meaning of the Russian word *yurodivy,* with its many historical and cultural overtones.

The *yurodivy* has the gift to see and hear what others know nothing about. But he tells the world about his insights in an intentionally paradoxical way, in code. He plays the fool, while actually being a persistent exposer of evil and injustice. The *yurodivy* is an anarchist and individualist, who in his public role breaks the commonly held "moral" laws of behavior and flouts conventions. But he sets strict limitations, rules, and taboos for himself.

The origins of *yurodstvo* go back to the fifteenth century and even earlier; it existed as a noticeable phenomenon until the eighteenth century. During all that time, the *yurodivye* could expose things and remain in relative safety. The authorities recognized the right of the *yur-*

odivye to criticize and be eccentric—within limits. Their influence was immense. Their confused prophetic words were heeded by tsars and peasants alike. *Yurodstvo* was usually innate, but it might also be taken on voluntarily, "for Christ's sake." A number of educated men became *yurodivye* as a form of intellectual criticism, of protest.

Shostakovich was not the only one to become a "new *yurodivy*." This behavior model had gained a certain popularity in his cultural milieu. The young Leningrad Dadaists, forming the Oberiu Circle, behaved like *yurodivye*. The popular satirist Mikhail Zoshchenko created a consistent *yurodivy* mask for himself, and he had a deep effect on Shostakovich's personal manner and expression.

For these modern *yurodivye* the world lay in ruins and the attempt to build a new society was—at least for the time being—an obvious failure. They were naked people on a naked earth. The lofty values of the past had been discredited. New ideals, they felt, could be affirmed only "in reverse." They would have to be conveyed through a screen of mockery, sarcasm, and foolishness.

These writers and artists chose unremarkable, crude, and purposely clumsy words to express the most profound ideas. But these words did not carry a simple meaning; they had double or triple implications. In their works, street speech grimaced and clowned, taking on mocking nuances. A joke was transformed into a parable, a child's ditty into a terrifying examination of *"la condition humaine."*

It goes without saying that the *yurodstvo* of Shostakovich and his friends could not be as consistent as that of their historical models. The *yurodivye* of the past had abandoned culture and society forever. The "new *yurodivye*" left in order to remain. Their attempt to rehabilitate traditional culture with methods borrowed from the arsenal of anticulture, even though it had deliberate moralizing and sermonizing overtones, took place in a secular context.

Shostakovich set great store by this bond with Mussorgsky, who, wrote the musicologist Boris Asafiev, "escaped from some internal contradiction into the region of semi-preaching, semi-*yurodstvo*." On a musical plane, Shostakovich had seen himself as Mussorgsky's successor; now he tied himself to him on a human level as well, occasionally playing the "idiot" (as even Mussorgsky's closest friends had called him).

Stepping onto the road of *yurodstvo,* Shostakovich relinquished all responsibility for anything he said: nothing meant what it seemed to, not the most exalted and beautiful words. The pronouncement of familiar truths turned out to be mockery; conversely, mockery often contained tragic truth. This also held for his musical works. The composer deliberately wrote an oratorio "without envoi," in order to force the audience to seek out the message in what appeared at first glance to be an insignificant vocal work.

His decision was not made suddenly, of course; it was the result of much vacillation and inconsistency. Shostakovich's everyday behavior was determined to a great degree—as was the behavior of many authentic old Russian *yurodivye* "for Christ's sake"—by the reaction of the authorities, which were sometimes more intolerant, sometimes less. Self-defense dictated a large portion of the position of Shostakovich and his friends, who wanted to survive, but not at any cost. The *yurodivy* mask helped them. It is important to note that Shostakovich not only considered himself a *yurodivy*, but he was perceived as such by the people close to him. The word *"yurodivy"* was often applied to him in Russian musical circles.

Shostakovich periodically returned throughout his life to this *yurodstvo*, with its traditional concern for oppressed people. It took on various forms as the composer's body and spirit matured and then withered. When he was young, it set him apart from the leaders of "left" art, such as Meyerhold, Mayakovsky, and Eisenstein. Pushkin has a famous line about "calling for mercy for the fallen." Shostakovich could claim to share Pushkin's concern for the fallen after 1927; for this theme is important in the composer-*yurodivy*'s two operas— *The Nose,* based on the Gogol story (completed in 1928), and *Lady Macbeth of Mtsensk District,* based on the Leskov story (completed in 1932).

In Gogol's story the characters are treated as masks, but Shostakovich turns them into human beings. Even the Nose, who separated himself from his owner, Major Kovalyov, and strolled about Petersburg in uniform, takes on realistic traits in Shostakovich's treatment. The composer is interested in the interaction between the faceless crowd and the individual; he carefully explores the mechanism of mass psychosis. We care about the Nose, driven to death by frenzied townspeople, and we care about "noseless" Kovalyov.

Shostakovich used the story plot merely as a springboard, refracting events and characters through the prism of a completely different writer with a different style—Dostoevsky.

In *Lady Macbeth of Mtsensk District* (the opera was called *Katerina Izmailova* in a later, second edition) the connection with Dostoevsky is also apparent. An example is the depiction of triumphant, all-pervasive police power. As in *The Nose*, Shostakovich brings his characters into collision with the police machine.

In both instances a criminal case is used to draw the "stations of the cross" of his characters with more clarity. He vulgarizes the already vulgar and intensifies colors by the use of harsh, strident contrasts.

In *Lady Macbeth*, Katerina Izmailova murders for love and Shostakovich exonerates her. In his interpretation, the heartless, oppressive, and powerful men who are killed by Katerina are actually criminals and Katerina is their victim. The finale of the opera is very important. The *katorga* (labor camp) scene is a direct musical embodiment of certain pages from Dostoevsky's *The House of the Dead*. For Shostakovich the convicts are *neschastnen'kie,* or "poor little wretches," and judges at the same time. Katerina suffers from her conscience and her intonations coincide, almost blend, with the melodies of the prisoners' chorus; that is, the individual and sinful dissolves into the general, the ethical. This concept of redemption and cleansing is cardinal in Dostoevsky; in *Lady Macbeth* it is expressed with almost melodramatic frankness. Shostakovich does not hide his sermonizing intentions.

The road traveled by Shostakovich from *The Nose* to *Lady Macbeth* is the distance between a young man of great promise and a widely known composer. *Lady Macbeth* was an enormous—and unparalleled—success for a contemporary work. It was given thirty-six times in the five months after its premiere in Leningrad in 1934, and in Moscow it had ninety-four performances in two seasons. It was presented almost immediately in Stockholm, Prague, London, Zurich, and Copenhagen; Toscanini added fragments from it to his repertoire. The American premiere under Artur Rodzinski created great interest; Virgil Thomson's article in *Modern Music* (1935) was titled "Socialism at the Metropolitan."

Shostakovich was hailed as a genius.

Then calamity. Stalin came to see *Lady Macbeth* and left the theater in a rage. On January 28, 1936, the devastating editorial "Muddle Instead of Music" appeared in the official Party organ, *Pravda*, dictated in fact by Stalin. "The listener is flabbergasted from the first moment of the opera by an intentionally ungainly, muddled flood of sounds. Snatches of melody, embryos of musical phrases, drown, escape, and drown once more in crashing, gnashing, and screeching. Following this 'music' is difficult, remembering it is impossible."

This was a time when terror raged across the land. Purges took on immense proportions. A new country was growing within the country—the "Gulag Archipelago." Within this context, Stalin's warning to Shostakovich in *Pravda*—"This is playing at abstruse things, which could end very badly"—was clearly and directly threatening. And one week later a second editorial appeared in *Pravda*, this time berating Shostakovich's music for a ballet produced by the Bolshoi Theater. The composer and everyone around him were certain that he would be arrested. His friends maintained their distance. Like many other people at that time, he kept a small suitcase packed and ready. They usually came for their victims at night. Shostakovich did not sleep. He lay listening, waiting in the dark.

The newspapers of the period were filled with letters and articles demanding death for "terrorists, spies, and conspirators." They were signed by almost everyone who hoped to survive; but whatever the risk, Shostakovich would not sign such a letter.

Stalin had made a private decision concerning Shostakovich that would never be rescinded; Shostakovich was not to be arrested, despite his closeness to such "enemies of the people" ruthlessly destroyed by Stalin as Meyerhold and Marshal Tukhachevsky. In the framework of Russian culture the extraordinary relationship between Stalin and Shostakovich was profoundly traditional: the ambivalent "dialogue" between tsar and *yurodivy*, and between tsar and poet playing the role of *yurodivy* in order to survive, takes on a tragic incandescence.

A wave of Stalin's hand created and destroyed entire cultural movements, not to mention individual reputations. The article in *Pravda* was the start of a vicious campaign against Shostakovich and his confreres. The epithet used was "formalism," which was shifted from an aesthetic lexicon to a political one.

In the history of Soviet literature and art there is not a single even slightly significant figure who has not been at one time or another branded a "formalist." It was an entirely arbitrary accusation. Many of those accused of it perished. After the "Muddle" article, Shostakovich was in despair, near suicidal. The constant anticipation of arrest affected his mind. For nearly four decades, until his death, he would see himself as a hostage, a condemned man. The fear might increase or decrease, but it never disappeared. The entire country had become an enormous prison from which there was no escape.

(In many respects, much of Shostakovich's hostility toward and mistrust of the West comes from this period, when the West was doing its best not to notice the Gulag. Shostakovich never did have friendly contacts with a foreigner, with the possible exception of the composer Benjamin Britten. It was no accident that he dedicated to Britten his Fourteenth Symphony, for soprano, bass, and chamber orchestra, in which the protagonist, thrown into jail, cries out in prostration: "Here above me is the crypt, here I am dead to all.")

A premonition of reprisal made Shostakovich postpone the premiere of the Fourth Symphony, which he had finished in 1936; he was afraid to tempt fate anew.* In 1932, after a stormy courtship, the composer had married Nina Varzar, a beautiful and energetic young woman and a gifted physicist. In 1936 their daughter, Galya, was born, and in 1938, their son, Maxim. So Shostakovich was now responsible not only for himself but for his family as well.

The situation was becoming increasingly dangerous. All dictators try to create an apparatus for managing "their" art; the one that Stalin built is still the most effective the world had ever known. He secured from Soviet creative figures an unprecedented degree of submissiveness in the service of his continuingly shifting propaganda goals. Stalin strengthened and perfected the system of "creative unions." Within the framework of this system, the right to work (and therefore to live as an artist) comes only to those officially registered and approved. The creative unions of writers, composers, artists, et al. were formed, begin-

---

* The premiere took place over a quarter century later. For all those years the composer patiently listened to press reports that he was keeping the symphony under wraps because he was dissatisfied with it; he even encouraged this nonsense. Yet when the symphony was finally rehearsed once more, he didn't change a single note. The conductor, who had suggested a few cuts, was refused categorically: "Let them eat it," Shostakovich said. "Let them eat it." The Fourth Symphony was a resounding success, as were revivals of other works long forbidden. His music stood the test of time.

ning in 1932, as bureaucratic organizations with strictly defined ranks and with equally strong accountability and constant cross-checking. Every organization had a branch of "security services," or secret police, as well as innumerable unofficial informers. The practice continues to this day. Any attempt to circumvent one's union ended badly: various forms of pressure and repression were always ready. Moreover, obedience was rewarded. Behind this well-oiled and smoothly running mechanism stood the figure of Stalin, an inevitable presence that often gave events a grotesque, tragicomic coloration.

In Shostakovich's life and work his relationship with Stalin was a decisive factor. In a country in which the ruler has total sovereignty over the fate of his subjects, Stalin inflicted severe trials and public humiliations on Shostakovich; yet almost simultaneously he rewarded him with the highest titles and honors. Paradoxically, the honors and defamations both produced unparalleled fame for the composer.

November 21, 1937, can be considered a watershed day in the musical fate of Shostakovich. The hall of the Leningrad Philharmonic was overflowing: the cream of Soviet society—musicians, writers, actors, artists, celebrities of every kind—had gathered for the premiere of the disgraced composer's Fifth Symphony. They were waiting for a sensation, a scandal, trying to guess what would happen to the composer, exchanging gossip and jokes. After all, social life went on despite the terror.

And when the last notes sounded, there was pandemonium, as there would be at almost all later Soviet premieres of Shostakovich's major works. Many wept. Shostakovich's work represented the effort of an honest and thoughtful artist confronted by a decisive choice under conditions of great moral stress. The symphony is riddled with neurotic pulsations; the composer is feverishly seeking the exit from the labyrinth, only to find himself, in the finale, as one Soviet composer put it, in "the gas chamber of ideas."

"This is not music; this is high-voltage, nervous electricity," noted a moved listener of the Fifth, which to this day remains Shostakovich's most admired work. The symphony made it clear that he spoke for his generation, and Shostakovich became a symbol for decades. In the West his name took on an emblematic quality for both the right and the left. Probably, no other composer in the history of music had been placed in so political a role.

Shostakovich had revived the dying genre of the symphony: for him it was the ideal form in which to express the emotions and ideas that possessed him. In the Fifth he finally reworked the influences of the new Western composers, Stravinsky, Prokofiev, and primarily Gustav Mahler, to create his own inimitable, individual style.

Most characteristic of Shostakovich's music are its strained, seeking melodics. Themes usually grow throughout the symphony, creating new "branches" (the source of the integrated quality of Shostakovich's symphonic canvases, often huge and almost always diverse).

Another important element in Shostakovich's music is his rich, three-dimensional, varied rhythm. He sometimes uses rhythm as an independent means of expression, building large symphonic sections with it (for instance, the famous "march" episode in the Seventh ["Leningrad"] Symphony).

Shostakovich imparted great significance to orchestration. He was able at once to imagine music as played by an orchestra and he wrote it down in score form from the start, not in piano reduction as many composers do. The orchestral timbres were individuals for him, and he liked personifying them (say, the predawn voice of the flute in the "dead kingdom" of the first movement of the Eleventh Symphony). The monologues of solo instruments in his orchestral works often resemble an orator's speech; at other times they are associated with intimate confession.

There is also much in Shostakovich's symphonies that evokes analogies with the theater and with film. There is nothing reprehensible in this, although many critics still seem to think so. In its day the "pure" symphonic music of Haydn, Mozart, and Beethoven incorporated the programmatic images of the Enlightenment, and Tchaikovsky and Brahms, each in his own way, reworked the material of Romantic literature and drama. Shostakovich took part in the creation of the musical mythology of the twentieth century. His style, to use the words Ivan Sollertinsky applied to Mahler, is truly Dostoevsky retold by Chaplin.

The music of Shostakovich combines lofty expressiveness, grotesquerie, and penetrating lyricism with the unpretentiousness of narrative.

The listener can almost always follow the "plot" of the music, even if he does not have much musical erudition and experience.

In the article "Muddle Instead of Music," along with the mocking jibes, there was a revealing slip: the statement that Shostakovich was not in the least untalented and that he knew how to express simple and powerful emotions in music. Unquestionably this observation is connected with Stalin's reaction to films for which Shostakovich had written the scores. These films had been very successful in their day, not only in the Soviet Union, but in the West among the left-wing intelligentsia (though now they are rarely remembered), and certainly the longest-lived element in them is Shostakovich's music.

Stalin, who had a superlative appreciation of the propaganda potential of art, paid special attention to film. He saw that Soviet movies had a powerful emotional effect, which was much enhanced by Shostakovich's music. Thus his film scores met with Stalin's approval. For Shostakovich, writing for the movies was his "rendering unto Caesar"; it seemed an effective and relatively harmless way of staying alive and at work on his own music. The authorities greeted the Fifth and many subsequent compositions matter-of-factly. Some of these works were even honored with Stalin Prizes—the highest awards of the period, given annually and with Stalin's personal approval.

But the greatest propaganda value was extracted by Stalin from Shostakovich's so-called military symphonies, the Seventh and Eighth, which appeared during World War II. The circumstances surrounding the creation of the Seventh were publicized around the world: the first three movements were written during a month or so in Leningrad while it was under fire from the Germans, who had reached the city in September 1941. The symphony was thus seen as a direct reflection of the events of the first days of the war. No one recalled the composer's manner of working. Shostakovich wrote very fast, but only after the music had taken final form in his head. The tragic Seventh was a reflection of the prewar fate of both the composer and Leningrad.

Nor did the first audiences link the famous "march" from the Seventh's first movement to the German invasion; that was done by later propaganda. The conductor Yevgeny Mravinsky, the composer's friend in those years (the Eighth is dedicated to him), reminisced that when he heard the march from the Seventh on the radio in March

1942 he thought that the composer had created a universalized image of stupidity and crass tastelessness.*

The popularity of the march episode has overshadowed the obvious fact that the first movement—indeed, the entire work—is full of mournful emotions in the manner of a requiem. Whenever the opportunity presented itself, Shostakovich stressed the fact that for him the requiem mood held the "central position" in this music. But the composer's words were deliberately overlooked. The prewar period, in truth filled with hunger and fear and the mass deaths of innocent people in the Stalinist terror, was now painted in official propaganda as luminous and carefree, an idyll. Why should the symphony not be transformed into a "symbol of struggle" with the Germans?

It was harder to do this with the Eighth Symphony, first played a year and a half later. Ilya Ehrenburg wrote: "I came home from the performance astounded: I had heard the voice of an ancient chorus from Greek tragedy. Music has a great advantage: without mentioning anything, it can say everything." Ehrenburg later remembered the war years as a time of relative freedom for Soviet creativity: "You could depict grief and destruction," for the fault lay with foreigners, the Germans. In peacetime unclouded optimism was required of art; under such circumstances Shostakovich's "requiems" would certainly have been subjected to annihilating criticism. Ironically, the war rescued the composer.

Another temporary shield was offered by the ever-increasing popularity of Shostakovich in the Allied countries. In England, sixty thousand listeners welcomed the Seventh rapturously when it was performed under the baton of Sir Henry Joseph Wood at Albert Hall. In the United States, leading conductors—Leopold Stokowski, Eugene Ormandy, Serge Koussevitzky, Artur Rodzinski—vied for the right to present the premiere of the sensational symphony. They wrote letters and sent telegrams to the Soviet embassy; their friends and agents campaigned to persuade the Soviet representatives to give the right of first

---

* From a purely musical point of view, it's not difficult to understand where this impression came from: the march theme assimilates a popular tune from Lehar's operetta *The Merry Widow*. For Shostakovich's close friends there was an "in joke" in that theme of the Seventh Symphony: in Russia the melody was sung with the words *"poidu k Maksimy ya"* ("I'll go see Maxim") and probably it was often addressed within the family to Shostakovich's small son, Maxim.

performance to "their" conductors, at the same time relating whatever "compromising" information they could about the other competitors.

Arturo Toscanini entered the fray late, but he had the power of NBC behind him and won. He received the first copy of the score, on film brought to the United States by military ship. The radio premiere of the work was broadcast from Radio City in New York on July 19, 1942, and was heard by millions of Americans.

That first season the symphony was performed sixty-two times in the United States. It was broadcast by 1,934 United States stations and ninety-nine Latin American ones. In September 1942 a festival of Shostakovich's music was held in San Francisco, with the best American orchestras participating. Toscanini repeated the Seventh Symphony there in a vast outdoor amphitheater. CBS paid the Soviet government ten thousand dollars for the right to the first broadcast of the Eighth Symphony.

In those years Western audiences grew familiar with Shostakovich's face through photographs, portraits, and magazine covers: wary eyes behind round glasses, thin, tight lips, the boyish facial contours, and the eternal cowlick. (Much later, the corners of the mouth lowered, while the eyebrows rose; old age was trying to change the face's blueprint. The mask of fear was sharper.) Shostakovich responded to applause clumsily and grotesquely. He bowed convulsively, awkwardly, his foot jerking to the side. Shostakovich did not "look like a composer," but they liked that too.

Stalin paid close attention to the propaganda he directed to the Allies. For a time he held his xenophobic instincts in check, but when friendly relations with the Allies ended after World War II, the explosion of anger was that much stronger. On Stalin's orders a campaign began against "cosmopolitanism" and "kowtowing to the West." This was a political campaign. The millions of Soviet citizens who during the war had come into contact with another world and another way of life, who had learned to take risks and be brave, to assert an initiative, had to be brought back into a state of submission. Mass arrests and deportations began again; several harsh anti-Jewish drives were carried out. Simultaneously, Russian nationalism was celebrated at every opportunity.

The regime devoted particular "attention" to culture. Beginning in

1946, one Party resolution after another was proclaimed, containing attacks on books, plays, and films; the first victims were Mikhail Zoshchenko and Anna Akhmatova. The culmination was the Resolution of the Central Committee of the Communist Party of February 10, 1948, "On the Opera *The Great Friendship* by V. Muradeli." According to a contemporary Soviet commentary, the "historical world significance" of this unfortunately famous resolution lay in the fact that "having shown the true path of the development of the greatest musical culture of our times, it at the same time brought a decisive blow to the aesthetics of bourgeois decadence, exposing its putrid essence to the millions of simple people of all the countries of the world." The commentator added gleefully: "Bourgeois modernism will not survive this blow."

The "historical resolution" attacked composers "maintaining a formalistic, anti-people tendency." Shostakovich, Prokofiev, Khachaturian, Shebalin, Gavriil Popov, and Miaskovsky were listed as composers "in whose work formalist perversions and antidemocratic tendencies in music, alien to the Soviet people and its artistic tastes, were particularly glaring." The resolution erased the most talented figures in Soviet music, foremost among these Shostakovich and Prokofiev. The hack Muradeli and his colorless opera condemned in the "historical resolution" were only an excuse. Stalin was particularly angry at Shostakovich—both because of his popularity in the West and because of his refusal to present Stalin with a majestic triumphal Ninth Symphony at the end of the war that would have hailed the genius and wisdom of the leader. Instead, in 1945, Shostakovich had written a symphony full of sarcasm and bitterness. The *yurodivy* wept at the festivities, when the majority thought that life would be cloudless. And his sad prophecy, as everyone could see, was correct.

After 1948, Shostakovich withdrew into himself. The split into two personae was complete. He continued making occasional mandatory public appearances, hurriedly and with visible revulsion reading confessions or pathos-filled pronouncements he had not written. This time he was not traumatized as he had been in 1936, because he was prepared for the worst. Events hurtled past him without impact; he seemed to watch them as from a distance. His works disappeared from the repertory—no reaction; the newspapers were full of "letters from workers" condemning his music—no reaction; in school, children memorized texts about the "great harm" Shostakovich had brought to art—also no reaction.

He felt himself alone—his friends died or disappeared, or worked on their careers—but he was used to that too. He lived in Moscow now—a city that had never become home to him. His family remained a small bastion, but that last sanctuary was given a short life by fate: his beloved wife Nina Varzar died in 1954; his children grew independent. A second, unhappy marriage to Margarita Kainova quickly ended in divorce. And through it all, it seemed as though the witch hunt would go on forever. The world turned permanently gray. It was a world of betrayal, of fear, which had become as unremarkable as rain on the window.

But Shostakovich also composed privately, as the Russians put it, "for his desk." One work, which mocked Stalin and his henchmen for organizing the "antiformalist" campaign of 1948, has yet to be performed or published. Other compositions became widely known later. Among them are several major works (the First Violin Concerto, the vocal cycle *From Jewish Folk Poetry,* the Fourth Quartet) in which Shostakovich speaks, using echoes of Yiddish folklore, with compassion about the fate of the Jews—exiles on the brink of extinction who miraculously survived. This theme blended into an autobiographical motif: the lone individual against the raging, stupid mob.*

It was also a period of contradictions, as is clear in Shostakovich's astounding dialogue with Stalin, to be found in this book. On the one hand Shostakovich's major works were not performed—and yet Stalin personally telephoned him to urge him to make the journey to New York in March 1949, to attend the Cultural and Scientific Conference for World Peace as a leading representative Soviet artist. Despite his heated exchange with Stalin, he went—and it was a profoundly unhappy experience for him. He played the scherzo from the Fifth Symphony on the piano to a huge audience at Madison Square Garden. But he felt like a pawn in a cynical political game. Except for his visit

* Shostakovich came out openly against anti-Semitism in his Thirteenth Symphony. It was 1962 then and Khrushchev was in power, not Stalin, but the official attitude toward Jews was, as always, hostile. The moralizing Thirteenth (which incorporated Yevgeny Yevtushenko's famous poem "Babi Yar") was the cause of the last sharp and well-known conflict between Soviet power and the composer.

to Warsaw for a piano competition as a young man, with a side trip to Berlin, this was his first trip abroad, and in the uncomfortable role of a mock celebrity to boot. His attitude had already formed toward things "Western" as being inimical and alien to his inner strivings. His brief American stay, which took place under extremely harried circumstances (like subsequent visits, in 1959 and 1973), merely reinforced his prejudice. Shostakovich was particularly traumatized by the aggressiveness of American reporters, and the bleakness of his life upon his return seemed almost welcome to him.

In 1953, Stalin died, leaving the country in shock. The Soviet Union began changing, tentatively, cautiously, but in a direction that the browbeaten intelligentsia had never let themselves dream of—that is, for the better and not for the worse. The "thaw" began. An enormous world power stood at a crossroads; and many human beings saw themselves at a crossroads too.

Shostakovich summed up Stalin's era in the Tenth Symphony (1953). The second movement is inexorable, merciless, like an evil whirlwind—a "musical portrait" of Stalin. In the same work he introduced his own musical monogram, DSCH (the notes D, E flat, C, B), which would take so important a place in his subsequent compositions. It was almost as though with the dictator's death the *yurodivy* could begin to assert his own identity in his work.

It goes without saying that Shostakovich stood wholeheartedly with the liberals. When Khrushchev dethroned Stalin in 1956, the facts he made public came as no surprise to Shostakovich. All it meant was that one could now talk about the crimes of the "leader and teacher" openly, though this freedom would prove to be short-lived. Shostakovich wrote music for the very progressive (by Soviet standards) poet Yevtushenko; he wrote and signed petitions for the "rehabilitation" of musicians who had been sentenced to the camps by Stalin, and helped the survivors return and find work; he tried to influence the relaxation of harsh cultural edicts established by Stalin. A new Party resolution, made on Khrushchev's orders in 1958, announced that Stalin was "subjective" in his approach to works of art; this removed the label "formalist" from Shostakovich and noticeably improved his standing. The composer devoted the greater part of his time to helping ordinary people in many ways, defending them against bureaucracy.

When the authorities decided to appoint Shostakovich to the post of first secretary of the proposed "Russian" division of the national Composers' Union, he had to join the Party for the first time. On September 14, 1960, the open meeting of the Composers' Union, convened for the admission of Shostakovich into the Party, attracted a large group of people expecting something unusual: they anticipated a spectacle from the *yurodivy*. And they were right. Shostakovich mumbled his prepared text without lifting his eyes from the paper, except for one moment when he suddenly raised his voice dramatically: "For everything good in me I am indebted to . . . ." The audience expected the standard and obligatory "the Communist Party and the Soviet government," but Shostakovich cried out, ". . . to my parents!"

Six years later, on the eve of his sixtieth birthday, he wrote a small vocal work, full of painful self-irony, titled "Preface to the Complete Collection of My Works and a Brief Meditation on This Preface," with his own text. A major element in this work is a mocking list of the composer's "honorific titles, extremely responsible duties and assignments." These are grotesque jokes for those in the know. To understand them one must know the rules of the game.* But despite his titles and awards, the Russian intelligentsia itself did not see the composer as part of the official system until the late 1960s. For decades the emotional truth of his music had helped them survive morally. Russia had no other Shostakovich.

In the years of the "thaw" Shostakovich wrote several major works that had a noticeable resonance in Soviet society; and other compositions, previously inaccessible to audiences, were performed—among them *Lady Macbeth* (retitled *Katerina Izmailova*), the Fourth Symphony, and instrumental and vocal works of the late 1940s. However, a gulf gradually formed between the greatest living Russian composer and the most freethinking intellectuals.

A brief chronology indicates the tension of developing events. In 1962 the journal *Novy mir* printed Aleksandr Solzhenitsyn's *One Day in the Life of Ivan Denisovich*. In 1966 the writers Andrei Sinyavsky and Yuli Daniel, who had printed their satirical works in the West,

* For instance, in order to appreciate fully the meaning of Opus 139, *March of the Soviet Police* for band, composed in 1970 between the Thirteenth Quartet and the Fifteenth Symphony, one must be aware that the writer Mikhail Zoshchenko, Shostakovich's idol, had served briefly on the force in his youth. The list of such private jokes in the composer's works is long.

were tried in Moscow. This trial rocked the Soviet creative elite. Dissent mounted throughout the "Prague Spring" and the Warsaw Pact troops' invasion of Czechoslovakia in August 1968. That same year academician Sakharov made public his essay "On Progress, Peaceful Coexistence, and Intellectual Freedom." The essay was widely distributed in samizdat, which by then had won for itself the status of a "parallel" Russian literature, at home and abroad, often much more influential than the official one.

Dissidence was turning into a political movement. Shostakovich watched with interest and sympathy, but he could not join in. The *yurodivy* cannot infringe on the social order. He confronts people, not conditions. He protests in the name of humanity and not in the name of political changes. Shostakovich was a moralist—eventually, as is clear in this book, a very embittered one—but he never had a political program.*

Moreover, his compositions became more and more introspective as he entered his "late" period. The theme of reflection, of self-analysis, always characteristic of his music, took on a different sound: before it was music for others, about himself in conflict and interrelationships with others; now it was about himself *for* himself.

The composer's health, never very good, was failing rapidly. In 1966 he developed heart trouble, the next year he broke his leg; his bones had become fragile and a careless sharp movement could have painful consequences. His condition was never definitively diagnosed. Treatment brought only temporary relief.

Now Shostakovich appeared in public only with his young third wife, Irina Supinskaya. She had to help him to sit and stand, would hand him his coat. His mouth could be seen to tremble, as though he were about to cry. Public appearances were extremely difficult for him. At home he seemed much calmer and more self-confident. Yet playing his compositions on the piano cost him great pain; when he offered his right hand, he supported it with his left. He was seriously training himself to write with his left hand, in case his right gave way completely.

The image of death now dominated his works. The influence of

---

* In his last years he wrote to me: "Music is good, not evil. Poetry is good, not evil. Primitive, but oh, so true!"

Mussorgsky's *Songs and Dances of Death* is profoundly reflected in his Fourteenth Symphony (1969). The music is permeated with inconsolable anguish; "Death is all-powerful," the soloist in this symphony proclaims. Aleksandr Solzhenitsyn could not accept this, as a dissident and as a deeply religious Christian. He and Shostakovich had a falling out, despite their cordial relations up to then.* The dissidents demanded political action rather than introspection. The government was for them a much more urgent antagonist than death. Moreover, Shostakovich's refusal to put his signature on the dissidents' political statements was, they felt, nothing less than capitulation. For the first time, the composer was seen as an opportunist rather than a *yurodivy*.

He was dying. His long, lonely journey was coming to an end, but he saw it as having gone nowhere. In that sense, as in many others, he was a true Dostoevsky hero—the man who, moving forward with dizzying velocity, is actually, if you look closely, motionless. His music of this final period expressed fear before death, a numbness, a search for a final sanctuary in the memory of future men; explosions of impotent and heartbreaking anger. Sometimes Shostakovich seemed most to fear that people would think he was repenting, asking for forgiveness. He was dying an "underground man."

Shostakovich died at the Kremlin Hospital—reserved for the elite—on August 9, 1975, of heart failure, according to the physicians. The obituaries in the West were unanimous: "One of the greatest twentieth-century composers and a committed believer in Communism and Soviet power" (London *Times*); "He contributed a decisive statement to the musical history of the century" (*Die Welt*); "A committed Communist who accepted sometimes harsh ideological criticism" *(The New York Times)*.

We live in a world without mercy. It sees the artist as gladiator and demands from him, in the words of Boris Pasternak, "total death, seriously." And the artist complies, offering his death as the price of his achievement. It was a price Shostakovich paid long before he died.

---

* Shostakovich was ambivalent toward Solzhenitsyn. He thought highly of him as a writer, and felt that his life had been extraordinarily courageous. But he also felt that Solzhenitsyn was creating an image of "luminary" for himself, aspiring to be a new Russian saint. This ambivalence was reflected in two of his compositions, which were produced in quick succession after Solzhenitsyn's expulsion to the West in 1974. In the vocal suite on the poems of Michelangelo, Shostakovich used the poet's angry lines about the expulsion of Dante from Florence to address Solzhenitsyn with poignant music. And then appeared the satiric piece "Luminary" with parodic words from Dostoevsky's *The Possessed*.

TESTIMONY

THESE are not memoirs about myself. These are memoirs about other people. Others will write about us. And naturally they'll lie through their teeth—but that's their business.

One must speak the truth about the past or not at all. It's very hard to reminisce and it's worth doing only in the name of truth.

Looking back, I see nothing but ruins, only mountains of corpses. And I do not wish to build new Potemkin villages on these ruins.

Let's try to tell only the truth. It's difficult. I was an eyewitness to many events and they were important events. I knew many outstanding people. I'll try to tell what I know about them. I'll try not to color or falsify anything. This will be the testimony of an eyewitness.

Of course, we do have the saying "He lies like an eyewitness." Meyerhold* liked to tell this story from his university days. He studied

*Vsevolod Emilyevich Meyerhold (1874–1940), director and actor, theorist of the avant-garde theater, a friend and patron of Shostakovich. In 1928 Shostakovich was responsible for the music in the Theater of Meyerhold and later he wrote the music for the premiere of Mayakovsky's comedy *The Bedbug*. (Subsequently Shostakovich invariably refused Meyerhold's proposals of collaboration.) Not only were Meyerhold's productions extremely popular, but his name was

3

law at Moscow University, you know. A professor was lecturing on testimony when a hooligan rushed into the classroom and created a disturbance. A fight broke out, they called in the guards, who removed the troublemaker. The professor suggested that the students recount what had just happened.

It turned out that each told a different story. Everyone had his own version of the fight and his own description of the hooligan, and some even maintained that there had been several hooligans.

Finally the professor admitted that the whole incident had been staged to demonstrate that future lawyers should know what eyewitness testimony was worth. They were young people with good eyesight and their accounts of what had just transpired varied. But witnesses were sometimes elderly. And they described things that happened long ago. How can you expect them to be accurate?

But nevertheless, there are courts of law where one seeks the truth and where everyone gets his just deserts. And that means that there are witnesses who testify before their own consciences. And there is no more horrible judgment than that.

I didn't spend my life as a gaper, but as a proletarian. I worked hard since childhood, not at seeking my "potential," but in the physical sense of the word. I wanted to hang around and look, but I had to work.

Meyerhold used to say, "If there's a rehearsal at the theater and I'm not there yet, if I'm late—look for the nearest row. I adore rows." Meyerhold held that rows were a school for artists, because when people fight they reveal their most basic traits and you can learn a lot.

Probably Meyerhold was right. While I didn't spend much time on the streets, I did see enough rows. Small ones and bigger ones too. I can't say that it enriched my life, but it has given me a lot to tell.

I had not expressed a desire to study music before I began taking lessons, although I had some interest in music and listened ear to the wall when a quartet met at the neighbors'.

My mother, Sofia Vasilyevna, saw this and insisted that I begin

known throughout the Soviet Union and among leftist circles of the Western intelligentsia. Despite that fact, Meyerhold disappeared without a trace in the years of the "great terror." In the fifteen years that followed, if Meyerhold was written about at all, it was usually in this vein: "All the work of Meyerhold, ringleader of formalism in the theater, is a betrayal of Russia's great culture and a groveling before the bourgeois unprincipled art of the West." During the "thaw," Shostakovich was one of the first to work toward Meyerhold's "rehabilitation."

learning the piano, but I hedged. In the spring of 1915 I attended the theater for the first time and saw *The Legend of Tsar Saltan*. I liked the opera, but it still wasn't enough to overcome my unwillingness to study music.

The root of study is too bitter to make learning to play worthwhile, I thought. But Mother had her way and in the summer of 1915 began giving me lessons. Things moved very quickly, I turned out to have absolute pitch and a good memory. I learned the notes quickly, and I memorized easily, without repetition—it came on its own. I read music fluently and made my first attempts at composing then too.

Seeing that things were going well, Mother decided to send me to the music school of Ignatiy Albertovich Gliasser (he died in 1925). I remember that at one recital I played almost half the pieces in Tchaikovsky's *Children's Album*. The next year, 1916, I was promoted into Gliasser's class. Before that I had been studying with his wife, O. F. Gliasser. In his class I played sonatas by Mozart and Haydn, and the following year, Bach's fugues.

Gliasser treated my composing quite skeptically and didn't encourage me. Nevertheless, I continued composing and wrote a lot then. By February 1917 I lost all interest in studying with Gliasser. He was a very self-confident but dull man. And his lectures already seemed ridiculous to me.

At the time I was studying at the Shidlovskaya Gymnasium. There was no certainty yet in the family that I would be a musician and they planned for me to become an engineer. I was a good student in all my subjects, but music began taking up more and more time. Father had hoped that I would be a scientist, but I didn't.

I was always a diligent student. I wanted to be a good student, I liked getting good grades, and I liked being treated with respect. I've been like that since childhood.

That may be the reason I left Gliasser's school. Mother was against it, but I held my ground. I make decisions of that kind instantly. I decided not to go—and I didn't. And that was it.

My parents were, without a doubt, *intelligent*s. And consequently had the required subtle spiritual make-up. They liked Art and Beauty. And incidentally, they had a special affinity for music.

Father sang, he sang gypsy romances, things such as "Ah, it's not you I love so passionately" and "The chrysanthemums in the garden have faded." Magical music, they called it, and it was a great help to me later on when I banged away in cinemas.

I don't renounce my interest in gypsy songs. I don't see anything shameful in it, as opposed to, say, Prokofiev, who pretended to be enraged when he heard such music. He probably had a better musical education than I did. But at least I'm not a snob.

Mother studied at the Petersburg Conservatory with Rozanova, the same woman to whom she later took me. She played the piano rather well. There's nothing particularly significant in that, for in those days there were many more amateur musicians than there are now. Take my neighbors' quartet, for instance.

In an old book I read, the local dignitaries—governor, police chief, and so on—got together and played the Mendelssohn Octet. And that was in some small town. If the chairman of the city council, the police chief, and the Party chief of Ryazan or some place like that were to get together today, what do you think they could play?

I rarely reminisce about my childhood. Probably because it's boring to reminisce alone, and the number of people with whom I could talk about my childhood is diminishing.

The young aren't interested in my childhood. And they're absolutely right. It may be interesting to know about Mozart's childhood, because it was unusual, and because his creative life began so early. But in my biography the events that could possibly be of some interest come much later. My childhood had no significant or outstanding incidents. The most uninteresting part of the biography of a composer is his childhood. All those preludes are the same and the reader hurries on to the fugue. The one exception to this is Stravinsky. In his memoirs the most interesting part is his childhood.

There's one thing that displeases me greatly: why did Stravinsky say such bad things about his parents? You get the impression that he's taking revenge for his childhood.

You can't take revenge on your parents. Even if your childhood wasn't very happy. You can't write a denunciation of them for your descendants, to the effect that Father and Mother were terrible people and I, poor child, had to put up with their tyranny. There's something despicable about that. I do not wish to listen to people denouncing their parents.

Sometimes I think that I've forgotten what my childhood was like. I have to strain to remember small scenes from my early years and I don't think that they are of any interest to others.

After all, I wasn't dandled on Leo Tolstoy's knee. And Anton Pavlovich Chekhov didn't tell me stories. My childhood was totally average. There was nothing extraordinary about it and I just can't seem to remember any special, earth-shaking events.

They say that the major event in my life was the march down to the Finland Station in April 1917, when Lenin arrived in Petrograd. The incident did take place. Some classmates from Shidlovskaya and I tagged along with the small crowd that was marching to the station. But I don't remember a thing. If I had been told ahead of time just what a luminary was arriving, I would have paid more attention, but as it is, I don't remember much.

I remember another incident more clearly. It took place in February of the same year. They were breaking up a crowd in the street. And a Cossack killed a boy with his saber. It was terrifying. I ran home to tell them about it.

There were trucks all over Petrograd, filled with soldiers, who were shooting. It was better not to go out in those days.

I didn't forget that boy. And I never will. I tried to write music about it several times. When I was small, I wrote a piano piece called "Funeral March in Memory of the Victims of the Revolution." Then my Second and Twelfth Symphonies addressed the same theme. And not only those two symphonies.

I also remember that there were a lot of prostitutes in Petrograd. They came out in flocks onto Nevsky Prospect in the evening. This began with the war, they serviced the soldiers. I was afraid of the prostitutes too.

Our family had Narodnik* leanings—and, naturally, liberal views. We had a definite understanding of right and wrong.

In those days I thought the whole world was that way. But now I see that our family was rather daringly freethinking, as compared with

---

*Narodnichestvo (from narod, "the people") was a radical political movement in nineteenth-century Russia, which encompassed broad circles of the intelligentsia. The central idea of the Narodniki was peasant democracy as the "Russian" path to socialism. The Narodniki fought autocracy through agitation and terrorist acts. In the Stalinist period, the activities of the Narodniki were hushed up and distorted.

the atmosphere at Prokofiev's house: they were much more reactionary there. To say nothing of the Stravinskys. After all, the family was supported by the Imperial Maryinsky Theater.

Our family discussed the Revolution of 1905 constantly. I was born after that, but the stories deeply affected my imagination. When I was older, I read much about how it all had happened. I think that it was a turning point—the people stopped believing in the tsar. The Russian people are always like that—they believe and they believe and then suddenly it comes to an end. And the ones the people no longer believe in come to a bad end.

But a lot of blood must be shed for that. In 1905 they were carting a mound of murdered children on a sleigh. The boys had been sitting in the trees, looking at the soldiers, and the soldiers shot them—just like that, for fun. Then they loaded them on the sleigh and drove off. A sleigh loaded with children's bodies. And the dead children were smiling. They had been killed so suddenly that they hadn't time to be frightened.

One boy had been torn apart by bayonets. When they took him away, the crowd shouted for weapons. No one knew what to do with them, but patience was running out.

I think that many things repeat themselves in Russian history. Of course, the same event can't repeat itself exactly, there must be differences, but many things are repeated nevertheless. The people think and act similarly in many things. This is evident, for example, if you study Mussorgsky or read *War and Peace*.

I wanted to show this recurrence in the Eleventh Symphony. I wrote it in 1957 and it deals with contemporary themes even though it's called "1905." It's about the people, who have stopped believing because the cup of evil has run over.

That's how the impressions of my childhood and my adult life come together. And naturally, the events of my mature years are more meaningful.

For some reason no one writes about the humiliations of childhood. They reminisce tenderly: I was so small and already independent. But in reality, they don't let you be independent when you're a child. They dress and undress you, wipe your nose roughly. Childhood is like old age. A man is helpless when he's old too. And no one speaks tenderly of old age. Why is childhood any better?

8

Childhood injuries last a lifetime. That's why a child's hurts are the most bitter—they last his whole life. I still remember who insulted me in the Shidlovskaya Gymnasium and even before that.

I was sickly as a child. It's always bad to be sick, but the worst time to be sick is when there's not much food. And there were some very bad times with food. I wasn't very strong. The trolleys ran infrequently. When the trolley finally came, the cars were packed, and the crowds still tried to push in.

I rarely managed to get in. I didn't have the strength to push. The saying "The pushy ride cushy" was coined then. That's why I always left early to get to the Conservatory. I didn't even think of the trolley. I walked.

That's how it always turned out. I was always walking, and the others rode by on the trolley. But I didn't envy them. I knew that there was no way that I could have got on, I was too weak.

I learned how to assess people, a rather unpleasant pastime, since it inevitably leads to disillusionment.

The supposedly marvelous years of youth are made for seeing the world through rose-colored glasses. For seeing merry things and beautiful objects. Clouds, and grass, and flowers. You don't want to notice the shady sides of glorious reality. You want to think that they're an optical illusion, as was once suggested by a sarcastic writer.*

But willy-nilly you begin looking closer. And then you notice certain ugly phenomena, you begin to see what moves what, as Zoshchenko† put it, and what pushes what. And that makes you rather sad.

Well, not enough to plunge you into despair and pessimism, but a few doubts start gnawing at your youthful brain.

I worked in my youth as the piano player at the Bright Reel Theater—now called the Barricade. Every Leningrader knows the place.

*Daniil Ivanovich Kharms (Yuvachev; 1906–1942), Dadaist writer, one of the most eccentric figures of Petrograd/Leningrad during Shostakovich's youth. He earned his living writing children's poetry. Kharms disappeared during the years of Stalinist terror. In the 1960s his absurdist "anecdotes" were widely distributed in samizdat.

†Mikhail Mikhailovich Zoshchenko (1895–1958), satirist and playwright, a friend of Shostakovich. A brilliant stylist, he gained unheard-of popularity while still quite young. Zoshchenko noted dryly: "I write with compression. My sentences are short. Accessible to the poor. Perhaps that's why I have so many readers." After World War II, Zoshchenko was viciously attacked by the Party; "thoroughly rotten and decayed sociopolitical and literary physiognomy," "vile, lustful animal," "unprincipled and conscienceless literary hooligan," were a few of the official descriptions of Zoshchenko. "Let him get out of Soviet literature," a Party leader demanded, and the order was carried through. Zoshchenko's original literary style had a decided influence on Shostakovich's manner of expressing himself.

My memories of the Bright Reel are not very pleasant. I was seventeen and my work consisted in providing musical accompaniment for the human passions on the screen.

It was disgusting and exhausting. Hard work and low pay. But I put up with it and looked forward to receiving even that paltry sum. That's how hard up we were then.

The owner of the theater was not an ordinary man. He was famous, no more and no less than an honorary citizen of Milan. And he received that citizenship for his scholarly work on Leonardo da Vinci.

The honorary citizen of Milan was called Akim Lvovich Volynsky, also known as Flekser. And he was, as I've said, a famous man, a critic in various fields of the arts. Before the Revolution, Volynsky headed a highly respectable journal, printed Chekhov and even Leo Tolstoy. After the Revolution, Volynsky started a ballet school, because he knew the field inside out. You might say the entire ballet world trembled in anticipation of his lengthy, innumerable articles. The articles were long-winded and abstruse. The ballet world read them with trepidation.

Every day the honorary citizen of Milan showed up at the ballet school and looked at the girls with satisfaction. This was Volynsky's little harem. He was about sixty then. He was a short man with a large head and a face like a prune.

He gave his harem good publicity, by the way. He published *A Book of Rejoicing*. The title in capitals. And in rejoicing, Volynsky prophesied world fame for his protégées. Nothing came of it. It turned out that Volynsky's patronage wasn't enough, you needed some talent as well.

My month of labor at the Bright Reel didn't fly by, it dragged. And then I went to see Volynsky for my salary. The honorary citizen of Milan ran from me as from the plague. But I finally caught up with him. I dragged him away from his contemplation of the ballet girls.

Volynsky looked at me with disdain. He was, let's be honest, extraordinarily august in his pre-Revolutionary frock coat. Once upon a time, that coat had been made for him, and not badly. His oversized head was propped up by a dirty collar. Volynsky looked down at me, even though that was difficult.

He asked me, "Young man, do you love art? Great, lofty, immortal art?" I felt uncomfortable, and I replied that I did. That was a fatal mistake, because Volynsky put it this way: "If you love art, young man, then how can you talk to me now about filthy lucre?"

He gave me a beautiful speech, itself an example of high art. It was passionate, inspired, a speech about great immortal art, and its point was that I shouldn't ask Volynsky for my pay. In doing so I defiled art, he explained, bringing it down to my level of crudity, avarice, and greed. Art was endangered. It could perish if I pressed my outrageous demands.

I tried to tell him that I needed the money. He replied that he couldn't imagine or understand how a man of the arts could be capable of speaking about such trivial aspects of life. He tried to shame me. But I held my own.

I hated art by then. It made me sick. We were desperate for money, I had worked hard, and now they didn't want to pay me for that work.

I was seventeen, but I knew that I was being cheated. It disgusted me. All the fine words of the world taken together were worthless—so I thought. What right does that man have to lecture me? Let him pay me my money. And I'll go home. Had I worked so hard in order to support Volynsky's harem? Not at all.

But Volynsky didn't give me my money. I came to see him a few more times, in vain. He lectured me but didn't give me the money. Finally he paid part of it. I had to sue for the rest.

Naturally, I left the Bright Reel, and it goes without saying that I didn't harbor any warm feelings for Volynsky after that business. I read his high-flown articles on ballet and other exalted matters with revulsion.

And then my First Symphony was performed and I acquired a certain fame. As a result, one fine day I received an invitation. At first I was insulted, because the invitation was to a memorial evening for Volynsky, who had died by then. They were planning to memorialize his creative activity with a gala evening and they wanted me to appear with my reminiscences of him, since I had had contact with him at the Bright Reel.

I was angry at first. But then I thought about it and decided why not? Why shouldn't I appear with my reminiscences? I had a story to tell and I went. There was a large audience. The master of ceremonies was Fyodor Kuzmich Sologub, a very famous man, a poet and writer. At the time Sologub was chairman of the All-Russian Writers' Union.

Anyone with the slightest interest in Russian literature knows Sologub. In those days he was a living classic. No one was reading his books by then, but a strange and mysterious occurrence in Sologub's life was making the rounds.

Sologub had a wife. Not just a wife, but a second Sologub. Sologub's wife was unquestionably an outstanding woman. They say that she collaborated with him on many of his novels and she also wrote many erudite articles on her husband's work. Not limiting herself to that, she put together an entire anthology in his honor. In other words, she was more than the ideal wife. Every artist should have such a wife.

Sologub wrote often about death. Of course, even that theme can pay off. You can set yourself up comfortably, write about death, and live well.

Mr. and Mrs. lived very well. But one day mystical vapors thickened in their house or they had a fight. In either case, one not very fine autumn evening Sologub's wife left the house and didn't return.

This was, of course, a tragedy. And in view of Sologub's fame, and the mystical nature of his work, this tragedy was given special significance. You could only venture a guess as to what happened to his wife, who had disappeared so mysteriously.

Someone had seen a woman throw herself into the Neva River from a bridge on that fateful night. Her body wasn't recovered. Perhaps that had been Sologub's wife.

The poet suffered and emoted. He languished for his wife. They say he set a place for her at dinner every night. Many members of the city's intelligentsia suffered and emoted along with Sologub. Winter passed and spring arrived. The ice on the Neva broke and right in front of Sologub's house, by the Tuchkov Bridge, a drowned woman surfaced.

They came for Sologub, he had to identify the body. "Yes, it's she," the poet said glumly, turned, and walked away.

This story was much discussed. There was something mysterious about it. Why had the body surfaced right in front of Sologub's house? "She came to say farewell," one writer decided.

Zoshchenko heard about this. It was too much for him and he wrote a parody. There were similarities: an unearthly love, a drowned woman, and so on. The commentary went something like this: "Maybe she had lived with this backward element for years and years and then went and drowned herself. And maybe it was because he filled her head with his mysticism. But that's really unlikely. Actually, if you want a psychological explanation, she slipped on the logs and drowned."

The hero of Zoshchenko's parody was an engineer, not a writer, but when they brought him to view his drowned wife he behaved exactly like Sologub.

The whole business of the poet's wife who floated over to the house to bring him a greeting from the other world grated on Zoshchenko. And with a laugh he concluded: "And this unfortunate incident has proved conclusively that all this mysticism, this idealism, all kinds of unearthly love, and so on are just absolute garbage and nonsense. Let us rise in honor of the memory of the drowned woman and the profound unearthly love for her and then let's move on to current events. Particularly since these are not the times to spend a lot of time on drowned citizens." Zoshchenko called his parody "The Lady with the Flowers."

And so it was this famous Sologub who was in charge of the evening for the great idealist and ballet lover Volynsky. I came out and started telling my story. I heard a murmur go through the audience.

Naturally, my performance was out of tune with the other orators. They remembered primarily what an exalted personage Akim Lvovich had been. And here I was with my crude materialism, talking about money. One didn't bring up money on memorial evenings. And if one did, it was only to remind those present what a selfless man the dear departed had been.

I violated decorum on all fronts. A scandal was brewing.

By the way, there was a scandal with Zoshchenko when he published his parody. The intelligentsia who sprang to Sologub's defense maintained that the mockery of the man was too blatant. Yet Zoshchenko hadn't intended to mock Sologub at all. He was laughing at people who wove all sorts of nonsense out of a sad and altogether prosaic event. "How can you laugh when the lady drowned?" That's from Zoshchenko. So she drowned. Why turn Sologub and his wife, Chebotarevskaya, into Tristan and Isolde?

I shared my memories. The audience was in an uproar, and I

thought, Even if you drag me off the stage, I'll finish my story. And I did.

And as I left I heard Sologub ask his neighbor loudly, "Who is that young bastard?" I bowed to him politely. For some reason, he didn't respond.

And so what might have been our historic meeting didn't take place that evening. He didn't pass his torch to me and now I can't boast that I continue Sologub's treatment of death.

Sologub died soon after.

Zoshchenko tried a materialistic approach to the issue. He thought that if he wrote about death ironically he would stop fearing it. For a while I was in complete agreement with Zoshchenko, I even wrote a composition on the theme—"McPherson Before Execution," based on a poem by Robert Burns. But later I decided that Zoshchenko apparently had been unable to rid himself of the fear of death. He only wanted to convince himself and others that he had succeeded. In general, my feelings on the subject changed with the years. But more about that later.

Zoshchenko created his own method of psychoanalysis. He called it self-healing. He treated himself for hysteria and melancholia. Zoshchenko didn't trust doctors.

He thought that you could free yourself of melancholy and depression. You only had to understand what it was you feared. When a man realizes the reason for his fears, depression will flee. You have to untangle your fears.

Zoshchenko was right about a lot. He was wrong, I suppose, only in that he sought the causes of fears in early childhood. After all, he himself said that catastrophes are more likely to occur at a mature age, because neuroses come to a head when you're at a mature age. True fear comes at a mature age.

Of course, fear is always with us. It's with us from earliest childhood. But you don't fear in childhood as you do as an adult.

As a child, Zoshchenko was afraid of beggars. More precisely, he was afraid of outstretched hands. He was afraid of water. He was also afraid of women.

I, apparently, was also afraid of outstretched hands. A hand can grab you. That's the fear of being grabbed. And besides, a stranger's hand might take away your food. And thus the fear of being hungry.

I was also afraid of fire. A story I read as a boy left a deep impression on me. The clown Durov told it. It happened in Odessa before the Revolution. There was an outbreak of plague. They decided that it was being spread by rats, and the mayor of Odessa gave the order to destroy rats.

The rat hunt began. Durov was walking down an Odessa side street and saw that some boys had set fire to several rats they had caught. The rats were running around in a frenzy, the boys were cheering. Durov yelled at the boys and managed to save one of the rats. It was covered with burns, but somehow survived. Durov named the rat Finka. Finka hated people. Durov moved Finka in with him, and fussed over it a long time, treating it. It was very hard for him to win the rat's trust, but finally Durov succeeded.

Durov felt that rats were smart and talented animals. He cited examples. He said that a dislike of rats was one of man's many superstitions. Tukhachevsky* had a mouse living in his office. He was very used to the animal and fed it.

Setting fire to animals is horrible. But unfortunately, these things happen even in our day. A talented director,† a young man, was making a film and he decided that what he needed in this film was a cow engulfed by flames. But no one was willing to set fire to a cow—not the assistant director, not the cameraman, no one. So the director himself poured kerosene over the cow and set fire to her. The cow ran off bawling, a living torch, and they filmed it. They were shooting in a village and when the peasants found out about it they almost killed the director.

When I hear about someone else's pain, I feel pain too. I feel pain for everything—for people and animals. For all living things.

I'm afraid of pain too, and I'm not too thrilled about death. But I'll live a long time, I know that, because I've learned to be calmer about

---

*Mikhail Nikolayevich Tukhachevsky (1893–1937), Soviet marshal, a patron of Shostakovich. He had a brilliant career from the start, with a series of important military victories, including the rout of the anti-Bolshevik Kronstadt Uprising in 1921. The uprising had a profound impact in nearby Petrograd and was remembered vividly by Shostakovich. Stalin saw Tukhachevsky as a possible competitor and had him shot, using as an excuse false documents supplied by the Gestapo that named Tukhachevsky as a German spy.

†A reference to Andrei Arsenyevich Tarkovsky (b. 1932), a leading Soviet film director. This episode took place during the filming of *Andrei Rublyov* (1966), a film well received in the West.

death. When I was a child I was terrified of death, maybe because of the war, I don't know.

I was afraid of corpses when I was a child. I thought that they would jump out of their graves and grab me. Now I know that unfortunately corpses don't jump out of graves. You can't jump out of there.

Of course, there was an incident in the late thirties that made me ready to believe that the dead fled their coffins. For some reason or other, they dug up Gogol's grave, and Gogol wasn't in his coffin. The lid was thrown back and the coffin was empty. A great corpse had run off.

Unpleasant rumors began circulating throughout Leningrad—it goes without saying—to the effect that the times were so bad even Gogol took off, couldn't stand it. And naturally, the appropriate departments took an interest: How could he have run off? What did this signify?

They cordoned off the burial place and conducted a search. It turned out that Gogol hadn't gone far. He lay nearby, headless. His head was next to him. And everything was cleared up simply.

It seemed that on some anniversary of Gogol's, they decided to erect a monument. It was made of brick and the bricks broke through the coffin, knocking off the lid. There were so many bricks that they knocked the body out of the grave and tore off Gogol's head.

Well, they put him back. The moral: Don't put too many bricks on the graves of great men. The deceased don't like it. And if you are going to put bricks above a grave, then at least don't dig around inside. It will be better that way.

No, I don't feel like digging around in my childhood. Let's leave that to others. If others, that is, have the time and the inclination.

I've worked at remembering a few times. Not for amusement, but following Zoshchenko's method. Nothing good ever came of it, my sickness got worse, and I couldn't sleep at night, I fell apart completely. Those who wish to know what I was like should take a good close look at my portrait by Kustodiev.* I think it's a good portrait. A good

*Boris Mikhailovich Kustodiev (1878–1927), painter, illustrator, and theater designer, famous for his colorful, rather exaggerated depiction of Russian life: heavily bearded merchants, voluptuous sloe-eyed wives, dashing artisans. His is a world of fairs, troikas, and bars. He could achieve both pathos and irony in his paintings, and this combination is found in Shostakovich's opera *Lady Macbeth*.

likeness. I think it's the best one of me, the most truthful one, and yet at the same time, not an insulting one. I like it very much.

The portrait is done in charcoal and sanguine. I had just turned thirteen. It was a birthday present from Kustodiev.

I don't feel like talking about the portrait. It seems to me that it speaks for itself. And I, an old man, sit at my desk and keep looking at it. It hangs on the wall to the side, it's easy to look at.

The portrait is not only a reminder of the way I was at thirteen, it's also a reminder of Kustodiev, and the suffering that befalls man.

Fate, higher powers—all that is meaningless. What explanation can there be for Kustodiev's lot? Now he is probably the most popular Russian artist. The least educated person, seeing any drawing or painting of his, will say, "A-a-ah, that's Kustodiev." That's what's called the "Kustodiev style." In bad times they used to call it "Kustodievism."

When a person finds himself in an ancient Russian city or sees typical Russian countryside, he says, "Just like a Kustodiev landscape." And a full-figured, voluptuous woman walks by and he says, "There's a Kustodiev type." And this whole movement was created by a hopelessly sick man, a paralytic.

The diagnosis, if I'm not mistaken, was sarcoma of the spinal cord. There's a man the doctors abused as they wished. He was treated, by the way, by the best doctors. The last operation—the fourth—was done by the same surgeon who had treated Lenin. He removed the growth on Kustodiev's spine.

The operation lasted five hours, Kustodiev said, the last hours without anesthetic. It was local anesthetic and it wore off quickly. That was a form of torture, plain and simple.

Almost none of my friends avoided torture. They tortured Meyerhold, and Tukhachevsky, and Zhilayev.* You know how things turned out.

I never knew Kustodiev as a healthy man. I saw him only in his wheelchair, which, I must say, he used with unusual ease. Sometimes he gritted his teeth—from pain—and then his face divided sharply into

*Nikolai Sergeyevich Zhilayev (1881–1942), composer and musicologist, Shostakovich's mentor. An eccentric and mysterious figure, a friend of Marshal Tukhachevsky, Zhilayev was taken by the secret police right after Tukhachevsky's arrest and killed.

two: one half turned red, the other stayed white.

And it was in that pathetic state that Kustodiev painted his famous portrait of Chaliapin, larger than life-size. It has Chaliapin, and his bulldog, and two of his daughters, Marfa and Marina, and a coachman with a horse. Chaliapin came to pose for Kustodiev after his performances. And they made the bulldog pose by putting a cat on the wardrobe; when it mewed, the dog froze.

Chaliapin felt that this portrait was the best representation of him. He took Kustodiev to all his performances. He came for him, took him out of his wheelchair, and carried him down from the fifth floor. And then he drove Kustodiev to the Maryinsky Theater, where he settled him in his box. After the performance, Chaliapin brought him back.

I was taken to Kustodiev by his daughter Irina, with whom I studied at the 108th Labor School. I wasn't eager to go to a strange house, but I was told that Kustodiev was a very sick man who loved music and I had to play for him.

I wrote down the titles of everything I knew and took the list with me. Kustodiev, leaning back in his chair, listened closely. He had kittens cuddling inside his jacket, dozing in ecstasy. When the music bored them, the kittens jumped noisily to the floor.

Kustodiev liked to listen to me play. He told me many things about art and Russian painters. And he was very pleased to be able to tell me something I didn't know. He told me and grew happy, pleased that now I also knew.

I was deeply impressed by Kustodiev's passion for voluptuous women. Kustodiev's painting is thoroughly erotic, something that is not discussed nowadays. Kustodiev made no secret of it. He did blatantly erotic illustrations for one of Zamyatin's* books.

If you dig deeper into my operas *The Nose* and *Lady Macbeth*, you can find the Kustodiev influence in that sense. Actually, I had never thought about it, but recently in conversation I remembered a few things. For instance, Leskov's† story "Lady Macbeth of Mtsensk Dis-

---

*Yevgeny Ivanovich Zamyatin (1884–1937), writer, author of the utopian novel *We;* he was branded a counterrevolutionary after *We* was published in the West. When the campaign against him was at its peak, Zamyatin wrote to Stalin, who eventually allowed him to emigrate. He died in Paris. *We* is still banned in the Soviet Union.

†Nikolai Semyonovich Leskov (1831–1895), short-story writer and novelist, whose artistic world is related in some ways to that of Kustodiev (who liked to illustrate Leskov's stories). His stylized prose depicts Russia in bold transformation and bright colors. Shostakovich wrote an opera based on Leskov's short story "Lady Macbeth of Mtsensk District."

trict" was illustrated by Kustodiev, and I looked through the drawings at the time I decided to write the opera.

The Nose was designed in Leningrad by Vladimir Dmitriev, a marvelous artist, who seemed to be stuck on Kustodiev: he made fun of him all the time but couldn't get away from him.

Parody and stylization are one and the same, after all. Dmitriev either stylized the production after Kustodiev or parodied Kustodiev— but the result was the same: Kustodiev on stage. The same thing happened with *Katerina Izmailova* in Nemirovich-Danchenko's* production. The designer was also Dmitriev.

These names are connected for me—Kustodiev, Zamyatin, Leskov. Zamyatin wrote a play, *The Flea*, based on a Leskov story. It was produced in Leningrad at the Bolshoi Dramatic Theater. The sets and costumes were by Kustodiev.

The play and the production made a great impression on me. I even turned to Zamyatin when I decided to write my opera *The Nose*. I asked him to help with the libretto. Zamyatin knew of me from Kustodiev and so he agreed. But it didn't work, Zamyatin couldn't do it, he just didn't understand what was needed. But I'm grateful to him for a few ideas.

As for Kustodiev, I grew further and further away from him with the years. For a while I was in love with animation. Actually, with Mikhail Tsekhanovsky, a talented director. I consider him our most talented animator. It's a pity that he's been forgotten.

I wrote two small operas for Tsekhanovsky. They're listed as music for cartoons, but actually the films were made for my music, real operas, small—*The Story of the Priest and His Worker Balda*, based on the Pushkin poem, and *The Story of the Silly Mouse*. There was a lot of music. Too bad it's all been lost somewhere.

The Story of the Priest was completely anti-Kustodiev. It depicted a drunkard selling pornographic postcards at a fair. And the cards were a painting by Kustodiev, called *Venus Without Shirt and with Fat Thighs*. That was an obvious reference to Kustodiev's popular *Russian Venus*.

*Vladimir Ivanovich Nemirovich-Danchenko (1858–1943), director and playwright, who with Stanislavsky founded the famous Moscow Art Theater. In 1934 he produced the Moscow premiere of Shostakovich's opera *Lady Macbeth* in the music theater he headed. In his late years Nemirovich insisted that Shostakovich was a genius and he never retreated from that position.

Crippled Kustodiev painted his voluptuous nudes using a special contraption to move the canvas toward him so that he could reach it with his brush. He tilted the canvas and then returned it to its vertical position.

I watched in awe as he worked. Kustodiev liked my sister Marusya, and he used her in the painting *Blue House*. The picture depicts several scenes: a boy with his pigeons, a young couple in love, three friends talking. The painting also has a coffin-maker reading. That's life—the boy on the roof, the coffin-maker in the cellar.

Kustodiev grew tired of living. He couldn't work any more. Voluptuous women no longer brought him any pleasure. "I can't live any more, I don't want to," he used to say.

And he died, not of his disease, but of exhaustion. From a cold, which was naturally only an excuse. Kustodiev was forty-nine then, but to me he seemed an old man.

Kustodiev's example had a profound effect on me, something that I've become aware of now. Because I see that you can be the master of your body. Of course, you can't really be the master in the sense that if your legs don't work, then they don't work, and if your hands don't move, then they don't move. But you must try to continue your work, you must train and figure out feasible working conditions.

Kustodiev went on working even though he was seriously ill. This is a question of vital importance for me now.

You must try to work always, under any circumstances. It can sometimes save you. For instance, I can say that work saved Glazunov;* he was so busy that he never had time to think of himself.

After the Revolution, everything around Glazunov changed and he lived in a terrible world that he didn't understand. But he thought that if he died, important work would perish. He felt responsible for the lives of hundreds of musicians, so he didn't die himself.

Once Glazunov listened to a friend and myself sight-read Brahms's Second Symphony. We were reading badly, because we didn't know

*Alexander Konstantinovich Glazunov (1865–1936), composer, head of the Petersburg/Petrograd/Leningrad Conservatory from 1906 to 1928. In this position he earned general respect. A musician of conservative bent (he wrote lush, colorful symphonies and stylized ballets), Glazunov nevertheless was sympathetic toward Shostakovich. Placed under strong pressure at the Conservatory by radical teachers and students to ease the Conservatory's academic traditions, Glazunov went abroad on a business trip in 1928 and never returned to Russia. He died in France.

the music. Glazunov asked whether we knew it, and I answered honestly, "No, we don't." And he sighed and said, "You're so lucky, young men. There are so many beautiful things for you to discover. And I already know it all. Unfortunately."

Glazunov, like Kustodiev, liked watching the young learn. Performers—violinists, cellists, pianists, harpists—came to his house every day. And of course, singers. They brought him invitations and tickets to their recitals, each of which was described as being a decisive recital, vitally important for the performer. And Glazunov's opinion would be the ray of light in the darkness that . . . And so on, the same old nonsense.

Actually, Glazunov's opinion as such was not that indispensable for a young artist. I'm talking about his opinion on the essential point, the music. But there were other considerations—publicity—at work.

A recital is greatly enhanced, as every pushy artist knows, by the presence of celebrities. They always tried to seat Glazunov in the first row. And some very resourceful ones even managed to haul him on stage, where they set up chairs for particularly honored guests.

And the audience this way had double pleasure. For the same money they could watch the struggling performer and his famous guests. A circus.

And how lovely afterward: the green room, the violinist (or pianist or harpist) stands there pleasantly excited, accepting his due from his fans. And then the celebrity makes his way through the excited crowd and either shakes the performer's hand or kisses it, depending on the musician's sex. And pronounces a few pretty words, which immediately become known to the broad musical community. Cheap and satisfying, as they say.

I had to go through all that and more myself. Not with such frequency as Glazunov, who certainly holds the record. But they say that Glazunov had recourse to illegal means to make the record, to use a sports analogy.

It's said that when he came to a recital Glazunov stuffed cotton in his ears and sat and thought his own thoughts. I must admit that he thought prodigiously, and the process was very impressive to behold. And his neighbors were certain that Glazunov was listening diligently to the sounds pouring from the stage.

And when it was time to go backstage to the green room to congratulate the "subject of the festivities," Glazunov surreptitiously slipped the cotton from his ears and muttered a few noncommittal but definitely laudatory generalities. "Marvelous, and such a stylish touch in the first part . . ."

Of course, to continue the sports metaphor, he should have been disqualified. But no one guessed, or they all pretended not to. Everyone had something to gain from this comedy.

The greatest paradox lay in the fact that Glazunov's taste in music was on the highest level. He was actually a very strict and demanding appraiser.

How can this be explained? And it's very important to me that it be explained, because if I can explain Glazunov's position on this issue, it will clear up much confusion about my own evaluations and reviews.

I know that my reviews and opinions are greeted skeptically by some comrades. A complex game is being played here. On the one hand, people try to get a recommendation or review from me. And on the other . . .

And on the other hand, I was once told about the words of one of our outstanding conductors.* He's supposed to have said about me, "Ah, that *yurodivy,* who says 'Very good, very good' about any performance."

First of all, it seems to me sometimes that this magnificent conductor (I hold his talent in high esteem) has more reason to be called *yurodivy* than I. I'm referring to his religious fanaticism. But I'm not talking about him here. Isn't it perfectly clear that there are many occasions when shooting a cannon at sparrows is completely unnecessary and pointless?

There is a severe critic inside all of us. It's not so hard to be tough, but is it worth airing your aural preferences before everyone? When it's necessary I can express myself—and have—very sharply, when it comes to the performance of both other people's music and my own.

As a youth I was very harsh and intolerant. The slightest deviation

---

*A reference to Yevgeny Alexandrovich Mravinsky (b. 1903), appointed chief conductor and musical director of the Leningrad Philharmonic orchestra in 1938 and still in this post. He led the first performances of the Fifth, Sixth, Eighth (which is dedicated to Mravinsky), Ninth, and Tenth Symphonies of Shostakovich, and for many years was a close friend of the composer. His relationship with Shostakovich deteriorated in the last years of the composer's life.

from the planned performance of one of my works irritated me extremely.

This lasted a fairly long time, and included collisions that had a fatal effect on the future of my works. I feel that this was part of the problem with my Fourth Symphony, and it's painful for me to think about it.

These and other circumstances and also, naturally, age have changed my position somewhat. I certainly haven't become more complaisant, but I have begun expressing my point of view in such a way that the point is made without mortally insulting the performer.

A major factor is that more attention is paid to my opinion. Before, in order to be heard, I had to be extreme. Later, musicians began to understand mere hints. It became easier for me to speak with musicians. But harder at the same time. Why harder? Because when a single word carries more weight it also hits harder.

I hear many mediocre musicians. A great many. But they have the right to live. It's only song-and-dance ensembles like the Red Army Chorus that drive me crazy. If I were suddenly to become minister of culture, I would immediately disband all these ensembles. That would be my first order. I would naturally be arrested immediately for sabotage, but they would never reorganize the scattered ensembles.

Before, when I spoke, people didn't pay too much attention, even when it concerned my own compositions. In order to overcome the performer's resistance, I had to be more aggressive than I would have liked. I had to scream where a normal voice should have done.

Most often I encountered an insulting condescension. But there were also highly irritable citizens, who became nervous at my modest requests and were rude to me.

Now I can't abide rudeness, even in so-called great artists. Rudeness and cruelty are the qualities I hate most. Rudeness and cruelty are always connected, I feel. One example out of many is Stalin.

As you know, Lenin in his "political will"* said that Stalin had only one fault—rudeness. And that everything else was in good shape.

*A reference to the so-called Letter to the Congress, dictated by the gravely ill Lenin in late December 1922–early January 1923; in it, Lenin, addressing the Party leaders, gave comparative evaluations of his possible successors, including Stalin. Published in the West in 1926, this important document, now widely known as Lenin's "political will," was denounced as a forgery at the time by Soviet leaders. It was not published in the Soviet Union until 1956, when it was officially included in the complete works of Lenin.

As we know all too well now, the Party leadership didn't feel the need to remove Stalin from his post as head of the Party because, in their opinion, what kind of fault was rudeness? On the contrary, it was almost like valor.

I remember reading in a commentary to some notes of Lenin's that important Party leaders (I think it was Ordzhonikidze* and some other Georgian) traded insults and slapped each other. A little joke among friends.

And we know how it all ended. No, don't expect anything good from a rude man.

And it doesn't matter in what field the boor is, politics or art. It doesn't matter where, he always tries to become a dictator, a tyrant. He tries to oppress everyone. And the result, as a rule, is very bad.

What galls me is that these sadists always have fans and followers— and sincere ones at that. The typical example of this is Toscanini.

I hate Toscanini. I've never heard him in a concert hall, but I've heard enough of his recordings. What he does to music is terrible, in my opinion. He chops it up into a hash and then pours a disgusting sauce over it. Toscanini "honored" me by conducting my symphonies. I heard those records too, and they're worthless.

I've read about Toscanini's conducting style and his manner of conducting a rehearsal. The people who describe this disgraceful behavior are for some reason delighted by it. I simply can't understand what they find delightful.

I think it's outrageous, not delightful. He screams and curses the musicians and makes scenes in the most shameless manner. The poor musicians have to put up with all this nonsense or be fired. And they even begin to see "something" in it.

Naturally, you must grow accustomed to it. For if you are mocked every day you either get used to it or you go mad. Only a strong person can remain between these two extremes, yet are there many truly strong people among orchestra players? The habit of group playing breeds the herd instinct. Not in everyone, of course, but in many. And

*Grigori (Sergo) Konstantinovich Ordzhonikidze (1886–1937), one of the leaders of the Communist Party. He committed suicide when the "great terror" began. The official version attributed his death to a heart attack. His relatives and friends suffered under the repressions, but Stalin thought it useful to maintain Ordzhonikidze's image as a "loyal Stalinist." Nevertheless, Stalin's hatred of Ordzhonikidze was so great that it played a part in his denunciation of the opera *The Great Friendship* by Muradeli, the hero of which was Ordzhonikidze.

they are the ones who exalt Toscanini.

Toscanini sent me his recording of my Seventh Symphony and hearing it made me very angry. Everything is wrong. The spirit and the character and the tempos. It's a lousy, sloppy hack job.

I wrote him a letter expressing my views. I don't know if he ever got it, maybe he did and pretended not to—that would be completely in keeping with his vain and egotistical style.

Why do I think that Toscanini didn't let it be known that I wrote to him? Because much later I received a letter from America: I was elected to the Toscanini Society! They must have thought that I was a great fan of the maestro's.

I began receiving records on a regular basis—all new recordings by Toscanini. My only comfort is that at least I always have a birthday present handy. Naturally, I wouldn't give something like that to a friend. But to an acquaintance—why not? It pleases them and it's less trouble for me. That's one of life's most difficult problems—what to give for a birthday or anniversary to a person you don't particularly like, don't know very well, and don't respect.

Conductors are too often rude and conceited tyrants. And in my youth I often had to fight fierce battles with them, battles for my music and my dignity.

Some of them tried to become my "patrons." Thanks a lot. Patronage makes me sick to my stomach. It was usually a poorly disguised attempt to foist their will on me, and I had to cut off these patrons brusquely, that is, put them in their place.

To respond to someone's rudeness in a way to end his desire to be rude once and for all is not easy. It's an art. I had good teachers. Naturally, Sollertinsky* was the best, but I tried to learn from others as well. I'm always happy to see that I've put down a boor.

An actor friend was appearing in a cabaret called Crooked Jimmy (this was in Moscow during the New Economic Policy). He came out on stage and wanted to begin, but he couldn't. A fat man was standing in front of the first row, berating someone in the audience. Time

*Ivan Ivanovich Sollertinsky (1902-1944), musicologist, Shostakovich's closest friend from 1927. He had an enormous influence on the formation of Shostakovich's tastes, and not only musically. A man of jovial and eccentric nature, Sollertinsky made brilliant appearances, and his pre-concert commentaries were often as appreciated as the music that followed. During the anti-formalist campaign of 1936, he was put under great pressure, but continued to defend Shostakovich. His only concession was the promise "to begin studying Georgian." Sollertinsky knew dozens of languages and dialects, including Sanskrit and Ancient Persian.

passed and finally my friend lost his patience and said, "Allow me to start, comrade . . ." only to hear the obnoxious and too familiar reply: "A goose is no comrade to a pig!"

My friend flapped his arms like wings and said, "In that case, I'm flying away. . . . " And tiptoed off the stage like a dying swan from *Swan Lake*.

That's a quick wit. The audience laughed so loud that the boor shot out of there like a bullet.

Once, in my presence, Sollertinsky cut a haughty and obnoxious woman down to size. She herself was nothing, but her husband was a Leningrad big shot. At a banquet for an opera premiere at the Maly Theater, Sollertinsky came up to this woman. And wanting to compliment her, he said in his usual excited, spluttering manner, "How wonderful you look, you are absolutely ravishing today!"

He was just getting ready to enlarge on his dithyramb when the lady interrupted, "Unfortunately, I can't say the same for you." (She had Sollertinsky's face in mind, as well as his rather extravagant manner of dressing.)

But Sollertinsky kept his wits about him and replied, "Why don't you do what I did? Lie."

Being rude is, in essence, easy; being sharp is significantly harder. I hope that the differences between these two manifestations of temperament are clear. The hardest, though, is telling the truth without being either rude or sharp. The ability to express yourself in this way comes only with years of experience.

But there is another danger here—that you begin expressing yourself obliquely. You begin lying.

In the last few years people have completely stopped being rude to me. It's good and it's bad. It should be obvious why it's good, and it's bad for two reasons.

First of all, people seem to be "protecting" me. They must be afraid that I'll shatter from a rude remark and they won't be able to glue me back together, not even in the best Kremlin hospital. They're sorry for me.

But the important part is this: the absence of rudeness today certainly doesn't mean that they won't be rude tomorrow or the next day with added gusto. Because boorishness as such is alive and flourishing and almost anything at all can happen at any time.

And you're no longer what you were, you grow soft. You're used to being treated well, you've lost your immunity. And then they'll trample you, poor naked devil, trample you to dust.

But at the present I sense a desire for restraint in their treatment of me, an avoidance of rudeness. And this inspires in me, a man brought up in the spirit of St. Petersburg, the desire to soften my opinions. And I immediately think of Glazunov.

Here's a man who listened to much more music than he needed to. I can't say anything as kind about myself. Glazunov always had a review ready, and not an overly severe one at that. Why should I do any less?

Plutarch was a great man, his parallel biographies are a marvelous thing. And now my own life seems better and more attractive through various kinds of parallels. In these pleasant surroundings I swim like a sardine in oil. Much honor, but little use.

Did Glazunov restrain himself consciously? Or was it just difficult to provoke him? I know of only a few times when Glazunov grew so angry that everyone noticed. Once I was involved, another time Prokofiev.

The incident of Prokofiev happened when I was still very young. But it was talked about later too, and the story became imbued with portent and considered almost symbolic, though as far as I'm concerned nothing particularly symbolic happened. Glazunov simply got up and left the hall during a performance of Prokofiev's *Scythian Suite*.

It was well known that Glazunov hated Prokofiev's music. But I'm ready to argue that in this case there was no demonstration intended. For Glazunov had listened, without leaving his seat or letting any expression cross his impassive face, to hundreds upon hundreds of works that were alien to him. What was the explanation, then?

A very simple one—*The Scythian Suite* was too loud for Glazunov and he feared for his hearing apparatus. The orchestra was trying too hard. After the premiere, the percussionist presented Prokofiev with the broken skin of the kettledrums.

And there's one other aspect, a very important one. Glazunov would never have left a concert hall during a performance—even if his life were in danger—unless he was sure that this would not upset the composer in the least. And Glazunov, undoubtedly, was right.

Prokofiev, as you know, got over his lack of success with Glazunov easily. He even put the occasion on his list of successes, so to speak. In this sense our reactions to the opinions of our Conservatory mentors differed radically.

Once, Prokofiev was showing his assignments in orchestration to Rimsky-Korsakov. This was always done in front of the entire class. Rimsky-Korsakov found a number of mistakes in Prokofiev's work and grew angry. Prokofiev turned to the class triumphantly—there, the old man is mad. He thought that it somehow increased his esteem. But as he later told it, his friends' faces remained serious; he didn't find support in this instance. And by the way, he never did learn how to orchestrate properly.

Prokofiev set himself at odds with the Conservatory almost from the very beginning. He was thirteen when he entered the St. Petersburg Conservatory. I was also thirteen, but I entered the Petrograd Conservatory, which was no longer the same place. In general, it's a question of discipline and character and a fix on the past and the future.

This may in part explain why Glazunov lost his temper a second time. It had to do with me, but he wasn't attacking me, he was defending me.

I hope I will be understood. I'm not bragging; on the contrary, this story shows me in a rather comic light and Glazunov as a highly decent man, while in the story with Prokofiev, it's Prokofiev who comes off well and Glazunov who looks a little silly.

But that seems to be my fate. Compared to me, Prokofiev always made more of a splash and seemed more interesting. Prokofiev always struck the more effective pose, so to speak, and took care with the background, wanting his almost classical profile to look as attractive as possible against it.

So the story that had to do with me took place five years later than the "Prokofiev" one. My teacher, Steinberg,* told me about it. Stein-

*Maximilian Oseyevich Steinberg (1883–1946), composer and teacher, son-in-law of Rimsky-Korsakov. For over forty years he was a professor at the Petersburg (later Petrograd and then Leningrad) Conservatory. Shostakovich studied composition with Steinberg from 1919 to 1930. The relations between teacher and student deteriorated as Shostakovich became more and more independent of Steinberg's teaching.

berg was present when they were going over the lists of scholarship recipients for the following year at the Conservatory. This was an important event, much more important than exams, so the entire staff was there.

This was a period of terrible famine. The gist of the scholarship was that its possessor was able to receive some groceries. In a word, it was a question of life and death. If you're on the list, you live. If you're crossed off, it's quite possible that you may die.

Naturally, they tried to pare the lists as much as possible. The longer the list, the less likely the government was to give the Conservatory anything at all.

My name was on the list, which was in the hands of Glazunov's assistant on administrative and organizational affairs. The list was a long one and they kept shortening it. The discussion was polite. Each professor defended the candidacy of "his" student, and they were all irritable, but they tried to control themselves. The atmosphere was charged.

The storm broke when they finally got to my name. It was the last one on the list. The assistant suggested dropping me. "This student's name says nothing to me." And Glazunov erupted. They say that he was a wild man and that he shouted something like, "If the name says nothing to you, then why are you sitting here with us at all? This is no place for you!"

Well, I'll omit the praise that he heaped on me since he shouted it out in a frenzied state. But this time his anger worked for me and I retained the scholarship. I was saved.

But these outbursts were very rare in Glazunov. And perhaps it's too bad that they were so rare. So many unsaid things collect in the soul, so much exhaustion and irritation lie as a heavy burden on the psyche. And you must, you *must* unburden your spiritual world or risk a collapse. Sometimes you feel like screaming, but you control yourself and just babble some nonsense.

As I reminisce about this major Russian musician and great Russian man I become agitated. I knew him and I knew him well. And today's generation virtually doesn't know him at all. For today's young musicians, Glazunov is like some Slavic wardrobe from Grandfather's furniture.

I appreciate Glazunov's greatness, but how can I make others understand it? Especially the young. The young students pass the bust of Glazunov in the Leningrad Conservatory every day, and they don't even turn their heads—I've watched.

The bust stands, but there is no love or understanding. You can't force love, the saying goes. And what's a bust or a monument, when you think about it? When they erected a monument in Moscow to "the best, the most talented" Mayakovsky,* as Stalin proclaimed him, a wag said, "You call that a monument? Now, if he were seated on a horse, then you'd be talking!" Must Glazunov be put on a horse? So that the students trip on the hoofs? Memory slips through one's fingers like sand.

A man dies and they want to serve him up to posterity. Serve him, so to speak, trussed up for our dear descendants at the table. So that they, napkin tucked under chin and armed with knife and fork, can dig in to the freshly deceased.

The deceased, as you know, have the inconvenient habit of cooling off too slowly; they're burning hot. So they are turned into aspics by pouring memories over them—the best form of gelatin.

And since deceased greats are also too large, they are cut down. The nose, say, is served separately, or the tongue. You need less gelatin that way. And that's how you get yesterday's classic as freshly cooked tongue in aspic. With a side dish of hoofs, from the horse he used to ride.

I'm trying to remember the people I knew without the gelatin. I don't pour aspic over them, I'm not trying to turn them into a tasty dish. I know that a tasty dish is easier to swallow and easier to digest. You know where it ends up.

I think Pushkin wrote, "Oblivion is the natural lot of anyone who is not present." It's horrible, but true. You have to fight it. How can it be? You're no sooner dead than forgotten.

*Vladimir Vladimirovich Mayakovsky (1893–1930), Futurist poet, one of the leaders and symbols of "left" art in Soviet Russia. With Meyerhold and Sergei Eisenstein, he supported Soviet power from the beginning, and wrote talented, innovative poetry that praised state trade, the secret police, and the first trials. Increasing creative difficulties led to his suicide. After his death his popularity began to decline, but Stalin's personal intervention assured Mayakovsky's role as official poet number one. Boris Pasternak said: "Mayakovsky was introduced forcibly, like the potato in the reign of Catherine the Great. That was his second death. This one was not his fault."

Take Miaskovsky,* for example. He wrote a number of symphonies, it seemed that the air was filled with them. He taught others, but now Miaskovsky is not played. He's forgotten.

I remember Miaskovsky used to tell his students: "What you have there isn't polyphony, it's muchyphony." Of course, he himself gave muchyphony its due, but he is forgotten unjustly.

And Ronya Shebalin?† He left a lot of excellent music, for example a fine violin concerto. And many of his quartets are fine. But is it possible to hear a work by Shebalin on the concert stage today? Oblivion, oblivion.

What about Misha Sokolovsky?‡ He was a marvelous director, I'd go so far as to call him a genius. He created a wonderful theater, he was adored, idolized. Everyone said that Sokolovsky was a director of genius. And now he's forgotten.

It's so unfair. People suffered, worked, thought. So much wisdom, so much talent. And they're forgotten as soon as they die. We must do everything possible to keep their memories alive, because we will be treated in the same way ourselves. How we treat the memory of others is how our memory will be treated. We must remember, no matter how hard it is.

---

*Nikolai Yakovlevich Miaskovsky (1881–1950), composer, a professor at the Moscow Conservatory for thirty years. He composed twenty-seven symphonies—an unparalleled output among musicians of the last century and a half—and holds an honorable position in the history of modern Russian music as head of the "Moscow" school of composition. In 1948, with Shostakovich and Prokofiev, he was branded a composer of "anti-people formalist tendencies."

†Vissarion (Ronya) Yakovlevich Shebalin (1902–1963), composer, a student of Miaskovsky and a friend of Shostakovich (who dedicated his Second Quartet to Shebalin). He was head of the Moscow Conservatory, but was ousted in 1948 at Stalin's request as another representative of "anti-people formalist tendencies."

‡ Mikhail Vladimirovich Sokolovsky (1901–1941), theater director, creator of the Leningrad Theater of Young Workers (TRAM), an avant-garde collective close to the aesthetics of the early Brecht and Piscator, in which Shostakovich worked in the late 1920s and early 1930s (see p. 112). In 1935, Sokolovsky left the theater under duress; soon afterward, TRAM was shut down. During World War II, Sokolovsky went to the front with the People's Volunteer Brigade and died near Leningrad (as did Shostakovich's student Fleishman).

STRAVINSKY is one of the greatest composers of our times and I truly love many of his works. My earliest and most vivid impression of Stravinsky's music is related to the ballet *Petrouchka*. I saw the Kirov Theater of Leningrad production many times, and I tried never to miss a performance. (Unfortunately, I haven't heard the new edition of *Petrouchka* for a smaller orchestra. I'm not sure that it is better than the earlier one.) Since then this marvelous composer invariably has been at the center of my attention, and I not only studied and listened to his music, but I played it and I made my own transcriptions as well.

I recall with pleasure my performance in the premiere of *Les Noces* in Leningrad, extraordinarily well performed by the Leningrad Choir under the direction of the outstanding choirmaster Klimov. One of the four piano parts—the second piano—was entrusted to me. The numerous rehearsals turned out to be both pleasant and beneficial for me. The work amazed everyone by its originality, sonority, and lyricism.

I also performed the *Serenade in A*. At the Conservatory we often played the piano concerto transcribed for two pianos. My student days hold another memory of a work by Stravinsky—the excellent opera *The Nightingale*. Of course, my acquaintance with it was made under "fatal" circumstances: during an exam on reading scores. I'm a little angry with the opera for that. It was like the Spanish Inquisition—a cruel sight. But I managed somehow and conquered *The Nightingale*.

Stravinsky gave me a lot. It was interesting to listen to him and it was interesting to look at the scores. I liked *Mavra,* I remember, and *L'Histoire du soldat*, particularly the first parts; it's too boring to listen to the work in its entirety. It's fashionable now to speak disparagingly of Stravinsky's opera *The Rake's Progress*, and that's a shame. The work is deeper than a first glance would lead you to believe. But we've become lazy and lack curiosity.

I have special memories of the *Symphony of Psalms*. I transcribed it for four-hand piano as soon as I got my hands on the score, and showed it to my students. I must note that it has its problems in terms of construction. It's crudely worked out, crudely. The seams show. In that sense the *Symphony in Three Movements* is stronger. In general, Stravinsky often has this problem; his construction sticks out like a scaffolding. There's no flow, no natural bridges. I find it irritating, but on the other hand, this clarity makes it easier for the listener. That must be one of the secrets of Stravinsky's popularity.

I like his violin concerto, and I love his mass—that's marvelous music. Fools think that Stravinsky began composing more poorly toward the end. That's calumny and envy speaking. To my taste, it's just the reverse. It's the early works I like less—for instance, *Sacre du printemps*. It's rather crude, so much of it calculated for external effect and lacking substance. I can say the same for *Firebird*, I really don't like it very much.

Still, Stravinsky is the only composer of our century whom I would call great without any doubt. Perhaps he didn't know how to do everything, and not everything that he did is equally good, but the best delights me.

It's another question as to how Russian a composer Stravinsky is.*

*Igor Fyodorovich Stravinsky (1882-1971) lived primarily outside Russia after 1908, and in 1914 moved abroad permanently—first to Switzerland, then to France, and finally to the U.S.A. For many years, Stravinsky's music was not performed in the Soviet Union at all. In 1962 the aged composer visited Leningrad and Moscow. The visit was accompanied by maximal official pomp, and Premier Khrushchev received the composer. Stravinsky's visit to the U.S.S.R. was a signal for his "rehabilitation" after several decades of sanctioned attacks. However, the question of Stravinsky's "Russian roots" is still an awkward one for Soviet criticism.

He was probably right not to return to Russia. His concept of morality is European. I can see that clearly from his memoirs—everything he says about his parents and colleagues is European. This approach is foreign to me.

And Stravinsky's idea of the role of music is also purely European, primarily French. My impressions of contemporary France were mixed. I personally felt that it was quite provincial.

When Stravinsky came to visit us, he came as a foreigner. It was even strange to think that we were born near each other, I in Petersburg and he not far from it.

(I don't know if anyone's paid any attention to this, but both Stravinsky and I are of Polish extraction. So was Rimsky-Korsakov. And we all belong to the same school, even though we expressed ourselves, so to speak, differently. Sollertinsky also came from a Russified Polish family. But that's just an aside. I don't think this has any serious import.)

The invitation to Stravinsky was the result of high politics. At the very top it was decided to make him the number one national composer, but this number didn't work. Stravinsky hadn't forgotten anything—that he had been called a lackey of American imperialism and a flunky of the Catholic Church—and the very same people who had called him that were now greeting him with outspread arms.

Stravinsky offered his walking stick instead of his hand to one of those hypocrites, who was forced to shake it, proving that he was the real lackey. Another kept hanging around, but didn't dare come up to him. He knew that he was at fault, so he stayed in the foyer the whole time, just like a lackey.* "Lackey, stay in the foyer, I'll deal with your master," as Pushkin once said.

I assume that all this disgusted Stravinsky so much that he left earlier than planned. And he did the right thing. He didn't make the mistake of Prokofiev, who ended up like a chicken in the soup.

Prokofiev and I never did become friends, probably because Prokofiev was not inclined toward friendly relations in general. He was a hard man and didn't seem interested in anything other than himself and his music. I hate being patted on the head. Prokofiev didn't like it either, but he allowed himself to be quite condescending to others.

*The references are to Boris Mikhailovich Yarustovsky (1911–1978) and Grigori Mikhailovich Shneyerson (b. 1900), musicologists who were both apparatchiks directing Soviet culture.

I doubt that a final summing up of Prokofiev's music is possible now. The time hasn't come for it yet, I imagine.

It's quite strange, but my tastes keep changing, and rather radically. Things that I liked quite recently I now like less, considerably less, and some I don't like at all. So how can I speak of music that I heard for the first time several decades ago? For instance, I remember Shcherbachev's piano suite, *Inventions*, written long ago, in the early twenties. At the time it seemed rather good to me. I recently heard it by chance on the radio. There's no inventiveness there at all.

And it's the same with Prokofiev. So many of his works that I liked once upon a time seem duller now.

A new period seemed to begin in his work just before his death, he seemed to be feeling his way along new paths. Perhaps this music would have been more profound than what we have, but it was only a beginning and we don't know the continuation.

Prokofiev had two favorite words. One was "amusing," which he used to evaluate everything around him. Everything—people, events, music. He seemed to feel that "amusing" covered *Wozzeck*. The second was "Understood?" That's when he wanted to know whether he was making himself clear.

Those two favorite words irritated me. Why the simple-minded cannibal's vocabulary? Ellochka the Cannibal, from Ilf and Petrov's story,* had a third vocabulary word in her arsenal: "homosexuality." But Prokofiev managed with just two.

Prokofiev was lucky from childhood, he always got what he wanted. He never had my worries, he always had money and success and, as a result, the personality of a spoiled *Wunderkind*.

Chekhov once said, "The Russian writer lives in a drainpipe, eats woodlice, and sleeps with washerwomen." In that sense, Prokofiev was never a Russian, and that's why he was stunned by the turn his life took.

Prokofiev and I could never have had a frank talk, but I feel that I know him, and I can imagine very well why that European man preferred to return to Russia.

Prokofiev was an inveterate gambler and, in the long run, he always

*Ilya Ilf (Ilya Arnoldovich Fainsilberg; 1897–1937) and Yevgeny Petrov (Yevgeny Petrovich Kataev; 1903–1942), popular satirists and collaborators. Sentences and jokes from their novels *The Twelve Chairs* and *The Golden Calf* are widely quoted in Soviet life; several characters from these novels have taken on the aura of folklore.

won. Prokofiev thought that he had calculated perfectly and that he would be a winner this time too. For some fifteen years Prokofiev sat between two stools—in the West he was considered a Soviet and in Russia they welcomed him as a Western guest.

But then the situation changed and the bureaucrats in charge of cultural affairs started squinting at Prokofiev, meaning, Who's this Parisian fellow? And Prokofiev decided that it would be more profitable for him to move to the U.S.S.R. Such a step would only raise his stock in the West, because things Soviet were becoming fashionable just then, they would stop considering him a foreigner in the U.S.S.R., and therefore he would win all around.

By the way, the final impetus came from his cardplaying. Prokofiev was deeply in debt abroad and he had to straighten out his financial affairs quickly, which he hoped to do in the U.S.S.R.

And this was where Prokòfiev landed like a chicken in soup. He came to Moscow to teach them, and they started teaching him. Along with everyone else, he had to memorize the historic article in *Pravda* "Muddle Instead of Music." * He did look through the score of my *Lady Macbeth*, however. He said, "Amusing."

I don't think that Prokofiev ever treated me seriously as a composer; he considered only Stravinsky a rival and never missed a chance to take a shot at him. I remember he started telling me some vile story about Stravinsky. I cut him off.

There was a period when Prokofiev was frightened out of his wits. He wrote a cantata with words by Lenin and Stalin—it was rejected. He wrote songs for solo, chorus, and orchestra, also praising Stalin— another failure. Meyerhold began work on Prokofiev's opera *Semyon Kotko*—and he was arrested. And then, to top it off, Prokofiev ran over a girl in his Ford. It was a new Ford and Prokofiev couldn't handle it. Moscow pedestrians are undisciplined, plow right under cars. Prokofiev called them suicidal.

Prokofiev had the soul of a goose; he always had a chip on his shoulder.

Prokofiev had to swallow many humiliations, and somehow he man-

*The sadly famous editorial article in *Pravda* "Muddle Instead of Music" (January 28, 1936), inspired by Stalin, attacked Shostakovich's opera *Lady Macbeth* and began the broad government campaign against formalism in various fields of literature and art (see Introduction).

aged. He wasn't allowed abroad, his operas and ballets weren't produced, any clerk could give him orders. And the only thing he could do was give them the finger in his pocket.

A characteristic example is the orchestration of Prokofiev's ballets—to this day the Bolshoi does not use his orchestrations. Even accepting the fact that orchestration was not Prokofiev's forte (I made corrections when I performed his First Piano Concerto at a very young age) and that orchestration was always work for him, and hard work, which Prokofiev always tried to palm off on someone else, the Bolshoi treated his ballets barbarically. It should be known that their production of *Romeo and Juliet* has Pogrebov as Prokofiev's co-composer. *The Stone Flower* too. A striking man, that Pogrebov, a percussionist and hussar of orchestration. He orchestrated with hellish speed and solidity.

For a while he was taken with the idea of writing an opera based on a Leskov story, that is, a Prokofiev *Lady Macbeth.* He wanted to show me up and prove that he could write a real Soviet opera, without the crudity and naturalistic touches. But he dropped the idea.

Prokofiev was always afraid that he was being overlooked—cheated out of his prizes, orders, and titles. He set great store by them and was overjoyed when he received his first Stalin Prize. This naturally did not further our relationship, or improve the friendly atmosphere, so to speak.

The animosity was revealed during the war. Prokofiev wrote several weak opuses, for instance the 1941 Suite and "Ballad of the Boy Who Remained Unknown." I expressed an opinion of these works that was commensurate with their worth. Prokofiev did not remain in my debt for long.

In general, he scanned my works without a close reading, but he voiced rather definitive-sounding opinions on them. In his lengthy correspondence with Miaskovsky, Prokofiev makes quite a few disparaging remarks about me. I had an opportunity to see the letters, and it's a shame they haven't been published. It must be the will of Mira Alexandrovna Mendelson.* She probably didn't want Prokofiev's harsh judgments made public. I was not the only one he criticized in

*Mira Alexandrovna Mendelson-Prokofieva (1915–1968), Prokofiev's second wife. The correspondence between Prokofiev and Miaskovsky was published after Shostakovich's death. As was to be expected, it was bowdlerized.

his letters, there were many other composers and musicians.

Personally, I don't see why his sharpness should be an obstacle to their publication. After all, they can use ellipses. Say, if Prokofiev wrote "that idiot Gauk,"* they could print it as "that . . . Gauk."

I'm rather cool about Prokofiev's music now and listen to his compositions without any particular pleasure. I suppose *The Gambler* is the opera of his that I like the most, but even it has too many superficial, random effects. Prokofiev sacrificed essential things too often for a flashy effect. You see it in *The Flaming Angel* and in *War and Peace*. I listen and remain unmoved. That's how things are now. Once it was different; but this was a long time ago. And then my infatuation with Mahler pushed Stravinsky and certainly Prokofiev into the background. Ivan Ivanovich Sollertinsky insisted that Mahler and Prokofiev were incompatible.

Everyone knows about Sollertinsky now, every idiot, but this is not the kind of popularity that I would have wished for my late friend; they've turned him into a laughingstock. It's the fault of Andronikov† and his television appearances in which he depicts Sollertinsky as some kind of fool.

Actually Sollertinsky was a great scholar who knew over twenty languages and dozens of dialects. He kept his diary in ancient Portuguese to keep it safe from prying eyes. Naturally, he was fluent in Ancient Greek and Latin.

And what do people remember about him now? That his tie was askew and that a new suit on him looked old in five minutes. Andronikov's nonsense made him ludicrous.

We were introduced three times and it was only on the third time that he remembered me, which is strange considering his prodigious memory. When something interested Sollertinsky he remembered it instantly and forever. He could glance at a page of Sanskrit and recite it from memory. Obviously, I didn't interest him very much the first two times.

That's understandable. The first time we met on the street and the

---

*Alexander Vasilyevich Gauk (1893–1963) conducted the premieres of Shostakovich's Third Symphony and two of his ballets. He headed the best orchestras of the Soviet Union.

†Irakli Luarsabovich Andronikov (b. 1908), literary historian, whose "oral stories" became extremely popular on radio and television; in them he brilliantly imitates the celebrities he knew, including Sollertinsky.

second time under truly ridiculous circumstances—at an exam on Marxism-Leninism. We were both taking the exam. He went in first and came out and scared all of us, saying that the questions were unbelievably hard. We almost died of fright.

There were a lot of us there, guinea pigs. We had only the vaguest notion of the science we were being tested on, and Sollertinsky announced that they wanted to know about Sophocles as an example of a materialistic tendency. He was just joking, of course. But we didn't even know in which century Sophocles had lived.

By the way, about Marxism-Leninism. Somewhere in the mid 1920s the conductor Gauk and his wife, a ballerina (Elizaveta Gerdt), were made Honored Artists of the R.S.F.S.R.,* a title that was considered an honor in those days and bestowed on only a few people. Gauk and his wife gave a series of receptions to celebrate. People came, ate and drank, and while they were at it, congratulated their hosts.

At one of the soirees, Sollertinsky and I were among the guests. Good food and many compliments. Then Sollertinsky stood, glass in hand, and gave a toast congratulating the hosts on such a high honor and hoping that they would pass the test and be confirmed in their titles.

Gauk panicked: "What test?" Now it was Sollertinsky's turn to be surprised. What, didn't his dear hosts know that first you had to pass a test on Marxism-Leninism? You didn't get the title until you'd passed.

Sollertinsky spoke with such seriousness that the Gauks didn't suspect a thing. They were both in a state of panic, for a test on Marxism-Leninism was no joke.

We calmly finished eating and drinking and departed, leaving the gloomy couple at the empty table.

Gauk was a rare specimen of stupidity; we used to call him "Papa Gauk," which sounded like *popugai* [parrot]. It's thanks to Gauk that the manuscripts of my Fourth, Fifth, and Sixth Symphonies are lost. And he replied to my feeble objections with: "Manuscripts? So what? I lost a suitcase with my new shoes, and you're worried about manuscripts."

*The Russian Soviet Federated Socialist Republic, one of the fifteen republics of the U.S.S.R.

Sollertinsky never prepared his jokes, he improvised. I was present at many of his improvisations, for we spent a lot of time together. He often took me along when he lectured. I sat quietly, waiting for the lecture to be over, when we would go for a walk. We strolled down Nevsky Prospect or went to drink beer at the People's House. It had marvelous attractions, including a roller coaster.

Well, at one of his lectures Sollertinsky was talking about Scriabin, whom he didn't like very much. He shared my opinion that Scriabin knew as much about orchestration as a pig about oranges. Personally, I think all of Scriabin's symphonic poems—the "Divine," and the "Ecstasy," and "Prometheus"—are gibberish.

Sollertinsky decided to have some fun and to amuse me. And with a tremor in his voice he declared from the stage, "In the brilliant constellation of Russian composers—Kalafati, Koreshchenko, Smirensky, and others—Scriabin was if not first, then far from the last." And went on.

I almost choked on my laughter, but no one else noticed. Sollertinsky pronounced the names with such grandeur.

By the way, about Kalafati, Koreshchenko, et al. (there is no composer by the name of Smirensky). Once Glazunov asked me to sort out his sheet music, that is, to put all the Beethoven together, the Brahms, the Bach, and then file them all under "B." And the Glinka and Gluck under "G," and so on.

I came to his house and began going through the music. And I saw that under "I" were obviously misfiled a number of composers whose names began with many different letters.

They included Kalafati, Koreshchenko, and Akimenko, as well as Ivanov. I asked Glazunov why all these composers were under "I" and he said, "Because they are all insignificant composers."

Once at a lecture I heard Sollertinsky field a question from the audience: Was it true that Pushkin's wife had been a mistress of Nicholas II? Sollertinsky, without pausing to think for a second, replied, "If Pushkin's wife, Natalya Nikolayevna, had died eight years later than she had, and if Nicholas II had been capable of performing sexual intercourse at the age of three, then in that case, what my respected questioner is asking could have taken place."

As soon as I got home I made a point of checking Sollertinsky's dates. He hadn't made an error, they were exactly right. Sollertinsky had a prodigious memory, containing masses of numbers.

But the idiocy of his listeners could give pause even to Sollertinsky. He lectured at the Conservatory and there was always a question period afterward. Sollertinsky was invariably brilliant. One time a huge lummox rose and asked, "Tell me, who is Karapetian?" Sollertinsky thought. A sensation—Sollertinsky didn't know the answer.

He said, "He must be a fifteenth-century Armenian philosopher. I'll find out by our next class, comrade." The student rose at the next lecture and asked, "Tell me, who is Karapetian?" "I don't know." "I'm Karapetian," the student announced. The class tittered. Sollertinsky said, "Ah, now I know who Karapetian is. He's a fool."

This Karapetian was a tenor and had a reputation in his own right. He was doing *Eugene Onegin* at the Opera Studio, singing the well-known couplets of Triquet. The performance was under way, everything was going well, but when he was cued, Karapetian didn't open his mouth. The conductor started over but Triquet kept silent.

They rang down the curtain and the conductor attacked Karapetian backstage. "What's the matter, did you forget your words?" "No, the tune."

(Much later I was at a performance at the Yerevan Opera House and a good-looking man came up to me: "Don't you recognize me? Karapetian.")

The lecturing tired Sollertinsky's vocal cords and he decided to see a teacher to help his voice. As usual, the vocal teacher performed his magic with disastrous results. Sollertinsky's voice was ruined and he became hoarse.

Once Sollertinsky was handed a note from the audience. He opened it, smiling, and read, "Enough wheezing." Sollertinsky shut up and left the stage.

Composers had a great fear of Sollertinsky, who was famous for his wit. Asafiev,* for instance, never did recover from Sollertinsky's re-

*Boris Vladimirovich Asafiev (1884–1949), musicologist and composer. It would be no exaggeration to say that Asafiev is the most important representative of Russian thought on music throughout the country's musicological history. (His work is only now becoming known in the West.) Unfortunately, high scruples were not among the character traits of this brilliant scholar and critic. It is important to stress Asafiev's significance because the reader of this book might easily come away with an inaccurate picture of his impressive accomplishments. Some of the best

mark about one of his ballets that had been given a lush production: "I'd be happy to watch, I just can't stand listening."

Once I was at the Philharmonic, where they were playing Stravinsky's *Nightingale*. Sollertinsky came on with a brief introduction. He began listing musical works dealing with China and said, "Well, there's also Glière's *Red Poppy*, forgive the expression." Glière was sitting next to me and turned color. He went backstage in the intermission and said, "Why do you apologize for mentioning *Red Poppy?* My composition isn't a swear word, you know."

The Red Poppy, staged by Lopukhov* at the Kirov Theater, was immensely popular. Glière wasn't a bad fellow, but he was a mediocre composer. Yet his ballet stayed on the boards endlessly, for decades. In the fifties they changed the name to *The Red Flower*, when it was discovered that in China the poppy was the raw material for opium and not the symbol of revolutionary fervor that Glière had thought.

Another of Glière's works that has unflagging popularity is "Hymn to a Great City." I shudder every time I get off the Red Arrow Express at the Leningrad Station because Glière's composition blares from every loudspeaker. The travelers duck their heads and walk faster.

Sollertinsky was mostly right in his attitude toward Western music. He never tried to run ahead of progress, as Asafiev did, and therefore he didn't have to change his opinions as often as Asafiev. Sollertinsky's love of Mahler speaks for itself. In that sense he opened my eyes.

Studying Mahler changed many things in my tastes as a composer. Mahler and Berg are my favorite composers even today, as opposed to Hindemith, say, or Křenek and Milhaud, whom I liked when I was young but cooled toward rapidly.

It's said that Berg's *Wozzeck* influenced me greatly, influenced both my operas, and so I am often asked about Berg, particularly since we have met.

It's amazing how lazy some musicologists can be. They write books

---

pages ever written about Shostakovich belong to Asafiev, though the two men's relationship varied at different times. Shostakovich could not forgive Asafiev for the position he took in 1948, when he allowed his name to be used in an attack on the "formalist" composers. Shostakovich told me that he destroyed his correspondence with Asafiev. Asafiev used the pseudonym "Igor Glebov" for his critical pieces; whence the references in this book to "Igors and Borises."

*Fyodor Vasilyevich Lopukhov (1886–1973), avant-garde choreographer, produced Shostakovich's ballets *Bolt* and *Bright Stream*.

that could cause a cockroach infestation in their readers' brains. At least, I've never had the occasion to read a good book about myself, and I do read them rather carefully, I think.

When they serve coffee, don't try to find beer in it. Chekhov used to like to say that. When they listen to *The Nose* and *Katerina Izmailova* they try to find *Wozzeck*, and *Wozzeck* has absolutely nothing to do with them. I liked that opera very much and I never missed a performance when it played in Leningrad, and there were eight or nine performances before *Wozzeck* was removed from the repertory. The pretext was the same one they used with my *Nose*—that it was too hard for the singers to stay in condition and they needed too many rehearsals to make it worthwhile; and the masses weren't exactly beating down the doors.

Berg came to Leningrad to see his *Wozzeck*. Musically, Leningrad was an avant-garde city, and our production of *Wozzeck* was one of the first, I think right after the Berlin production.

It was known beforehand how pleasant a man Berg was because the critic Nikolai Strelnikov told everyone. Strelnikov wrote innumerable operettas and was sure that he was a great opera composer manqué. I can imagine how he bored Berg in Vienna, for in Leningrad he practically ran him to the ground. He dragged Berg to a rehearsal of one of his operettas and then told everyone how Berg had praised him. And really, Berg turned out to be exquisitely polite. Everyone liked Berg; he was nice and he didn't behave like a visiting guest star. He was rather shy and kept looking behind him.

We later learned the cause of his shyness. Berg had been terrified of coming to Leningrad. He didn't know what awaited him and he feared that there would be some sort of scandal with *Wozzeck*. And there was more. Just before the premiere he received a telegram from his wife begging him not to enter the opera house because she had learned that they would throw a bomb at him.

You can imagine his condition. He had to go to the rehearsal and he kept waiting for the bomb. And the officials who greeted Berg seemed quite grim. That's why he kept looking around. But when Berg realized that there probably wouldn't be any bomb he grew bolder, even asking to conduct his own work.

A composer conducting his own work usually looks ridiculous.

There are a few exceptions, but Berg didn't add to the list. As soon as he started waving his arms, the wonderful Maryinsky Theater orchestra disintegrated, each member pulling in his own direction.

It did not bode well, but the situation was saved by Vladimir Dranishnikov, the theater's chief conductor. He stood behind Berg and signaled the orchestra. Berg didn't notice a thing because he was so engrossed in the process of conducting.

The premiere of *Wozzeck* went brilliantly. The composer's presence added to the excitement. But why had he been welcomed so coldly? I learned the reason later. It turned out that the singer who was supposed to play Marie developed angina. In any other country they probably would have postponed the premiere, but not here. How could we fall flat on our faces in front of foreigners?

It only appears that we despise foreigners and everything foreign. Morbid contempt is the reverse face of morbid adulation. And contempt and adulation coexist in one soul. A good example of that is Mayakovsky. In his poems he spat on Paris and America, but he preferred to buy his shirts in Paris and he would have been willing to climb under a table to get his hands on an American fountain pen.

And it's the same with musicians. We all talk about having our own school, but the performer who is the most highly regarded here is one who's made a name for himself in the West. I'm still surprised that the pianists Sofronitsky and Yudina* gained such unheard-of popularity with almost no appearances in the West.

So this business with Berg was typical. They ordered the singer to sing despite her throat problems. And she sang even though her career as a singer was in jeopardy. It's no joke singing with a sick throat.

Berg didn't notice anything amiss there either. Shaporin† gave a re-

*Vladimir Vladimirovich Sofronitsky (1901–1961) and Maria Veniaminovna Yudina (1899–1970), pianists, who with Shostakovich were students of Leonid Vladimirovich Nikolayev (1878–1942), a professor at the Leningrad Conservatory. Shostakovich dedicated his Second Piano Sonata to Nikolayev. The creative path of Sofronitsky and Yudina is unusual in many ways. Both consciously set themselves against the Soviet musical establishment and became the objects of a cult following among Soviet audiences. Biographical facts of Sofronitsky's life include his marriage to the daughter of Alexander Scriabin (he is considered the best Russian interpreter of that composer); numerous subsequent romantic and scandalous entanglements; and an addiction to drugs and alcohol, which led to his death. Yudina's life was dominated by religious principles, which overshadowed her entire performing career. She actively promoted avant-garde music in the Soviet Union in those years when such music was officially frowned upon. Recordings by both Sofronitsky and Yudina, now issued in great numbers in Russia, are sold out immediately.

†Yuri Alexandrovich Shaporin (1887–1966), academically traditional composer and pedagogue, widely beloved for his gentleness.

ception in his honor after the premiere, and Berg said little, mostly praising the production and particularly the singers.

I sat and said nothing, partly because I was young and mostly because my German wasn't very good.

However, it turned out later that Berg had remembered me. I learned just recently that he had heard my First Symphony in Vienna and seemed to like it. Berg wrote me a letter about it.

They tell me that he sent the letter via Asafiev. I never received the letter and I never heard a word about it from Asafiev, which says that much more about the man.

Berg, it seemed to me, left Leningrad with relief. "So fly off . . . the sooner the better," as Pushkin wrote. But Berg left two legends behind. The source of one legend was a critic and fan of Scriabin. Berg supposedly told him that he owed everything as a composer to Scriabin. The other legend came from a critic who didn't care for Scriabin. Supposedly Berg told *him* that he had never heard a note by Scriabin.

Over forty years have passed, but both men still repeat with a thrill what Berg said to them. So much for eyewitness accounts.

But there's no reason to be upset that they lie about Berg. He's a stranger, a visitor, you're supposed to lie about him, for foreigners lie about us (I don't mean Berg personally). What hurts is that here they lie about their own Russian musicians.

Lately I've been thinking about my relationship with Glazunov. This is a special topic that's very important to me. As I see, it's also popular among those who are becoming interested in my humble self. They're writing about our relationship. Quite a bit, and it's all wrong.

And perhaps, therefore, it would be a good idea to spend some time on this point. Because Glazunov is, after all, one of the major figures of Russian music whom I've met.

Glazunov played an important role in my life. But the scribblers who like the theme are painting saccharine pictures. There are lots of them by now. People bring me magazines or books with some new story about Glazunov and me. It's getting so that there's no point to them any more.

It's like Glazunov and the famous choreographer Marius Petipa and Glazunov's ballet *Raymonda*. They worked on it and worked on it. The ballet was produced and was very successful. One day the composer and the choreographer ran into each other. Glazunov asked Petipa, "Tell me, do you know the plot of *Raymonda?* What's the plot?" Petipa replied, "Of course..." Then he thought and said, "No, I can't remember. Can you?" Glazunov said, "No."

And it's so simple. When they worked, they created pretty pictures. Glazunov thought about the music, Petipa dreamed about the *pas*, and they forgot about the plot.

And the pictures that depict Glazunov and me obeying the popular ditty and "marching through life with a song" are also pointless. Probably the authors of such sentimental stories would like everything in life to be pretty and edifying and touching—you know, this century and the century past. Or as a schoolchild wrote about Chekhov, "He had one foot in the past and with the other he welcomed the future."

And this nonsense has a glorious tradition in Russia—for how is cultural history written here? Everyone embraces everyone else, everyone blesses everyone else. They write sweet notes on laurel wreaths: "To my conquering student from his conquered teacher," as Zhukovsky wrote to Pushkin. And then there's always: "And descending into the grave, he gave his blessing." Quotes from Pushkin's famous poem ring in my ears.

And naturally, they forget to add that before "old man Derzhavin"* noticed Pushkin, he asked the servant, "Where's the can around here?"

I think the can is indispensable to this historic scene. It adds the missing realistic touch that makes it possible to believe that this event, found in all the primers and textbooks, really took place.

On the other hand, the can should not take up the entire stage. "The dawn of a new age" and all the sentimental tripe is vile. But digging around in shit is also vile. What choice is there?

I choose the truth. And perhaps it's hopeless and a mistake, because the truth always brings problems and dissatisfactions. Insulted citizens howl that you've hurt their most noble feelings and didn't spare the finest strings of their exalted soul.

But what can you do? "I walk out onto the road alone," as the poet† said. As you know, nothing good came of his walking out alone.

---

*In the poem, the great poet Gavriil Romanovich Derzhavin (1743–1816) visits young Pushkin's lycée and predicts a glorious future for him.

†The poet is Mikhail Yuryevich Lermontov (1814–1841), who was killed in a duel that was the inevitable result of a chain of events and circumstances which included a confrontation with Tsar Nicholas I. Shostakovich quotes Lermontov's most famous lyric poem ironically.

The whole point is that it only seems that you're alone when you go out. A wise man reminds us, "Man is not alone. Someone is always watching him." It's like that with the road. You walk and someone's already lying in wait for you.

I love Glazunov and that's why I'm telling the truth about him. Let anyone who doesn't know better lie about Glazunov. They can take their laurel wreaths with sweet messages and shove them. For them, Glazunov is fiction, the Bronze Horseman. They see only the horse's hoofs.

My good relationship with Glazunov developed on an excellent basis—alcohol.

You must not think that Glazunov and I used to sit around and drink and eat. After all, he was over fifty and I was thirteen when our paths crossed. We could hardly have become drinking partners. And I must add that Glazunov didn't simply enjoy drinking. He suffered from incessant thirst. Some people have such unfortunate constitutions. Of course, under normal circumstances, it wouldn't have been a problem. Why not drink to slake thirst? You just stop at the store and buy a few bottles, particularly since I think that Glazunov couldn't have managed more than two bottles at a time, his health wouldn't have permitted it.

But here enter those extreme, abnormal circumstances, also known as that "unforgettable year 1919," or "military communism."

Those two words say little to the young generation now, but they meant a great deal, including the complete absence of an opportunity to drink and eat. No, no, not even on the day of your former saint, because there was a complete and total disappearance of food, and of wine and liquor products because of a strict ban on alcohol.

Now when I think back I just don't want to believe that year ever existed. It's unpleasant to remember. And it must be because so many don't like to think about it that I haven't seen any references to the sorry circumstances of our lives back then. All the memoirists must have amnesia caused by malnutrition.

All right, let's put the food problem aside and concentrate on the vodka. For many its disappearance was a tragedy, and for Glazunov the sad fact constituted a catastrophe.

How did other people react to this? Life dictates its laws and you must obey. Let's bear up, comrades, and so on. Probably Glazunov tried to march in step with the times. He probably thought, Well, I can't drink, so I won't. And he went an hour without a drink, two hours. He probably went outside to breathe some fresh air. The air in Petrograd was wonderful then—pine- and fir-scented, since most of the factories were shut down, thus reducing the air pollution considerably. And he saw that life couldn't go on like this, because he was suffering too much.

You know that you have to find the cause for any disease and then beat the hell out of it with a log. That's the advice all the healers in Russia gave from time immemorial. And now we hear the same valuable advice from our physicians.

Glazunov realized that the cause of his distress was the absence of the precious liquid. And therefore he had to get hold of some. Even without a log, since logs in those unforgettable and highly romantic days were also in short supply. (Firewood was invaluable then, people even gave logs as birthday presents. You could certainly bring a bundle as a present, in fact such a valuable gift was quite welcome.)

A joke's a joke, but this was serious, they didn't have what could be called the last solace in life. And without it, as Zoshchenko used to say, speech grew difficult, breathing irregular, and nerves frazzled.

Since there was no vodka, you had to get raw alcohol, that was obvious even to a child. But there was no alcohol. It was given out in only two cases: as medical aid for the wounded and for scientific defense experiments. And the last of the cologne had been consumed long ago.

I'm coming to the gist of the story. Glazunov met my parents and they talked about this and that, when it came out that my father had access to state alcohol.*

Glazunov had lost a lot of weight by then and looked peaked. His face was yellow and unhealthy, with a myriad of tiny lines under the eyes. It was obvious that the man was suffering. And so they came to an agreement: Father would help Glazunov out with alcohol. He would get it for him, from state reserves.

While I studied at the Conservatory I often ran errands for Gla-

---

*Shostakovich's father worked at the Institute of Standards, which was concerned, among other matters, with establishing a universal metric system in Russia. He was assistant to the manager and had broad powers, and therefore he had access to "scarce" matériel and products.

zunov, delivering letters to various places—offices, the Philharmonic. But I particularly remember his other letters, the ones he asked me to deliver to my father, because I knew that they contained the usual request for alcohol. "Dear Dmitri Boleslavovich, could you please spare . . . " and so on.

Why did I take note of these occasions? Because I wasn't a child any more and I understood everything. And first and foremost, I knew that this was serious.

In those days every person had some sort of shady business going. You had to survive somehow, and everyone was walking close to the edge. But in this case Father could have got into a real mess. Alcohol was worth its weight in gold, even more. Because what was gold? Only metal. They were planning to build toilets out of it, as Lenin promised, and no one had really planned to abolish alcohol. It was like life itself, and people caught in business involving alcohol were deprived of their lives.

Back then it was called being sentenced to the "highest measure of punishment," which, translated, meant "to be shot." And people used to joke then, "Anything but the highest measure. I'm allergic to the highest measure." In those heroic times there were a lot of synonyms for the simple word "shoot," including "expend," "send to the left," "send to Dukhonin's staff," "liquidate," and "lay down." There were many more. It's amazing that there were so many expressions for a single ugly, unnatural act. Why were people afraid to call it by its name?

For no matter what you call it, it's still shooting. And Father was risking his life then. It must run in the family—taking risks.

I worried about Father, I really did. It was a good thing that I wasn't asked to take the alcohol to Glazunov, for I could have dropped the bottle or done so many other stupid things. And what if I had been caught?

Glazunov used to come to our house for it. It was done with the greatest conspiratorial air possible. When I think about it now my heart rate goes up, it's like watching a frightening movie. Sometimes I dream about Glazunov's visits.

Later, much later, when my father was no longer alive and Glazunov lived abroad, rumors started around Leningrad about this whole business. I must have carelessly told someone and I never did lack well-wishers. People began saying things like, "Well, naturally he's got no talent. He bought Glazunov with alcohol. And all his excellent grades at the Conservatory were lubricated with alcohol. What a fraud, and a composer to boot!"

They suggested taking away my diploma, but nothing came of it.

All right, go ahead, kick me, I won't say a word, I thought then. But now I'd like to say the following in my defense: I studied honestly and worked honestly. I was lazier at first and less so later. And there were no stories about me like the ones about the legendary Anatol Liadov.

As a youth, Liadov played the violin and gave it up, then he played piano and dropped that too. He paid little attention to his composition studies. For instance, he would be assigned to write a fugue and he knew ahead of time that he wouldn't do it. And he would tell his sister, with whom he lived, "Don't give me dinner until I've written the fugue." Dinnertime would roll around and the fugue would be unwritten. "I won't feed you because you haven't completed the assignment. You asked me to do that yourself," Liadov's sister, a kind woman, would say. "As you like," our marvelous young man would reply. "I'll dine with Auntie." And leave.

I wrote my Conservatory fugues honestly; Glazunov didn't let composers off lightly on the exams, though he was more liberal with performers. He always gave them high marks. A talented person could get a 5+ [A+] without much effort.

But composition was another matter. He could be very fussy and could argue long and hard about whether a student should get a 3 or a 3− or perhaps a 2+. A teacher was overjoyed if he managed to get his student an extra half grade. And I'd like to show that I had trouble with him too, despite the notorious alcohol.

There was an examination on the fugue. Glazunov gave the theme and I had to write a fugue with a stretto. I sat and puffed over it, I was soaked with perspiration, but I couldn't do the stretto. You could kill me, but it didn't work. I thought there was a catch in it, maybe there wasn't supposed to be a stretto. So I handed in the fugue without one, and I received a 5−. I was hurt. Should I go and talk to Glazunov? That wasn't done, but on the other hand, it looked as though I hadn't passed well enough. I went to see him.

Glazunov and I began looking it over and it turned out that I had incorrectly copied down the theme. I got a note wrong. That's why I couldn't do the stretto. That miserable note changed everything. If I had written it down correctly, I could have done all kinds of stretti. At a fourth, or a fifth, or an octave. I could have written canon by augmentation or diminution or even retrograde canon. But only on the condition that I had the theme copied correctly, and I had made a mistake.

But Glazunov didn't change my grade, instead he scolded me.

I remember his lecture, word for word, to this day: "Even if you had mistaken that note, young man, you should have realized that it was a mistake and corrected it."

I studied honestly at the Conservatory, working harder than many others. I didn't pretend to be a genius and I attended all the classes.

Being a diligent student wasn't easy in those days. The times were hard, even the teachers didn't make much effort. For instance, Nikolayev, my professor, was a refined man, more than refined, in fact, and his tastes were recherché as well. Consequently he couldn't allow himself to appear at the Conservatory bundled up in rags. But it was cold at the Conservatory, there was no heat, so Nikolayev came up with this solution—he came late. The students would tire of waiting and leave. But I sat and waited.

Sometimes another stubborn student, Yudina, and I would get four-hand transcriptions from the library and play to pass the time.

Yudina was a strange person, and very much a loner. She gained immense popularity, first in Leningrad and then in Moscow, primarily because of her distinction as a pianist.

Nikolayev often said to me, "Go and listen to how Marusya plays." (He called her Marusya and me Mitya.) "Go and listen. In a four-voice fugue, every voice has its own timbre when she plays."

That seemed astounding—could it be possible? I would go and listen, hoping, naturally, to find that the professor was wrong, that it was just wishful thinking. Most astounding was that when Yudina played, each of the four voices really had its own timbre, difficult as that is to imagine.

Yudina played Liszt like no one else. Liszt is a very verbose composer. In my youth I played a lot of Liszt but then I cooled toward him completely, even from the point of view of sheer pianism. My first solo recital had a mixed program, but my second was all Liszt. But then I grew tired of Liszt—too many notes.

Yudina was wonderful at those Liszt pieces that didn't have quite so many notes, for instance, "Les Cloches de Genève," which I think is his best piano work.

Once Yudina stung me rather badly. I had learned Beethoven's *Moonlight* and *Appassionata* Sonatas and I performed them often, particularly the *Appassionata*. And Yudina said to me, "Why do you keep playing them? Take on the *Hammerklavier*."

I was hurt by the mockery and I went to Nikolayev, who agreed to let me learn the *Hammerklavier*. Before bringing it to Nikolayev, I played it for Yudina several times, because she had a marvelous understanding of Beethoven. I was especially impressed by her performance of Beethoven's last sonata, opus 111. The second part is extremely long and extremely boring, but when Yudina played I didn't seem to notice.

It was thought that Yudina had a special, profoundly philosophical approach to what she played. I don't know, I never noticed that. On the contrary, I always thought that much of her playing depended on her mood—the way it is with every woman.

Externally, there was little in Yudina's playing that was feminine. She usually played energetically and forcefully, like a man. She had powerful and rather masculine hands with long, sturdy fingers. She held them in a unique way so that they resembled an eagle's claws, to use a trite metaphor. But of course, Yudina remained a woman and all the purely feminine feelings played an important role in her life.

When she was young, she wore a floor-length black dress. Nikolayev used to predict that when she was old she would appear on stage in a diaphanous peignoir. Luckily for her audience, Yudina did not follow his prophecy, she continued wearing her shapeless black dress.

I had the impression that Yudina wore the same black dress during her entire long life, it was so worn and soiled. But in her later years, Yudina added sneakers, which she sported summer and winter. When Stravinsky was in the U.S.S.R. in 1962, she came to the reception for him in her sneakers. "Let him see how the Russian avant-garde lives."

I don't know if Stravinsky saw, but I doubt that her sneakers had the desired effect on him.

Whatever Yudina played, she played "not like everyone else." Her numerous fans went wild, but there were some interpretations that I didn't understand and when I asked about these I usually got the reply, "I feel it that way." Now, what kind of philosophy is that?

I showed Yudina my works; I was always curious to learn her opinion. But in those days, it seemed to me, she wasn't particularly enthusiastic about them, she was mostly interested in the new piano music from the West. It was Yudina, after all, who introduced us to the piano music of Křenek, Hindemith, and Bartók. She learned Křenek's Piano Concerto in F minor and it made a great impression on me in her interpretation. When I looked over the music in my older years, it didn't have the same effect.

In those days, I remember, I enjoyed playing second piano for Yudina and then going to the orchestra rehearsals. This was, if memory serves, around 1927, when the performance of new music was still permitted. The conductor Nikolai Malko* treated Yudina very rudely. He blatantly mocked her and her eccentricities, and used to say, "What you need is a good man, Marusya, a man." I remember being shocked that Yudina, who raised her hackles over the least trifle, didn't seem to get angry with Malko. Personally, I wouldn't have let it go.

Later Yudina must have changed her mind about my music, because she played quite a bit of it, particularly the Second Piano Sonata. There's a recording of it, and everyone seems to think it's the best interpretation of the sonata. I think that Yudina plays my sonata badly. The tempos are all off and there's a free, shall we say, approach to the text. But perhaps I'm wrong, I haven't heard the recording in a while.

In general, I didn't like seeing Yudina—whenever I did I got embroiled in some unpleasant and confused story. Strange things kept happening to her. Once I ran into Yudina in Leningrad at the Moscow Station. "Ah, hello, hello. Where to?" "Moscow," I said. "Ah, how good, how handy. I have to give a concert in Moscow but I can't possibly go there. Please, go in my place and please give the concert."

*Nikolai Andreyevich Malko (1883–1961), conductor who led the premieres of the First and Second Symphonies, as well as other works by Shostakovich. He emigrated in 1929 and did much to promote Shostakovich's symphonies abroad. On a bet with Malko, Shostakovich arranged Vincent Youmans's fox trot "Tea for Two," called "Tahiti Trot" in Russia. For more information see Solomon Volkov, "Dmitri Shostakovich and 'Tea for Two,'" *The Musical Quarterly*, April 1978, pp. 223–228.

I was naturally taken aback by this unexpected proposal. I said, "How can I go in your place? I don't know your program. And this is rather strange. Why should I play in your place? What's your program anyway?"

Yudina told me her program. "No, I can't. How could I? That would be rather strange." And I hurried into my compartment.

From the window of the train, I saw Yudina wandering along the platform, probably looking for another pianist who was going to Moscow and who would agree to her odd proposal.

Yudina, as far as I know, always drew overflow crowds. She deserved her fame as a pianist completely. But they also used to say that she was a saint.

I was never a crude antireligionist. If you believe, then believe. But Yudina apparently did believe that she was a saint, or a female prophet. Yudina always played as though she were giving a sermon. That's all right, I know that Yudina saw music in a mystical light. For instance, she saw Bach's *Goldberg Variations* as a series of illustrations to the Holy Bible. That's also excusable, though it can be terribly irritating at times.

Yudina saw Mussorgsky as a purely religious composer. But Mussorgsky isn't Bach, after all, and it's a rather controversial reading, I think. And then there was the business of reading poetry at her concerts. Either you play or you read poetry, not both. I realize that she read Pasternak and at a time when he was banned. But nonetheless, the whole thing reminded me of a ventriloquist's act. And naturally, the result of the famous readings—between Bach and Beethoven, I think—was another huge scandal in the series of Yudina's scandals.

There was just too much deliberate hysteria in Yudina's behavior. Too much, really. She came to see me once and said that she was living in a miserable little room where she could neither work nor rest. So I signed a petition. I went to see various bureaucrats, I asked a lot of people to help, I took up a lot of people's time. With great difficulty we got an apartment for Yudina. You would think that everything was fine. Life could go on. A short time later she came to me again and asked for help in obtaining an apartment for herself.

"What? But we got an apartment for you. What do you need another one for?"

"I gave the apartment away to a poor old woman."

Well, how can anyone behave that way?

It was the same with money, she was always borrowing from everyone. And after all, she was paid rather well; first she had a professor's salary and then a professor's pension. And Yudina made quite a few recordings and radio appearances, but she gave her money away as soon as she got it and then her phone would be disconnected for nonpayment.

I was told the following story about Yudina. She went and asked for a loan of five rubles. "I broke a window in my room, it's drafty and so cold, I can't live like that." Naturally, they gave her the money. It was winter out there.

A while later they visited her and it was as cold in her room as it was outside and the broken window was stuffed with a rag. "How can this be, Maria Veniaminovna? We gave you money to fix the window." And she replied, "I gave it for the needs of the church."

What is this? The church can have various needs, but the clergy doesn't sit around in the cold, after all, with broken windows.

Self-denial should have a rational limit. This behavior smacks of the behavior of *yurodivye*. Was Professor Yudina a *yurodivy?* No, she wasn't. Then why behave like one?

I can't wholly approve of such behavior. Naturally, Yudina had many unpleasant incidents in her life, and one can sympathize, of course. Her religious positions were under constant artillery and even cavalry attack, so to speak. For instance, she was kicked out of the Leningrad Conservatory even before I was.

It happened this way. Serebriakov,* the director then, had a habit of making so-called "raids of the light brigade." He was a young man—not even thirty—and it was easy for him to get around the entire Conservatory. He checked to see that everything was in order in the institution that had been entrusted to him.

The director received many denunciations of Yudina, and he must have written some himself. He realized that Yudina was a first-class pianist, but he wasn't willing, apparently, to risk his own position.

*Pavel Alexeyevich Serebriakov (1909–1977), pianist, for many years rector of the Leningrad Conservatory, which he ran using police methods. Serebriakov was called "the best Chekist [Cheka agent] among the pianists and the best pianist among the Chekists." In 1948 he dismissed Shostakovich from his professorship at the Conservatory.

One of the charges of the light brigade was made specifically against her.

The cavalry rushed into Yudina's class and demanded of Yudina: Do you believe in God? She replied in the affirmative. Was she promoting religious propaganda among her students? She replied that the Constitution didn't forbid it.

A few days later a transcript of the conversation made by "an unknown person" appeared in a Leningrad paper, which also printed a caricature: Yudina in nun's robes surrounded by kneeling students. And the caption was something about preachers appearing at the Conservatory. The cavalry trod heavily, even though it was the light brigade. Naturally, Yudina was dismissed after that.

For some reason, our papers like to print caricatures involving priests, monasteries, and so on. And most often it's done quite unconvincingly and not to the point. For example, when Zhdanov* was berating the poet Akhmatova† in Leningrad after the war, he described her like this for some reason: "Either a nun or a slut." And then he added, "Rather, both a slut and a nun, who mixes fornication with prayer." It's a nice turn of phrase, but meaningless. I for one could never get Zhdanov to tell me precisely what he meant by it. Did Akhmatova misbehave in some way? He did hint at something in one of his speeches in Leningrad. He said that Akhmatova had "shameful ideas on the role and calling of woman." What did that mean? I don't know either.

But there were certainly enough caricatures of Akhmatova in those days, trying to depict her simultaneously as a whore and a nun. I remember they drew me as a monk once, in the magazine *Sovetskaya muzyka*. Now, what kind of monk would I make? You see, I drank and smoked and was not without other sins. And even read prepared

*Andrei Alexandrovich Zhdanov (1896–1948), Communist Party leader. The term "Zhdanovism" is well known in the West. It refers to the harsh regimentation of literature and art in postwar Russia. It is not clear whether or not Zhdanov was merely carrying out Stalin's orders in his "aesthetic" pronouncements, but as a result of them Zhdanov acquired so much prominence that Stalin began envying him. It is now thought that Stalin had Zhdanov killed and then cast blame for his death on the Jewish doctors.

†Anna Andreyevna Akhmatova (Gorenko; 1889–1966), poet. She maintained her popularity from prerevolutionary years until her death, despite extremely formidable pressures against her. All kinds of tactics (short of arrest and physical extermination) were used on Akhmatova: total literary ostracism; a vicious and insulting campaign in the official press; and the exile and murder of people close to her. A great part of Akhmatova's legacy, including her poem *Requiem*, about the "great terror," has still not been published in the Soviet Union. Shostakovich and Akhmatova had many creative bonds, and this connection was particularly strong in the late years.

speeches about works of genius by composers I couldn't stand. And so on. But nevertheless, the Composers' Union put me down as a monk too. Yet despite our appearance in cartoons in similar garb, Yudina and I couldn't always find a common language.

I remember I had a lot of problems when I was young—I dried up as a composer, and I had no money, and I was sick. In general, I had a very gloomy outlook on life. And Yudina suggested, "Let's go see the bishop, he'll help. He'll definitely help. He helps everyone." And I thought, All right, let her take me to the bishop, maybe he will help.

We got there. A rather well-fed, good-looking man sat before me, and a bunch of women were making a spectacle of themselves in front of him, throwing themselves at his hand to kiss it. There was a bottle-neck near his hand, each of the ladies wanted to be first. I looked and saw that Yudina was in ecstasy, and I thought, No, I won't kiss his hand for anything. And I didn't.

The bishop gave me a rather sympathetic look, but I didn't give a damn about his sympathy. He didn't help me at all.

Nikolayev's other favorite student was Vladimir Sofronitsky, whom Nikolayev called Vovochka. Nikolayev adored him and this is how their lessons went. Vovochka would play Schumann's *Symphonic Études* in class. Nikolayev would say, "Marvelous, Vovochka! Next time prepare Liszt's sonata, please."

A cult sprang up around Sofronitsky almost immediately. Meyerhold dedicated one of his finest productions to him, *The Queen of Spades*. Sofronitsky's reputation grew constantly and his popularity peaked just before his untimely death. But I don't think that Sofronitsky's life was a very happy one; it had everything in it—alcohol, drugs, complicated involvements and relationships. He might drink a bottle of cognac before a performance and collapse; the concert would be canceled, of course. Sofronitsky never toured abroad, although I think he did go to Warsaw once and once to France. In 1945 Stalin ordered Sofronitsky to go to Potsdam for the conference. They dressed him in a military uniform and took him there. When he came back he said nothing about it; I don't think many people know about the trip. But once Sofronitsky showed me how President Truman played the piano.

Sofronitsky was like Yudina in that you never knew what to expect from him. In 1921 they were graduating from the Conservatory and both were playing Liszt's B Minor Sonata. Their recitals were a sensation, all of Petrograd was there. Suddenly Nikolayev came out on stage and said, "Student Sofronitsky is ill and begs your indulgence." I was rather surprised. Sofronitsky played brilliantly, as was expected, but after the examination I went up to Nikolayev and asked what that was all about. If you're sick, don't play. And if you do play, then why announce that you're sick. For sympathy?

Nikolayev told me, I remember, that Sofronitsky went on with a high fever. To tell the truth, I don't set much store by that.

Sofronitsky and I played together several times, performing Nikolayev's Variations for Two Pianos. Nikolayev thought himself a composer but he really didn't have much basis for thinking this. We played the Variations and laughed to ourselves. We laughed, but we played.

Sofronitsky liked to tell this story about Glazunov. A messenger rushed up to him: Hurry to Glazunov's, he has to see you urgently. Sofronitsky dropped what he was doing and raced to Glazunov's house. He got there, was taken in to see Glazunov, who was napping in his armchair, his head lolling on his fat stomach.

Silence. Glazunov opened one eye and stared at Sofronitsky for a long time and then, his tongue moving slowly, asked, "Tell me, please, do you like the *Hammerklavier?*" Sofronitsky replied readily that of course, he liked it very much. Glazunov was silent for a long time. Sofronitsky stood and waited until Glazunov muttered softly, "You know, I can't stand that sonata." And went back to sleep.

Things like that happened to me too. You could say that I'm a student of Glazunov's. In my day Glazunov taught only chamber music at the Conservatory and naturally I studied with him. He had his own style of teaching, which would have looked bizarre to a stranger.

We went to his office on the first floor. Bulky Glazunov sat at his desk and we played. He never interrupted. We finished the piece (perhaps it was a Schubert trio) and Glazunov muttered to himself, without rising from his desk, quietly and briefly. It was hard to tell exactly what he was saying and most of the time we didn't know.

The trouble was that I was at the piano and my friends were next to me. Glazunov remained at his desk, that is, at a considerable distance from us. He never stood up or came closer and he spoke so softly. It seemed wrong to ask him to repeat himself and it also seemed wrong to move closer to him. It was a strange situation.

So we would repeat the work from beginning to end, guessing at changes. There was never any objection to our initiative. After the repeat performance Glazunov gave another speech, even softer and even shorter, after which we left.

At first I was extremely put out by this method of instruction, and particularly surprised by the fact that Glazunov never left his desk and came over to us, not even to glance once at the music. But with time I worked out the secret of his strange behavior.

This is what I noticed. During the lessons Glazunov sometimes leaned over with a grunt toward his large director's desk, remained in that position for some time, and then straightened out with some difficulty.

Interested, I increased my observations of our beloved director's actions and came to this conclusion: Glazunov really did resemble a large baby, as so many people liked to say. Because a baby is always reaching for a nipple and so was Glazunov. But there was an essential difference. And the difference was that first of all, Glazunov used a special tube instead of a nipple, a rubber tube if my observations were correct, and second, instead of milk he was sipping alcohol.

These are not my conjectures, these are facts that I determined and confirmed through repeated observation. Without this fortification, Glazunov was incapable of giving the lesson. That's why he never rose from his desk and that's why his instructions to the class grew more indistinct and shorter.

You might get the impression that there was nothing to be learned from Glazunov. You would be mistaken. He was an excellent pedagogue, but first one had to learn how to learn from him. I think I mastered that art, I learned the secret. And so I have every right to call Glazunov one of my teachers. In order to really study with Glazunov you had to meet with him as often as possible, catch him wherever possible—at concerts, at people's houses, and naturally, at the Conservatory.

First and foremost, at the Conservatory, for Glazunov spent almost all his free time there. This is hard to believe now, but he was present at every single Conservatory examination, without exception. He even went to the exams of the percussionists, and often Glazunov was the only outsider there.

What did I learn from Glazunov? Many things, many essential things. Of course, I could have learned more from him, but I was only a boy, diligent and hard-working but still a boy. There's much that I regret now.

Glazunov's erudition in music history was outstanding for those days. He knew, as few others did, the wonderful music of the great contrapuntalists of the Flemish and Italian schools. It's only nowadays that everyone is so smart and no one doubts the genius and viability of fifteenth- and sixteenth-century music. But in those days, let's be frank, the picture was completely different, that music was hidden beneath seven seals. Even Rimsky-Korsakov felt that music began with Mozart, and Haydn was dubious; Bach was considered a boring composer. What, then, of the pre-Bach period? For my comrades it was nothing but a desert.

Glazunov delighted in Josquin des Prés, Orlando di Lasso, Palestrina, and Gabrieli, and willy-nilly, I began to find delight in them too, even though at first I thought their music difficult and boring. It was also very interesting to listen to how Glazunov evaluated this music, for he never limited himself to general delight, he truly knew and loved these composers. And it seemed to us that he could always distinguish between the general "style of the era" and the individual composer's insights, the truly marvelous examples of musical genius.

For today all the old music is praised indiscriminately. Before, they didn't know any old composers and forgot them all. Now they've remembered them all and praise them all. They write "the forgotten ancient composer"—perhaps he's a justly forgotten ancient composer who should never have been remembered?

It's terrifying to think how much terrible contemporary music will someday fall into the category of "ancient." And excerpts from Ivan Dzerzhinsky's opera *The Quiet Don* (based on the forgotten novel by Nobel Prize-winner Sholokhov—a fact too embarrassing to be remembered!) will be performed with the subtitle "once forgotten." It would be better if they played only the things that didn't become forgotten, I think that would be more logical. Let them spare the innocent listeners. Actually, it's the listeners' own fault; people shouldn't try to pass themselves off as experts. It's always the snobs who fall for the bait first.

But when Glazunov talked about ancient music, there wasn't a whiff of snobbery. He never resorted to generalities, he evaluated this music as he did any other, with full responsibility for his words and with complete seriousness, which spread to those around him. And so we learned to imbue seemingly simple labels with exact meaning.

For instance, if Glazunov called a composer a "master," we remembered it for life, because there was a great deal of mental effort behind that brief description. We were witnesses to that effort and to the best of our ability we tried to do the same ourselves, that is, to come to the same conclusions as Glazunov, to recreate his mental processes.

When Glazunov said after listening to, say, a Schumann symphony, "technically not irreproachable," we also understood what was meant, we didn't need any long explanations.

This was a period of verbosity, an ocean of words. They depreciated before your eyes. Glazunov reestablished the value of the simple word. It turned out that when a professional, a master, spoke about music simply, without fancy words and curlicues, it made a powerful impression, much more powerful than the flood of pseudo-musical eloquence of Igor Glebov, in the real world Boris Asafiev.

This was a good education for me because it was then that I began to appreciate the power of a brief word about music, the power of a simple, uncomplicated, but expressive opinion, and the importance of such an opinion for professionals in a professional milieu. As I recall, Glazunov made the word "worthless" very expressive.

It became quite popular in the Conservatory, thanks to Glazunov, where previously, in imitation of Rimsky-Korsakov, professors said "not very pleasing" about poor compositions. In Glazunov's day they used the more concise and simple "worthless." And the appellation wasn't reserved for music; the weather might be worthless, or an evening spent visiting, or even a pair of new shoes that pinched.

Glazunov spent all his time thinking about music and therefore, when he spoke about it, you remembered for life. Take Scriabin, for instance. My attitude toward him was greatly influenced by one of

Glazunov's favorite thoughts: that Scriabin used the same methods in writing his symphonies that he did in his piano miniatures. This is a very fair assessment of Scriabin's symphonies. Glazunov also suggested that Scriabin had religious and erotic fixations, with which I agree completely.

I remember quite a few musical opinions that Glazunov gave on a variety of subjects, such as: "The finale of Mozart's *Jupiter* Symphony is like the cathedral of Cologne." Honestly, to this day I can't think of a better description of that amazing music.

Many other comments that Glazunov carelessly tossed off have been useful: for instance, on "excesses" in orchestration, an important issue on which one must have one's own opinion and be firm. Glazunov was the first to convince me that a composer must make the performers submit to his will and not the other way around. If the composer doesn't need a triple or quadruple complement of brass instruments for his artistic vision, that's one thing. But if he starts thinking about practical matters, economic considerations, that's bad. The composer must orchestrate in the way he conceived his work and not simplify his orchestration to please the performers, Glazunov used to say. And for instance, I still feel that Stravinsky was mistaken in doing new orchestral editions of *Firebird* and *Petrouchka,* because these reflected financial, economic, and practical considerations.

Glazunov insisted that composing ballets was beneficial because it developed your technique. Later I learned that he was right about that, as well.

Glazunov gave me a good piece of advice once regarding the symphonic scherzo as part of a symphony. He felt that the main object of the scherzo was to interest the listener and everything must serve that goal—melody, rhythm, and texture. Everything must be attractive in the scherzo, and most important, unexpected. That was good advice and I told my own students something like it.

Naturally, there was much with which I disagreed then and disagree now. Glazunov once said in my presence that music was written by the composer for himself and, as he put it, "a few others." I am categorically opposed to that statement. And I couldn't possibly agree with him in his attacks against the "recherché cacophonists," which is what he called the new Western composers, beginning with Debussy.

Once, looking over a score of Debussy's (it was "Prélude à l'Après-midi d'un Faune"), Glazunov noted with deep thought, "It's orchestrated with great taste. . . . And he knows his work. . . . Could it be that Rimsky and I influenced the orchestration of all these contemporary degenerates?"

On Schreker's opera *The Distant Peal,* which was staged in Leningrad, Glazunov pronounced, *"Schrekliche Musik!"*

But I must say, to his credit, that even after relegating a composition to the detested "cacophonic style," Glazunov did not stop listening to the work once and for all. He tried to comprehend all music, for he was a composer, not a bureaucrat.

Glazunov liked to recount how he "penetrated" Wagner. "I listened to *The Valkyrie* the first time, understood absolutely nothing, and didn't like it at all. I went a second time. Nothing again. And a third—the same. How many times do you think I went to hear that opera before I understood it? Nine times. On the tenth, finally, I understood it all. And I liked it very much."

When I heard Glazunov tell this story the first time, I laughed to myself, even though I maintained a serious expression. But now I respect him for it deeply. Life has taught me many things.

In our time Glazunov was going through the same thing with Richard Strauss. He went to see *Salome* many times, getting used to it, penetrating it, studying it. And his opinion of Strauss began changing—before, Strauss had been on the list of "damned cacophonists." By the way, Glazunov had always adored Johann Strauss, and this is just one more proof that he was no musical snob. I think that I learned that from him too—it's very important not to be a snob.

In general, however paradoxical this might seem, Glazunov was not dogmatic in music. His dogmatism was more aesthetic. Flexibility was not one of his qualities, which may not be such a bad thing. We've all seen what "flexibility" in questions of art is and what it leads to.

Of course, Glazunov had more than enough inertia, but he was an honest man and he didn't hang political labels on his aesthetic enemies, who, alas, resorted to such unfair practices often.

This is a good place to bring up the polemics between Nemirovich-Danchenko and Meyerhold. Nemirovich didn't understand or like Meyerhold. He began disliking him when Meyerhold was his student.

When the Art Theater opened, their first production was *Tsar Fyodor Ivanovich,* and Stanislavsky wanted Meyerhold to play Fyodor. Nemirovich insisted on Moskvin.

Meyerhold later told me, laughing, that he almost went crazy then with jealousy of Moskvin and hatred of Nemirovich. He laughed, all right, but his dislike of Nemirovich remained forever.

But all that isn't so important, this is: In the many years of polemics, Meyerhold invariably attacked the Art Theater and Nemirovich, using the most varied, and usually unfair, methods. Meyerhold always tried to hang some "current" political label on the old man. But Nemirovich never stooped to that, even though in our conversations Nemirovich always referred to Meyerhold with extreme irritation.

Nemirovich considered Meyerhold a side-show man, a showoff. He was convinced that Meyerhold was leading the theater down false paths, but he never used the terminology of newspaper headlines or political jargon.

And yet it would have been much easier for Nemirovich to do it than for Meyerhold, for by the time I met Nemirovich it was obvious that the future of the Theater of Meyerhold was threatened, and at the same time, everyone knew that the Art Theater had Stalin's powerful support. In that situation you would think that Nemirovich would be sorely tempted to get rid of his daring opponent once and for all. What could be easier than to publicly accuse Meyerhold of some political crime? Quite simple. In those days everyone did it—or almost everyone.

But Nemirovich shunned as distasteful even the possibility of such an action. The old man couldn't even imagine how it might be possible.

Here is a typical episode. In 1938, when Meyerhold's theater was shut on Stalin's personal command, an anti-Meyerhold campaign was smeared all over the pages of the press. This wasn't the first such campaign, but it was a particularly vicious one. They printed numerous articles as well as interviews with men of Soviet culture, who were united in their pleasure at an outstanding cultural event like the closing of a theater.

They called up Nemirovich and asked for an interview. The obnoxious newspaper people were sure that the old man wouldn't miss an opportunity to dance on the fresh grave of his opponent. But Nemiro-vich refused, adding, "And it's stupid to ask me what I think about the closing of the Theater of Meyerhold. That's like asking the tsar what he thinks about the October Revolution."

To return to Glazunov, he did not like my music, particularly the later music. He lived long enough to see the publication in *Pravda* and other papers of the article "Muddle Instead of Music." He was in Paris by then and no one from *Pravda* could come to him for an inter-view, but I'm certain that the old and sick Glazunov would not have said anything that would please them. There was no vileness in him.

An important circumstance for me personally was the fact that Gla-zunov never presented his thoughts and pronouncements in an admin-istrative form, that is, what he said never sounded like a "directive from the director of the Conservatory." It is a great misfortune that he was the last director to behave that way. Let's not even mention what went on beyond the walls of the Conservatory, I mean in the field of culture and other areas.

In general, I'm grateful to the Conservatory. I got what I wanted from it. I didn't force myself to study. I can't say that everything went smoothly, for I lived in very difficult material circumstances and I was sickly. And then I had to make a difficult decision—would I be a pia-nist or a composer? I chose composing.

Rimsky-Korsakov used to say that he refused to acknowledge any complaints from composers about their hard lot in life. He explained his position thus: Talk to a bookkeeper and he'll start complaining about life and his work. Work has ruined him, it's so dull and boring. You see, the bookkeeper had planned to be a writer but life made him a bookkeeper. Rimsky-Korsakov said that it was rather different with composers. None of them can say that he had planned to be a book-keeper and that life forced him to become a composer.

It's that kind of a profession. You can't complain about it. If it's too tough, become a bookkeeper or a building manager. Don't worry, no one will force you to keep at the hard work of composing.

I had a period of doubt and despair when I was young. I decided that I couldn't compose music and that I would never write a single note. It was a difficult moment, which I would prefer not to think about. And indeed I wouldn't except for one thing. I burned a lot of my manuscripts then. Imitating Gogol I was, silly young fool. Well, Gogol or no Gogol, I burned an opera then, *The Gypsies,* based on Pushkin's poem.

It may be because of that business, but I recall my teacher of composition, Steinberg, without any particular joy. He was a dry and didactic person, and I remember him primarily for two things. One was that Steinberg was Rimsky-Korsakov's son-in-law and the other was that he passionately hated Tchaikovsky. Rimsky-Korsakov's family, I must say, did not have a high regard for Tchaikovsky and his treatment was a sore point for them. It was a much sorer point, of course, for Nikolai Andreyevich himself. You don't need to dig around in the archives, just take a look at the works Rimsky-Korsakov composed and everything becomes clear.

Tchaikovsky kept Korsakov from composing, interfered simply by existing. This may sound blasphemous, but it's a fact. Rimsky-Korsakov tensed up because Tchaikovsky was composing next to him and he couldn't write a note. And like the old saying, a disaster came to the rescue—Tchaikovsky died and Korsakov's crisis ended.

For ten years Rimsky-Korsakov couldn't write an opera and after Tchaikovsky's death he wrote eleven operas in fifteen years. And it's interesting that this flood began with *Christmas Eve.* As soon as Tchaikovsky died, Korsakov took a theme already used by Tchaikovsky and rewrote it his way. Once he affirmed himself, the writing went smoothly.

But the hostility remained. Prokofiev said that he found a mistake in the score of Tchaikovsky's First Symphony—the flute had to play a B flat. He showed it to Rimsky-Korsakov, who was gratified by this error and said, laughing into his beard, "Yes, Pyotr Ilyich really confused things here, he did."

I've never met a family like Korsakov's, words cannot describe their reverence for his memory. And naturally, Steinberg was no exception. He and his wife, Nadezhda Nikolayevna, spoke only of Nikolai Andreyevich, they quoted and referred to him alone.

I remember November of 1941. It was wartime. I was sitting writing the Seventh Symphony, when there was a knock at the door. I was being called to the Steinbergs', urgently. All right, I dropped my work and went. When I got there I could see that a tragedy had befallen the house. Everyone was subdued and grim, with tear-stained eyes. Steinberg himself was darker than a storm cloud. I thought that he would want to ask me something about evacuation, which was the most important issue of the day. And he did, but I could tell that that wasn't why I was there. Then Steinberg began talking about some composition of his. What composer doesn't like talking about his music? But I listened and I thought, This isn't it, obviously this isn't it.

Finally Steinberg could stand it no longer. He led me to his study, locked the door and looked around. He pulled out a copy of *Pravda* from his desk drawer and said, "Why did Comrade Stalin name Glinka and Tchaikovsky in his speech? And not Nikolai Andreyevich? Nikolai Andreyevich has more significance for Russian music than Tchaikovsky. I want to write to Comrade Stalin about it."

Here was the story. All the papers had just printed Stalin's speech. This was his first major speech since the war began and he spoke, in part, about the great Russian nation—the nation of Pushkin and Tolstoy, Gorky and Chekhov, Repin and Surikov...and so on. You know, two of every living creature. And of the composers, Stalin singled out only Glinka and Tchaikovsky for praise. This injustice shook Steinberg to the very foundations of his being. Steinberg was seriously consulting me on how best to write to Stalin, as though it could have any meaning.

Years had passed, epochs changed, God knew what was going on, but nothing could shake the sacred enmity of Korsakov's family for Tchaikovsky.

Naturally, this is insignificant, a minor weakness. The main problem was that Steinberg was a musician of limited scope. He shone in reflected light and therefore his words and opinions didn't elicit particular trust, while whatever Glazunov said elicited trust, primarily because he was a great musician. A living classic, so to speak. (And in my day, he was the only such exhibit at the Conservatory.)

But in the final analysis, Glazunov's works could be seen then—as now—in various lights. There was something much more important for us and that was that each student (or pupil, as they were called then) could see for himself Glazunov's marvelous, even unique, abilities as a musician.

First there was his pitch. Glazunov had perfect, absolute pitch. His ear terrified the students. Say there was an exam in harmony and part of it called for playing a modulation on the piano. Steinberg had trained us well for harmony. We could play a given modulation unbelievably fast, in the tempo of a virtuoso Chopin étude.

You went to the exam, Glazunov was there. You played and it was fantastic, you were even pleased yourself. After a pause came Glazunov's mutter, "And why did you allow parallel fifths between the 6/5 chord of the second degree and the 6/4 tonal chord?" Silence.

Glazunov caught all false notes, flawlessly, no matter where they were. Just before he left the country, however, he complained that he was hearing a half tone higher than the actual sound. He thought it was sclerosis. But it might not have been. The pitch to which instruments are tuned might have risen, it's rising all the time, you know. Anyone who has lived in music for over fifty years notices that. Recording is partly to blame. When you think about it, it's awful. You crank it faster, it sounds higher. Crank slower and it's lower. We're used to that now, but it's nothing less than a mockery of the human ear.

The other way in which Glazunov amazed us was with his memory. Musical memory, naturally. There are many stories about that. I remember some of Glazunov's tricks, and I even tried to imitate them to a degree.

One of his more famous ones went something like this: Taneyev had come to Petersburg from Moscow to show his new symphony, and the host hid the young Glazunov in the next room. Taneyev played. When Taneyev finished and rose from the piano, he was surrounded by the guests, who congratulated him, naturally. After the obligatory compliments, the host suddenly said, "I'd like you to meet a talented young man. He's also recently written a symphony." What was that?

They brought Glazunov from the next room. "Sasha, show your symphony to our dear guest," the host said. Glazunov sat down at the piano and repeated Taneyev's symphony, from beginning to end. And he had just heard it for the first time—and through a closed door. I'm not so sure that even Stravinsky could do Glazunov's trick. And I know for certain that Prokofiev couldn't.

I remember that people said Stravinsky had trouble with pitch when he was studying with Rimsky-Korsakov; but perhaps that was just slander, maybe they were just angry with an insubordinate student. For such tricks the most important thing a musician needs is a good ear. And daring. These things are usually done on a bet. Sollertinsky used to goad me into recreating Mahler's symphonies that way, and it worked all right.

I managed a more minor bit of hooliganism. I was a guest in the home of a conductor when I was in my early twenties. They turned on the gramophone and played a popular record with a fox trot. I liked the fox trot but I didn't like the way it was played.

I confided my opinion to the host, who suddenly said, "Ah, so you don't like the way it's played? All right. If you want, write down the number by heart and orchestrate it and I'll play it. That is, of course, if you can do it and in a given amount of time. I'm giving you an hour. If you're really a genius, you should be able to do it in an hour."

I did it in forty-five minutes.

Glazunov naturally knew all his Conservatory students by their last names. That wasn't so surprising, for a memory for faces and names isn't such a rarity. Military men have it. What was more important for us was that Glazunov remembered each of us as a musician. He remembered when and what a student had played, and what the program had been, and how many false notes there had been.

This is not an exaggeration. Glazunov really did remember how many times and exactly where a given student had made mistakes during an examination. And this examination might have taken place three or four years earlier.

And the same applies to composers. Glazunov remembered them all—the talented, the mediocre, the worthless, and the hopeless. And all their compositions—past, present, and future—even if they studied there for twenty years.

Incidentally, some did manage to spend twenty years and more at the Conservatory. Eternal students, we called them. But there weren't many left in my day, they were gradually being smoked out.

But you could apply to the Conservatory as many times as you liked, trying to prove that you weren't retarded. There was one stubborn fellow champing at the bit to get into the composition department. And Glazunov astounded him. The applicant played a piano sonata, Glazunov listened to it and said dreamily, "If I'm not mistaken, you applied a few years ago. Then, in another sonata, you had quite a good secondary theme." And with those words, Glazunov sat down and played a large chunk of the old sonata by the hapless composer. The secondary theme was rubbish, of course, but the effect was enormous.

And Glazunov played the piano well, I must add. In an original manner, but well. He didn't have a real piano technique and he often played without removing his famous cigar from his right hand. Glazunov held the cigar between his third and fourth fingers. I've seen it myself. And yet he managed to play every note, absolutely everything, including the most difficult passages. It looked as though Glazunov's fat fingers were melting in the keys, drowning in them.

Glazunov could also sight-read the most complicated score and make it sound as though an excellent orchestra were playing. In Glazunov's living room there were two good Koch grand pianos, but he didn't use them. Glazunov played on an upright piano that had been pushed into a small, narrow room. Before the Revolution it had been the maid's room, and after the Revolution it turned out to be the only habitable room in the apartment. There was enough wood to heat it, while the rest of his apartment stood cold.

Coming to his house, you could find him dressed in fur coat and boots. The respected Elena Pavlovna, his mother, bustled about, tucking a blanket around the baby. It didn't help, Glazunov shivered pitifully.

Elena Pavlovna was about eighty then and sometimes I came across her darning her baby's socks. Of course, the new conditions of life were difficult for Glazunov to bear. He was amazed that singers, despite the cold, had stopped catching colds. That was a miracle, and it gave him comfort.

So Glazunov sat at the piano in his fur coat, in the more or less warm maid's room, and played his works for visiting celebrities. It was an exotic thrill for them and a safety valve for him. Besides, Glazunov apparently thought it wise to maintain friendly relations with major foreign musicians, since, I assume, he had given more than a passing thought—even then—to emigrating to the West. It was there that Glazunov hoped, not without basis, to satisfy his fading needs and desires without risking his life.

A marvelous picture—Glazunov in his fur coat, playing, and a famous guest, also in fur coat, listening. Then some social chitchat, clouds of steam coming from their mouths. Steam came from the mouth of Felix Weingartner, and Hermann Abendroth, and Artur Schnabel, and Joseph Szigeti. So all these visiting celebrities returned home to the West, enriched by unheard-of impressions of a frozen country—darkness and cold.

The celebrities were amazed by Glazunov, and he by them. For instance, Glazunov was awed and astounded by the physical endurance of Egon Petri, which he talked about for a long time. And why not? Petri played an all-Liszt program, this is one concert, mind you—*Don Juan* and two sonatas (the B minor and the *Dante*). It was a champion performance, the result of good nutrition and a peaceful life for three generations.

Glazunov was an admirer of Liszt, whom he had met in Weimar, I believe. Liszt played Beethoven for him. Glazunov liked to tell about the interpretation and juxtapose Liszt's playing to Anton Rubinstein's. Glazunov often referred to Rubinstein when he spoke of piano timbres and quoted him as saying, "You think that the piano is one instrument. It's really a hundred." But in general, he didn't like the way Rubinstein played, and preferred Liszt's manner.

In Glazunov's telling, Liszt's manner differed vastly from what we are used to imagining as such. When we hear the name we usually picture banging and ballyhoo, gloves tossed in the air, and so on. But Glazunov said that Liszt played simply and accurately and transparently. Of course, this was the late Liszt, so to speak, and he wasn't performing on stage but playing at home, where he didn't have to impress assorted women and young ladies.

The sonata in question, as I recall, was Beethoven's C-sharp minor and Glazunov said that Liszt played it steadily and with control and that the tempos were extremely moderate. Liszt revealed all the "inner" voices, which Glazunov liked very much. He liked to remind us that the most important element in composition is polyphony. When Glazunov sat down to demonstrate something on the piano, he always stressed the accompanying voice and chromatics, the ascending and descending progressions, which gave his playing fullness and life.

Personally, I feel that this is one of the great secrets of pianism, and

71

the pianist who understands this is on the threshold of great success.

A major concert performer once complained to me that it was so difficult to play the war-horses. "It's so hard to find a fresh approach," he confided. I immediately had a contradictory reaction to this announcement. First I thought what an unusual person is sitting next to me, because the great majority of performers don't think at all when they play their *Pathétique* or *Moonlight* Sonata or their Hungarian Rhapsodies. (The list of works can be enlarged or shortened, it doesn't change the point.) These performers do not play what the composer intended, nor do they demonstrate their own relationship to the work, since their own relationship to it simply does not exist. Then what do they play? Just notes. Basically, by ear. It's enough for one to start and all the rest pick it up. The list of literature played by ear nowadays has expanded to include Prokofiev's sonatas and works by Hindemith, but the essential approach to the music by these stars has not changed as a result.

So while at first I was simply delighted by the self-critical announcement, my next thought was much calmer. And it went something like this: How can you complain that it's hard to find a "fresh approach"? What is it, a wallet full of money? Can you find a "fresh approach" walking down the street—someone drops it and you pick it up? This pianist must have taken Sholom Aleichem's joke seriously. You know, Aleichem said, "Talent is like money. You either have it or you don't." And I think that the great humorist is wrong here. Because money comes and goes, today you don't have any, tomorrow you do. But if you don't have talent, then the situation is serious and long-lasting.

Therefore you can't find a fresh approach, it has to find you. A fresh approach to a work of music, as I have seen time and time again, usually comes to those who have a fresh approach to other aspects of life, to life in general—for example, Yudina or Sofronitsky.

But let's return to my pianist friend who naïvely sought a fresh approach without changing his own life. I didn't want to upset him with my considerations, why upset the man? I had to help him, and I remembered Glazunov's advice about polyphony in playing.

And I said to him, "Why don't you show the polyphonic movement in every piece you play, show how the voices move. Look for the secondary voices, the inner movements. That's very interesting and should bring joy. When you find them, show them to the audience, let them be happy too. You'll see, it'll help a lot, the works will come alive immediately."

I remember that I made an analogy with the theater. Most pianists have only one character in the foreground—the melody—and all the rest is just a murky background, a swamp. But plays are usually written for several characters and if only the hero speaks and the others don't reply, the play becomes nonsense and boring. All the characters must speak, so that we hear the question and the answer, and then following the course of the play's action becomes interesting.

And that was my advice to the then already famous pianist, and to my great astonishment, he took it and acted upon it. Success, as they say, was not far behind. He had been considered merely a virtuoso without any particular depth in his playing, but now everyone was proclaiming how intellectual and deep he was. His reputation grew considerably and he even called me to say, "Thank you for a fortunate piece of advice." I replied, "Don't thank me, thank Glazunov."

Glazunov himself loved to sit down at the piano, and once he started playing it was hard to stop him, in fact it was almost impossible. He usually played his own works and he was capable of playing two or three symphonies in a row. I sometimes had the feeling that he went on playing because it was hard for him to get up. That's how sedentary Glazunov was—it was easier to sit and continue playing.

When Glazunov did stand up he invariably mentioned Leopold Godowsky, who always refused to play in company, saying that his fingers stopped moving in a living room. But as soon as he sat down, Godowsky forgot his warning and then it became impossible to drag him away from the piano. I don't know about Godowsky, but as for Glazunov, I was surprised at his childlike desire to play—and to play his own compositions. This trait is common among composers who write by improvising at the piano. This musicmaking holds pleasant memories and associations for them and they readily move their fingers over the keys. The guests are snoring and the hostess is in a panic, but the venerable composer at the piano sees and hears nothing.

But Glazunov, as you know, did not compose at the piano. Here we were in total agreement—for a change--on composing. Glazunov also had to suffer when musical ideas sprang into his head during endless meetings. In fact, many of my acquaintances from the ranks of what are called "creative workers" complain that the most marvelous ideas and concepts come to them during meetings. As a man who has spent many hundreds and perhaps thousands of hours in meetings, I believe them gladly. There must be a special muse—the muse of meetings.

Glazunov usually waited until the composition had formed in his mind and then wrote it down in a final draft. But he did allow for the possibility of corrections or new editions, and so on. Strange, I agree with him about writing only a final draft but not about corrections. It's strange because if you were to base your opinion of us on these points, you would get the false impression that Glazunov worked hard and that I was free as a bird. Actually, just the reverse is true. Glazunov was and remained a squire when it came to composing and I was a typical proletarian.

It's hard to win the respect of young and rather brazen people, in fact it's almost impossible. But Glazunov earned our respect. His practical knowledge in the important area of musical instruments was invaluable. For too many composers, this area remains terra incognita; they have theoretical textbook knowledge and understanding, but no practical knowledge. Glazunov, for instance, learned to play the violin while writing his violin concerto. You must admit that's a heroic deed. I know for a fact that Glazunov played many wind instruments, for example, the clarinet.

I always told my students this story. Once Glazunov was in England, conducting his own works there. The British orchestra members were laughing at him. They thought he was a barbarian, and probably an ignoramus, and so on. And they began sabotaging him. I can think of nothing more horrible than an orchestra that has gone out of control at rehearsal. I wouldn't wish it on an enemy. The French horn player stood up and said that he couldn't play a certain note because it was impossible. The other orchestra players heartily supported him. What would I have done in Glazunov's place? I don't know, probably I would have walked out of the rehearsal. But here's what Glazunov did. He silently walked over to the horn player and took his instrument. The stunned musician didn't object. Glazunov "took aim" for a while and then played the required note, the one that the British musician insisted was impossible.

The orchestra applauded, the insurrection was broken, and they continued the rehearsal.

I think that for me the most serious obstacle on the path to conducting was just that—the resistance of the orchestra, which I always expected. I was used to it from my very first steps, from my First Symphony. Overcoming it is the work of born dictators. I don't like feeling that I'm distrusted. That disgusting professional condescension, such confidence, such aplomb and the constant desire to judge, to anathematize, constant distrust and disdain. And incidentally, the higher the orchestra's pay, the more it has of that impenetrable, stubborn . . . professionalism? No, I would say professional snobbery.

Glazunov liked to say that amateurs would make the best musicians, adding after some thought, "If they only knew how to play."

Do you know the line from Chukovsky's children's story about how hard it is to pull a hippo from a swamp? Well, I'm pulling a hippo from the swamp of my memory, and the hippo's name is Glazunov. He is a good, kind, and helpful hippo.

The work of memory goes on and I often think about its meaning. Sometimes I'm sure that the meaning will not be understood by anyone. Other times I'm more optimistic and I think that I'm guaranteed at least one reader who will know what it's about—myself. I'm explaining various people to myself, people whom I knew in various ways—not well, well, and very well. And in one case, perhaps better than anyone else on earth.

I spoke of these people, my acquaintances, in various ways throughout my life. Occasionally I contradicted myself—and I'm not ashamed of that. I changed my mind about these people and there's nothing shameful in that. There would have been, had I done so because of external pressures or to make my life better. But that was not the case. These people simply changed and so did I. I listened to new music and grew to know the old better. I read, I was told many things, I suffered from insomnia and I spent my nights ruminating. All this affected me.

And that's why today I don't think about people the way I did thirty, forty, or fifty years ago.

When I was younger, I often used swear words in conversations with friends. With the years I came to use them less and less. I'm getting old, death is near, you might say that I'm looking it in the eye. And now I think that I understand my past better. It, too, has come closer to me and I can look it in the eye as well.

Yuri Olesha,* when we were still friends, told me this parable in a didactic voice. A beetle fell in love with a caterpillar and she returned his love, but she died and lay still, wrapped in a cocoon. The beetle grieved over his beloved's body. Suddenly the cocoon opened and a butterfly appeared. The beetle decided to kill the butterfly because it disturbed his meditations over the body. He rushed over to her and saw that the butterfly's eyes were familiar—they were the caterpillar's eyes. He had almost killed her, for after all, everything was new except the eyes. And the butterfly and beetle lived happily ever after.

But you need to look things in the eye for that, and not everyone can do it, and sometimes a lifetime isn't long enough.

*Yuri Karlovich Olesha (1899–1960), writer and playwright, whose brilliant style resembles Nabokov's. Olesha stopped writing fiction for a long time after the publication of his long story "Envy" (1927), in reaction to the sociopolitical situation, which was not conducive to creative work. He esteemed Shostakovich, but after the article "Muddle Instead of Music" appeared, he publicly criticized his work, declaring that "Leo Tolstoy would have signed the article in *Pravda,*" and that Shostakovich's music "humiliated" him, Olesha. Later the critic Arkady Belinkov commented: "His speech was one of the earliest and most brilliant examples of betrayal of the 1934–53 model."

I THINK of Meyerhold too frequently, more frequently than I should, because we are now neighbors of sorts. I often walk or drive past the memorial plaque that depicts a repulsive monster and I shudder. The engraving says: "In this house lived Meyerhold." They should add, "And in this house his wife was brutally murdered."

I met Meyerhold in Leningrad in 1928. Vsevolod Emilyevich called me on the telephone and said, "This is Meyerhold speaking. I want to see you. If you can, come to me. Hotel So-and-so, room such-and-such."

I don't remember what we talked about. I only remember that Vsevolod Emilyevich asked if I would like to join his theater. I agreed immediately and a short time later I went to Moscow and began working in the Theater of Meyerhold in a musical capacity.

But I left the same year: it involved too much technical work. I couldn't find a niche for myself that satisfied both of us, even though it was very interesting to be part of the theater. Most fascinating were

Meyerhold's rehearsals. Watching him prepare his new plays was enthralling, exciting.

My work in the theater, basically, was playing the piano. Say, if an actress in *The Inspector General* was called upon to sing a romance by Glinka, I donned tailcoat, went on as one of the guests, and sat down at the piano. I also played in the orchestra.

I lived at Vsevolod Emilyevich's apartment on Novinsky Boulevard. In the evenings we often spoke of creating a musical drama. I was working hard then on my opera *The Nose*. Once there was a big fire at Vsevolod Emilyevich's apartment. I wasn't home at the time, but Meyerhold grabbed my music and handed it to me perfectly intact. My score survived thanks to him—a magnificent deed, for he had things much more valuable than my manuscript.

But everything ended well; I don't think that his property was heavily damaged either. If it had been, he would have had to answer to his wife, Zinaida Nikolayevna Raikh.

My feelings for Raikh are subjective and probably stem from the following fact: Meyerhold himself tried to underplay the difference in our situations and ages. He never would have dared to raise his voice to me. But his wife yelled at me now and then.

Raikh was an energetic woman, rather like the sergeant's widow in *The Inspector General*. She imagined herself a social lioness. This reminds me of a poem by Sasha Cherny.* It notes a certain rule of life. While a celebrity, Cherny says, may casually give you his hand, his wife at best will proffer two fingers. And this could have been written about Zinaida Nikolayevna.

Meyerhold loved her madly. I had never seen anything like it. It's hard to imagine that such a love could exist in our day. There was something ominous about it—and it did end badly.

It makes you think: the best way to hold on to something is to pay no attention to it. The things you love too much perish. You have to treat everything with irony, especially the things you hold dear. There's more of a chance then that they'll survive.

*Sasha Cherny (Alexander Mikhailovich Glikberg; 1880–1932), satirical poet. He died in France. Shostakovich loved Cherny's mocking poems and wrote a vocal cycle based on his texts in 1960. His prerevolutionary poems turned out to be so relevant more than four decades later that the first performance of the cycle created havoc among the apparatchiks of the Ministry of Culture.

That is perhaps one of the greatest secrets of our life. The old men didn't know the secret. That's why they lost everything. I can only hope that the young people will be luckier.

Meyerhold liked to dress elegantly and to surround himself with beautiful things—paintings, porcelain, crystal, and so on. But it was nothing compared to Zinaida Nikolayevna's passion for luxury. Raikh was a very beautiful woman, but perhaps a bit on the heavy side, which was particularly evident on stage. She moved with astounding clumsiness on stage.

Raikh loved her own beauty. And she knew how to make herself look good, how to frame her beauty. Everything in the Meyerhold house served that purpose: the furniture, the décor, everything. And of course, the jewels.

Almost immediately after Meyerhold's disappearance,* bandits came to Raikh's house. They killed her. Seventeen knife wounds; she was stabbed in the eyes. Raikh screamed for a long time, but none of the neighbors came to her aid. No one dared to go into Meyerhold's apartment. Who knew what was going on? Maybe Raikh was being battered by the iron fist of an official thug. Better keep away from trouble. And so they killed her and got away with all the jewels.

Raikh was of Lutheran stock, and a noblewoman at that, but I would never have thought so to look at her. She seemed a typical Odessa fishwife. I wasn't very surprised to learn that she was born in Odessa. Her Odessa heritage overshadowed the rest. Zinaida Niko- layevna often frequented a secondhand shop, the one near Novinsky Boulevard, where former ladies sold remnants of their past. Raikh was an excellent haggler.

Raikh's attitude toward me was, I suppose, one of the reasons that I left the Theater of Meyerhold. Because she let me know that I was liv- ing on Meyerhold's charity like a sponger. Naturally, it was never ar- ticulated, but it was obvious in her treatment of me. And I didn't like it.

Meyerhold was my benefactor. He heard about me from Arn-

---

* "Disappearance" refers here to Meyerhold's arrest on June 20, 1939. People often simply disappeared in those days, without any official word on their fate; when this happened, relatives knew enough to make inquiries of the secret police. The subsequent fate of those arrested often remained unknown for many years, and in most cases the dates of death are approximate.

shtam.* In Meyerhold's production of *The Teacher Bubus,* Arnshtam sat in a shell over the stage. He wore tails and he played pieces by Chopin and Liszt. Including the *Dante* Sonata ("After Reading Dante"), which ended the play. *The Teacher Bubus* was a rather wild and clumsy play. The shell in which poor Arnshtam was enthroned was gilded. Candles burned on the grand piano. And voluptuous Raikh marched heavily to Chopin's music.

Arnshtam was planning to leave Meyerhold, since he was being drafted. Meyerhold had heard my First Symphony. He didn't like it very much, but still he knew my name. Arnshtam recommended me as a pianist. It was a good deed for Meyerhold. He thought along these lines: Here's a young man with nothing to eat. I'll take him into my theater. And he did. But being a noble spirit, he didn't hold his good deed against me. Not like Zinaida Nikolayevna.

Raikh was the one who destroyed Meyerhold. I'm absolutely convinced of it. It was she who made him stay close to the rulers, close to Trotsky, Zinoviev,† et al. Meyerhold dedicated one of his plays to Trotsky (he called his plays opuses). And it backfired.

Meyerhold's admirers included Bukharin and Karl Radek.‡ But to Meyerhold's credit, he never felt on friendly footing with the authorities. Important guests had a terrible effect on him. I can attest to that. And naturally, Meyerhold would never lower himself to the role of Stalin's flunky. Stalin hated Meyerhold. It was a hatred by default, you might say, because Stalin had never been present at a single production of Meyerhold's. Not a one. Stalin based his feelings for Meyerhold completely on denunciations.

---

*Leo Oskarovich Arnshtam (b. 1905), film director, a friend of Shostakovich. In his youth, he worked as a piano player at the Theater of Meyerhold. Shostakovich wrote the scores for five of Arnshtam's films, including *Girlfriends* (1936), which was a success in the United States.

†Grigori Evseyevich Zinoviev (Radomyslsky; 1883–1936), a leader of the Communist Party and the Comintern. As Chairman of the Petrograd City Soviet, he was notorious for his cruelty (including executions of hostages). An artist who knew him recalled that Zinoviev told him: "The Revolution, the Internationale—they are major events, that's true. But I'll burst out crying if they touch Paris!" He was shot on Stalin's orders for being a "terrorist."

‡Nikolai Ivanovich Bukharin (1888–1938), a Communist Party leader. In his "political will" Lenin described Bukharin as "not only the most valued and most important theoretician of the Party, but also justly the favorite of the Party." He was shot by Stalin. The same fate awaited the major Party worker and journalist Karl Berngardovich Radek (Sobelson; 1885–1939), who in his day was hailed as the best fabricator of anti-Soviet jokes.

Just before the Theater of Meyerhold was shut down, Kaganovich*
came to a performance at the theater. He was very powerful. The theater's future depended on his opinion, as did Meyerhold's future.

As was to be expected, Kaganovich didn't like the play. Stalin's
faithful comrade in arms left almost in the middle. Meyerhold, who
was in his sixties then, ran out into the street after Kaganovich. Kaganovich and his retinue got in the car and drove off. Meyerhold ran
after the car, he ran until he fell. I would not have wanted to see
Meyerhold like that.

A strange thing happened with Meyerhold. He certainly wasn't a
pedagogue, more of an antipedagogue, in fact. If an extremely curious
person pestered him with questions, it led to a grandiose scene.
Meyerhold attacked the innocent person, shouting that he was being
spied upon, that his best creative discoveries were being stolen from
him, and so on, bordering on insanity.

But even people who spent a very brief time with Meyerhold learned
something. And even if Meyerhold threw them out on their ears, they
still came away enriched, unless, of course, they were complete idiots.

When I lived with Meyerhold on Novinsky Boulevard, he occasionally shared his ideas with me. I sat in on many rehearsals and I saw
many of his productions. If I start thinking, there was *Tarelkin's
Death, The Teacher Bubus, Trust D.E., The Forest, The Mandate,
Commander of the Second Army, The Inspector General, The Last Decision, Thirty-Three Swoons, The Baths,* and *The Lady of the Camel-
lias.* I saw Meyerhold's production of Tchaikovsky's *Queen of Spades*
at the Maly Theater, I saw a revival of *The Masquerade,* I wrote music for *The Bedbug,* I was in charge of the music for *Woe to Wit,*† and
I learned a few things, I would think, from Meyerhold.

Some of his ideas took root in me then, and they turned out to be
important and useful. This, for example: You must strive for some-

‡Lazar Moiseyevich Kaganovich (b. 1893), a leader of the Communist Party. Stalin was married to Kaganovich's younger sister, Rose. Kaganovich's signature appeared on multitudes of
death warrants in Stalin's time. In 1957 Khrushchev removed him from power as a member of
an "anti-Party group."
†In Meyerhold's production of Alexander Griboyedov's classic comedy *Woe from Wit,* the title was *Woe to Wit* (as the author himself had called the original draft)—a small touch illustrat-
ing Meyerhold's eternal desire to confuse and astound the audience.

thing new in each work, so that each new work stuns. Set a new technical goal in every work. Meyerhold followed this rule of his with maniacal stubbornness. Today such a rule may seem a commonplace, but in those days, at that time, it was a major discovery for me. We had never been taught anything like that. At the Conservatory it was: So you compose? Well, go ahead, however you please. Of course, follow certain rules. But nothing more than that.

And this leads to the second rule, Meyerhold's second lesson. You must prepare for every new composition. Look through a lot of music, search—maybe there was something similar in the classics. Then you must try to do it better, or at least in your own way.

All these considerations helped me very much in that period. I quickly forgot my fears about never turning into a composer. I began thinking through each composition, I had more confidence in what I was writing, and it was harder to throw me off the track.

And one more Meyerhold rule helped me to be calmer in the face of criticism of my work. This is Meyerhold's third lesson, and it is useful for others, not just me. Meyerhold stated it more than once: If the production pleases everyone, then consider it a total failure. If, on the other hand, everyone criticizes your work, then perhaps there's something worthwhile in it. Real success comes when people argue about your work, when half the audience is in raptures and the other half is ready to tear you apart.

In general, when I remember Meyerhold I feel sad. And not only because of the horrible fate that befell him. When I think of his end, it merely hurts. The sadness comes because Vsevolod Emilyevich and I didn't do anything together. Nothing came of the vast plans we made to collaborate. Meyerhold wanted to stage my opera *The Nose;* it didn't work. He also wanted to put on *Lady Macbeth;* that didn't work out either. I wrote the music for one of his productions, Mayakovsky's *The Bedbug,* yet essentially, I felt great antipathy for that play. I had fallen under Meyerhold's spell.

I refused Meyerhold's other proposals because I was angry with him over *The Bedbug.* I didn't work with him on Mayakovsky's awful play *The Baths,* which was a failure. I even refused to write the music for his play *Thirty-Three Swoons,* based on Chekhov. And naturally, I didn't write the music for Meyerhold's production of *One Life.* That was a terrible creation based on Ostrovsky's horrible novel *How the Steel Was Tempered*. Meyerhold wanted to disassociate himself from formalism* with this play. He ordered realistic scenery so that everything looked real. But it was too late for disassociation. His list of ideological sins was too long. And the authorities, seeing the realistic sets, decreed, "This is intentional, the better to mock realism."

The play was banned, and they shut the Theater of Meyerhold.

It's like the Ilf and Petrov story: Come on over, the Petrovs won't be here. Neither will the Ivanovs. Come over, do. The Sidorovs won't be here either. No matter what I think of, it's the same: it didn't happen, we didn't have the time, we didn't do this because we were afraid, that we just didn't do at all. You look, and your whole life is gone.

Meyerhold wanted to do an opera with me based on Lermontov's *A Hero of Our Time*. He planned to write the libretto himself. Then we thought about doing an opera with Lermontov's *Masquerade*. And he proposed that I write an opera on *Hamlet,* which he also planned to produce. It's very sad. Though I can imagine what we would have got for doing *Hamlet,* since Meyerhold's ideas on that were as wrong as they could be for those times. We would have been decried for formalism.

It's a shame that it didn't work out with Meyerhold. I ended up writing music for a *Hamlet* anyway, for a most formalistic one. I'm very unlucky with that formalism. An artistic project is planned, I'm asked to be the composer, and then there's always a scandal. It must be fate. "Fateful eggs," like Bulgakov's story.

One of the most "fateful eggs" was the first of the three productions of *Hamlet* with which I was involved. The production was scandalous, the most scandalous, they say, in the history of Shakespeare. It may be so, I don't know. In any case, there was a great hue and cry. And of course, it was over the same old thing: formalism.

* "Formalism" has been a "cant" word in Soviet art and literature since the 1920s. As history has shown, this word has almost no real aesthetic content. It has been an epithet for the most varied creative figures and tendencies, depending on the political line and personal tastes of the leaders of the Soviet Union at a particular time. Let us quote one typical Soviet definition of "formalism": "Formalism in art is the expression of bourgeois ideology that is hostile to the Soviet people. The Party did not cease its vigilant struggle even for a moment against any even minute manifestation of formalism." It therefore is not strange that all kinds of punishments were brought upon those branded as "formalists," up to and including extermination.

Akimov* was doing *Hamlet* at the Vakhtangov Theater. He's five years older than I, and that's an enormous difference, especially when you're young. This was in the early 1930s, and *Hamlet* was Akimov's first independent production. Daring, wouldn't you say? Particularly if you bear in mind what kind of *Hamlet* he wanted to show the audience.

To this very day, that scandalous production is a nightmare for Shakespearian scholars. They blanch at the mention of the production, as though they're seeing the Ghost. Incidentally, Akimov got rid of the Ghost. I think that this must have been the only version of *Hamlet* without him. The production had a materialistic base, so to speak.

Meyerhold, as you know, adored *Hamlet*. He considered it the best play of any time and any country. He said if all the plays ever written suddenly disappeared and only *Hamlet* miraculously survived, all the theaters in the world would be saved. They could all put on *Hamlet* and be successful and draw audiences.

Meyerhold may have overstated the case a bit. But really, I love *Hamlet* too. I "went through" *Hamlet* three times from a professional standpoint, but I read it many more times than that, many more. I read it now.

I'm particularly touched by Hamlet's conversation with Rosenkrantz and Guildenstern, when Hamlet says that he's not a pipe and he won't let people play him. A marvelous passage. It's easy for him, he's a prince, after all. If he weren't, they'd play him so hard he wouldn't know what hit him.

Another Shakespeare play I love is *King Lear*. I met "the prince" three times and "the king" twice, and in one case I shared their music—*King Lear* shared with *Hamlet*.† Crowned personages, I thought, would work it out between them.

In *King Lear* the important thing as I see it is the shattering of the miserable Lear's illusions. No, not shattering. Shattering comes all at once, and it's over; that wouldn't make it tragedy. It wouldn't be inter-

---

*Nikolai Pavlovich Akimov (1901–1968), theater director and artist, perpetually charged with "formalism." His 1932 production of *Hamlet* was highly regarded in its day in the American literary press.

†The director Grigori Mikhailovich Kozintsev (1905–1973) used Shostakovich's music, written earlier for his production of *King Lear,* in his staging of *Hamlet*. Later Shostakovich wrote the scores for Kozintsev's famous films of *Hamlet* and *King Lear*.

esting. But watching his illusions slowly, gradually crumbling—that's another thing. That's a painful, morbid process.

Illusions die gradually—even when it seems that it happened suddenly, instantaneously, that you wake up one fine day and you have no more illusions. It isn't like that at all. The withering away of illusions is a long and dreary process, like a toothache. But you can pull out a tooth. Illusions, dead, continue to rot within us. And stink. And you can't escape them. I carry all of mine around with me.

I think about Meyerhold. There were many tragedies in his life. His whole life was tragic, and one of the tragedies was that he never directed *Hamlet*. Meyerhold liked to discuss how he would stage this or that scene from *Hamlet*. His ideas had much in common with Akimov's concept. Meyerhold had thought of it all earlier and carried it around in his head. Then he shouted on every corner that Akimov had robbed him. Of course, he hadn't. Akimov thought of everything himself. But it's significant that the idea of staging *Hamlet* as a comedy was in the air.

Meyerhold wanted Hamlet to be played by two actors, perhaps a man and a woman, and for one Hamlet to read the tragic monologues and the other to bother him. The second Hamlet would be comic. I think that Raikh would have read the tragic monologues. Meyerhold had already tried her as Hamlet.

Meyerhold was worried by the Ghost. He didn't believe in ghosts. But more important, the censors didn't believe in ghosts. And so Meyerhold thought about how to present him. He demonstrated how the Ghost would climb out of a huge old trunk, creaking and groaning. The Ghost would wear glasses and galoshes and sneeze constantly. It was damp in the trunk and he had caught cold. Meyerhold was very funny talking about the Ghost. And then Akimov had a *Hamlet* without the Ghost. That's interesting too.

But at the time I was going through a serious crisis.* I was in terrible shape. Everything was collapsing and crumbling. I was eaten up

*In 1931, when Shostakovich was writing *Lady Macbeth,* a series of painful failures befell him: his ballet *Bolt* was taken out of the repertoire and the music to several plays and films did nothing to enhance his reputation (one production set to Shostakovich's music included circus horses and Alma the Trained Dog). He wanted to create "high art" and he was angry with all the pressures that were distracting him from his real work. His courtship of Nina Vasilyevna Varzar, his future wife, was going through a difficult and strained period at this time too.

inside. I was writing my second opera then. My second finished one. We'll talk another time about my unsuccessful operatic projects. There were enough of them. They cluttered up my mind and exhausted my spirit. But this one seemed to be going well and I wanted to complete it. But I was being pulled in all directions. I was being bothered.

It was a bad period in general. And Akimov kept after me. I had agreed to write the music, and, it's important to note, the theater had paid my advance. Akimov was a very vitriolic man, and persistent, and he kept seducing me with tales about how scandalous his *Hamlet* would be.

The point is that in those days, *Hamlet* was banned by the censors. You may believe it or not. In general, our theater has had trouble with Shakespeare, particularly with *Hamlet* and *Macbeth*. Stalin could stand neither of these plays. Why? It seems fairly obvious. A criminal ruler—what could attract the leader and teacher* in that theme? Shakespeare was a seer—man stalks power, walking knee-deep in blood. And he was so naïve, Shakespeare. Pangs of conscience and guilt and all that. *What* guilty conscience?

All that is conventional, naïve, and beautiful. At times, Shakespeare speaks to us like a small child. When you talk with a child, the words aren't important. What's important is what lies behind the words—the mood, the music.

When I speak to small children I often don't delve into the meaning of their babble, I just listen to timbres. It's the same with Shakespeare. When I read Shakespeare, I give myself up to the flow. It doesn't happen often. But those are the best moments. I read—and listen to his music.

Shakespeare's tragedies are filled with music. It was Shakespeare who said that the man who doesn't like music isn't trustworthy. Such a man is capable of a base act or murder. Apparently Shakespeare himself loved music. I'm always taken with one scene in *Lear,* in which the sick Lear awakens to music.

Stalin didn't give a damn about all these refinements, naturally. He simply didn't want people watching plays with plots that displeased

* "Leader and Teacher" is one of the traditional formulas invariably appended to Stalin's name in his lifetime. Among the other epithets were "Great Railroad Engineer," "Friend of Children," "Great Gardener." These expressions are still part of the ironic vocabulary of the Soviet intelligentsia.

Eighteen-year-old Shostakovich (standing second from left) among other students of his professor in piano at the Leningrad Conservatory, Leonid Nikolayev (seated fourth from left). Note two other major figures: the pianists Maria Yudina (standing third from left) and Vladimir Sofronitsky (seated first from right). Leningrad, 1924.

The young Shostakovich: "I like to be treated with respect."

The Leningrad Conservatory, the oldest and most prestigious musical academy in Russia. In front is the monument to Rimsky-Korsakov.

The director of the Leningrad Conservatory, Alexander Glazunov, the "Russian Brahms." He had been a *Wunderkind* himself, and as such, understood Shostakovich especially well. 1920s.

With his friend and mentor Vsevolod Meyerhold at the director's Moscow apartment. Shostakovich was writing *The Nose* in this period. Ten years later Meyerhold would disappear forever behind Stalin's prison walls. Moscow, 1928.

Holding up the music for the production of Vladimir Mayakovsky's comedy *The Bedbug*. Seated (left to right): Shostakovich and Meyerhold; standing (left to right): Mayakovsky (who shot himself in 1930) and avant-garde artist Alexander Rodchenko. Moscow, 1929.

Shostakovich's patron,
Marshal Mikhail
Tukhachevsky, and his
wife, Nina. Stalin had
Tukhachevsky destroyed.

Director Nikolai Akimov.
Shostakovich wrote the music for
his scandalous production of
Hamlet. 1932.

The satirical writer Mikhail
Zoshchenko, Shostakovich's
friend. In 1946, Party leader
Andrei Zhdanov would call him
an "abominable, lustful animal."

After a stormy romance, Shostakovich married Nina Varzar in 1932. The opera *Lady Macbeth of Mstensk District,* which provoked Stalin's wrath, was dedicated to her. Nina died in 1954.

With his closest friend, the musicologist Ivan Sollertinsky.

The distinguished musicologist Boris Asafiev. Shostakovich was never able to forgive his betrayal.

A rare photograph: Stalin at the bier of Leningrad Party leader Sergei
Kirov, killed, it is now believed, on Stalin's orders. Stalin used Kirov's
murder as an excuse for massive repressions. Next to Stalin is Andrei
Zhdanov, later the Party ideologist on cultural matters. For many years
their tastes determined the official attitude toward Shostakovich's music.
Leningrad, 1934.

During World War II, Shostakovich in a fire fighter's helmet was a symbol of Russian resistance to Hitler's armies. *(Copyright 1942, Time Inc. All rights reserved.)*

The composer Veniamin Fleishman (seated second from right), a student of Shostakovich's, who died during the war in the battle defending Leningrad. Stunned by his death, Shostakovich completed and orchestrated Fleishman's opera *Rothschild's Violin*, based on the Chekhov story.

Three titans of Soviet music: they were enemies, they were friends.
From the left: Sergei Prokofiev, Dmitri Shostakovich,
Aram Khachaturian. Moscow, 1945.

With bomber pilots
(1942). Shostakovich
took his wartime
obligations seriously.

Tikhon Khrennikov, appointed by Stalin to administer Soviet music, attacks Shostakovich at the first Composers' Congress: "Armed with clear Party directives, we will put a final end to any manifestations of anti-People formalism and decadence, no matter what defensive coloration they may take on." Moscow, 1948.

The Congress "unanimously" condemned "formalists": Shostakovich, Prokofiev, Khachaturian, and other leading composers.

him; you never know what might pop into the mind of some demented person. Of course, all the people knew once and for all that Stalin was the greatest of the great and the wisest of the wise, but he banned Shakespeare just in case. What if someone decided to play Hamlet or Macduff?

I remember how they stopped a rehearsal of *Hamlet* at the Moscow Art Theater. It was, if you can put it that way, Stalin's "favorite" theater. More precisely, it was the only theater that the leader approved fully and entirely. For the actor playing Hamlet, the banning of the play became a real tragedy. Hamlet had been his dream, everyone around him understood that this would have been a fantastic Hamlet. But Stalin's word was law, and the leader and teacher didn't even have to give a written order. There was no order, just a wish. Why forbid? You might go down in history with a less than noble image. It's better to merely ask, as Stalin did, "Why is this necessary—playing *Hamlet* in the Art Theater, eh?" That was all, that was enough. The play was removed and the actor drank himself to death.

And for many long years *Hamlet* was not seen on the Soviet stage. Everyone knew about Stalin's question directed at the Art Theater and no one wanted to risk it. Everyone was afraid.

And *King Lear?* Everyone knows that our best Lear was Mikhoels* in the Jewish Theater and everyone knows his fate. A terrible fate. And what about the fate of our best translator of Shakespeare—Pasternak?

Almost every name bears a tragedy, more tragic than anything in Shakespeare. No, it's better not to become involved with Shakespeare. Only careless people would take on such a losing proposition. That Shakespeare is highly explosive.

But back then, in my youth, I gave in to Akimov's exhortations. He was a unique director, a siren with a cabbage head. Akimov was always elegantly dressed and extremely polite, but it was better not to be the butt of his wit or his pen. Akimov was a mean artist. His caricatures were lethal. I think I got off lightly.

*Solomon Mikhailovich Mikhoels (Vovsi; 1890-1948), Jewish actor and director. He was brutally murdered on Stalin's orders and the murder was said to be an attack by hooligans. In 1943, when Mikhoels was chairman of the Jewish Anti-Fascist Committee (later disbanded by Stalin), he came to America on Albert Einstein's invitation. In New York he appeared with Mayor La Guardia in the Polo Grounds before a crowd of 50,000.

Akimov obtained provisional permission for a production of *Hamlet*. This was a major victory. The problem was that the previous Moscow production of the play was deemed totally inadmissible by the censors. The legendary Mikhail Chekhov played Hamlet. He, as you know, was an anthroposophist, and he imbued his theater with anthroposophy. *Hamlet* was staged that way. Mikhail Chekhov set the play in Purgatory. Literally. That is, Chekhov thought that Shakespeare had written a purely symbolic play, that everyone was actually dead. The courtiers were the souls of the dead and the protagonists were anthroposophic symbols.

Probably Mikhail Chekhov sincerely believed that Shakespeare really was an anthroposophist, and that's how he played Hamlet. The atmosphere was otherworldly. The actors were brilliant, after all, and Chekhov was simply a genius. The audience came away from this strange *Hamlet* with the feeling that it had just come from the other world. You see what mysterious ideas artistic people can have. You might call them delirious. Officials saw the play and, horrified, banned *Hamlet* immediately as a reactionary, pessimistic, and mystical play.

Akimov, as I said, was a mean man, but a jolly one. He saw Mikhail Chekhov's interpretation of Hamlet and was outraged. He told me, "I look at the stage and think, Could the author of this morose delirium really be Shakespeare?" Akimov developed a passionate desire to stage his own *Hamlet*. That often happens: inspiration from the contrary, so to speak. For example, Meyerhold conceived his version of *The Queen of Spades* under the influence of a terrible production he had seen. He later told me that he would have been ready to strangle the tenor who sang Gherman if he had run into him in a dark alley.

Akimov suffered mightily during Chekhov's *Hamlet* and it was the final straw that led to his own conception of the play. The concept was, I must say, revolutionary. Akimov decided to stage it as a comedy. A comedy of struggle for power. Akimov gave the part to a rather famous comic actor. The actor was stocky and fat, a man who loved food and drink. I might note that this corresponds to the text of the play, which mentions Hamlet's corpulence. But the audience is completely unused to it. It's used to exalted Hamlets, to sexless Hamlets, I would say. Or rather, to androgynous ones in black, thigh-hugging tights. Women have played Hamlet—Asta Nilsen, I think. And Zinaida

Raikh planned to play it. With *her* body. I think it's the only male role in world literature that women have attempted. And now suddenly a fat Hamlet. With a loud voice, full of vitality.

When Akimov informed the theater authorities of his project, they were also surprised. There didn't seem to be anything to forbid here. And in any case, this concept didn't reek of reactionary mysticism. On the contrary, it gave off the healthy smell of alcohol. For Hamlet, according to Akimov, was a merry, cheerful, and hard-working man who enjoyed his drink. Actually, there wasn't anyone who didn't in this unique version. Gertrude, Claudius, Polonius, even Ophelia, drank. In Akimov's version, Ophelia drowns because she's drunk. In the language of a medical examiner's report: "an autopsy revealed traces of heavy alcoholic intoxication." The gravediggers spoke thus: "To drink or not to drink—that is the question." The doubter was set straight: "What question? Of course, to drink." The dialogue was written specially for this scene.

Now about the struggle for power. This struggle became the central theme of *Hamlet* for Akimov. The struggle for the crown. And none of the traditional pangs of guilt, the doubts, and so on. I'm sick of that struggle for power, the eternal theme of art. You can't get away from it. Particularly in our times. So. Hamlet pretends to be mad the better to trick Claudius. Akimov calculated that in the play Hamlet feigns madness seventeen times. Akimov's Hamlet wages a persistent and clever fight for the throne. There is no Ghost, as I said. Hamlet himself impersonates the Ghost. He does that to frighten and terrorize the courtiers. Hamlet wants to present an important witness for his side, from the other world, to have the witness confirm that Claudius is on the throne illegally. And so the scene of the Ghost's appearance was staged as pure comedy.

As for "To be or not to be," Hamlet spoke the lines weighing the crown in his hands. He tried it on, twirled it every which way. His relations with Ophelia, a bitch and a spy, were unambiguous. Hamlet was screwing her. And Ophelia, pregnant, got drunk and drowned herself.

Polonius was marvelous. This was perhaps the acting triumph of Akimov's production (another of his paradoxes). The famous Boris Shchukin played the role. Later Shchukin became even more famous as the first actor to portray Lenin on the screen. Or rather, as the first professional actor upon whom such a historic mission was bestowed.

Shchukin, like Akimov, was a very nasty man. He tried various approaches to the role of Polonius. But nothing seemed to work at first. I later got to know Shchukin better, when he was putting on a Balzac play in his theater and asked me to write the music. It was then that Shchukin revealed a small secret of his success in *Hamlet*.

I think the story is interesting and quite educational for actors. A small lesson in the art of acting. I laughed heartily when I heard it. Shchukin wanted to get away from the clichés. Polonius's part isn't very clear. He seems clever and at the same time rather stupid. He can be a "noble father," that's how he behaved with his son. But in relation to his daughter he's a panderer. Usually Polonius's appearances are boring for the audience. But the audience is used to it and bears it. The feeling is that if it's a classic, you have to bear certain things. You must have respect for the classics.

This was Shchukin's method. He found traits and characteristics in his friends that would help him create a role, and that's what he did with Polonius. He took something from one friend and something else from another. And then at a rehearsal Shchukin tried reading Polonius's monologue as though he were Stanislavsky.

And suddenly the role began taking shape. Everything fell into place. Even the most difficult parts of the role, when spoken in the manner and from the persona of Stanislavsky, suddenly sounded convincing. Shchukin copied Stanislavsky impeccably. You could cry laughing. The result was something majestic and slightly stupid. The man lives comfortably, very well, yet he prattles on with this nonsense. That's how Shchukin portrayed Stanislavsky.

There were many jokes about Stanislavsky then. He understood nothing about what they call "surrounding reality." Sometimes when Stanislavsky appeared at rehearsal in the Art Theater (and that was becoming rare), the actors were horrified by his stupid questions, particularly if they were rehearsing a play about Soviet life.

One of the comedies, *Squaring the Circle,* for instance, revolved around the fact that two families were living in one room. Well, two weren't that many in those days. If the room was large, it could be divided into three and even four sections. And there was no talk of a luxury like an apartment. An apartment could hold ten or fifteen families. There was a housing shortage, what could you do?

Fine words: communal apartment. The phenomenon must be immortalized, so that even our distant descendants know what a communal apartment is. Zoshchenko is incomparable here. He sings this song: "Of course, having our own separate apartment is nothing but a petty-bourgeois dream. We must live together, in collective harmony, and not lock ourselves up in our own fortresses. We must live in communal apartments. You're surrounded by people. There are people to talk to. To advise. To punch."

And it's easier to make a statement or, to put it bluntly, a denunciation, about your neighbor, since your neighbor's life is on display. Everything is visible—who came, what time he left, who visited whom, who his friends are. What a person cooks for dinner is also visible, since the kitchen, obviously, is communal. You can peek into your neighbor's pot when he steps out. You can pour in more salt. Let him eat something salty if he's so smart. And you can add something else. For his appetite, for better taste.

There are plenty of diversions in a communal kitchen. Some like to spit into the neighbor's pot. Others limit spitting to teapots. It calls for certain skills, after all. You have to wait for the person to leave the kitchen, rush over to the teapot, pull off the cover, and cough up lots of sputum. It's important not to scald yourself. There is the element of risk. The person might come back any second. If he catches you, he'll punch you in the face.

It's as Zoshchenko said: learned secretaries should be housed with learned secretaries, dentists with dentists, and so on. And people who play flutes should be settled outside of town. Then life in communal apartments will shine in its full glory.

Yes, we need, we really do need, epochal and monumental works on the deathless theme of the communal apartment. The communal apartment must be captured, depicted, glorified, and proclaimed. This is the duty of our art, of our literature.

I confess here that I also tried to take part in the common cause. To wit, to depict this misery in music. I tried to create a musical composition on this immortal theme. I wanted to show that you can kill a man in many ways, not just physical ones. Not only by shooting, say, or through hard labor. You can kill the human being in a man through simple things, by life style, for example, by the infernal communal apartment or *kommunalka,* as we all call it. May it rot in hell.

This is not a theme for comedy. I mean, not for chuckles and laughter. It's a theme for satire. But the Art Theater staged a comedy on the topic. They decided to have a pleasant laugh over it when they should have been weeping, as I've said. And Stanislavsky, to general amazement, didn't even comprehend the mechanism of the plot. He asked, "What's the point? Why are all these people living in one room!" Stanislavsky lived in a town house.

They told Stanislavsky, "They don't have individual apartments." Stanislavsky didn't believe it. Stanislavsky's famous "I don't believe it." Actors of the world, start trembling. Stanislavsky said, "It can't be! It can't be that people don't have their own apartments. You're pulling my leg."

They tried to convince Stanislavsky that this was the unadulterated truth, that there were some citizens living in these abnormal conditions. The old man became upset. They calmed him down. And then Stanislavsky made the brilliant decision: "All right, in that case we'll put in the posters that this is a comedy about people who don't have their own apartments. Otherwise the audience won't believe it."

This is a true story about one of the great directors of our time. Now, it's clear that Stanislavsky lived in his own world. He was an exalted man with an artistic soul. He received groceries from an exclusive distributor, as did all geniuses and Party workers bringing outstanding benefit to the state.

But in his naïveté, the old man called the exclusive distributor his "secret provider." People in the theater talked about it with a smirk. Stanislavsky really did think that it was a great secret. But it was no secret. Everyone knew about exclusive distributors. Everyone knew that important people got their groceries from a different source than other citizens, in special places set up just for them. Everyone was used to this fact of our life, as though that was the way it was supposed to be. And everyone kept quiet, thinking he was keeping the "great secret."

One Leningrad con man made a lot of money over it. He took both circumstances into account, as it were, and used them. The circumstance that everyone knew about exclusive distribution and the circumstance that everyone kept quiet about it. The ones who didn't get groceries kept quiet so that they wouldn't end up behind bars for spreading slander, and as for the ones who got groceries, it's obvious why they kept quiet.

The con man operated this way. He read the paper, paying special attention to the obituaries. When he saw that the Party organization of some plant or office "expressed condolences to the family of the deceased," he clipped it, got the phone number, and sometime later called the number. The con man represented himself as the head of an exclusive distribution concern and said that they had received "orders from above" to provide the family of the deceased with "everything necessary." "Since the deceased had performed such great services for them," the con man added. He asked them to place an order for whatever they wanted—eggs, butter, meat, sugar, even cocoa and chocolate. All at fantastically cheap prices. And why not—an exclusive distributor, just for deserving comrades.

Waiting for a few more days, the con man called again and said the order was ready. He asked the honored relatives of the deceased to appear for the groceries at such-and-such a place, and when the trusting people came to the appointed spot for the order, he took the money, promised immediate delivery, and disappeared.

The scoundrel got away with it for a long time, even though he pulled the trick dozens and perhaps hundreds of times, because he had worked it out so well—the plan was simple, but a work of genius. If the crook had come to a worker's family with such a proposition, they simply wouldn't have believed him. But a bureaucrat's family—they believed and how, because they knew very well that exclusive distribution existed, that it functioned openly, that it was done covertly, and that they shouldn't talk about it.

The new life style brought so many new and fresh conflicts. The exclusive distributor. The communal apartment. In previous eras a man might wander around a castle with a sword, looking for a ghost. In our times a man wanders around a communal apartment with an ax in his hands, keeping watch for the resident who doesn't turn out the light in the toilet. Imagine a novel of secrets and horrors of the new era. Here's my hero, ax in hand, threatening to chop up the sloppy resident if he catches him in the act. I feel that I didn't sing his praises enough, that is to say, I didn't portray him fully enough.

I'm not indulging in irony now. For some reason, people think that music must tell us only about the pinnacles of the human spirit, or at least about highly romantic villains. But there are very few heroes or villains. Most people are average, neither black nor white. They're gray. A dirty shade of gray.

And it's in that vague gray middle ground that the fundamental conflicts of our age take place. It's a huge ant hill in which we all crawl. In the majority of cases, our destinies are bad. We are treated harshly and cruelly. And as soon as someone crawls a little higher, he's ready to torture and humiliate others.

That is the situation that needs watching, in my opinion. You must write about the majority of people and for the majority. And you must write the truth—then it can be called realistic art. Who needs the tragedies? There's an Ilf and Petrov story about a sick man who washes his foot before going to the doctor. When he gets there he notices that he washed the wrong one. Now, that's a real tragedy.

To the extent of my ability I tried to write about these people, about their completely average, commonplace dreams and hopes, and about their suspicious tendency toward murder.

I regret that I wasn't consistent enough, perhaps, in that regard. I didn't have Zoshchenko's determination and will power. Zoshchenko plainly rejected the idea of a Red Leo Tolstoy or a Red Rabindranath Tagore, and that sunsets and dawns had to be described in flowery prose.

But I do have one great excuse. I never tried to flatter the authorities with my music. And I never had an "affair" with them. I was never a favorite, though I know that some accuse me of it. They say that I stood too close to power. An optical illusion. What was not, was not.

It's simplest to look at the facts. Lenin, as it is easy enough to surmise, never heard my music. And if he had, I doubt that he would have liked it. As far as I can tell, Lenin had specific tastes in music. He had a rather distinctive approach to it, more peculiar than is usually imagined.

Lunacharsky* used to speak of it in this way: Lunacharsky often invited Lenin to his house to listen to music, but Lenin was always busy and refused. Once, tired of Lunacharsky's invitations, he said directly, "Of course, it's very nice to listen to music. But can you imagine, it depresses me, I find it hard to bear." You see, poor Lenin was saddened by music. A telling fact, if you think about it.

Chief of Petrograd Zinoviev didn't become a fan of my music. Zinoviev was replaced by Kirov,† and I had no luck with him either.

In his time, Zinoviev ordered all the opera houses in Leningrad closed. He explained it something like this: The proletariat doesn't need opera houses. They are a heavy burden for the proletariat. We Bolsheviks can't carry the heavy burden any more. (Lenin, if you recall, also called opera a "piece of purely upper-class culture.")

Kirov, on the contrary, often attended the opera. He liked being a patron of the arts. But that didn't help my opera *The Nose* any. Kirov had a strongly negative reaction to *The Nose* and the opera was taken out of repertory. They blamed it on the fact that it needed too many rehearsals. The artists, they said, got tired. At least they didn't shut down the theater. They had planned to squash the opera house completely over Křenek's operas.

I don't need to speak of Stalin, Zhdanov, or Khrushchev here. Everyone knows of their dissatisfaction with my music. Should I have been upset? It seems a strange question. Of course not! That would be the simplest answer. But the simple answer isn't enough. These weren't mere acquaintances, men on the street. They were men wielding unlimited power.

And the comrade leaders used that power without thinking twice about it, particularly if they felt that their refined taste was offended. An artist whose portrait did not resemble the leader disappeared forever. So did the writer who used "crude words." No one entered into

*Anatoly Vasilyevich Lunacharsky (1875–1933), a Communist Party leader, People's Commissar of Education. The first and last educated Soviet "culture boss," he wrote many lively articles on music and would never have given orders, as did a later minister of culture, to organize "a quartet of ten men." In 1921, on Lunacharsky's personal orders, young Shostakovich was awarded food rations.

†Sergei Mironovich Kirov (Kostrikov; 1886–1934), a Communist Party leader, the "boss" of Leningrad. He was killed by a terrorist (the murder is now thought by most historians to have been engineered by Stalin), and Stalin used this terrorist act as an excuse for a wave of massive repressions, long remembered by Leningraders. In 1935 the famous Maryinsky Theater of Opera and Ballet was renamed after Kirov.

aesthetic discussions with them or asked them to explain themselves. Someone came for them at night. That's all.

These were not isolated cases, not exceptions. You must understand that. It didn't matter how the audience reacted to your work or if the critics liked it. All that had no meaning in the final analysis. There was only one question of life or death: how did the leader like your opus. I stress: life or death, because we are talking about life or death here, literally, not figuratively. That's what you must understand.

Now you see why it's impossible to answer the question was I upset. Of course I was.

Upset is the wrong word, but let's let it stand. Tragedies in hindsight look like farces. When you describe your fear to someone else, it seems ridiculous. That's human nature. There was only one single person with supreme power who sincerely liked my music, and that was very important for me. Why it was important should be self-evident. He was Marshal Tukhachevsky, the "Red Napoleon," as they liked to call him.

When we met, I wasn't even nineteen and Tukhachevsky was over thirty. But the main difference between us wasn't age, of course. The main difference was that by then Tukhachevsky had one of the most important positions in the Red Army and I was just a beginning musician.

But I behaved very independently. I was cocky, and Tukhachevsky liked that. We became friends. It was the first and last time that I was friends with a leader of the country, and the friendship was broken tragically.

Tukhachevsky was probably one of the most interesting people I knew. Of course, his military glory was irresistible. Everyone knew that at twenty-five Tukhachevsky was commander of the army. He seemed to be fate's favorite. He had fame, honors, high rank. It lasted until 1937.

Tukhachevsky enjoyed being attractive. He was very handsome and he knew it. He was always dressed flashily. I really liked that about him. When I was young I enjoyed dressing well myself. I rather envied another of his qualities—his unshatterable health. I had a long way to go to be like him. I was a sickly youth, while Tukhachevsky could put a man on a chair and then lift the chair, yes, lift the chair and its occupant by one leg with his arm outstretched. His office in Moscow had a gym with beams, a horizontal bar, and other incomprehensible equipment.

Undoubtedly, Tukhachevsky was a man of outstanding ability. It's not for me to judge his military talent, and I didn't always feel like falling into raptures over some of Tukhachevsky's famous military operations—for instance, the suppression of the Kronstadt Uprising.

But I often witnessed people singing dithyrambs to his military achievements. He had more than enough flatterers around him. I kept quiet.

Tukhachevsky was a very ambitious and imperious person—a typical military man. In these traits the marshal resembled Meyerhold, who adored military masquerade. He wore a Red Army uniform. Meyerhold proudly bore the ridiculous title "Honored Red Army Soldier." He had a passion for cannons, decorations, drums, and all the other military paraphernalia.

That was Meyerhold's weakness, let's put it that way. Tukhachevsky's weakness was art. Meyerhold looked silly in a uniform, but many were impressed. Tukhachevsky looked just as silly when he picked up his violin, but many were charmed. By the way, we're dealing here with pure and simple phoniness in both cases.

Strange: Meyerhold played the violin and so did Tukhachevsky. (Tukhachevsky also made violins with great passion.) Each of them recalled the craft not long before his tragic death. That, of course, is merely a coincidence. One of life's cruel jokes.

Meyerhold, as he awaited arrest, regretted that he hadn't become a violinist. "I'd be sitting in some orchestra now, sawing away at my fiddle, and I wouldn't have a care," Meyerhold said with bitterness and fear. He was sixty-five then. Forty-four-year-old Tukhachevsky said almost the same thing before his arrest. "How I wanted to learn the violin as a child! Father didn't buy me a violin. He never had the money. I would have been better off as a violinist."

The coincidence amazes and horrifies me. A renowned director and a famous military leader—both suddenly wanting to become little, unnoticeable. Just sit in some orchestra and saw at a fiddle. The marshal and the maître would have traded their biographies with almost anyone, with any drunkard who amused the crowds in the cinema lobbies. But it was too late.

Tukhachevsky liked being a patron of the arts. He liked finding "young talents" and helping them. Perhaps because the marshal himself had been a military *Wunderkind*, or perhaps because he liked demonstrating his enormous power.

From the very first day we met, Tukhachevsky demanded that I play my compositions for him. He praised them and criticized some. Often he asked me to repeat things—which is torture if music gets on your nerves. So Tukhachevsky probably did like my music.

Sometimes I think about how my life would have been if Tukhachevsky hadn't been shot on Stalin's orders. Maybe everything would have gone differently? Better, happier? But let's cast off dreams. After all, Stalin didn't consult Tukhachevsky. When the wise leader and teacher had them harass me over *Lady Macbeth*, Tukhachevsky hadn't known anything beforehand. He learned it with everyone else, in a notorious article in *Pravda*. And what could he have done? Talked Stalin out of it?

Tukhachevsky's future at that moment seemed radiant. Only a few months earlier he had become Marshal of the Soviet Union. Sounds impressive? And a year and a half later he was shot. And by chance I remained alive. Which of us was luckier?

Back at that time, in 1936, I was called to Moscow for a show whipping. Like the sergeant's widow, I had to declare to the whole world that I had whipped myself. I was completely destroyed. It was a blow that wiped out my past. And my future.

To whom could I turn for advice? To whom could I go? I went to Marshal Tukhachevsky. He had recently returned from his triumphant visit to London and Paris. *Pravda* wrote about him every day. And I was a leper, people were afraid to come up to me. I was shunned. Tukhachevsky agreed to see me. We locked ourselves in his office. He turned off his phones. We sat in silence. And then we started talking very softly. I spoke softly because my grief and despair wouldn't let me speak in my normal voice. Tukhachevsky spoke softly because he feared prying ears.

Even then you had to take a guest to the bathroom to tell him a

98

joke. You turned on the water full force and then whispered the joke. You even laughed quietly, into your fist. This marvelous tradition did not die out. It continues in our day.

But we were in no mood for jokes then. Tukhachevsky knew Stalin incomparably better than I. He knew that Stalin pursued a man to the end. In those days it looked as though that would happen to me. A second article in *Pravda*, destroying my ballet this time, confirmed my direst fears.

Tukhachevsky promised to do what he could. He spoke carefully. I could see him controlling himself when the talk turned to Stalin. And what could he have said then?

Tukhachevsky's plans have remained a mystery. Had he wanted to become a dictator? Why not, I think now. But I doubt that it would have been possible under those conditions. Now it's well known that Tukhachevsky was destroyed through the joint action of Stalin and Hitler. But one mustn't exaggerate the role of German espionage in this matter. If there hadn't been those faked documents that "exposed" Tukhachevsky, Stalin would have got rid of him anyway. The Germans just played into Stalin's hands. It was an accompaniment. Whether there was a reason or not—what was the difference? Tukhachevsky's fate was sealed.

Tukhachevsky's recommendations on military matters always rankled Stalin, and yet it was Stalin who decided which recommendations to approve. I know that Tukhachevsky had to resort to trickery. He and his deputy would plan it this way: They would appear together before Stalin. Tukhachevsky would make his proposal and the deputy would "correct" him. This always made Stalin very happy. Stalin would add to and develop the "correction." He liked the fact that Tukhachevsky was "wrong." In the end the idea would be accepted. But it was no longer Tukhachevsky's, it was Stalin's idea. Another marvelous illustration of where Stalin's ideas came from.

They sometimes say that Tukhachevsky was powerless before Stalin, that Stalin was more clever. That's nonsense. Stalin attacked from around the corner, like a bandit. You don't need to be cleverer for that. You just have to be meaner.

Tukhachevsky was alone. He had no friends, only fawners and companions for amorous expeditions. Tukhachevsky was attacked by the "old cavalrymen": Budyonny and Voroshilov.* Tukhachevsky maintained, after all, that the next war would be won by tanks and aviation. As we all know, the marshal was right. But the former cavalrymen didn't want to listen. They thought that they could easily gallop over to Paris and Berlin.

Tukhachevsky, who discussed the meaning of Einstein's theory of relativity as it applied to warfare, stuck in their craw. It was easier for Stalin to talk with the cavalrymen. They looked up to him. That allowed Voroshilov, for instance, to live through all the unpleasant events. Of course, in his last days, Stalin began saying that Voroshilov was a British spy, but he didn't remember what he was saying any more. Voroshilov survived.

Voroshilov loved choral singing. He sang himself, he was a tenor, and that's probably why he felt he was as much a specialist in music as Zhdanov. He longed to give valuable advice to composers and performers. His favorite works were Ukrainian folk songs. He used to sing them with his puny tenor voice. One of my actor friends told me how he sang with Stalin, Voroshilov, and Zhdanov after a reception. The soloists of the Bolshoi modestly sang along with the leaders. A horrible dissonance hung in the air. Stalin conducted. He wanted to command even here. Of course, they were all quite drunk.

It's obvious to everyone that I'm no judge in military matters. I'm a total amateur in the field and very happy that it's so. But I heard a lot about various military matters from Tukhachevsky. He naturally realized that it was stupid to discuss military affairs with me, but he couldn't stop himself.

We met often, and went out a lot. He liked driving to the country and he used to take me with him. We would leave the car and go deep into the woods. It was easier to talk freely there.

Tukhachevsky was always professional, everywhere, in any situation. He wanted to be a patron of the arts, but his mind swirled with military affairs. Sometimes he told me a thing or two.

In those moments I liked him and didn't like him. I liked him because he talked about the subject he knew. I don't care for dilettantes.

*Semyon Mikhailovich Budyonny (1883–1973) and Kliment Efremovich Voroshilov (1881–1969), marshals of the Soviet Union, both of whom began their careers as cavalrymen. Budyonny, famed for his huge mustache and his outstanding stupidity, became a figurehead even before World War II, but Voroshilov continued on top almost until his death.

I find professionals more simpatico. But Tukhachevsky was a specialist in a terrible profession. His profession was walking over the dead. Tukhachevsky strove to do it as successfully as possible, and his enthusiasm for military matters repelled me.

Tukhachevsky loved impersonating Harun al-Rashid. Actually, the uniform became Tukhachevsky and he knew it. But he was recognized immediately in uniform, and therefore he often went into town in blatantly civilian clothes. His suit would also be well made. Tukhachevsky loved the cinema. He could have seen the films in private screening rooms for the top brass. But he preferred putting on his civilian clothes and going to a seedy movie house. Alone, without a bodyguard. It was more interesting for him that way.

Once Tukhachevsky went to a theater and saw that the piano player was the former music teacher from the Cadet Corps. He had taught Tukhachevsky. The piano player's name was Erdenko, and he was related to the famous violinist Mikhail Erdenko. The old man was in pathetic straits. Tukhachevsky decided to bestow favors on him. He went up to him and introduced himself. He said that he wanted to study with him again, that the lessons of his youth were so good that he, Marshal Tukhachevsky, still couldn't forget them.

Naturally, Tukhachevsky didn't start taking lessons from his old teacher. But the old man did get a tidy sum. Tukhachevsky paid for something like a year's lessons in advance. He wanted to help the old man in a gracious way, without insulting him. He liked looking gracious.

Once Tukhachevsky and I went to the Hermitage to look at the paintings. Actually, it was his idea. He was in mufti, of course. First we wandered around the museum on our own, then we tagged along with a group. The group had a guide. A young fellow and obviously not very educated. Tukhachevsky began correcting the guide. He said two words to the guide's one, and, I must admit, to the point. The people stopped listening to the guide, and listened only to Tukhachevsky. Finally the guide grew angry. He wouldn't even talk to Tukhachevsky. He approached me and said, "Who is that?" Meaning, why is he sticking his nose in my business?

Without blinking, I replied, "Tukhachevsky." It was like a lightning bolt. At first the guide didn't believe me. But then he looked closely, and of course recognized him. Tukhachevsky had an extremely distinctive face. Naturally, this not very educated worker at the Hermitage got scared. He feared for his job, that his children would starve.

And they would have fired him if Tukhachevsky had ordered it, or if he had merely complained. As commander of the military district, Tukhachevsky had great power in Leningrad.

The guide's feistiness was replaced by terrible fear. He began thanking Tukhachevsky for his priceless information. Tukhachevsky replied benignly, "Study, young man, study. It's never too late." And we headed for the exit. Tukhachevsky was very pleased with the adventure.

Once Tukhachevsky's security men discovered a man sitting in his car completely drunk, soused. He was trying to unscrew the door handles, for some reason. They were nickel-plated, very shiny, and apparently they had caught the citizen's eye. Well, the security men planned to take this citizen "where he should be." There is such a marvelous place, with very bad consequences, I might add.

Tukhachevsky interfered. He ordered them to let the drunkard go. Let him sleep it off. He turned out to be the composer Arseny Gladkovsky, a rather famous composer in his time, one of his operas was quite successful. The opera was just then being revived, after a long hiatus, and since it dealt with a military theme (the defense of Petrograd in 1919), Gladkovsky thought Tukhachevsky might be interested in hearing it. In his invitation he thanked Tukhachevsky for not sending him "where he should be."

Tukhachevsky saw the opera but didn't like it very much. Later he said to me thoughtfully, "Maybe I was mistaken in letting him go?" He was joking, of course.

They called Tukhachevsky the "greatest Soviet military theoretician." Stalin couldn't stand that. Stalin was also very suspicious of Tukhachevsky's friendship with Ordzhonikidze. When People's Military Commissar Frunze died suddenly—as they now suspect, Stalin had a hand in that death too—Tukhachevsky recommended Ordzhonikidze for the vacant post. Stalin didn't like that at all. That, too, played a part in future events.

On Stalin's personal orders Tukhachevsky was sent to Leningrad. This was a sort of exile for Tukhachevsky, but I got to see him much more. Tukhachevsky flew into a frenzy of activity in Leningrad, the results of which were apparent later, during the war—after Tukhachevsky had been shot.

During the war I thought of Tukhachevsky often. Naturally, we sorely lacked his clear mind. Now we know that Hitler didn't sign the Barbarossa plan* right away. He hesitated, and signed only because he thought that without Tukhachevsky the Red Army was powerless.

I thought of Tukhachevsky when I dug trenches outside Leningrad in July '41. They sent us beyond the Forelli Hospital, divided us into groups, and handed each of us a shovel. We were the Conservatory group. The musicians looked pathetic and worked, I might add, very badly. It was a hot July. One pianist came in a new suit. He delicately rolled up his trousers to his knees, revealing his spindly legs, which were soon covered with mud to the thigh. Another one—a highly respected music historian—kept setting aside his shovel every minute. He had arrived with a briefcase stuffed with books. Heading for a shady bush, he would pull out a thick volume from his briefcase.

Of course, everyone tried hard. So did I. But what kind of ditchdiggers were we? All this should have been done before. Much earlier and more professionally. It would have had more effect. The little that had been done earlier in terms of defense had been done under Tukhachevsky.

When Tukhachevsky insisted on increasing the number of planes and tanks, Stalin called him a harebrained schemer. But during the war, after the first crushing defeats, Stalin caught on. It was the same with rockets. Tukhachevsky began rocketry while in Leningrad. Stalin later had all the Leningrad rocketry experts shot, and then they had to start from scratch.

The war became a terrible tragedy for everyone. I saw and lived through a great deal, but the war was probably the hardest trial. Not for me personally, but for the people. For composers and, say, poets, perhaps, it wasn't so hard. But the people suffered. Think how many perished. Millions.

War was inevitable, of course. It's a terrible, dirty, and bloody business. It would be better if there were no war and no soldiers. But if

---

*Hitler's plan of attack on the Soviet Union, named after Frederick I "Barbarossa" (Red Beard), the Holy Roman Emperor who had marched east in 1190.

there is war, then the professionals should take care of it. Tukhachevsky was a war professional and naturally he would have done his work better than the inexperienced or incompetent military leaders who led our troops after all the purges.

Tukhachevsky told me how he had fought in the First World War. He was more than skeptical of the tsar and yet he fought, and fought passionately, bravely. Tukhachevsky, fighting the Germans, felt that he was defending the people and not the tsar. It would have been worse for the people under the Germans than under the tsar.

I often remembered those words of Tukhachevsky's. They became real for me during the war. I hate war. But you have to defend your country from invasion by the enemy. You have only one motherland.

Tukhachevsky had spent time as a German prisoner of war. By present-day standards, the camp was like a sanatorium. The prisoners were allowed to walk around the camp without guards; a written agreement not to run away was enough. An officer's word, so to speak. Tukhachevsky asked another officer to sign in his place, and escaped. He told me about it with a smile. But Tukhachevsky didn't manage to get away from Stalin.

When Tukhachevsky was introduced to Lenin, his first question was how did Tukhachevsky manage to get away from the German prison camp? Apparently he thought that the Germans had "helped" Tukhachevsky escape, just as they had "helped" Lenin appear in Russia right after the Revolution.

Lenin sensed that Tukhachevsky was a kindred spirit. He delegated the most responsible jobs to the obscure lieutenant. As you know, Tukhachevsky's army reached Warsaw, but it failed and had to retreat. Lenin forgave Tukhachevsky his failure. Tukhachevsky reminded me of that before my trip to Warsaw for a competition. Tukhachevsky had attacked Warsaw in 1920. We were leaving for Warsaw in January 1927, just some six years later. There were three of us. We played our competition programs for Tukhachevsky. Tukhachevsky put up with it and said something to the effect that we should be brave. Nothing terrible would happen even if we lost. After all, he hadn't been beheaded for his failure, and neither would we.

I wonder who plays the violins that Tukhachevsky made, if they survived at all, that is. I have the feeling that the violins emit a pathetic sound. I was very unlucky in life. But others were unluckier. When I think of Meyerhold or Tukhachevsky, I think of the words of Ilf and Petrov: "It's not enough to love Soviet power. It has to love you."

I worked on *Lady Macbeth* for almost three years. I had announced a trilogy dedicated to the position of women in various eras in Russia. The plot of *Lady Macbeth of Mtsensk District* is taken from the story of the same name by Nikolai Leskov. The story amazes the reader with its unusual vividness and depth, and in terms of being the most truthful and tragic portrayal of the destiny of a talented, smart, and outstanding woman, "dying in the nightmarish conditions of prerevolutionary Russia," as they say, this story, in my opinion, is one of the best.

Maxim Gorky once said: "We must study. We must learn about our country, her past, present, and future"; and Leskov's story serves this purpose. *Lady Macbeth* is a true treasure trove for a composer, with its vividly drawn characters and dramatic conflicts—I was attracted by it. Alexander Germanovich Preis, a young Leningrad playwright, worked out the libretto with me. It followed Leskov almost in its entirety, with the exception of the third act, which for greater social impact deviates slightly from the original. We introduced a scene at the police station and left out the murder of Ekaterina Lvovna's nephew.

I resolved the opera in a tragic vein. I would say that *Lady Macbeth* could be called a tragic-satiric opera. Despite the fact that Ekaterina Lvovna is a murderer, she is not a lost human being. She is tormented by her conscience, she thinks about the people she killed. I feel empathy for her.

It's rather difficult to explain, and I've heard quite a bit of disagreement on the matter, but I wanted to show a woman who was on a much higher level than those around her. She is surrounded by monsters. The last five years were like a prison for her.

Those who criticize her harshly do so from this point of view: if she's a criminal, then she's guilty. But that's the common consensus, and I'm more interested in the individual. I think it's all in Leskov. There are no general, standardized rules of conduct. Everything depends on the situation and on the person. A turn of events is possible in which murder is not a crime. You can't approach everything with the same measure.

Ekaterina Lvovna is an outstanding, colorful person and her life is sad and drab. But a powerful love comes into her life, and it turns out that a crime is worth committing for the sake of that passion, since life has no meaning otherwise anyway.

Lady Macbeth touches on many themes. I wouldn't want to spend too much time on all the possible interpretations; after all, I'm not talking about myself in these pages and certainly not about my music. In the long run, you can just go to see the opera. In the last few years it's been produced frequently, even abroad. Of course, all the productions are bad, very bad. In the last few years I can point out only one good production—in Kiev under the direction of Konstantin Simeonov, a conductor who has a wonderful feel for music. And he starts from the music, not the plot. When his singers started overpsychologizing their parts, Simeonov shouted, "What are you trying to do, set up the Moscow Art Theater here? I need singing, not psychology. Give me singing!"

They don't understand that too well here, that singing is more important in opera than psychology. Directors treat the music in opera as something of minor importance. That's how they ruined the film version, *Katerina Izmailova.* The actors were magnificent, particularly

Galina Vishnevskaya,* but you can't hear the orchestra at all. Now, what is the point of that?

I dedicated *Lady Macbeth* to my bride, my future wife, so naturally the opera is about love too, but not only love. It's also about how love could have been if the world weren't full of vile things. It's the vileness that ruins love. And the laws and proprieties and financial worries, and the police state. If conditions had been different, love would have been different too.

Love was one of Sollertinsky's favorite themes. He could speak for hours on it, on the most varied levels: from the highest to the very lowest. And Sollertinsky was very supportive of my attempt to express my ideas in *Lady Macbeth*. He spoke of the sexuality of two great operas, *Carmen* and *Wozzeck,* and regretted that there was nothing comparable in Russian opera. Tchaikovsky, for instance, had nothing like it—and that was no accident.

Sollertinsky believed that love was the greatest gift and the person who knew how to love had a talent just as does the person who knows how to build ships or write novels. In that sense Ekaterina Lvovna is a genius. She is a genius in her passion, for the sake of which she is prepared to do anything, even murder.

Sollertinsky felt that contemporary conditions were not conducive to the development of talents in that area. Everyone seemed worried about what would happen to love. I suppose it will always be like that, it always seems that love's last days are here. At least, it always seems that everything is different today from what it was yesterday. And it will all be different tomorrow. No one knows how, but it will be different.

Love for Three was a success in the movies, the theaters were running plays like *The Nationalization of Women,* and there were debates on free love. Debates were very popular, and they debated the theory of "the glass of water." It used to be said that having sexual inter-

*Galina Pavlovna Vishnevskaya (b. 1926), soprano. Shostakovich's vocal cycle *Satires* and his instrumentation of Mussorgsky's *Songs and Dances of Death* are dedicated to her. She sang the premieres of these works and sang in the first performance of the Fourteenth Symphony. In 1978 she and her husband, cellist and conductor Mstislav Rostropovich, were stripped of Soviet citizenship for "systematic acts that bring harm to the prestige of the Soviet Union." Thereafter, Vishnevskaya's name was removed from all Soviet reference works.

course should be as simple as having a glass of water. At TRAM, in some play, the heroine said that satisfying your sexual needs was the only important thing, and that drinking from the same glass all the time gets boring.

There were also debates on a popular book, *Moon from the Right,* by Sergei Malashkin. It's a terrible book, but the readers didn't care. The point was that it described orgies with young Komsomol girls. And so they tried the heroes of this book—with appointed counsel and judges. The question they were hotly debating was can a young woman have twenty-two husbands?

This problem was on everyone's lips, even Meyerhold was taken with it, and he was a man of excellent taste. This is just further proof of what the atmosphere was like then. Meyerhold planned to stage Tretyakov's* play *I Want a Baby* and even began rehearsals, but the play was banned. He tried for two years to get permission and failed. The censors felt that the play was too frank. Meyerhold, in defense, insisted that if you wanted to remove all vulgar words from the stage you'd have to burn all of Shakespeare and leave only Rostand.

Meyerhold wanted to put on Tretyakov's play as a debate too. In fact, things seemed to be moving toward the abolition of love. One good woman in a play said as much: "The only thing I love is Party work." And love can fall by the wayside. From time to time, we'll give birth to healthy children, naturally pure from a class point of view, of a good Aryan, I mean proletarian, background.

This is not a happy business. Tretyakov dreamed of how everyone would give birth by plan, and they destroyed him. And it went on Meyerhold's record that "he stubbornly persisted in staging the play *I Want a Baby* by enemy of the people Tretyakov, which was a hostile slander of the Soviet people."

So you see that even though my opera's plot did not deal with our glorious reality, actually there were many points of contact, you only have to look for them. In general, a heroine like Ekaterina Lvovna is not very typical for Russian opera, but there are some traditional

*Sergei Mikhailovich Tretyakov (1892–1939), avant-garde playwright, who worked with Meyerhold, Eisenstein, and Mayakovsky. Bertolt Brecht considered Tretyakov one of his teachers in the field of Marxism. He was shot during the "great terror."

things in *Lady Macbeth* and I think they're very important. There's the scrawny little man, something like Grishka Kuterma,* and the entire fourth act, with the convicts. Some of my friends objected that the fourth act was too traditional. But that was the finale I had in mind, because we're talking about convicts.

In the old days a convict was called *neschastnen'kii,* or "poor little wretch"; people tried to help them, to give them something. But in my day the attitude toward the arrested had changed. If you got yourself in jail, you no longer existed.

Chekhov went to Sakhalin Island to better the lot of criminal convicts. As for political prisoners—they were all heroes in the eyes of cultured men. Dostoevsky recalled how a little girl gave him a kopeck when he was a convict. He was a poor wretch in her eyes.

And so I wanted to remind the audience that prisoners are wretched people and that you shouldn't hit a man when he's down. Today you're in prison, tomorrow it might be me. That's a very important moment for me in *Lady Macbeth*, and incidentally, a very traditional one for Russian music. Recall *Khovanshchina,* for instance—Prince Golitsyn is an extremely unsympathetic character, but when he's taken away into exile, Mussorgsky sympathizes with him. That's as it should be.

I think it was a great stroke of luck for me that I found the plot of *Lady Macbeth*, even though there were many factors promoting it. For one, I like Leskov, and for another, Kustodiev did good illustrations for *Lady Macbeth* and I bought the book. And then I liked the film that Cheslav Sabinsky made of the story. It was roundly criticized for being unscrupulous, but it was vivid and engrossing.

I composed the opera with great intensity, which was enhanced by the circumstances of my personal life.

When I write vocal music I like to picture concrete people. Here's a man I know—how will he sing this or that monologue? That's probably why I can say about any of my characters, "That's So-and-so and she's So-and-so." Of course, that's just my personal feeling, but it does help me compose.

---

*Grishka Kuterma is the character in Rimsky-Korsakov's opera *Tale of the City of Kitezh* who symbolizes betrayal and repentance. Lunacharsky wrote of "the almost Wagnerian, yet Slavic, Russian Orthodox power of the sinner Kuterma."

Naturally, I think about tessituras and such, as well. But first of all I think about personality and that may be why my operas don't have an *emploi* and sometimes it's hard for the performers to find themselves. It's the same with my vocal cycles.

For instance, I have rather complicated feelings about Sergei from *Lady Macbeth*. He's a bastard, of course, but he's a handsome man and, more importantly, attractive to women, while Ekaterina Lvovna's husband is a degenerate. I had to show Sergei's flashy sex appeal through my music. I couldn't resort to mere caricature because it would be psychologically false. The audience had to understand that a woman really couldn't resist a man like that. So I endowed Sergei with several characteristics of a close friend of mine, who naturally wasn't a Sergei at all, but a very intelligent person. He missed nothing when it came to ladies, though; he was quite persistent in that regard. He says many beautiful things and women melt. I gave that trait to Sergei. When Sergei seduces Ekaterina Lvovna, in intonation he's my friend. But it was done in such a way that even he—a subtle musician—didn't notice a thing.

I feel it's important to use real events and real people in the plot. When Sasa Preis and I did our first drafts of *Lady Macbeth*, we wrote all kinds of nonsense drawn from the personalities of our friends. It was amusing and it turned out to be a big help in our work.

The opera was a huge success. I wouldn't bring it up at all, of course, but later events turned everything around. Everyone forgot that *Lady Macbeth* ran for two years in Leningrad and for two in Moscow under the title *Katerina Izmailova* at Nemirovich-Danchenko's theater. It was also produced by Smolich* at the Bolshoi.

Worker correspondents wrote incensed letters about *The Nose*. And the ballets *The Golden Age* and *Bolt* were also denounced in every way. But it wasn't like that with *Lady Macbeth*. In both Leningrad and Moscow the opera played several times a week. *Katerina Izmailova* ran almost a hundred times in two seasons at Nemirovich-Danchenko's and as often in Leningrad. You might say that that's good for a new opera.

You must understand that I'm not indulging in self-praise here. The

*Nikolai Vasilyevich Smolich (1888–1968), opera director, avant-gardist, who directed the premieres of *The Nose* and *Lady Macbeth of Mtsensk District*.

point isn't only in the music and in the productions themselves, which in both Leningrad and Moscow were done with talent and care. The general atmosphere was important too, and for the opera it was good.

This may have been the happiest time for my music, there was never anything like it before or after. Before the opera I was a boy who might have been spanked, and later I was a state criminal, always under observation, always under suspicion. But at that moment everything was comparatively fine. Or to be more accurate, everything seemed to be fine.

This essentially unfounded feeling arose after the breakup of RAPP and RAPM.* These unions had been on everybody's back. Once the Association came to control music, it seemed that Davidenko's "They wanted to beat, to beat us"† was going to replace all available music. This worthless song was performed by soloists and choirs, violinists and pianists, even string quartets did it. It didn't get as far as a symphony orchestra, but only because some of the instruments were suspect—the trombone, for instance.

You can see there was plenty of reason to fall into despair. It looked as though neither orchestral music nor the opera had any prospects at all. And most musicians were in a terrible mood. One after another, with bowed heads, they joined the ranks of RAPM. For instance, my friend Ronya Shebalin suddenly began singing the praises of Davidenko. I protected myself by working at TRAM.

RAPM had turned the screw so tight that it seemed things couldn't possibly be any worse. (Later it turned out that they could be a lot worse.) And when RAPM disappeared, everyone heaved a sigh of relief. For a time, professionals were in charge of things; I mean, naturally they had no power, but their suggestions were taken into account, and that was quite something.

I went to Turkey as part of a semiofficial cultural delegation. They were trying to improve relations with Turkey and President Kemal

*The Russian Association of Proletarian Writers (1920–1932) and its "musical" offshoot, the Russian Association of Proletarian Musicians (1923–1932), arose as instruments of the cultural policies of the Party. The influence of these unions was almost overwhelming at the end of the 1920s and into the early 1930s. They often turned out to be greater royalists than the king, and were disbanded by Stalin when he decided that the organizations had served their function.

†This song by one of the leaders of RAPM, Alexander Davidenko, was written in late 1929, after Soviet-Chinese conflict in the Far East. One of the first successful examples of the popular Soviet propaganda song, "They Wanted to Beat Us" remained popular right up to World War II, when its dashing tone seemed inappropriate.

Ataturk, who arranged endless receptions for us. All the men received inscribed gold cigarette cases and all the women got bracelets. They fussed over us greatly. Turkey's musical life was in an embryonic stage then. David Oistrakh and Lev Oborin, who were part of the delegation, needed some sheet music—I think it was Beethoven—and it couldn't be found in all of Ankara. They played everything they could remember by heart.

I learned to wear a tuxedo in Turkey, since I had to wear one every evening, and when I got home I showed it off to my friends and acquaintances. I was rewarded for my tuxedo sufferings with a soccer game between Vienna and Turkey. When the Austrians made a goal there was absolute silence in the stadium, and the match ended in a huge brawl.

But it was fun. We drank coffee and then didn't sleep—not from the coffee, but from its price. I went into a store to buy a pair of glasses. The owner demonstrated how strong the glasses were by flinging them down onto the floor; twice they didn't break. He wanted to show me a third time. I said, "Don't bother, it's all right." He didn't listen to me, threw them down a third time, and broke them.

After my trip to Turkey, which got a lot of coverage in the Soviet papers, I was offered guest performances at very flattering terms. I went on one of these trips, to Arkhangelsk, with the cellist Viktor Kubatsky. He played my cello sonata. On January 28, 1936, we went to the railroad station to buy a new *Pravda*. I opened it up and leafed through it—and found the article "Muddle Instead of Music." I'll never forget that day, it's probably the most memorable in my life.

That article on the third page of *Pravda* changed my entire existence. It was printed without a signature, like an editorial—that is, it expressed the opinion of the Party. But it actually expressed the opinion of Stalin, and that was much more important.

There is a school of thought that holds that the article was written by the well-known bastard Zaslavsky.* It might have been written down by the well-known bastard Zaslavsky, but that's another matter

*David Iosifovich Zaslavsky (1880–1965), a journalist, whom Lenin, before the Revolution, had called a "notorious slanderer" and a "blackmailing pen for hire." He became a trusted Stalin crony and died a respected member of the staff of *Pravda*. The last well-known article by Zaslavsky is "Ballyhoo of Reactionary Propaganda Around a Literary Weed," which appeared in *Pravda* in 1958 and marked the beginning of the campaign against Pasternak.

entirely. The article has too much of Stalin in it, there are expressions that even Zaslavsky wouldn't have used, they were too ungrammatical. After all, the article appeared before the big purges. There were still some fairly literate people working at *Pravda* and they wouldn't have left in that famous part about my music having nothing in common with "symphonic soundings." What are these mysterious "symphonic soundings"? It's clear that this is a genuine pronouncement of our leader and teacher. There are many places like that in the article. I can distinguish with complete confidence Zaslavsky's bridges from Stalin's text.

The title—"Muddle Instead of Music"—also belongs to Stalin. The day before, *Pravda* had printed the leader and teacher's brilliant comments on the outlines of new history textbooks, and he talked about muddles there too.

This text by the Leader of the Peoples and Friend of Children was printed over his signature. Obviously, the word "muddle" stuck in his mind, something that often happens to the mentally ill. And so he used the word everywhere. Really, why call it a muddle?

All right, the opera was taken off the stage. Meetings were organized to drum the "muddle" into everyone's head. Everyone turned away from me. There was a phrase in the article saying that all this "could end very badly." They were all waiting for the bad end to come.

It went on as if in a nightmare. One of my friends, whom Stalin knew, thought that he might be of some help, and he wrote a desperate letter to Stalin. His letter maintained that Shostakovich wasn't a lost soul after all, and that besides the depraved opera *Lady Macbeth of Mtsensk District,* which was criticized with perfect justification by our glorious organ *Pravda,* Shostakovich had also written several musical works singing the praises of our socialist homeland.

Stalin attended a ballet with my music called *Bright Stream,* which was being done at the Bolshoi. Lopukhov had staged the ballet in Leningrad, where it had been popular, and he was invited to stage it in Moscow. And after doing this ballet, he was named director of ballet for the Bolshoi Theater. The results of the leader and teacher's cultural outing are known—not even ten days after the first article in

Pravda, another appeared. It was written more grammatically, with fewer nuggets, but that didn't make it any more pleasant as far as I was concerned.

Two editorial attacks in *Pravda* in ten days—that was too much for one man. Now everyone knew for sure that I would be destroyed. And the anticipation of that noteworthy event—at least for me—has never left me.

From that moment on I was stuck with the label "enemy of the people," and I don't need to explain what the label meant in those days. Everyone still remembers that.

I was called an enemy of the people quietly and out loud and from podiums. One paper made the following announcement of my concert: "Today there is a concert by enemy of the people Shostakovich." Or take this example: In those years my name wasn't welcomed enthusiastically in print unless, of course, it was used in a discussion about struggles against formalism. But it happened that I was assigned to review a production of *Otello* in Leningrad and in my review I did not say ecstatic things about the tenor Nikolai Pechkovsky. I was swamped with anonymous letters saying in effect that I, enemy of the people, did not have long to tread on Soviet soil, that my ass's ears would be chopped off—along with my head.

They really loved Pechkovsky in Leningrad. He was one of those tenors who know three things to do with their hands while singing: gesture toward yourself, away from yourself, and to the side. When Meyerhold heard Pechkovsky in the role of Gherman in *The Queen of Spades,* he told everyone, "If I run into him in a dark alley, I'll kill him."

A German musicologist came to Leningrad before the war—and nothing interested him, not music, not concerts, nothing. Everyone at the Composers' Union was sick and tired of him. What could they do with the man? Finally someone suggested, Would you like to go to see Pechkovsky? The German brightened. "Ohh! The famous pervert!" and hurried off. Everyone sighed in relief, Pechkovsky had saved the day.

Actually, Pechkovsky's life took an unfortunate turn and he spent quite a lot of time in the camps. If I had known that ahead of time I would never have permitted myself to say anything negative about him. But in those days I stood a greater chance of ending up in the camps than he did.

Because after the articles came the "Tukhachevsky affair." It was a terrible blow for me when Tukhachevsky was shot. When I read about it in the papers, I blacked out. I felt they were killing me, that's how bad I felt. But I wouldn't like to lay it on too thick at this point. It's only in fine literature that a person stops eating and sleeping because he's so overwrought. In reality, life is much simpler, and as Zoshchenko noted, life gives little material to fiction writers.

Zoshchenko had a firm philosophy on the matter—a beggar stops worrying as soon as he becomes a beggar, and a roach isn't terribly upset about being a roach. I wholeheartedly agree. After all, life goes on, I had to live and feed my family. I had an infant daughter who cried and demanded food and I had to guarantee food for her as best I could.

"The author's feelings before the grandeur of Nature are indescribable." Naturally, without sparing color and in broad strokes, I could describe my depressed condition, my moral torment, my constant strong fear, not only for my own life but for the lives of my mother, sisters, wife and daughter, and later my son. And so on. I don't want to deny that I went through a bad period. Perhaps the careful reader will understand that or perhaps he'll just skip all this drivel and think, munching a piece of candy, "Whatever made me read this book? It's just upsetting me before bedtime."

When I picture an idiot like that, I don't even want to go on reminiscing. I just sit with a feeling of guilt, when there isn't anything really that I'm guilty of.

The greatest specialist in depression, despair, melancholy, and such, of all the people I've met in my life, was Zoshchenko. I think I'm talking too much about myself, and these memoirs are not about me, they're about others. I want to talk about others first and about me only tangentially.

So, about Zoshchenko. It's a fact that cobblers go about without shoes, and there's no better confirmation of the truism than Zoshchenko. He was the most popular humorist of my youth and he's just as popular now, despite all the bans and persecution. Millions of people laughed over his stories. Perhaps they weren't very aware or cultured readers, maybe they laughed when they should have cried. They laughed over those works of Zoshchenko's that I personally consider tragic. But my opinion isn't important here. Zoshchenko was considered a great humorist, but in fact he was a man thoroughly riddled by depression and melancholy.

I'm not referring now to his tragic literary fate or to the fact that he was forced to write more and more poorly, so that I can't read his last works without a feeling of bitterness and disillusionment.

No, Zoshchenko was dying of depression when there was nothing to foreshadow his sad fate, when he had fame and money. Zoshchenko's ennui wasn't a literary affectation. He really did nearly die of depression—he couldn't leave the house and he couldn't eat. They gave him medicine and injections, but to no avail. Zoshchenko was still a young man, just twenty-seven, and he decided to battle his illness on his own, without the help of doctors, because the doctors, he was sure, didn't understand the cause of his terrible and extraordinary depression.

Laughing sadly, Zoshchenko told me about his visit to a psychiatrist. Zoshchenko described his dreams, in which he saw tigers and a hand reaching out toward him. The doctor was a specialist in psychoanalysis and immediately replied that the meaning of these dreams was very obvious to him. In his opinion, little Zoshchenko had been taken to the zoo at too tender an age and an elephant frightened the child with his huge trunk. The hand was the trunk, and the trunk was a phallic symbol. And therefore Zoshchenko had a sexual trauma.

Zoshchenko was certain that the doctor was mistaken. His fear of life stemmed from other causes, he felt, because not all our impulses can be reduced to sexual attraction. Fear can take root in a man's heart for social reasons too.

Zoshchenko maintained that fear based on social causes could be even more powerful and could take over the subconscious. I agree with him completely. It's true that sex plays an important part in this world and no one is free of its effect. But illness can spring from other causes and fear can be produced by other forces.

Fear arises from cruder and more substantial causes—fear of losing food, or fear of death, or fear before a horrible punishment. Zoshchenko said that a man ill with this kind of fear can remain basically normal and reveal his illness in just a few bizarre actions, that is, a few eccentricities. He felt that these eccentricities were a better guide to the cause of the illness than dreams, because the bizarre behavior was almost always infantile. The adult behaved like a child, or rather, he tried to be one. This playing at being a child seems to help the adult avoid danger, helps him avoid contact with dangerous objects and dangerous forces.

The patient begins to maneuver every which way, and when the disease takes this turn everything hinges on the strength of the patient's psyche as against the strength of the illness. Because if the fear grows, it can lead to a total collapse of the personality.

The person tries to avoid dangerous phenomena and that leads to thought of suicide. What is suicide? Zoshchenko explained it to me. He explained that death can look like salvation. The point is that a child doesn't understand what death is, he only sees that death is absence. He sees that you can escape danger, can get away and hide from danger. And that escape the child calls death, because death is not frightening to him.

When a man is sick, his feelings are the feelings of a child. That's the lowest level of his psyche, and a child fears danger much more than death. Suicide is a hurried escape from danger. It is the act of a child who has been scared by life.

In my unhappy life there were many sad events, but there were periods when danger gathered ominously, when it was particularly palpable, and then my fear augmented. In the period about which we were talking just now, I was near suicide. The danger horrified me and I saw no other way out.

I was completely in the thrall of fear. I was no longer the master of my life, my past was crossed out, my work, my abilities, turned out to be worthless to everyone. The future didn't look any less bleak. At that moment I desperately wanted to disappear, it was the only possible way out. I thought of the possibility with relish.

And in that critical period my familiarity with Zoshchenko's ideas helped me greatly. He didn't say that suicide was a whim but he did say that suicide was a purely infantile act. It was the mutiny of the lower level against the higher level of the psyche. Actually, it's not a mutiny, it is the victory of the lower level, complete and final victory.

Naturally, it wasn't only Zoshchenko's thoughts that helped me in that desperate hour. But these and similar considerations kept me from making extreme decisions. I came out of the crisis stronger than I went in, more confident of my own strength. The hostile forces didn't seem so omnipotent any more and even the shameful treachery of friends and acquaintances didn't cause me as much pain as before.

The mass treachery did not concern me personally. I managed to separate myself from other people, and in that period it was my salvation.

Some of these thoughts you can find, if you wish, in my Fourth Symphony. In the last pages, it's all set out rather precisely. These thoughts were also present in my mind later, when I was writing the first part of the Sixth Symphony. But the Sixth in a way had a much happier fate than the Fourth. It was played right away and criticized moderately. The Fourth was played twenty-five years after it was written. Maybe that was for the best, I don't know. I'm not a great adherent of the theory that musical compositions should lie in the ground waiting their time. Symphonies aren't Chinese eggs, you know.

In general, music should be played right away, and that way the audience gets pleasure in time and it's easier for the composer to tell what's what. And if he has made mistakes, he can try to correct them in the next work. Otherwise it's just nonsense, like the business with the Fourth.

Now some people say that I was to blame for the whole incident, that I stopped the performance of my symphony, that I whipped myself, like the sergeant's widow, and that I have no right to point at others. It's easy to judge from afar. But if you had been in my shoes, you'd sing a different tune.

It seemed then as if every performance of my works caused nothing but trouble. The Maly Opera Theater brought *Lady Macbeth* to Moscow—and there was "Muddle Instead of Music." The Bolshoi Theater staged my ballet—and there was another *Pravda* editorial, "Balletic Falsity." And what would have happened if the Fourth had been performed then too? Who knows, perhaps no one would have said a word, and my song would have been sung for good.

The conditions were grave, fatal. There's no point in thinking about it. Besides, Stiedry's* rehearsals weren't merely bad—they were outrageous. First of all, he was scared to death, because no one would have spared him either. In general, conductors aren't the bravest men on earth. I've had many opportunities to confirm this opinion. They're brave when it comes to yelling at an orchestra, but when someone yells at them, their knees shake.

Secondly, Stiedry didn't know or understand the score, and he expressed no desire to grapple with it. He said so straight out. And why be shy? The composer was an exposed formalist. Why bother digging around in his score?

This wasn't the only time Stiedry behaved this way, and it wasn't only my music he treated carelessly. In his time, Stiedry truly upset Glazunov. He was supposed to conduct Glazunov's Eighth Symphony. He came to Leningrad and then it became clear that he was confusing the Eighth with Glazunov's Fourth—quite literally, probably because they are both in the key of E flat.

This didn't embarrass Stiedry in the least. He didn't give a damn. As long as Glazunov sat in the auditorium, he rehearsed a little. But Glazunov had to leave, because he was called to court. He was having an argument with the tenants' committee of his building and not paying his rent. As soon as Glazunov left the auditorium, Stiedry perked up and ended the rehearsal. He said, "It'll do like this."

Someone could say to me: Why are you complaining about others? What about you? Weren't you afraid too? I answer honestly that I was afraid. Fear was a common feeling for everyone then, and I didn't miss my share.

Then he might say: What were you afraid of? They didn't touch musicians. I'll reply: That's not true, they did touch them—and how. The story that the musicians weren't touched is being spread by Khrennikov† and his henchmen and since men of the arts have short

*Fritz Stiedry (1883–1968), conductor, Mahler's assistant in the Vienna Opera. In 1933 he emigrated to the U.S.S.R., where he was chief conductor of the Leningrad Philharmonic. He led the premiere of Shostakovich's First Piano Concerto. After the war he was one of the principal conductors of the Metropolitan Opera in New York.

†Tikhon Nikolayevich Khrennikov (b. 1913), composer, head of the Composers' Union of the U.S.S.R. from the time of its First Congress (1948). He was appointed to the post by Stalin (as were leaders of the analogous unions of writers, artists, etc.). In the Stalinist years the duties of the head included approval of lists of the union's members marked for repression. Khrennikov is the only original union leader of the "creative" unions to retain his post to this day. For many years he attacked Shostakovich and Prokofiev viciously. He has received all the highest Soviet orders and prizes.

memories, they believe him. They've already forgotten Nikolai Sergeyevich Zhilayev, a man I consider one of my teachers.

I met Zhilayev at Tukhachevsky's; the two were friends. Zhilayev taught at the Moscow Conservatory, but most of the lessons were given in his home. Whenever I was in Moscow, I dropped in on him and showed him my latest works. Zhilayev never made a comment merely to say something. By that time there was no point in showing my work to Steinberg, my teacher at the Conservatory, for he simply didn't understand the kind of music I was writing then. Zhilayev replaced my teacher as much as possible.

He had a large picture of Tukhachevsky in his room, and after the announcement that Tukhachevsky had been shot as a traitor to the homeland, Zhilayev did not take the picture down. I don't know if I can explain how heroic a deed that was. How did people behave then? As soon as the next poor soul was declared an enemy of the people, everyone destroyed in a panic everything connected with that person. If the enemy of the people wrote books, they threw away his books, if they had letters from him, they burned the letters. The mind can't grasp the number of letters and papers burned in that period, no war could ever clean out domestic archives like that. And naturally, photographs flew into the flames first, because if someone informed on you, reported that you had a picture of an enemy of the people, it meant certain death.

Zhilayev wasn't afraid. When they came for him, Tukhachevsky's prominently hung portrait amazed even the executioners. "What, it's still up?" they asked. Zhilayev replied, "The time will come when they'll erect a monument to him."

We forgot about Zhilayev too quickly, and the others. Sergei Popov died, a very talented man. Shebalin introduced us. He recreated Tchaikovsky's opera *Voyevode,* which the composer had burned in a fit of despair. When they took Popov away, the score was destroyed a second time. Lamm* resurrected it once more.

Or Nikolai Vygodsky, a talented organist. The same story. And they've forgotten Boleslav Pshibyshevsky, the director of the Moscow

---

*Pavel Alexandrovich Lamm (1882–1951), musicologist, famed for his work on the academic texts of the operas of Mussorgsky (with Asafiev) and Borodin. Lamm wrote the orchestrations for many important works of Prokofiev, including *The Betrothal in the Convent* and *War and Peace,* as well as the music for the films *Alexander Nevsky* and *Ivan the Terrible* (see the recent Soviet reference work *Avtografy S. S. Prokof'eva,* Moscow, 1977).

Conservatory. He was the son of the famous writer. And they've forgotten Dima Gachev.

Gachev was a good musicologist, and after completing some difficult work he decided to take a rest and went to a sanatorium, where he shared a room with several others. Someone found an old French newspaper. To his misfortune, Gachev read French. He opened the paper and began reading aloud, just a few sentences, and stopped—it was something negative about Stalin. "Ah, what nonsense!" But it was too late. He was arrested in the morning. Someone from the room turned him in, or perhaps they all did.

Before his arrest, Gachev had corresponded with Romain Rolland, who liked the work Gachev had written on him. Rolland praised Gachev. I wonder, did the great French humanist ever inquire what happened to his admirer and researcher? Where he suddenly disappeared to?

I think Gachev got five years. He was a strong man and he got through the five years of hard labor, naïvely hoping that he would be released when his term was up. A few days before the end Gachev was told that he had got an additional ten years. It broke him and he died soon after.

Everyone wrote denunciations then. Composers probably used music paper and musicologists used plain. And as far as I know, not one of the informers has ever repented. In the middle of the 1950s some of the arrested began returning, the lucky ones who survived. Some of them were shown their so-called files, which included the denunciations. Nowadays the informers and former prisoners meet at concerts. Sometimes they bow.

Of course, one of the victims didn't turn out to be so polite. He publicly slapped the informer. But everything sorted itself out, the informer turned out to be a decent sort and didn't file a complaint with the police. The former prisoner died a free man, for his health had been seriously undermined by camp life. The informer is alive and thriving today.* He's my biographer, you might say, a Shostakovich specialist.

I was lucky then, I wasn't sent to the camps, but it's never too late.

*A reference to an incident involving Viktor Yulyevich Delson (1907–1970), pianist and musicologist, who spent almost twenty years in Stalin's camps, and Lev Vasilyevich Danilyevich (b. 1912), the author of several works on Shostakovich's music.

After all, it depends on how the new leader and teacher feels about your work. In my case, my music. They're all patrons of arts and refined literature—that's the general opinion, the voice of the people, and it's hard to argue with that voice.

Tyrants like to present themselves as patrons of the arts. That's a well-known fact. But tyrants understand nothing about art. Why? Because tyranny is a perversion, and a tyrant is a pervert. For many reasons. The tyrant sought power, stepping over corpses. Power beckoned, he was attracted by the chance to crush people, to mock them. Isn't the lust for power a perversion? If you're consistent, you must answer that question in the affirmative. At the moment when the lust for power arises in you, you're a lost man. I am suspicious of every candidate for leadership. I had enough illusions in my misty youth.

And so, having satisfied his perverted desires, the man becomes a leader, and now the perversions continue, because power has to be defended, defended against madmen like yourself.

For even if there are no such enemies, you have to invent them, because otherwise you can't flex your muscles completely, you can't oppress the people completely, making the blood spurt. And without that, what pleasure is there in power? Very little.

An acquaintance with whom I went drinking once poured out his heart to me that night. He stayed overnight, but we got no sleep. He began confessing to me that he was tormented by one desire. One nightmare. And this is what I discovered. You see, since his childhood he had enjoyed reading descriptions of torture and executions. That was his strange passion. He had read everything that was written on this vile subject. He listed them for me, and it was a rather long list. Strange, I thought, that when they torture in Russia, they try not to leave any traces. I don't mean on the body—those remain, even though there is a science now of torturing without leaving marks on the body. I'm referring to written traces. But it turns out that there has been literature on the subject in Russia as well.

There's more. The man confessed that his interest in descriptions of torture was just covering up his real passion: he wanted to torture people himself. Before, I had thought that this man was a fair musician. But the longer his story went on the less I believed he was. And he kept talking, panting and trembling.

This acquaintance of mine had probably not even killed a fly in his life, but judging by what he said, it was not because he found executions and death repugnant. On the contrary, blood and everything that might make it flow excited and attracted him. He told me many things that night, for instance how Ivan the Terrible's famous henchman Malyuta Skuratov dealt with his victims and their wives. He made the women sit astride a thick cable and then started sawing them in half with the cable. Back and forth, pulling their legs one way and then the other, until they were sawn in half.

Another horrible method used in those times was described this way. The *oprichniki** found two young trees that stood in an empty field not too far from each other. They climbed up and bent the trees down, so that their crowns almost touched. Then they tied a man to the crowns, making a living knot of the person. They released the trees, tearing the victim in half. They amused themselves that way with horses too, tying a man to two steeds and setting them off galloping in different directions.

This was the first I had heard of Malyuta Skuratov's sadistic exercises, even though I had known many other things about him. And it was the first that I heard of trials of animals. They had those too, people thought that it wasn't enough to torture only human beings. Of course, animals are tortured all the time, by anyone who has the energy. But this seemed particularly vicious. Not just torturing them, but hiding under the pretense of observing the law. I see a desire to drag animals down to the level of man, so that they can be dealt with like men. Actually, they tried to make men out of animals, and in doing so, the men turned into beasts.

All this torture took place not so long ago, a few centuries, that's all. They had court trials for cows and horses, dogs, monkeys, even mice and caterpillars. They thought they were devils. Enemies of the people. They tortured the animals, blood flowed in rivers, cows mooed and dogs howled and moaned, horses neighed. They were being interrogated and specialists in mooing acted as translators. I can imagine

Oprichniki were a kind of personal guard created by Tsar Ivan the Terrible (1530–1584) to fight the powerful feudal aristocracy. In Russian historiography and literature, the *oprichniki* were a symbol of lawlessness and terror. However, they were "rehabilitated" in the Stalinist period. The second part of Eisenstein's film *Ivan the Terrible* angered Stalin, in part because of the ambiguous portrayal of the *oprichniki*.

how it went. "Does the enemy of the people admit to such-and-such and so-and-so?" The cow is silent. They stick a spear into its side. It moos and the specialist translates, "It fully admits culpability in all the acts it performed against the people."

Silence is a sign of guilt and so is mooing. Bonfires, blood, overheated executioners. Time? Seventeenth century. Place? Russia, Moscow. Or perhaps it was yesterday? I don't know. Which is the beast here, which is the human being? I don't know that either. Everything is confused in this world. Later I heard about this more than once, the trials of animals. But that memorable night I stared in horror at the man, my guest. He was beside himself, his face blazing. He was usually calm and rational, but now there was another man before me. I clearly saw that he was of the same breed as the executioners, vile scum. He waved his arms, his voice trembled and broke, but not from indignation, from excitement.

And then he grew quiet, losing steam all at once. I looked at him with repugnance, but without pity. No, there was no pity. I thought, You're a finished man. You crave power, you dream of torturing others, and the only reason you don't become an executioner is that you're a coward.

And I told him this to his face. That's my rule, say it and say it all. He cried and repented, but from that moment he ceased to exist as a musician for me. I realized that I had been mistaken about him, because this craving for blood is a perversion and a perverted creature is incapable of understanding art, and music in particular.

Sometimes they say or write that the directors of the German death camps loved and understood Bach and Mozart. And so on. That they shed tears over the music of Schubert. I don't believe it. It's lies, made up by journalists. Personally, I've never met a single executioner who truly understood art.

But where do these persistent stories come from? Why are people so eager for tyrants to be "patrons" and "lovers" of art? I think there are several reasons. First of all, tyrants are base, clever, and cunning men who know that it is much better for their dirty work if they appear to be cultured and educated men rather than ignoramuses and boors. Let the ones who do the work be boors, the pawns. The pawns are proud to be boors, but the generalissimo must always be wise in all things.

And such a wise man has a huge apparatus working for him, writing about him and writing speeches for him and books too. A huge team of researchers prepares papers for him on any question, any topic.

So you want to be a specialist in architecture? You will be. Just give the order, beloved leader and teacher. Do you want to be a specialist in graphic arts? You will be. A specialist in orchestration? Why not? Or in languages. You name it.

And as for that death camp director who supposedly adored Mozart, he had an assistant in ideology. And that assistant had his own assistant. In general, just look for a victim who did actually say that Mozart was a good composer, and the executioner was on the spot. He strangled the victim and said the words about Mozart, but as though they were his own. He robbed the victim twice. He took his life and got an inheritance. And everyone around him said, "How cultured, how wise, how refined."

All the pawns, toadies, screws, and other tiny souls also desperately want their leader and teacher to be an undisputed and absolute titan of thought and pen. This is the second reason that these dirty inventions continue to live.

It's all marvelously simple. If the leader doesn't write books but cuts up people instead, then what is he? You don't need to look up the answer in an encyclopedia or wait for the next issue of the magazine with the answer to the crossword puzzle. The answer is simple: a butcher, a gangster. And that makes the toadies the henchmen of a butcher and gangster. And who wants to think of himself in those terms? Everyone wants to be clean, now that the new dawn has come.

(All tyrants always proclaim that the long-awaited dawn has come, always under the rule of the given tyrant. And in the darkest night people act out the comedy of the day that has come. Some enter their roles following Stanislavsky's precepts and that really impresses the uninitiated.)

It's a completely different picture when the leader loves Beethoven, is it not? That alters the landscape somehow. I've met many musicians who insisted seriously that Stalin loved Beethoven.

"Of course, he doesn't understand contemporary music," they said. "But then there aren't many who do. Even professionals don't, even many composers, and some good ones, who write in a more traditional style, consider the music of their more avant-garde colleagues to be delirium, muddles, and cacophony. You see, there is dissension among musicians on this complex issue. And Iosif Vissarionovich has many other concerns besides music, you know that. But he does love classical art. The ballet, for instance. And loves classical music, Beethoven, for instance. He loves everything exalted, like the mountains. Beethoven is exalted, that's why he loves him too."

I had my fill of speeches like that, thank you. It made my ears vomit. They shoved proof of Stalin's great love for the classics at us from all sides, front and back, above and below.

For instance, I heard the following story. Supposedly at the end of some Party Congress, it was decided to have a gala concert so that the delegates who had worked so hard could have a good rest. The program was a typical one for these occasions. "Ensembles of dance and prance," combined choirs—to give a volume level that will knock out windowpanes—and a full collection of swans. The dance of the little swans and the big ones, dying ones and recuperating ones, dances about swans and songs about eagles. You know, an avian, zoological theme for the program.

And they brought the program to Stalin for approval. Approving programs and lists was a hobby of his. The Party's program, lists of condemned men. He also liked approving menus, with Caucasian wine lists.

And now the story takes wing to the heavenly heights—a lackey's dream. Supposedly, Stalin rejected this mishmash with Caucasian wines, the menu displeased him. He had a taste for something different, something more exalted; instead of the Caucasian wines he wanted the Caucasian mountains. Stalin crossed out the swans and eagles and instead wrote in one composition: Beethoven's Ninth Symphony. Embrace, millions! He wrote it himself! With his own hand! The lackey's breath stops! How happy he made us, our benefactor! He made us happy! He made Beethoven happy!

I don't believe it for a minute. It's all lies.

First of all, no one has ever told me precisely at which congress it was that they ended with the Beethoven. Everyone gives me a different number.

Secondly, why was Beethoven given such honors only at this congress? Why did they dance and sing at the others? And they didn't sing "Millions embrace" either. They sang about Stalin the eagle, for there were always more than enough songs on that eternally fresh and captivating theme. I think there must have been some twenty thousand, maybe more. It would be interesting to work out how much money our leader paid out for songs about our leader.

Finally, even if this dubious fact of the Ninth Symphony did occur, it still doesn't prove anything, least of all Stalin's love of Beethoven. Should we consider the production of *The Valkyrie* at the Bolshoi, done before the war on Stalin's direct order, to be proof of his love of Wagner? Rather it was a declaration of his love for Hitler.

This story about *The Valkyrie* is so shameful that it's worth telling. The Molotov-Ribbentrop pact was in force. We were supposed to love Fascists. We loved belatedly, but as a result with greater passion, the way a middle-aged widow loves her husky young neighbor.

They were pushing Jews out of the more important positions so that they wouldn't irritate German eyes. Litvinov was removed from his position as People's Commissar of Foreign Affairs, for instance. But these were negative actions, so to speak, and positive actions were called for. Well, they gave Hitler several hundred German anti-Fascists and German Jews who were seeking asylum in the Soviet Union. But that was too modest, nothing on a grand scale, no publicity or fanfare. Just a business favor. And what was wanted were fanfares and a passionate Caucasian love. High emotions, "beautiful tea, and beautiful candy," as the poet said.* They remembered Wagner.

Funny things happen with Wagner in Russia. At first the Russian musicians got into fights with one another over him. Then they stopped fighting and learned from him. But this at least remained within the boundaries of a small group of professionals. Suddenly Wagner became popular. This was before World War I. The tsar, you see, ordered the production of *The Ring of the Nibelung* at the Imperial Maryinsky Theater. The court, the officers, and the clerks all fell in love with Wagner. And then suddenly the war came! A relative, you might say, and picking a fight. It hurt, it really did. Savages usually

---

*Shostakovich is quoting a popular line from the ironic poem by Nikolai Makarovich Oleinikov (1898–1942), who died in the Stalinist terror. He was one of Shostakovich's favorite poets. His collected works have not been published in the Soviet Union.

whip their graven images in these situations. In Russia they decided to whip Wagner. And he was thrown out of the repertory of the Imperial Maryinsky Theater.

After the Revolution they remembered Wagner again, because they needed an opera repertory that was commensurate with the epoch. The revolutionary operatic repertoire was limited. You couldn't permit tsars or boyars onstage, or "fancied-up ladies," as they used to call Tatiana from *Eugene Onegin* in those days. They decided that Western operas held less danger for the Revolution. They tried to learn *William Tell, Fiorella*, and *Le Prophète*. And they pulled out Wagner's *Rienzi*.

Meyerhold began staging *Rienzi*. He told me that for some purely internal theatrical reason, he didn't see the production through to the end. He always regretted it. I think the problem was money. Meyerhold told me about his conception, which was very interesting and had nothing to do with the music.

Finally, another director produced *Rienzi*. I don't like the opera very much, I find it pompous and overblown. The conception is not capable of standing alone and the music is mediocre. The plot is good for a revolutionary play, but that's not a primary prerequisite for an opera.

I felt differently toward Wagner at different stages of my life. He wrote some pages of genius, and a lot of very good music, and a lot of average music. But Wagner knew how to peddle his goods. The composer–publicity man is a type I found alien; it is certainly not in the tradition of Russian music. That may be the reason why Russian music is not as popular in the West as it should be. Glinka, our first professional composer, was also the first to say, replying to Meyerbeer, "I do not hawk my own works." And that was so. Not like Meyerbeer.

And then there was Mussorgsky, who refused to go to see Liszt despite all his invitations. Liszt planned to give him marvelous publicity, but Mussorgsky preferred to remain in Russia and compose. He was not a practical man.

There is one more example—Rimsky-Korsakov. Diaghilev was dragging him to one of his earliest concerts of Russian music in Paris. They were talking about *Sadko*. Diaghilev demanded cuts from Rimsky-Korsakov. He insisted that the French were incapable of listening to an opera from eight until midnight. Diaghilev said that the French couldn't even hear *Pelléas* to the end and fled in large crowds after eleven, creating a "murderous impression" (Diaghilev's words).

Korsakov replied thus: "I'm totally indifferent to the tastes of the French." And added, "If the weak-willed French audiences in tail coats, who drop in at the opera and who listen to the bought press and to claques, find it too difficult to hear the full *Sadko*, it shouldn't be offered to them." Not badly said.

After some clever maneuvering, Diaghilev managed to dig Korsakov out and drag him to Paris. Korsakov sent Diaghilev a postcard with his agreement, which said, "If we're going, then let's go, as the parrot said to the cat that was dragging him by the tail down the stairs."

Of the major Russian composers, only two have known how to sell themselves, Stravinsky and Prokofiev. But it's no accident that both are composers of a new era, and in a sense children, even though adoptive ones, of Western culture. Their love and taste for publicity, I feel, keep Stravinsky and Prokofiev from being thoroughly Russian composers. There's some flaw in their personalities, a loss of some very important moral principles.

Both took several lessons from the West too much to heart, lessons that perhaps should not have been learned at all. And in winning popularity they lost something just as valuable.

It's difficult for me to talk about this, I have to be very careful not to insult a man undeservedly. For Stravinsky, for example, may be the most brilliant composer of the twentieth century. But he always spoke only for himself, while Mussorgsky spoke for himself and for his country. But on the other hand, Mussorgsky didn't have a good publicity machine. Not at all.

Now, I hope, you'll see why I have ambivalent feelings towards Wagner. Russian composers learned a new way to orchestrate from him and not how to create publicity on a wide scale or to intrigue and infight. The forging of the sword in the first act of *Siegfried* is a moment of genius. But why mobilize an army of your proponents against Brahms? Badgering a colleague doesn't come from a fit of pique, it comes from an organic quality of the soul. And a mean soul will inevitably be reflected in music. Wagner is a convincing example of that, but far from the only one.

During the entire prewar period Wagnerian operas played in Russia, but somehow limply, weakly, and wanly. Various things got in the way. They found traces of idealism, mysticism, reactionary romanticism, and petty-bourgeois anarchism in his works and they wrote all kinds of insulting things about him. And then suddenly the situation changed once again. (The word "suddenly" appears here like a messenger in a bad play—when the plot needs to be thickened, the runner comes and announces, "Your beloved is dead!" or "The enemy has entered the city!" Suddenly. That's bad writing, used by bad playwrights. And I'm a bad raconteur. Naturally, nothing happens "suddenly.") It was just that Stalin wanted to give Hitler a tighter hug, with loud music in the background. Everything had to be on family footing, as of yore. Wilhelm and Romanov were blood relatives. Stalin and Hitler were spiritual relatives.

And the most appropriate composer to accompany Russo-German friendship turned out to be Wagner. They called Eisenstein and told him to quickly produce *The Valkyrie* at the Bolshoi. Why Eisenstein, a film director? They needed a famous name. Wagner's opera had to be dramatic, as loud as the music. And most important, the director had to be a Gentile. And Eisenstein's father was even German, a converted Jew.

Eisenstein didn't realize the point of the invitation right away. He called up Alexander Tyshler,* a Jewish artist, and asked him to be designer of the production.

Tyshler was a wise man. He said, "Are you mad? Don't you realize what this production is? They won't let you use my name on the poster. The production will have to be *Judenfrei*, free of Jews."

Eisenstein laughed. He still didn't want to understand what everyone else already did. Perhaps he was pretending, but anyway he said, "I guarantee you work on this production." He called back a few days later, and this time he didn't laugh. He apologized. "You were right," Eisenstein said to Tyshler, and hung up.

Why didn't Eisenstein refuse to work on the project when he saw what it really was? We often say about someone that he works not for

*Alexander Grigoryevich Tyshler (b. 1908), artist who designed some of the most famous productions in Soviet theater, including *King Lear* at the Moscow Jewish Theater (1935). Tyshler was one of the favorite painters of the poet Osip Mandelstam.

fear but for his conscience. Well, he had no conscience at all, but he did have fear, a lot of it. It turned out that Eisenstein was risking his head. They say that he was in torment and suffered greatly, but consoled himself with the thought that it would be interesting to work in the Bolshoi and that *The Valkyrie* was an opera of genius.

Recently I was talking to a musicologist, a friend of mine, and we brought up the shameful Wagnerian production. The musicologist defended Eisenstein, saying that he had long wanted to work in opera, that he had "thought a lot about the synthesis of the arts," and that he had managed to introduce some of his ideas—certainly not all of them—onto the stage of the Bolshoi.

But I reminded the musicologist that Eisenstein had had an opportunity to realize his marvelous ideas in another opera production, also in Moscow. And the opera was by his close friend Prokofiev. I'm referring to Prokofiev's *Semyon Kotko*. This opera deals with the occupation of the Ukraine by the Germans in 1918. The Germans are depicted as cruel butchers. When Prokofiev was writing the opera, this corresponded to the political setting.

Actually, this Prokofiev plot was distinguished by great ideological consistency. There were Bolsheviks and evil kulaks and a vow sworn by Red partisans over the grave of a commissar and even a people's uprising.

Semyon Kotko was put into production at the Stanislavsky Opera Theater by Meyerhold himself. It was his last work in the theater. In fact, he never finished it, he was arrested in the middle of it, and he was no longer Meyerhold, but "Semyonich." That was his alleged underground saboteur's nickname. That's quite ridiculous. It was probably the interrogator who invented the name, having read something about *Semyon Kotko* in the papers.

The director was arrested but the work went on as though nothing had happened. This was one of the terrible signs of the age, a man had disappeared but everyone pretended that nothing had happened. A man was in charge of the work, it had meaning only with him, under his direction. But he was no longer there, he had evaporated, and no one said a word.

The name Meyerhold immediately disappeared from conversations. That was all.

At first everyone shuddered. Each thought: I'm next. Then they prayed—I don't know to whom, but they prayed that the next one would be someone else. And since there was no order stopping the work, they could continue. It meant that high up they felt that the work was necessary, and perhaps in working they could save their lives.

Prokofiev turned to Eisenstein, his friend. The word "friend" is used as a convention here, particularly when it's used for two men like Eisenstein and Prokofiev. I doubt that either of them needed friends. They were both remote and aloof, but at least Prokofiev and Eisenstein respected each other. Eisenstein had also been a student of Meyerhold's, so Prokofiev asked the film director to bring the production of *Semyon Kotko* to completion.

Eisenstein refused. The political climate had changed by then, and in that wonderful era, attacks on Germans, if only in an opera, were forbidden. The opera's future looked doubtful. Why get mixed up in a politically dubious venture? So Eisenstein said, "I don't have the time." He found time, as we know, for *The Valkyrie*.

The subsequent history of both productions is interesting, very, very interesting. The premiere of *The Valkyrie* proceeded with all due pomp, and leaders from the Party and the state and the Fascist ambassador all attended. There were rave reviews. In a word, another victory on the arts front. *Semyon Kotko* barely squeaked into the world. Naturally, the Germans were gone from the production, replaced by some unnamed occupying force. But nevertheless, the powers that be were displeased. Stalin panicked at the thought of angering the Germans. Officials from the People's Commissariat of Foreign Affairs showed up at every rehearsal, frowned, and left, saying nothing. That was a very bad sign.

Finally, Vishinsky* himself appeared. He was Stalin's right-hand man, a bastard and a butcher. Obviously, the leader and teacher had sent him to determine just what seditious ideas were being preached from the stage of the opera theater named after a man whom Stalin respected. I mean Stanislavsky. Under the wise direction of Vishinsky,

*Andrei Yanuaryevich Vishinsky (1883–1954), one of the prime organizers of the political trials of the 1930s. In his memoirs Winston Churchill described Vishinsky's performance as state prosecutor in these trials as "brilliant."

the Procurator General of the U.S.S.R., the opera was brought into proper shape. He was satisfied that in terms of plot the opera was suitable; all it had required was playing down the Germans, or occupiers, or whoever. Let the White Guard be the enemy. "Where is the enemy?" as they sing in another opera, *A Life for the Tsar*, which was retitled *Ivan Susanin* in our day. As long as there are enemies, it's fine. Any enemy. As long as there is someone to fight, there's no need to get overly specific about who it is.

And so this half-dead production came to life and no one liked it. Everyone liked Wagner because Wagner, as was very obvious, was beloved by Stalin. And then suddenly, war again! And National Socialist Wagner was dropped from the repertory once more. He had fallen into bad company again. And all our professors and assistant professors and the leading and following music critics started teaching Wagner a thing or two, the way you do underage criminals in reform school colonies. They said Wagner had the wrong friends, went to the wrong places, and did the wrong things. And as for their love—it had never existed.

And so here is the sad story in two acts with a prologue and epilogue. History, as we see, repeats itself. You can see the same farce reenacted two, three, sometimes four times in a lifetime, particularly if you're lucky and if you've managed to live more than sixty years in our troubled times, jumping over several terrible barriers.

Every leap takes your last ounce of strength and you're sure that it's your last leap. But it turns out there's more life to live and you can take a rest and relax. And they show you the same old farce. You don't find it funny any more. But people around you are laughing, the young people who are seeing this vulgar show for the first time. It's pointless trying to explain anything to them, they won't understand anyway. You seek out spectators your own age, they know, they understand, and you can talk to them. But there aren't any, they have died off. And the ones who survived are hopelessly stupid, and that's probably why they survived. Or they pretend to be stupid, which also helps.

I will never believe that there are only idiots everywhere. They must be wearing masks—a survival tactic that permits you to maintain a minimal decency. Now everyone says, "We didn't know, we didn't understand. We believed Stalin. We were tricked, ah, how cruelly we were tricked."

I feel anger at such people. Who was it who didn't understand, who was tricked? An illiterate old milkmaid? The deaf-mute who shined shoes on Ligovsky Prospect? No, they seemed to be educated people—writers, composers, actors. The people who applauded the Fifth Symphony. I'll never believe that a man who understood nothing could feel the Fifth Symphony. Of course they understood, they understood what was happening around them and they understood what the Fifth was about.*

And this makes it even harder for me to compose. It must sound odd: it's hard to compose because the audience understands your music. It's probably the other way around in most cases: when they understand, it's easier to write. But here everything is back to front, because the larger the audience, the more informers there are. And the more people who understand what it's about, the more likely that they'll inform.

A very difficult situation arose, which became more difficult with time. It's sad to talk about it, unpleasant, but I must if I am to tell the truth. And the truth is that the war helped. The war brought great sorrow and made life very, very hard. Much sorrow, many tears. But it had been even harder before the war, because then everyone was alone in his sorrow.

Even before the war, in Leningrad there probably wasn't a single family who hadn't lost someone, a father, a brother, or if not a relative, then a close friend. Everyone had someone to cry over, but you had to cry silently, under your blanket, so that no one would see. Everyone feared everyone else, and the sorrow oppressed and suffocated us.

It suffocated me too. I had to write about it, I felt that it was my responsibility, my duty. I had to write a requiem for all those who died, who had suffered. I had to describe the horrible extermination machine and express protest against it. But how could I do it? I was constantly under suspicion then, and critics counted what percentage of

---

*The Fifth Symphony was composed and performed in 1937, at the height of mass terror. The premiere, at which many members of the audience wept, took place in Leningrad, a city that had suffered particularly harsh repressions.

my symphonies was in a major key and what percentage in a minor key. That oppressed me, it deprived me of the will to compose.

And then the war came and the sorrow became a common one. We could talk about it, we could cry openly, cry for our lost ones. People stopped fearing tears. Eventually they got used to it. There was time to become used to it—four whole years. And that is why it was so hard after the war, when suddenly it all stopped. And that's when I put many major works in my desk drawer, where they lay for a long time.

To be able to grieve is also a right, but it's not granted to everyone, or always. I felt that personally very strongly. I wasn't the only one who had an opportunity to express himself because of the war. Everyone felt it. Spiritual life, which had been almost completely squelched before the war, became saturated and tense, everything took on acuity, took on meaning. Probably many people think that I came back to life after the Fifth Symphony. No, I came back to life after the Seventh. You could finally talk to people. It was still hard, but you could breathe. That's why I consider the war years productive for the arts. This wasn't the situation everywhere, and in other countries war probably interferes with the arts. But in Russia—for tragic reasons— there was a flowering of the arts.

The Seventh Symphony became my most popular work.* It saddens me, however, that people don't always understand what it's about, yet everything is clear in the music. Akhmatova wrote her *Requiem* and the Seventh and Eighth Symphonies are my requiem. I don't want to linger on the brouhaha connected with these works. Much has been written about it, and from an external point of view, this is the best-known part of my life. And in the final analysis, this brouhaha had fateful repercussions for me. It was to be expected. And I had guessed that it would be so, almost from the very beginning.

At first it seemed that a wider celebrity might help me, but then I

* "The Seventh Symphony arose from the conscience of the Russian people, who unwaveringly accepted mortal combat with evil forces." This is a typical reaction to the symphony's premiere, from the writer Alexei Tolstoy. The symphony, written and performed during World War II, found itself a subject of world public opinion for many reasons. In the Soviet Union it was raised to the status of symbol, and excerpts from it can be heard in many films and plays devoted to the war. The American radio premiere of the symphony, conducted by Toscanini on July 19, 1942, was heard by millions of Americans. This was probably the first time in musical history that a symphony played so political a role. Shostakovich was not responsible for this, yet even to this day the political resonance of the Seventh interferes with an objective evaluation of its musical merits.

remembered Meyerhold and Tukhachevsky. They were much more famous than I, and it didn't help them one bit. On the contrary.

At first, everything developed normally, but then I realized there were too many articles, too much noise. They were turning me into a symbol. "Shostakovich's symphony" was thrown in where it was needed and where it wasn't and that was more than unpleasant, it was frightening. And I grew more and more frightened, especially when the West began making noise as well. I'm certain that the brouhaha was started with a specific goal. There was something artificial about it, a shade of hysteria.

You would think that the news that your music is enjoying success would bring nothing but pleasure, but I didn't have complete satisfaction. I was happy that they were playing my music in the West, but I would have preferred that they talk more about the music and less about tangential matters.

I didn't know all of this then, I was just uneasy. Later I saw how right I had been. The Allies enjoyed my music, as though trying to say: Look how we like Shostakovich's symphonies, and you still want something more from us, a second front or something.

Stalin was incensed. Wendell Willkie came to Moscow, when he was a presidential candidate. He was considered a big shot who could do much. He was asked about the second front and he replied, Shostakovich is a great composer. Mr. Willkie, naturally, thought that he was an extremely deft politician; see how he got out of that one. But he didn't think about the repercussions for me, a living human being.

I think that was what started it. They shouldn't have made such a fuss over my symphonies, but the Allies fussed, and fussed deliberately. They were creating a diversion, at least that's how it was interpreted here in Russia. The ballyhoo kept growing, which must have irritated Stalin. A situation in which someone else is much talked about was intolerable for him. "They don't like it here," Akhmatova once said. Everyone had to be constantly praising only Stalin; only he could shine in all spheres of life, creativity, and science. Stalin was at the very pinnacle of power, no one dared contradict him, and still it wasn't enough.

What I'm saying is a sober analysis and not a temperamental outburst. Stalin's envy of someone else's fame might sound crazy, but it did exist. And that envy had a disastrous effect on the lives and activity of many people. Sometimes it took only a trifle to make Stalin angry, a careless word. A man talked too much, or was, in Stalin's opinion, too educated, or carried out Stalin's orders too well. That was enough. He perished.

Stalin was a spider and everyone who approached his nets had to die. Some don't even deserve pity; they wanted to get close and be petted. They dirtied themselves with the blood of innocents, they fawned, and still they perished.

A man reporting to Stalin might read in his eyes, "Too nimble," and know that he was doomed. Sometimes all the ardent servitor had time to say at home was that the Master was displeased. They called him Master.

Stalin hated the Allies and feared them. He couldn't do a thing with the Americans. But almost immediately after the war he dealt cruelly with his citizens who had had relations with the Allies. Stalin transferred all his fear and hatred to them. This was a tragedy for thousands upon thousands. A man received a letter from America and was shot. And the naïve former Allies kept sending letters and every letter was a death sentence. Every gift, every souvenir—the end. Doom.

And the most loyal wolfhounds shared Stalin's hatred of the Allies. They felt the scent. They weren't allowed yet to attack and go for the throat. The wolfhounds merely snarled, but it was clear. Khrennikov was one of the wolfhounds, and his nose and brains were topnotch. He knew just what the Master wanted.

A Moscow musicologist told me this story: He was giving a lecture on Soviet composers, and in passing, praised my Eighth Symphony. After his lecture Khrennikov came up to him, bursting with rage. He was almost shouting. "Do you know whom you were praising? Do you? As soon as we get rid of the Allies we'll put your Shostakovich under our thumbnail!"

The war was still on and the Allies were still comrades in arms, as they were called officially. But the wolfhounds already knew that it meant nothing and they were preparing for the reprisals.

Khrennikov was trying very hard. He hated me. It's funny to talk about it now, but there was a time, until I heard Khrennikov's opera *Into the Storm*, when my picture stood on Khrennikov's desk. A bad opera. I considered Khrennikov a talented man and here was a weak imitation of Dzerzhinsky's terrible opera *The Quiet Don*. Khrennikov was obviously speculating. Everything in that opera fit the political situation. The libretto was based on a novel that Stalin liked very much and the music was based on an opera that Stalin had approved.

It was pallid music, uninteresting, with primitive harmonies and weak orchestration. Khrennikov clearly wanted to please the leader and teacher. I wrote a letter to Khrennikov about it. I wrote that he was stepping onto a dangerous path. I wanted to warn him. I went over his opera in detail, and the letter was a long one. Before sending it I showed it to a few friends, thinking it would be better to seek some advice. Perhaps I shouldn't send a letter like that, perhaps I was interfering for nothing. But they all approved of the letter, they said it was a necessary, beneficial letter from which they profited, so think how good it would be for Khrennikov.

But Khrennikov didn't see it that way. When he read my letter he tore it up and stamped on it in an excess of emotion. My picture was trampled at the same time. Khrennikov was terribly angry. I had thought that I was acting in the spirit of the Russian school—Russian composers had always conferred with one another and criticized one another, and no one took offense. But Khrennikov didn't see it that way. He thought that I was blocking his way to the awards and prizes and that I was going out of my way to lead him from the righteous path into the alleys of formalism. When the point wasn't even in the music, in the musical ideas, so to speak. His point was that Stalin wouldn't praise him for formalism, while a trip down the righteous road of primitivism might enable him to pick up the leader and teacher's approval and all the concomitant blessings.

The success of the Seventh and Eighth Symphonies was like a knife in the throat for Khrennikov and company. They thought that I was blocking their light, grabbing up all the fame and leaving none for them. It turned into a nasty story. The leader and teacher wanted to teach me a lesson and my fellow composers wanted to destroy me. And every report of the success of the Seventh or Eighth made me ill. A new success meant a new coffin nail.

The reprisals were being prepared ahead of time, the preparations began with the Seventh Symphony. They said that only its first part was effective, and that was the part, the critics pronounced, that depicted the enemy. The other parts were supposed to show the might and power of the Soviet Army, but Shostakovich lacked the colors for that assignment. They demanded something like Tchaikovsky's *1812 Overture* from me, and later on the comparison between my music and the overture became a popular argument, naturally not in my favor.

When the Eighth was performed, it was openly declared counter-revolutionary and anti-Soviet.* They said, Why did Shostakovich write an optimistic symphony at the beginning of the war and a tragic one now? At the beginning of the war we were retreating and now we're attacking, destroying the Fascists. And Shostakovich is acting tragic, that means he's on the side of the Fascists.

The dissatisfaction gathered and rose; they wanted a fanfare from me, an ode, they wanted me to write a majestic Ninth Symphony. It was very unfortunate, the business with the Ninth. I mean, I know that the blow was inevitable, but perhaps it would have landed later, or less harshly, if not for the Ninth Symphony.

I doubt that Stalin ever questioned his own genius or greatness. But when the war against Hitler was won, Stalin went off the deep end. He was like the frog puffing himself up to the size of the ox, with the difference that everyone around him already considered Stalin to be the ox and gave him an ox's due.

Everyone praised Stalin, and now I was supposed to join in this unholy affair. There was an appropriate excuse. We had ended the war victoriously; no matter the cost, the important thing was that we won, the empire had expanded. And they demanded that Shostakovich use quadruple winds, choir, and soloists to hail the leader. All the more because Stalin found the number auspicious: the Ninth Symphony.

Stalin always listened to experts and specialists carefully. The experts told him that I knew my work and therefore Stalin assumed that the symphony in his honor would be a quality piece of music. He would be able to say, There it is, our national Ninth.

I confess that I gave hope to the leader and teacher's dreams. I announced that I was writing an apotheosis. I was trying to get them off

*The Eighth Symphony (1943) vexed the apparatchiks of culture, but Shostakovich's world fame, and particularly the political ramifications of the Seventh, prevented an open attack. Later, in 1948, almost all of Shostakovich's works were censured officially, starting with the First Symphony. Even works that had been awarded the Stalin Prize were criticized—an unheard-of event.

my back but it turned against me. When my Ninth was performed, Stalin was incensed. He was deeply offended, because there was no chorus, no soloists. And no apotheosis. There wasn't even a paltry dedication. It was just music, which Stalin didn't understand very well and which was of dubious content.

People will say that this is hard to believe, that the memoirist is twisting things here, and that the leader and teacher certainly didn't have time in those difficult postwar days to worry about symphonies and dedications. But the absurdity is that Stalin watched dedications much more closely than affairs of state. For this was not only happening to me. Alexander Dovzhenko told me a similar story. He made a documentary film during the war and somehow overlooked Stalin in some way. Stalin was livid. He called Dovzhenko in, and Beria shouted at Dovzhenko in front of Stalin, "You couldn't spare ten meters of film for our leader? Well, now you'll die like a dog!" By some miracle, Dovzhenko survived.

I couldn't write an apotheosis to Stalin, I simply couldn't. I knew what I was in for when I wrote the Ninth. But I did depict Stalin in music in my next symphony, the Tenth. I wrote it right after Stalin's death, and no one has yet guessed what the symphony is about. It's about Stalin and the Stalin years. The second part, the scherzo, is a musical portrait of Stalin, roughly speaking. Of course, there are many other things in it, but that's the basis.

I must say that it's difficult work depicting the benefactors of humanity in music, evaluating them through music. Now, Beethoven managed it, from a musical point of view. He was mistaken from the point of view of history, however.

I understand that my Twelfth Symphony isn't a complete success in that sense. I began with one creative goal and ended with a completely different scheme.* I wasn't able to realize my ideas, the material put up resistance. You see how hard it is to draw the image of leaders and teachers with music. But I did give Stalin his due, the shoe fits, as they say. I can't be reproached for avoiding that ugly phenomenon of our reality.

However, when I was composing the Ninth, the leader's death

*According to Shostakovich's plan, the Twelfth Symphony (1961) was supposed to contain a musical portrait of Lenin.

wasn't close at hand, and my stubbornness cost me dearly. Why didn't Stalin hit me right away? Right then, in 1945? The answer is simple: first he had to deal with the Allies. And here a convenient opportunity presented itself. The wolfhounds had grown up and were baring their fangs. Our wolfhounds had missed their share of the meat. No one abroad demanded Khrennikov's compositions or the compositions of Koval* or Mikhail Chulaki. Orders came in for works by other composers. Terrible inequity. They thought they had destroyed formalism, and here it was rearing its ugly head.

The dissatisfied group showered Stalin with declarations, signed personally and collectively. As Ilf and Petrov noted once, "Composers denounce each other on music paper." They overrated composers, they wrote denunciations on plain paper.

One of the disgruntled was Muradeli,† a fact that is now forgotten. After the historic resolution "On the Opera *The Great Friendship*," Muradeli seemed to walk among the victims, but actually Muradeli was never a victim, and he was planning to warm his hands on his *Great Friendship*.

And he wanted more than just personal glory, he hoped to pull formalism out by the roots from music. His subsequently infamous opera was accepted for production in 1947 by almost twenty opera companies, and most important, the Bolshoi was doing it, and they were planning it for an important occasion—the thirtieth anniversary of the October Revolution. They were going to open at the Bolshoi on November 7, with Stalin attending.

Muradeli walked around and blustered, "He Himself will invite me into his box! I'll tell him everything! I'll tell him the formalists have been blocking my way. Something has to be done!" Everything seemed to augur success for Muradeli. The plot had ideology, from the lives of the Georgians and Ossetians. The Georgian Commissar Ordzhonikidze was a character in the opera, he was cleaning up the Caucasus.

---

*Marian Viktorovich Koval (Kovalev; 1907–1971), a composer and one of the group of musical "wolfhounds" who cleared the path for the "antiformalist" campaign of 1948. He was the author of a uniquely hostile article on Shostakovich, printed in the magazine *Sovetskaya muzyka* in 1948. This is a political denunciation that is frightening to read even today.

†Vano Ilyich Muradeli (1908–1970), a composer whose place in the history of Russian music is assured because he was grouped with Shostakovich and Prokofiev as a "formalist." Of course, Muradeli does have his own musical "record": a singing Lenin makes his first appearance in his opera *October* (1964). (A talking Lenin appeared in Soviet opera in 1939, in Khrennikov's *Into the Storm*.)

The composer was also of Caucasian descent. What more could you ask?

But Muradeli had miscalculated terribly. Stalin disliked the opera. First of all, he didn't like the plot, he found a major political error in it. According to the plot, Ordzhonikidze convinces the Georgians and Ossetians not to fight with the Russians. Stalin, as you know, was an Ossetian himself (and not a Georgian, as is usually thought). He took offense on behalf of the Ossetians. Stalin had his own view of the matter. He despised the Chechens and Ingush, who were just then being moved out of the Caucasus. That was a simple thing to do in Stalin's day. They loaded two nations into wagons and took them away to the devil. So Muradeli should have blamed all the evildoing on the Chechens and Ingush, but he didn't display the necessary mental nimbleness.

And then there was Ordzhonikidze. Muradeli showed his naïveté once more. He thought that it would be a good idea to have Ordzhonikidze in the opera, he didn't think that reminding Stalin of him was like stepping on a corn. At the time, the country had been informed that Ordzhonikidze had died from a heart attack. Actually, Ordzhonikidze shot himself. Stalin drove him to it.

But the main problem was with the *lezghinka*.* The opera was based on life in the Caucasus, so Muradeli crammed it full of native songs and dances. Stalin expected to hear his native songs, but instead he heard Muradeli's own *lezghinka*, which he had composed in a fit of forgetfulness. And it was that original *lezghinka* that angered Stalin the most.

There were black clouds, a storm was brewing. It just lacked an excuse, the lightning needed an oak to strike, or at least a blockhead. Muradeli played the part of the blockhead.

But in the end, Muradeli didn't get burned by the historic resolution "On the Opera *The Great Friendship*." † He was a clever man and he

*In the Stalin years, the sounds of the *lezghinka*, a national Georgian folk dance, as well as the melody "Suliko," Stalin's favorite Georgian folk song, were familiar to millions of Soviet people.

†"The year 1948 is a historical, watershed year in the history of Soviet and world musical culture. The Resolution of the Central Committee of All-Union Communist Party (Bolshevik) of February 10, 1948, On the Opera *The Great Friendship* by V. Muradeli, harshly condemning the anti-people formalist tendency in Soviet music, broke the decadent fetters that hobbled for so many years the creativity of many Soviet composers; for many years ahead the only correct path for the development of musical art in the U.S.S.R. has been determined." (From a collective work published in 1948 by the Composers' Union)

managed to profit even from the historic resolution.

As you know, the resolution drew heated interest among the toiling masses. Meetings and gatherings were held everywhere, in factories, communal farms, industrial cartels, and places of public food consumption. And the workers discussed the document with enthusiasm, since, as it turned out, the document echoed the spiritual needs of millions of people. These millions were united in their rejection of Shostakovich and other formalists. And so Muradeli added his babble to satisfy the spiritual interests of the workers . . . for money, of course.

Muradeli began making appearances at various organizations. He came to the people and repented. I was a so-and-so, a formalist and cosmopolite. I wrote the wrong *lezghinka*, but the Party showed me the way in time. And now I, the former formalist and cosmopolite Muradeli, have stepped onto the righteous road of progressive realistic creativity. And in the future I'm determined to write *lezghinka*s that are worthy of our great epoch.

Muradeli said all this in an agitated manner, with Caucasian temperament. The only thing he didn't do was dance the *lezghinka*. And then he sat at the piano and played excerpts from his future, yet-to-be-written works, worthy of our great epoch. The excerpts were melodious and harmonious, quite like the harmony exercises from the conservatory textbook.

Everyone was satisfied, the workers saw a live formalist, they had something to tell their friends and neighbors. Muradeli earned good money and met the Composers' Union's plan on self-criticism.

Why am I spending so much time on Muradeli? In a musical sense he was a rather pathetic figure and as a man he was extremely malignant. An excess of temperament might lead Muradeli to perform a good deed, but only by accident. For instance, once he got the wild idea of reconciling Prokofiev and me. He decided that if Prokofiev and I sat down at a table and started drinking Georgian wines and eating shashlik, we would become great friends. We had to, for who could resist Georgian wines and shashlik? Naturally, nothing came of that idea.

However, Muradeli played an important role in the business with formalism, albeit an extremely deplorable one. This was the situation. There was Shostakovich, who needed to be put in his place, and there

144

was Muradeli, whose opera *The Great Friendship* displeased Stalin. But the problem of formalism in music did not yet exist, the horrible picture of a formalist conspiracy had not yet formed. They could hit Shostakovich and hit Muradeli and be finished. Stalin might not have even taken aim at all of Soviet music.* The impetus to start a broadly based destruction of Soviet music came from Muradeli and him alone.

After the unhappy presentation of *The Great Friendship*, a meeting was called at the Bolshoi Theater, and at that meeting Muradeli repented and came up with the following theory: that he loved melody and understood melody and he would be more than happy to write melody alone, including melodious and harmonious *lezghinka*s, but it seems that he was kept from writing melodious *lezghinka*s because the formalist conspirators were everywhere—in the conservatories, in the publishing houses, in the press. Everywhere. And they forced poor Muradeli to write a formalist *lezghinka* instead of a melodious and harmonious one. Muradeli's *lezghinka* was the direct result of a conspiracy of enemies of the people, formalists, and toadies to the West.

And this version from Muradeli interested Stalin, who was always interested in conspiracies, an unhealthy interest that always had unpleasant consequences. The unpleasant consequences were quick to follow in this instance as well. One provocateur—Muradeli—had been found. But that wasn't enough. They gathered the composers, who began hanging one another. It was a pathetic sight that I would rather not recall. Of course, almost nothing surprises me, but this is one thing that's too repugnant to think about. Stalin designated to Zhdanov the task of compiling a list of the "main offenders." Zhdanov worked like an experienced torturer—he set one composer against the other.

Of course, Zhdanov didn't have to work too hard; the composers chewed one another up with glee. No one wanted to be on the list, it wasn't a list for prizes but for possible extermination. Everything had significance here—your position on the list, for instance. If you were first, consider yourself gone. Last—there was still hope. And the citizen composers knocked themselves out to avoid the list and did every-

*In order to appreciate Shostakovich's commentaries, one must picture the ubiquity of the "discussions" of formalism in music instituted in 1948. Unlike the "antiformalist" campaign of 1936, which had struck at many victims but then paled before the mass repressions, the "formalism" theme of 1948 became the most important issue in the public life of the times and dominated every conversation.

thing they could to get their comrades on it.* They were real criminals, whose philosophy was: you die today, and I'll go tomorrow.

Well, they worked and worked on the list. They put some names on, crossed others off. Only two names had the top spots sewn up. My name was number one, and Prokofiev's number two. The meeting was over, and the historic resolution appeared. And after that . . .

Meeting upon meeting, conference upon conference. The whole country was in a fever, the composers more than anyone. It was like a dam breaking and a flood of murky, dirty water rushing in. Everyone seemed to go mad and anyone who felt like it expressed an opinion on music.

Zhdanov announced, "The Central Committee of Bolsheviks demands beauty and refinement from music." And he added that the goal of music was to give pleasure, while our music was crude and vulgar, and listening to it undoubtedly destroyed the psychological and physical balance of a man, for example a man like Zhdanov.

Stalin was no longer considered a man. He was a god and all this did not concern him. He was above it all. The leader and teacher washed his hands of it, and I think he did so consciously. He was being smart. But I only realized this later. At the time it seemed as though my end had come. Sheet music was reprocessed; why burn it? That was wasteful. But by recycling all the cacophonic symphonies and quartets, they could save on paper. They destroyed tapes at the radio stations. And Khrennikov said, "There, it's gone forever. The formalist snake will never rear its head again."

All the papers printed letters from the workers, who all thanked the Party for sparing them the torture of listening to the symphonies of Shostakovich. The censors met the wishes of the workers and put out a blacklist, which named those symphonies of Shostakovich's that were being taken out of circulation. Thus I stopped personally offending Asafiev, that leading figure of musical scholarship, who complained, "I take the Ninth Symphony as a personal insult."

From now unto forever, music had to be refined, harmonious, and melodious. They wanted particular attention devoted to singing with

---

*The reference is in part to the desperate attempt by Dmitri Borisovich Kabalevsky (b. 1904) to replace his name in a blacklist, prepared by Zhdanov, of composers "who held formalistic, anti-People tendencies" with that of Gavriil Nikolayevich Popov (1904–1972). The attempt was successful. The final text of the Party's "historic resolution" does not mention Kabalevsky. The talented Popov eventually drank himself to death.

words, since singing without words satisfied only the perverted tastes of a few aesthetes and individualists.

Altogether this was called: The Party has saved music from liquidation. It turned out that Shostakovich and Prokofiev had wanted to liquidate music, and Stalin and Zhdanov didn't let them. Stalin could be happy. The whole country, instead of thinking about its squalid life, was entering mortal combat with formalist composers. Why go on talking about it? I have a musical composition on that theme, and it says it all.*

There were further developments: Stalin was rather deflated by the reaction in the West to the historic resolution. For some reason, he thought they'd be tossing their hats in the air as well, or at least be silent. But they weren't silent in the West. During the war, they had come to know our music a little better and thus they saw that the resolution was the delirium of a purple cow.

Naturally, Stalin didn't give a damn about the West, and the Western intelligentsia in particular. He used to say, "Don't worry, they'll swallow it." But the West did exist and he had to do something with it. They had started a peace movement, and they needed people for it. And Stalin thought of me. That was his style completely. Stalin liked to put a man face to face with death and then make him dance to his own tune.

I was given the order to get ready for a trip to America. I had to go to the Cultural and Scientific Congress for World Peace in New York. A worthy cause. It's obvious that peace is better than war and therefore struggling for peace is a noble effort. But I refused, it was humiliating for me to take part in a spectacle like that. I was a formalist, a representative of an antinational direction in music. My music was banned, and now I was supposed to go and say that everything was fine.

No, I said. I won't go. I'm ill, I can't fly, I get airsick. Molotov † talked to me, but I still refused.

---

*A reference to the still unpublished satiric vocal work of Shostakovich mocking the antiformalism campaign of 1948 and its main organizers. The existence of this composition is one of the reasons why the forthcoming multivolume collection of Shostakovich's works will not in fact be complete.

†Vyacheslav Mikhailovich Molotov (Skryabin; b. 1890), Soviet government leader. In 1949 Stalin sent Molotov's wife, Polina Zhemchuzhina, to the camps for "Zionist activities." Molotov's career ended in 1957, when Khrushchev had him removed from power as a member of an "anti-Party group."

Then Stalin called. And in his nagging way, the leader and teacher asked me why I didn't want to go to America. I answered that I couldn't. My comrades' music wasn't played, and neither was mine. They would ask about it in America. What could I say?

Stalin pretended to be surprised. "What do you mean, it isn't played? Why aren't they playing it?"

I told him that there was a decree by the censors, that there was a blacklist. Stalin said, "Who gave the orders?" Naturally, I replied, "It must have been one of the leading comrades."

Now came the interesting part. Stalin announced, "No, we didn't give that order." He always referred to himself in the royal plural— "We, Nicholas II." And he began rehashing the thought that the censors had overreacted, had taken an incorrect initiative: We didn't give an order like that, we'll have to straighten out the comrades from the censorship, and so on.

This was another matter, this was a real concession. And I thought that maybe it would make sense to go to America, if as a result they would play the music of Prokofiev, Shebalin, Miaskovsky, Khachaturian, Popov, and Shostakovich again.

And just then, Stalin stopped going on about the question of the order and said, "We'll take care of that problem, Comrade Shostakovich. What about your health?"

And I told Stalin the pure truth: "I'm nauseated."

Stalin was taken aback and then started mulling over this unexpected bulletin. "Why are you nauseated? From what? We'll send you a physician, he'll see why you are nauseated." And so on.

So finally I agreed, I made the trip to America. It cost me a great deal, that trip, I had to answer stupid questions and keep from saying too much. They made a sensation out of that too. And all I thought about was: How much longer do I have to live?

Thirty thousand people were jammed into Madison Square Garden when I played the scherzo from my Fifth Symphony on the piano, and I thought, This is it, this is the last time I'll ever play before an audience this size.

Even now I sometimes ask myself, How did I manage to survive? I don't think that the trip to America had anything to do with it. That wasn't it. I think it was the films. I am sometimes asked, "How could you participate in such film projects, you so-and-so, as *The Fall of*

Berlin and *Unforgettable 1919?* * And even accept prizes for these unseemly things?"

My reply is that I can expand the list of shameful enterprises with music composed by me, for instance the revue at the Leningrad Music Hall called *War Game "Casualties."* They used song and dance to agitate for antiaircraft defense. I wrote songs, fox trots, and so on. Chekhov used to say that he wrote everything but denunciations. And you see, I agree with him. I have a very unaristocratic point of view.

But naturally, there was another nuance, so to speak, in this case with the film industry, and that nuance turned out to be rather important. The point is that for us film is the most important art form. As you know, Lenin said that. And Stalin confirmed that profound and just thought and put it into action.

Stalin was in charge of the film industry personally. The results are known. And it's not my concern to delve into it. My own firm conviction is that film is an industry and not an art, but my participation in this industry of national importance saved me. More than once or twice.

Stalin wanted our film industry to put out only masterpieces. He was convinced that under his brilliant leadership and personal guidance it would do so. But let's not forget "The cadres determine everything." † So the leader and teacher worried about the cadres. He had his own confused notions about who could do what, and he decided that Shostakovich could write film scores. And he never changed his mind. Considering the situation, it would have been irrational for me to refuse to do film work.

Khrennikov, taking heart after the historic resolution, decided that my song was sung and my time was over. My operas and ballets were not being produced. My symphonies and chamber music were banned. Now all he had to do was squeeze me out of film work and then my end would be nigh.

---

*These films, praised by the press and glorified by awards, depict Stalin as a wise and brave leader. Stalin saw them many times, relishing his personal portrayal. Shostakovich wrote film scores throughout his creative life, beginning in 1928 (for the famous *New Babylon*). He worked on forty films, which is no mean feat. However, the true significance of this output will become clear when one remembers that in the Soviet Union there were years in which only a few films were released, and the production of each film was under the personal control of Stalin. Shostakovich received money and prizes for his film music, but his feelings in his late years about this form of art, and his participation in it, were ambivalent, to say the least.

† "The cadres determine everything" is one of Stalin's aphorisms.

And so Khrennikov and his friends actively brought my end closer. I wouldn't speak of this with such assurance if I hadn't learned about it accidentally. I don't like gossip and when people try to tell me who said what about me, I usually try to stop the conversation. I have been told about the moves Khrennikov made toward having me liquidated. I don't lend credence to these stories. But once I witnessed a rather interesting conversation.

Here's what happened. Khrennikov called me in to the Composers' Union on some matter. I came, and we had a leisurely conversation. Suddenly the phone rang. Khrennikov, on the intercom, said to his secretary: "I told you not to disturb us!" But her reply made our hereditary shop clerk quiver. He became so agitated that he jumped up and waited for his caller, holding the receiver respectfully.

Finally Comrade Khrennikov was put through. It was Stalin calling. These coincidences *do* happen in real life. Namely, Stalin was calling about me, and Khrennikov was so confused that he forgot to see me out of his office and I heard the entire conversation.

Out of politeness, I turned away and began a close examination of Tchaikovsky's portrait on the wall. I scrutinized Tchaikovsky, and he stared back. The classic and I studied each other, but to tell the truth, I was also listening closely to Khrennikov's conversation.

This was the situation. When Khrennikov learned that I had been commissioned to do the music for several important films, he wrote a complaint to the Party's Central Committee. He didn't realize that he was complaining to Stalin about Stalin. And Stalin was letting him have it. Khrennikov gulped and tried to say something in his defense. But what defense could there be—obviously, he admitted that he had been wrong. Ever since that day, I can reproduce Pyotr Ilyich's beard faultlessly.

But otherwise, films have generally meant nothing but trouble for me, beginning with my first one, *New Babylon*. I'm not talking about the so-called artistic side. That's another story, and a sad one, but my troubles on the political side began with *New Babylon*. No one remembers this any more and the film is considered a Soviet classic and has a wonderful reputation abroad. But when it was first shown, KIM* interfered. The KIM leaders decided that *New Babylon* was

*KIM—the Communist International of Youth, the young people's division of the Comintern.

counterrevolutionary. Things could have ended very badly, and I was only in my early twenties then. And there was trouble with every other film. When we were doing *Girlfriends*, *Pravda* published a list of fourteen people who had allegedly planned Kirov's death. Raya Vasilyeva was on that list. She was the screenwriter of *Girlfriends*. Now, you might ask: What does the screenwriter have to do with the composer? And I'll reply: And what did Raya Vasilyeva have to do with Kirov's murder? Nothing. But she was shot nevertheless.

Something worse happened with *Friends*, a film about Betal Kalmykov, a man famous in those days. They proclaimed Betal Kalmykov an enemy of the people, and all the people involved with the film shook in their boots. And so on.

No, this was more than I could take, particularly since I had to work with geniuses like Mikhail Edisherovich Chiaureli. Whenever he went over budget, Chiaureli called Beria* and explained the financial situation this way: "You know, we need more money. Films are complicated. A location shot, coming and going, and a million's gone. We need more money." And Beria would arrange it. He and Chiaureli understood each other.

Chiaureli also went to America, so that the progressive American community would have the opportunity to get to know this outstanding cultural leader. His elaborate creations made it possible for me to live through the hardest years.

Well, everything is still ahead. "I look ahead without fear," Pushkin said in the bad times of tsarism. I can't repeat his statement with confidence. Sometimes someone will subtly hint, After all, the historic resolution on the opera *The Great Friendship* has been rescinded.

First of all, one judges by actions, not words. And as for actions, there are plenty of sad examples. I won't talk about other composers now, let them speak for themselves. But the Thirteenth Symphony†

---

*Lavrenti Pavlovich Beria (1899–1953), for many years the head of the Soviet secret police. He was shot almost immediately after Stalin's death.

†The Thirteenth Symphony, for soloist, chorus, and orchestra (1962), is the last composition of Shostakovich to elicit open dissatisfaction from the authorities, including a ban on public performance. It was prompted primarily by his choice of the poem for the first movement, Yevtushenko's "Babi Yar," which is directed against anti-Semitism, an unfashionable theme in the U.S.S.R. since Stalin's time. Babi Yar was the site of the mass murder of Jews in 1943. The premiere of the Thirteenth Symphony in Moscow turned into an expression of antigovernment feelings.

speaks for itself. It had an unhappy fate. It is very dear to me, and it hurts to remember the ugly attempts to take the symphony out of circulation.

Khrushchev didn't give a damn about the music in this instance, he was angered by Yevtushenko's poetry. But some fighters on the musical front really perked up. There, you see, Shostakovich has proved himself untrustworthy once more. Let's get him! And a disgusting poison campaign began. They tried to scare off everyone from Yevtushenko and me. We had so much trouble with the bass singer. Unfortunately, the soloist in the Thirteenth is a bass. One after another, they dropped out of the running. They were all worried about their position, their reputation. They behaved shamefully, shamefully. They almost destroyed the premiere, which took place by sheer accident.

And the Thirteenth was not exceptional. I had the same problems with *The Execution of Stepan Razin* and with the Fourteenth Symphony. But why list them; the point isn't in the list, it's in the situation.

And here's another thing. When they tell me that the historic resolution has been rescinded, I like to inquire: When was it rescinded? I heard a strange reply, that the historic resolution was rescinded by another, no less historic resolution, ten years later, in 1958.*

But am I deaf or blind? It's hard for me to play the piano and write with my right hand,† but I still see and hear well, thank God. I've read the new historic resolution over and over and it says right there in black and white that the previous resolution played a positive role in the development of our culture and that formalism had been correctly condemned. And there's something added about the narrow circle of gourmand-aesthetes. So even the style is maintained. It's just as it was before. Everything is in order.

Why did this new historic resolution appear? Very simple. In 1951 Stalin reprimanded Alexander Korneichuk for writing a bad libretto to

*A reference to the Party resolution of May 28, 1958, "On Correcting Errors in the Appraisal of the Operas *Great Friendship, Bogdan Khmelnitsky,* and *From the Bottom of My Heart.*" Like almost all of Khrushchev's acts, this resolution was very ambivalent. Stalin's appraisals of the individual musical works and their composers were termed "unfair"; yet the criticism of formalism in 1948 was characterized as "just and timely." Actually, other Party resolutions of the postwar period (for instance, those attacking Akhmatova, Zoshchenko, and Eisenstein) have not been revoked to this day and thus formally are still in force.

†In the last years of his life Shostakovich suffered from heart problems, fragility of the bones, and an impairment of the right hand.

the opera *Bogdan Khmelnitsky*. The composer was in trouble too. The opera, naturally, was soundly denounced.

But Korneichuk was a friend of Khrushchev's and when Khrushchev became our leader, he decided to correct this gross injustice. He decided to rehabilitate Korneichuk's good name, and incidentally added Prokofiev and Shostakovich. That's the whole story.

Khrennikov was dumfounded at first, but quickly readjusted. Nothing terrible had happened, but just in case, he fired the editor * of *Sovetskaya muzyka* for revisionism.

Revisionism became the new insult, to replace formalism. Revisionism meant that the editor had tried to write about my compositions and Prokofiev's in a more polite manner. Khrennikov regrouped quickly and began his counterattack. The Party once again unquestioningly maintains that the historic resolution on the opera *The Great Friendship* . . . And so on, and so forth.

Everything repeated itself. Once Koval wrote in *Sovetskaya muzyka* something to the effect that the people bow down to and applaud the genius of our leader, Comrade Stalin, and Shostakovich has proved himself a dwarf. What was Shostakovich trying to prove when in his Ninth Symphony he created the image of a happy-go-lucky Yankee instead of the victorious Soviet man?

Ten years later our brilliant leader was no longer mentioned. They wrote simply and with taste: The Soviet people express dissatisfaction with the Ninth Symphony and recommend that I learn from our comrades in the People's Republic of China.

"The Party has once and for all knocked the ground out from under the feet of the revisionists," Khrennikov announced joyously. Right out from under them.

So let's not talk about correcting mistakes, because it will only make it worse. And more important, I like the word "rehabilitation." And I'm even more impressed when I hear about "posthumous rehabilitation." But that's nothing new either. A general complained to Nicholas I that some hussar had abducted his daughter. They even got married, but the general was against the marriage. After some thought, the emperor proclaimed: "I decree the marriage is annulled, and she is to be considered a virgin."

Somehow I still don't feel like a virgin.

*A reference to the musicologist Georgi Nikitich Khubov (b. 1902).

Is a musical concept born consciously or unconsciously? It's difficult to explain. The process of writing a new work is long and complicated. Sometimes you start writing and then change your mind. It doesn't always work the way you thought it would. If it's not working, leave the composition the way it is—and try to avoid your earlier mistakes in the next one. That's my personal point of view, my manner of working. Perhaps it stems from a desire to do as much as possible. When I hear that a composer has eleven versions of one symphony, I think involuntarily, How many new works could he have composed in that time?

No, naturally I sometimes return to an old work; for instance, I made many changes in the score of my opera *Katerina Izmailova*.

I wrote my Seventh Symphony, the "Leningrad," very quickly. I couldn't not write it. War was all around. I had to be with the people, I wanted to create the image of our country at war, capture it in music. From the first days of the war, I sat down at the piano and started work. I worked intensely. I wanted to write about our time, about my contemporaries who spared neither strength nor life in the name of Victory Over the Enemy.

I've heard so much nonsense about the Seventh and Eighth Symphonies. It's amazing how long-lived these stupidities are. I'm astounded sometimes by how lazy people are when it comes to thinking. Everything that was written about those symphonies in the first few days is repeated without any changes to this very day, even though there has been time to do some thinking. After all, the war ended a long time ago, almost thirty years.

Thirty years ago you could say that they were military symphonies, but symphonies are rarely written to order, that is, if they are worthy to be called symphonies.

I do write quickly, it's true, but I think about my music for a comparatively long time, and until it's complete in my head I don't begin setting it down. Of course, I do make mistakes. Say, I imagine that the composition will have one movement, and then I see that it must be continued. That happened with the Seventh, as a matter of fact, and with the Thirteenth. And sometimes it's the reverse. I think that I've started a new symphony, when actually things come to a halt after one movement. That happened with *The Execution of Stepan Razin*, which is now performed as a symphonic poem.

The Seventh Symphony had been planned before the war and consequently it simply cannot be seen as a reaction to Hitler's attack. The "invasion theme" has nothing to do with the attack. I was thinking of other enemies of humanity when I composed the theme.

Naturally, fascism is repugnant to me, but not only German fascism, any form of it is repugnant. Nowadays people like to recall the prewar period as an idyllic time, saying that everything was fine until Hitler bothered us. Hitler is a criminal, that's clear, but so is Stalin.

I feel eternal pain for those who were killed by Hitler, but I feel no less pain for those killed on Stalin's orders. I suffer for everyone who was tortured, shot, or starved to death. There were millions of them in our country before the war with Hitler began.

The war brought much new sorrow and much new destruction, but I haven't forgotten the terrible prewar years. That is what all my symphonies, beginning with the Fourth, are about, including the Seventh and Eighth.

Actually, I have nothing against calling the Seventh the Leningrad Symphony, but it's not about Leningrad under siege, it's about the Leningrad that Stalin destroyed and that Hitler merely finished off.

The majority of my symphonies are tombstones. Too many of our people died and were buried in places unknown to anyone, not even their relatives. It happened to many of my friends. Where do you put the tombstones for Meyerhold or Tukhachevsky? Only music can do that for them. I'm willing to write a composition for each of the victims, but that's impossible, and that's why I dedicate my music to them all.

I think constantly of those people, and in almost every major work I try to remind others of them. The conditions of the war years were conducive to that, because the authorities were less strict about music and didn't care if the music was too gloomy. And later all the misery was put down to the war, as though it was only during the war that people were tortured and killed. Thus the Seventh and Eighth are "war symphonies."

This is a well-rooted tradition. When I wrote the Eighth Quartet, it was also assigned to the department of "exposing fascism." You have to be blind and deaf to do that, because everything in the quartet is as clear as a primer. I quote *Lady Macbeth*, the First and Fifth Symphonies. What does fascism have to do with these? The Eighth is an autobiographical quartet, it quotes a song known to all Russians: "Exhausted by the hardships of prison."

And there is also the Jewish theme from the Piano Trio in this quartet. I think, if we speak of musical impressions, that Jewish folk music has made a most powerful impression on me. I never tire of delighting in it, it's multifaceted, it can appear to be happy while it is tragic. It's almost always laughter through tears.

This quality of Jewish folk music is close to my ideas of what music should be. There should always be two layers in music. Jews were tormented for so long that they learned to hide their despair. They express despair in dance music.

All folk music is lovely, but I can say that Jewish folk music is unique. Many composers listened to it, including Russian composers, Mussorgsky, for instance. He carefully set down Jewish folk songs. Many of my works reflect my impressions of Jewish music.

This is not a purely musical issue, this is also a moral issue. I often test a person by his attitude toward Jews. In our day and age, any person with pretensions of decency cannot be anti-Semitic. This seems so obvious that it doesn't need saying, but I've had to argue the point for at least thirty years. Once after the war I was passing a bookstore and saw a volume with Jewish songs. I was always interested in Jewish folklore, and I thought the book would give the melodies, but it contained only the texts. It seemed to me that if I picked out several texts and set them to music, I would be able to tell about the fate of the Jewish people. It seemed an important thing to do, because I could see anti-Semitism growing all around me. But I couldn't have the cycle performed then, it was played for the first time much later, and later still I did an orchestral version of the work.

My parents considered anti-Semitism a shameful superstition, and in that sense I was given a singular upbringing. In my youth I came across anti-Semitism among my peers, who thought that Jews were getting preferential treatment. They didn't remember the pogroms, the ghettos, or the quotas. In those years it was almost a mark of sangfroid to speak of Jews with a mocking laugh. It was a kind of opposition to the authorities.

I never condoned an anti-Semitic tone, even then, and I didn't repeat anti-Semitic jokes that were popular then. But I was much gentler about this unworthy trait than I am now. Later I broke with even good friends if I saw that they had any anti-Semitic tendencies.

But even before the war, the attitude toward Jews had changed drastically. It turned out that we had far to go to achieve brotherhood. The Jews became the most persecuted and defenseless people of Europe. It was a return to the Middle Ages. Jews became a symbol for me. All of man's defenselessness was concentrated in them. After the war, I tried to convey that feeling in my music. It was a bad time for Jews then. In fact, it's always a bad time for them.

Despite all the Jews who perished in the camps, all I heard people saying was, "The kikes went to Tashkent to fight." And if they saw a Jew with military decorations, they called after him, "Kike, where did you buy medals?" That's when I wrote the Violin Concerto, the Jewish Cycle, and the Fourth Quartet.

Not one of these works could be performed then. They were heard only after Stalin's death. I still can't get used to it. The Fourth Symphony was played twenty-five years after I wrote it. There are compositions that have yet to be performed, and no one knows when they will be heard.

I'm very heartened by the reaction among young people to my feelings on the Jewish question. And I see that the Russian intelligentsia remains intractably opposed to anti-Semitism, and that the many years of trying to enforce anti-Semitism from above have not had any visible results. This holds for the simple folk as well. Recently I went to the Repino station to buy a lemonade. There's a little store, a stall really, that sells everything. There was a line, and a woman in the line, who looked very Jewish and had an accent, began to complain out loud. Why is there such a line, and why are canned peas only sold with something else, and so on.

And the young salesman answered along these lines: "If you're unhappy here, citizeness, why don't you go to Israel? There are no lines there and you can probably buy peas just like that."

So Israel was pictured in a positive way, as a country without lines and with canned peas. And that's a dream for the Soviet consumer, and the line looked with interest at the citizeness who could go to a country where there are no lines and more peas than you could want.

The last time I was in America I saw the film *Fiddler on the Roof* and here's what astounded me about it: the primary emotion is homesickness, you sense it in the music, the dancing, the color. Even though the motherland is a so-and-so, a bad, unloving country, more a stepmother than a mother. But people still miss her, and that loneliness made itself felt. I feel that that loneliness was the most important aspect. It would be good if Jews could live peacefully and happily in Russia, where they were born. But we must never forget about the dangers of anti-Semitism and keep reminding others of it, because the infection is alive and who knows if it will ever disappear.

That's why I was overjoyed when I read Yevtushenko's "Babi Yar"; the poem astounded me. It astounded thousands of people. Many had heard about Babi Yar, but it took Yevtushenko's poem to make them aware of it. They tried to destroy the memory of Babi Yar, first the Germans and then the Ukrainian government. But after Yevtushenko's poem, it became clear that it would never be forgotten. That is the power of art.

People knew about Babi Yar before Yevtushenko's poem, but they were silent. And when they read the poem, the silence was broken. Art destroys silence.

I know that many will not agree with me and will point out other, more noble aims of art. They'll talk about beauty, grace, and other high qualities. But you won't catch me with that bait. I'm like Sobakevich in *Dead Souls*: you can sugar-coat a frog, and I still won't put it in my mouth. Zhdanov, a great specialist in the musical arts, also stood fast for beautiful and graceful music. Let anything at all go on around you, but serve high art, and nothing but, at the table.

It's amusing to see how pronouncements on art from people who consider themselves to be in opposite camps correspond. For example: "If music becomes ungainly, ugly, vulgar, it stops satisfying those demands for the sake of which it exists, and it ceases being music."

Now wouldn't any aesthete who campaigns for high art be willing to sign his name to that excerpt? And yet this was said by that brilliant music critic Zhdanov. Both he and the aesthetes are equally against music reminding people about life, about tragedies, about the victims, the dead. Let music be beautiful and graceful and let composers think only about purely musical problems. It'll be quieter that way.

I've always protested harshly against this point of view and I strove for the reverse. I always wanted music to be an active force. That is the Russian tradition.

There is another notable phenomenon that is characteristic of Russia. It is so notable that I would like to dwell on it, it needs to be detailed to make it more understandable. In one of Rimsky-Korsakov's letters I found words to which I have returned many times. They make one think. The words are: "Many things have aged and faded before our eyes and much that seems obsolete I think will eventually seem fresh and strong and eternal, if anything can be."

I'm delighted once more by the soundness and wisdom of that man. Of course we all, while still of sound mind, have our doubts about eternity. I'll be frank: I don't have much faith in eternity.

Once so-called eternal needles for Primus stoves were advertised, and Ilf said, "What do I need eternal needles for? I have no intention of living forever, and even if I did, will the Primus stoves exist forever? That would be very sad." That was how our famous humorist expressed himself on eternity, and I agree wholeheartedly.

Was Rimsky-Korsakov thinking about his music when he spoke of eternity? But why should his music have eternal life? Or any music, for that matter? Those for whom the music is written, the ones who are born with it—those people don't plan on living forever. How dreary to picture generation after generation living to the same music!

What I want to say is that what may remain "fresh and strong" may not be music at all, and not even creativity, but some other, more unexpected and prosaic thing, such as attentiveness toward people, toward their humdrum lives, filled with unpleasant and unexpected events, toward their petty affairs and cares, and toward their general lack of security. People have invented many curious things: the microscope, Gillette razor blades, photography, and so on and so forth, but they still haven't invented a way of making everyone's life tolerable.

Naturally, solving world problems by creating oratorios, ballets, and operettas is a noble undertaking. Of course, you address yourself to the lovers of these lofty genres, but you must also respond to the feelings of other, say, more average, people. And these people may be occupied with something quite different from the construction of the Volga-Don Canal and the re-creation of that momentous event via cantatas, oratorios, ballets, and such. Those miserable characters, so to speak, are concerned with a leaky toilet that the janitor won't fix, or the fact that their son passed the entrance exams but won't be accepted because he's the wrong nationality for the institute he wants to enter, and similar problems, not very exalted and therefore not appropriate for oratorios and ballets. Perhaps Rimsky-Korsakov's "freshness and strength" would lie in attention to these problems of average people in certain circumstances.

They'll say that this is all talk and that there's too much talk, and that the little action there is becomes silly. But I feel that the history of Russian music is on my side. Take Borodin, for instance, whose music I rate very highly taken as a whole, even though I don't always agree with the ideology behind it. But we're not talking about ideology now, and Borodin was highly gifted as a composer. Any Western composer

160

with such a gift would sit around and dash off symphony after symphony and opera upon opera, and live a life of ease.

But Borodin? Stories about him paint a picture that seems fantastic to an outsider, but is completely normal and customary for us. All right, everyone knows that besides music, Borodin was also a chemist and that Borodin made a name for himself in the field of catalysts and precipitates with his discoveries. I've met chemists who insisted that they are truly valuable discoveries. (However, one chemist told me it was all nonsense and that he would trade all Borodin's scientific discoveries for a second set of *Polovetsian Dances*. And then I had the thought that perhaps it was good that Borodin was interested in chemistry and didn't write a second set.)

But besides chemistry, there was also the women's movement. We don't have feminism in Russia now, we simply have energetic women. They work and earn money, with which they buy groceries, and then cook dinner for their husbands, and then do the dishes, and also bring up the children. So we have individual energetic women but no feminist movement. But if feminism did exist, a monument would certainly be erected to Borodin. I remember that in my early years, feminists and suffragettes treated the opposite sex with disdain, but in this case they would be willing to spend money for a monument. After all, we have a monument for Pavlov's dog, which served humanity—that is, was butchered in the name of humanity. Borodin would get one of those monuments too, because he plunged headlong into women's education and spent more and more time as he grew older on philanthropy, primarily for women's causes. And these causes butchered him as a composer.

Reminiscences of friends paint an educational picture. Borodin's apartment looked like a railway station. Women and girls came to him at any time of day, dragging him away from breakfast, lunch, and dinner. Borodin would get up—without finishing his meal—and go off to take care of all their requests and complaints. A too familiar picture.

It was impossible to find him at home or at his laboratory. Borodin was always out at some meeting on women's rights. He dragged himself from one meeting to another, discussing women's problems which could probably have been taken care of by a lesser composer than Borodin. To tell the truth, a man without any musical education could

161

have successfully understood the pressing women's issues. (Why was it that the musical ladies, who adored Borodin's music, were the ones who dragged him into this business? Why is it always like that? Whom and what do these ladies love most: music, charitable causes, or themselves?)

Borodin's apartment was a madhouse. I'm not exaggerating, this is not a poetic simile, so popular in our times, as in "Our communal apartment is a madhouse." No, Borodin's place was a madhouse without similes or metaphors. He always had a bunch of relatives living with him, or just poor people, or visitors who took sick and even—there were cases—went mad. Borodin fussed over them, treated them, took them to hospitals, and then visited them there.

That's how a Russian composer lives and works. Borodin wrote in snatches. Naturally, there was someone sleeping in every room, on every couch, and on the floors. He didn't want to disturb them with the piano. Rimsky-Korsakov would visit Borodin and ask, "Have you written anything?" Borodin would reply, "I have." And it would turn out to be another letter in defense of women's rights. And the same jokes came up with the orchestration of *Prince Igor*. "Did you transpose that section?" "Yes. From the piano to the desk." And then people wonder why Russian composers write so little.

In the long run, *Igor* is as much Borodin's as it is Rimsky-Korsakov's and Glazunov's. The other two tried not to stress the fact, saying that Glazunov wrote down this section "from memory," and that one too. The overture was written "from memory" and the entire third act. But when he was in his cups, and Glazunov got drunk very rapidly and became defenseless then, he would admit that it wasn't "from memory"—he simply wrote for Borodin. This says many good things about Glazunov, whose behavior I am going to talk about. It doesn't happen often that a man composes excellent music for another composer and doesn't advertise it (to talk while drinking doesn't count). It's usually the other way around—a man steals an idea or even a considerable piece of music from another composer and passes it off as his own.

Glazunov is a marvelous example of a purely Russian phenomenon: as a composer he can honestly and fairly hold a position in the history of Russian music that is not simply outstanding but unique, and not because of his compositions. Do we love Glazunov now for his music? Have his symphonies remained "fresh and strong," as Rimsky-Korsakov put it, or his quartets?

I recently listened—for the umpteenth time—to *Suite from the Middle Ages*. It has nothing to do with the Middle Ages; they would have scorned it. I think the masters were stronger then, even though I like this suite more than many of Glazunov's other works. And I suppose I value his Eighth Symphony more than the others, particularly the slow movement. The others make rather flabby music. Boring, actually. When I listen to his symphonies, I grow bored. I keep thinking, Let's have the recapitulation—oh, no, it's still the development.

Glazunov had a lot of trouble with finales, he did not create enough energy or tension. In fact, this characterizes almost all his compositions. I think that a decisive factor in this problem was a misfortune—in his youth Glazunov contracted a venereal disease. He picked it up from some ballerina in the Imperial Maryinsky Theater. He was awfully unlucky with that ballerina. He fell into a deep depression, they say, and went to Aachen for a cure. That was the famous German resort where all the syphilitics went. He wrote tragic letters from Aachen. They say that his tragic suffering is reflected in the Fourth Quartet. I know the Fourth, naturally, but I don't hear anything like that in it. In general, I like the Fifth Quartet much more, if it comes to that, even without the venereal suffering. Oh yes, I forgot, I also like parts of *Raymonda*.

Besides his music, Glazunov's private life was also affected by that incident. He never did marry and lived with his mother. Glazunov was well over fifty when his mother would still say to the laundry, "Do a good job on the child's underwear, now." And Glazunov was famous throughout Russia, the "Russian Brahms," the director of the best Russian conservatory. And he was good-looking, strong and massive, at least until the lean years of the Revolution.

Here's another popular story that circulated in my years at the Conservatory. Glazunov was planning to go out and called a hackney cab. His mother expressed her fears about whether the horse was docile enough, whether it would bolt, and she didn't want him to go. They say that even good-natured Glazunov lost his temper and asked, "Mother, do you plan to put a guardrail on the coach?"

But all these stories didn't keep us from feeling the greatest respect for Glazunov. Even adulation. It's only now that his compositions seem dull, but then they were heard in all our classes, at every student recital, and particularly at the examinations, which Glazunov invariably attended. And I don't think it was to suck up to Glazunov, either. You didn't have to tell Glazunov he was a marvelous composer to flatter him. You had to tell him he was a marvelous conductor. They played his works because they were convenient and effective, for instance, the Piano Variations in D, the Sonata in B Minor, and the Concerto in F Minor. The singers adored Glazunov's romances, and Nina's romance from Lermontov's *Masquerade* was something of a war-horse. It's popular today, we often hear it. I'm not very fond of it.

Everyone knows how Glazunov began. When his First Symphony was performed, it was a great success, and they called for the composer. The audience was stunned when the composer came out in a gymnasium uniform. Glazunov was seventeen. That's a record in Russian music. I didn't beat it, even though I began early enough.

Incidentally, the same rumors circulated about us both: to wit, "such a young man" couldn't have written such a symphony. They said that his wealthy parents had paid someone for Glazunov's symphony. And they said that mine was a collective effort. But no, we wrote them ourselves. I was even more independent. Balakirev reorchestrated pages of Glazunov's First Symphony. Glazunov put up with it, didn't dare contradict him, and later even defended Balakirev. And Glazunov wanted to fix up my First. Of course, he wasn't talking about pages, as far as I remember there were just a few unpleasant harmonies, as Glazunov thought, and he insisted that I change them, even suggesting his own variations.

I made one change at first, in the introduction, after the first phrases of the muted trumpet. I didn't want to hurt the old man's feelings, but then I thought, Wait a minute, this is my music, and not Glazunov's. Why should I feel ill at ease? There's a lot I don't like in his music, but I don't suggest he change it to suit me. And I reinstated the original before the first performance. Glazunov was very angry, but it was too late. So I wasn't as malleable as Glazunov had been in his day. Of course, he was two whole years younger at the time.

After his brilliant debut, Glazunov had a rosy and completely deserved future ahead of him. He lived well and peacefully. Not like me. He never had to worry about money, while that care always hung over my head. The wealthy Mitrofan Beliayev,* as you know, considered Glazunov the new musical messiah, and published whatever Glazunov wrote. He published quickly and paid generously. Patrons are always more generous than the state, at least so it seems to me. So Glazunov could devote himself exclusively to his music and particularly to his emotions, since, as I've told you, he had good reason to emote.

He lived that way, quietly and peacefully, as none of us ever has. Glazunov was totally indifferent to the social upheavals of the period, he saw the world only through music, not only his own but other music as well. He was a huge musical ear.

Mikhail Gnessin† and I were speaking of Glazunov once and Gnessin made a perceptive remark about the man he knew so well; he said Glazunov's basic emotion was delight in an exquisitely arranged universe. I've never experienced that delight.

Of course, Glazunov had many childish traits—his subordination to his mother, the revered Elena Pavlovna, when hundreds of people were subordinate to him, and that voice as quiet as a roach's, and that huge fish tank in his apartment. (Glazunov liked to feed his fish.) And his childish love of conducting. I think he always thought of the orchestra as a large shiny toy. But you can't play games with an orchestra. I tried a few times and gave it up. Why bother?

A miracle happened with Glazunov, one that can only happen in Russia. An edifying and mysterious evolution. This enormous elderly child gradually—gradually, not abruptly—became a public figure of immense significance. Glazunov began changing the moment he became director of the Petersburg Conservatory and eventually he turned into another person altogether.

This was a Glazunov who was simultaneously the old man and the new. The old Glazunov we knew from stories. But as I've said, there was no sharp, sudden change in his personality, so even in our times it

*Mitrofan Petrovich Beliayev (1836–1903), a millionaire merchant who devoted himself to disseminating Russian music. He used his money to establish a professionally run concert organization and a music publishing house.

†Mikhail Fabianovich Gnessin (1883–1957), composer, professor at the Leningrad Conservatory, one of the eminent representatives of twentieth-century Jewish music. Gnessin's behavior during the "antiformalist campaign" is an outstanding example of steadfastness and firmness of conviction.

was often possible to see and hear the old Glazunov. And yet he was also the new Glazunov—a figure of epochal public resonance, a historic figure without exaggeration.

In our own time Glazunov was a living legend. In the twenty or more years that he headed the Petersburg, later the Leningrad, Conservatory, thousands of students graduated, and I'm certain that it would be hard to name even one who wasn't indebted to Glazunov in some way.

I realize that this is hard to believe now, but it is really so. There is no false sentimentality in my recollections. I despise sentimentality, can't bear it, and I'm not reminiscing so that sensitive ladies can bring their scented hankies to their eyes. I'm remembering so that the truth will be recorded, the truth that I saw and remembered, so that the phenomena of our cultural life that I witnessed will not be forgotten. Glazunov was one of these phenomena.

He used to be a squire, and he became a man blessed for his good deeds by every working musician in the country. He composed when he really wanted to, for his own pleasure, without giving a thought to "ideological content." And he sacrificed everything for the Conservatory—his time, his serenity, and finally, his creativity. Glazunov was always busy. He told friends who wanted to see him that he could only be seen in their dreams. And it was so. They say that he was extremely passive in his youth. Of course, Glazunov didn't become assertive in my day either, but he did develop the necessary firmness—and not only toward his subordinates or students.

The firmness of a boss toward his underling is worthless. It only outrages me, this notorious firmness. Glazunov became firm and calm in his dealings with big shots, and that's quite a feat.

Gnessin told me that before the Revolution, Prime Minister Stolypin sent an inquiry to the Conservatory: How many Jewish students were there? And Gnessin, a Jew, elatedly gave me Glazunov's reply. Delivered with quiet satisfaction, it was "We don't keep count."

And these were the years of pogroms, when Jews were considered rabble-rousers and had strictly curtailed rights. They weren't permitted into institutions of higher learning. An independent and even challenging answer like that could have created problems for Glazunov. But he wasn't afraid. Anti-Semitism was organically alien to him. He followed the tradition of Rimsky-Korsakov in that sense, for Korsakov couldn't abide it either. He pointed with revulsion at Balakirev, who became rabid with the filthy trait in his old age. There's no need to bring up Mussorgsky here. It's a complex situation. But in "Korsakov's school" there was no room for anti-Semitism.

Here's another typical incident. An anniversary concert in Glazunov's honor was held in Moscow in 1922. He went, and after the gala, Lunacharsky, the People's Commissar of Education, gave a speech. He announced that the government had decided to give Glazunov living conditions that would facilitate his creativity and be commensurate with his achievements. What would any other man have done in the guest of honor's place? He would have thanked him. The times were hard and lean. Glazunov, who had once been a substantial and handsome man, had lost a catastrophic amount of weight. His old clothes sagged on him as though he were a hanger. His face was haggard and drawn. We knew that he didn't even have music paper on which to write down his ideas. But Glazunov manifested an absolutely amazing sense of his own dignity. And honor. He said that he needed absolutely nothing and asked not to be put in circumstances that differed from those of other citizens. But if the government had turned its attention to musical life, Glazunov said, well then, let it rest on the Conservatory, which was freezing. There was no firewood, nothing with which to heat the place. It caused a minor scandal, but at least the Conservatory received firewood.

I'm not painting a picture of an angel. That's not like me at all. There was much in Glazunov that I found laughable and incomprehensible. I'm not all that fond of his music, but I want to stress that man does not live by music alone. Even if it is the music by which you should be living—your own compositions. And I want to reiterate the following circumstance: Glazunov did not take on public roles because he lacked the gift for composing, or the technique. He was talented and a master of the art.

It is only nowadays that the people who want to attend meetings, make decisions, and command are the ones who are doing badly with their own work. And these bums, finally getting their administrative posts, use all their power to stifle talented music and bury it, while promoting their own worthless works.

It was just the reverse with Glazunov, he wasn't seeking profit for himself. He gave away his salary as director and professor to needy students. No one will ever be able to tally the number of his famous letters of recommendation. They gave people work, bread, sometimes saved lives.

I want what I am remembering now to be taken very seriously, for I am talking about a complex psychological and ethical problem which not many bother to think about. In such letters Glazunov did write what he really thought about the person quite often and praised the person with justification. But even more frequently—much more so—he helped people out of compassion. Many turned to him for help, often total strangers. They were in need and were oppressed by life, and he quickly took on the cares of each victim. Glazunov listened to their pleas by the hour, tried to understand their situation. And he did more than sign letters of request, he went to the big shots to plead their cases. Glazunov felt that no real harm would come to great and holy Art if some singer without a voice, the mother of children and without a husband, was given a job in the chorus of an operetta company.

Every Jewish musician knew that Glazunov would make the rounds to get him permission to live in Petersburg. Glazunov never asked the poor violinist to play for him, he felt firmly that everyone had the right to live wherever he pleased and art would not suffer as a result.

Glazunov didn't get on a soapbox or pretend to feel holy righteous wrath about this. He didn't demonstrate his high principles when it came to small and pathetic people. He saved this for more important people and more important incidents. In the long run, all things in life can be separated into the important and the unimportant. You must be principled when it comes to the important things and not when it comes to the unimportant. That may be the key to living.

Glazunov was sometimes childish, and sometimes he was very wise. He taught me a lot. I've thought about it a great deal and perhaps all of life goes toward finding out what is important in it and what isn't. It's tragic, but it's so.

I don't remember where I read an ancient prayer that goes, "Lord, grant me the strength to change what can be changed. Lord, grant me the strength to bear what can't be changed. And Lord, grant me the wisdom to know the difference."

Sometimes I love that prayer and sometimes I hate it. Life is ending for me and I have neither the strength nor the wisdom.

It's easy to ask for this and that, but you don't get it, even though you knock and bow as much as you can. You can't have it and that's that. You might get a medal or an order, or a pretty diploma. Recently I got a degree in America, in Evanston. I asked the dean what privileges or rights the diploma gave me. He gave me a witty answer: the diploma and twenty-five cents will buy me a ride on the bus.

I like honorary degrees, they're quite decorative and they look good on the wall. They're made of fine paper. I've noticed a curious thing: the smaller the country, the better the paper and the bigger the diploma. Sometimes, when I look at them all, I think that I've been given my allotment of wisdom. But that happens rarely. It happens when I finish a work, and then I feel that all the problems are solved and that I've answered all the questions—in music, naturally. But even that's a great deal. And now let people hear the music, and then they'll see what they have to do and how to separate the important from the unimportant.

But most often I think about the fact that none of this has helped—with or without the prayers. What I really want is a peaceful life, and a happy one. I remember old man Glazunov, that big, wise child. He spent his entire life thinking that he could separate the important from the unimportant. And he thought that the universe was created rationally. But at the end of his life, I think he began doubting it. Glazunov sincerely believed that the work to which he had devoted all his strength—Russian musical culture, the Conservatory—was doomed. That was his tragedy.

All values were confused, criteria obliterated. Glazunov ended up in Paris, where he was respected, but not, I think, much loved. He continued composing, not really knowing for whom and for what he was writing. I can't imagine anything more horrible than that. That's the end. But Glazunov was wrong. He had been given the wisdom and he had correctly separated the important from the unimportant, and his work turned out to be "fresh and strong."

When I was young, I enjoyed laughing at Glazunov—it was easy. At fifteen I was much more mature than Glazunov, a revered old man. The future belonged to me, not him. Everything that changed was

169

changing in my favor, not his. Music was changing, tastes were changing. All Glazunov could do was grumble offendedly.

But now I see how complicated it all really was. Now I suspect that there was eternal conflict in Glazunov's soul, a story typical of the Russian intelligentsia, of all of us. Glazunov was always tormented by the awareness of the injustice of his personal well-being. He was visited by many people who had been treated unfairly by life and he tried to help them; in turn even more came to him. But he couldn't help them all. He wasn't a miracle worker after all, none of us is, and that is a source of constant torment. Glazunov was also pestered by an enormous number of composers, who sent their work to him from all over Russia.

When they just send you music, it's not so bad, I know that from my own experience. You can glance through a score rather quickly, particularly if you see right off that it's hopeless. Of course, if you want to experience the music fully, you must sight-read it in the amount of time that it would take to perform, that's the only way to derive real satisfaction from reading it. But that's a method to be used only with good music. It's torture to "listen" with your eyes to bad music. You just glance through it. But what do you do when a talentless composer comes and plays his music from beginning to end?

The very worst is when the composer is neither a charlatan nor a scoundrel, but a diligent person with little talent. In those cases you listen and think, What can I possibly say to him? The music is written conscientiously, the composer did everything that he could, it's just that he can do very little. You might say he can do almost nothing. He was taught to write notes grammatically at the Conservatory, and that is all he can do. Yet such composers are often quite nice and often quite needy.

Well, what do you do with them? Tell the nice man that he's written a woeful work? Why, he won't even understand what's so wrong with his beloved child. After all, everything seems in order. It's pointless to try to explain, and if you do explain—a long, stubborn, and dull venture—and he does understand, then what? This person still can't do any better, you can't jump over your forehead, as they say. And so in those cases I tell my visitor, Well, it can be like that, why not?

I feel that Glazunov chose the right behavior for these situations. He praised such works moderately and quietly, looking at the music with thought. Sometimes he used his gold pencil on the second or fifteenth page to add a sharp or flat or make some other piddling change. "In general, this is all right, it's good; but here, perhaps, the shift from triple to quadruple time isn't very good. . . ." So that the composer wouldn't think that Glazunov didn't pay enough attention to the work.

Another form of musical torture through which Glazunov suffered was the obligatory attendance at recitals. This was almost a job for him. It is a torture that I understand very well, because I've been subjected to it more than once myself.

And this isn't as clear-cut as it might seem at first glance. The easiest response to all this is "poor fellow." If you look at it, Glazunov was a poor fellow, swamped with tons of sheet music, dragged to thousands of concerts. But there were times when I would have sworn that he liked it. I've caught myself liking it, strangely enough. A composer telephones and asks you to listen to his work and give your opinion. Well, you agree, cursing silently. And you think, why does this man exist, you think Sasha Cherny's thoughts about the pockmarked girl: "Why didn't she marry? Why—may a pole ram her between the shoulder blades—didn't she fall under a trolley on the way over here?"

And then the composer calls back and says that he can't make the appointment because he has to go to Tashkent or his uncle is sick. And you honestly feel sorry that the planned run-through won't take place.

After all, I like listening to music. That's not the same as simply liking music. Naturally, it's silly for me to say that I love music, that goes without saying. And I love all music—from Bach to Offenbach. But I love only good music, that is, what I consider good at any given time. But I like listening to any music, including bad music.

It's a professional disease, an addiction to notes. The brain finds sustenance in any combination of sounds. It works constantly, performing various composerly operations.

When I listen to orchestral music, I transcribe it for piano in my mind. I listen, while my fingers try it out to see if it fits the hand. And when I listen to piano music, mentally I run it through in an orchestral version. It's a disease, but a pleasant one. It's like scratching when you itch.

I'm spending time discussing the Russian composer-eccentrics deliberately. "The fairy tale is a lie, but it does contain a clue," as they sing in Rimsky-Korsakov's *Golden Cockerel*. It might seem that these eccentrics lived the wrong way, not like everyone else, and spent all their time on all the wrong things instead of composing. But they preferred to take this strange path. They may have lost, but art won. It became cleaner, purer, more moral—not in the hypocrite's sense of moral. A sensitive person will understand what I mean. You can be a syphilitic and still be a moral person. You can be an alcoholic. A clean bill of health from a hospital doesn't prove that a healthy man stands before us.

Many of today's composers can show a bill of health proving that they don't have VD, but they are rotten from within. Their souls stink. That's why I fight for the "fresh and strong" that Rimsky-Korsakov wrote about. I miss that feeling very much. If I were to bring up the "composer's morality" at a composers' meeting, I would be laughed at. They've forgotten what it is.

For instance, I'm astounded at how widespread plagiarism has become in our music. Where did this infection, this vileness, come from? I'm not talking about imitation or unconscious borrowings. One of my colleagues says that there is no music that consists of just itself, that is, music is not distilled water and it can't be stylistically crystal clear and pure. Every piece of music resembles other music in some way.

But I'm not talking about that, I'm talking about the most ruthless, blatant copying, and we have more than enough scandals with that. One woman, a member of the Composers' Union, simply took symphonies by American composers and copied them down, from first note to last, without any changes. And when she was caught—quite accidentally—she insisted that she was playing a joke. Some joke. I think that they had even planned on publishing these works, so appropriate for our socialistic art. In any case, the lady had been paid for them. And this nonentity was teaching composition at the Moscow Conservatory. I can imagine what she could have taught her students. It might have been a good idea: "Musical Plagiarism, Professor So-and-so, lab work Mondays and Thursdays."

I know people will say that's not a typical case. But I think it is. There was nothing accidental about this shameless theft except the fact that she was caught. The accident was that one erudite composer among our colleagues recognized William Schuman's work when our brazen lady showed her "composition" at the Composers' Union. He even happened to have the music at home. Now, that's not typical at all. An accident, you might say. Because most of our composers aren't willing to clutter their minds; at first it wasn't allowed and then when it was, it seemed like too much trouble. People were too lazy. It's easier to dismiss music as the rotten product of the decadent West.

I'm talking about contemporary Western music now. But unfortunately, their knowledge of classical Western music is very sketchy too. I keep running into people who have heard of Mahler and Bruckner but who have never actually looked at a score, not once. And they know only a few popular melodies from Wagner. Not only Wagner; they have only a vague idea of Schumann and Brahms too (except for the symphonies).

Naturally, you can't really quiz a colleague in private conversation, it's impolite and you might hurt his feelings. But I was chairman of the State Examination Commission in the Composition Division of the Moscow Conservatory. And as you know, student composers from the Conservatory become members of the Composers' Union upon graduation. They all have an impressive baggage of work—symphonies, operas—but they don't know music. Not only do they not know Western music, they don't know their own native music. And that is the result of another process. They vilified and hid Western music, lowered grades on exams for too much familiarity with it, and they shoved Russian music down the students' throats and said stupid things about it, like Russian music developing independently, on its own, related to nothing. You know, like "Russia is the homeland of elephants."*

As a result, the history of Russian music as taught by our institutions of higher learning has taken on an exceptionally ridiculous aspect, and the students' aversion to it is understandable, but not excusable. After all, pamphlets and lectures are one thing, but the real

*A reference to a nationalistic campaign, unfurled soon after the war, to fight "kowtowing before foreigners." Like all totalitarian campaigns, it took on grotesque dimensions. Children were taught in school that all important inventions had been made in Russia first; that Russian writers, composers, and artists had never borrowed anything from the West; French bread was renamed "city" bread. Inevitably, all these official claims gave rise to many jokes, like the one Shostakovich quotes.

music is another. The usual dichotomy between word and deed. And it's a shame that the students don't understand the dichotomy, and that they feel that being illiterate is a form of opposition. I've spoken with mature people who were proud of not knowing or liking Glinka.

This general musical illiteracy is naturally one of the factors that have helped plagiarism flourish, but obviously it's not the only one. There are so many reasons. Greed, for one, but also the certainty that no one will catch you. They're not afraid of being caught and shamed.

Entire tragedies unfold in whispers, lives are ruined. I had a friend who once confessed while drunk that he earned his living ghost-writing songs for a very popular composer. He told me which one.

"Our people love those songs, don't they?" he said with a wry smile. "They're all about heroic deeds, courage, nobility, and other marvelous things." He told me how they did it—a lovely picture straight out of Dostoevsky. The two "co-composers" met in a toilet. One handed over the money, the other the sheet music for the latest song about nobility. Then the conspirators flushed, for authenticity.

This was the lofty and poetic setting for the birth of another valuable work that was to elevate the moral level of the people.

I said to my friend, "I'll throw the bastard out of the union." (I was secretary of the Composers' Union of the R.S.F.S.R. then.) He sobered up and replied, "Just try. I'll say that you're slandering him."

"Why?" I asked. "You just told me about him yourself." And he replied, "I'll deny it, I'll say you're lying. I'll lose income because of you. He pays me well, and on time. I have to dun the others. This one lets me live, and thanks to him for that. I'll turn you into a slanderer—just try saying anything. You'll be a slanderer, everyone will call you a liar."

And I said nothing, I let it go. Why? I still don't know for sure. I shouldn't have, I know. I never seem to follow up on anything. I suppose I was afraid of being branded a liar. I hate hearing things like that about myself. I want to be an honest man in all respects.

Citizens, a new era has begun in musical history, new and unheard of. Now we are no longer dealing with simple plagiarism. In plagiarism the thief fears being caught. But now the person who knows the truth is the one who lives in fear. Because he faces a smoothly running operation, a large machine at work, and he, the fool, wants to stick his hand in it. Obviously, it will be chopped off.

I backed off, but I should have seen it through. I should have got rid of him. But then my friend would have lost his job. Of course, his job was perverse and he should have done something more worthwhile. But I felt sorry for him.

Perhaps I just washed my hands of it. There's no point in getting involved with plagiarists and scoundrels when they're in power. The whole world can shout that a man is a scoundrel and a bastard, and he'll just go on living and thriving. And not twitch a hair on his mustache, if he has one.

Take the astonishing rise of Mukhtar Ashrafi, famous composer, and not only in his native Uzbekistan. He is the recipient of two Stalin Prizes, is a People's Artist of the U.S.S.R., and a professor. He even has the Order of Lenin. The reason I know his title and awards so well is that I handled his case. He turned out to be a shameless plagiarist and thief. I was chairman of the commission that smoked him out. We dug around in shit, "analyzing" his music, hearing depositions from witnesses. We had Ashrafi up against the wall. It was exhausting work—and in vain, as it turned out. At first we seemed to have got some results. He was expelled from the Composers' Union. But recently I was thumbing through a magazine, I don't remember which, and I saw a familiar name. Ashrafi was giving an interview. He was in power again, sharing his creative plans, which were quite extensive. How can you keep from washing your hands of it, from saying to hell with it?

I think the greatest danger for a composer is a loss of faith. Music, and art in general, cannot be cynical. Music can be bitter and despairing, but not cynical. And in this country, they like to confuse cynicism with despair. If music is tragic, they say it's cynical. I've been accused of cynicism more than once, and incidentally, not only by government bureaucrats. The Igors and Borises of our country's musicologists added their two cents' worth too. But despair and cynicism are different, just as ennui and cynicism are different. When a man is in despair, it means that he still believes in something.

It's the smug little music that is often cynical. Quiet and calm it is, for the composer doesn't give a damn about anything. It's just drivel and not art. And it's all around us. It saddens me to talk about it, because cynicism is not characteristic of Russian music. We have never had the tradition. I don't want to be full of hot air and bore everyone with calls to good citizenship; I want to discover the causes of cynicism. In looking for the causes of many interesting phenomena, one must turn, I feel, to the Revolution, because the Revolution brought a turnabout in the consciousness of a significant number of people, a radical turnabout. I'm speaking now of the so-called cultural stratum.

The living conditions of this stratum changed sharply and the unexpected change caught many smack between the eyes. People were unprepared. They were professionally involved in literature and art. It was their work, their market, and suddenly everything in the market changed.

I'll never forget one incident that Zoshchenko told me about. It had made a strong impression on Zoshchenko and he often referred to it. He used to know a poet in Petersburg by the name of Tinyakov, a fair, even talented, poet. Tinyakov wrote rather recherché poetry about betrayals, roses, and tears. He was a handsome man, a dandy.

Zoshchenko met him again after the Revolution and Tinyakov gave him a copy of his latest book. There was nothing about love, flowers, and other lofty objects. They were talented poems, Zoshchenko felt they were works of genius, and he was a severe critic—Anna Akhmatova gave him her prose to read with trepidation. Tinyakov's new poems dealt with the poet's hunger—that was the central theme. The poet announced firmly that "I will perform any vile act for food."

It was a direct, honest statement, which didn't remain only as words. Everyone knows that a poet's words often diverge from his deeds. Tinyakov became one of the rare exceptions. The poet, who was not yet old and still handsome then, began begging. He stood on a heavily traveled corner in Leningrad, with a sign that said "Poet" around his neck and a hat on his head. He didn't ask, he demanded, and the frightened passers-by gave him money. Tinyakov earned a lot that way. He bragged to Zoshchenko that he was making much more than he had before, because people liked giving money to poets. After a hard day's work, Tinyakov headed for an expensive restaurant, where he ate and drank and greeted the dawn, whereupon he returned to his post.

Tinyakov became a happy man, he no longer had to pretend. He said what he thought and did what he said. He had become a predator and he wasn't ashamed.

Tinyakov is an extreme example, but not an exceptional one. Many thought as he did; it's just that other cultural figures didn't say it out loud. And their behavior didn't look as outrageous. Tinyakov promised in his poems to "lick his enemy's heels" for some food. Many cultural figures could have repeated Tinyakov's proud cry, but they preferred to keep silent and licked heels in silence.

The psychology of my contemporary *intelligent* had changed utterly. Fate made him fight for his existence, and he fought for it with all the fury of a former *intelligent*. He no longer cared who was to be glorified and who vilified. These trifles no longer mattered. The important thing was to eat, to tear off as sweet a hunk of life as possible while you're still alive. Calling this cynical is not enough—this is the psychology of a criminal. I was surrounded by many Tinyakovs; some were talented, others weren't. But they worked together. They were working to make our era cynical and they succeeded.

I REALLY love Chekhov, he's one of my favorite writers. I read and reread not only his stories and plays, but his notes and letters. Of course, I'm no literary historian and I can't give a proper assessment of the work of the great Russian writer, who I feel has not been thoroughly studied and certainly not always correctly understood. But if I were suddenly expected to write a dissertation on an author, I would choose Chekhov, that's how close an affinity I feel for him. Reading him, I sometimes recognize myself; I feel that anyone in Chekhov's place would react exactly as he did in confronting life.

Chekhov's entire life is a model of purity and modesty—and not a modesty for show, but an inner modesty. That's probably why I'm not a fan of certain memorial editions that can only be described as a spoonful of pitch in a barrel of honey. In particular, I'm quite sorry that the correspondence between Anton Pavlovich and his wife was ever published; it's so intimate that most of it should not be seen in print. I'm saying this with respect for the strictness with which the writer approached his work. He did not publish his works until he brought them to the level that he considered at least decent.

On the other hand, when you read Chekhov's letters you gain a better understanding of his fiction; therefore I am ambivalent on the question. Sometimes I feel that Chekhov would not have liked to see his letters in print, but at other times I think that he would not have been upset by it. Perhaps I'm prejudiced because I feel so possessive of what Chekhov has written, including his letters.

It was Chekhov who said that you must write simply, write about how Pyotr Semyonovich married Maria Ivanovna; and he added, "That's all." Chekhov also said that Russia is a land of greedy and lazy people who eat and drink prodigious amounts and like to sleep during the day and snore while they sleep. People marry in Russia to keep order in the house, and take mistresses for social prestige. Russians have the mentality of a dog—when they're beaten, they whimper softly and hide in the corner, and when they're scratched behind the ear, they roll over.

Chekhov didn't like talks on lofty topics, they nauseated him. A friend came to him once and said, "Anton Pavlovich, what can I do? Reflection is destroying me!" Chekhov replied, "Drink less vodka." I remembered his answer and used it often. When Zoshchenko and I used to meet at Zamyatin's house, he kept telling me about his reflections, giving a detailed account of why he was depressed and confiding his complicated plans for overcoming his reflectiveness. And I would say, "Just drink less vodka."

Zoshchenko also kept pestering me, wanting to rid me of my melancholy, saying, "Why are you so glum? Let me explain it to you, and you'll immediately feel better." To which I replied rudely, "Why don't we play some poker instead?"

I was a mentally healthy person, quite skeptical actually, with a healthy skepticism, but Zoshchenko kept on with his refrain: "Melancholy is characteristic of youth. Don't be melancholy." He kept exhorting me to look inward to chase away my melancholy, and so on. He didn't take offense when I cut him short, and he wasn't offended by my persistent mental health.

Zoshchenko reminded me of Chekhov except for one thing. Even though he had been so many things—a shoemaker and a policeman (I wrote "March of the Soviet Police" in his honor)—he missed medicine. But Chekhov was a doctor and that's why he despised medicine in all forms. He used to say, "What does it mean to heal according to the laws of science? We have the laws, but not the science." But Zoshchenko, on the other hand, had great respect for medical science. A mistake. Doctors are sure that all diseases come from colds. Chekhov said that too.

I'm delighted that Chekhov was a man free from hypocrisy. For instance, he wrote without embarrassment that when it came to girls, he was a pro. And in another letter, he describes how he and a professor from Kharkov decided to get drunk. They drank and drank and then gave up. Nothing happened and they awoke in the morning fit as fiddles. Chekhov could drink an entire bottle of champagne and then some cognac and not get drunk.

I read Chekhov greedily, because I know that I'm about to find some important thoughts on the beginning and the end. I remember that once I accidentally came across Chekhov's thoughts on how the Russian man only lives a real life until he's thirty. We rush when we're young, we think that everything is ahead, we hurry, pouncing on everything. We fill our soul with whatever comes our way. But after thirty our soul is filled with gray rubbish. That's amazingly true.

And Chekhov had sensible thoughts about the end. He thought that immortality, life after death in any form, was all nonsense, because it was superstition. He said we had to think clearly and daringly. Chekhov wasn't afraid of death. "As I was alone in life, so will I lie alone in the grave."

Now, Gogol died from a fear of death. I first heard about that from Zoshchenko. I checked it later, and it really was so. Gogol did not resist death, in fact he did everything he could to hasten it. The people around him noticed it and many reminiscences of Gogol mention it.

Fear of death may be the most intense emotion of all. I sometimes think that there is no deeper feeling. The irony lies in the fact that under the influence of that fear people create poetry, prose, and music; that is, they try to strengthen their ties with the living and increase their influence on them.

These unpleasant thoughts did not bypass me. I tried to convince myself that I shouldn't fear death. In that sense, I followed Zoshchenko's ideas, I tried to find help in them, but they seemed rather naïve to me. How can you not fear death? Death is not considered an appropriate theme for Soviet art and writing about death is tantamount to wiping your nose on your sleeve in company. That's where titles like *An Optimistic Tragedy* come from. Even though that's nonsense—a tragedy is a tragedy and optimism has nothing to do with it.

But I always thought that I was not alone in my thinking about death and that other people were concerned with it too, despite the fact that they live in a socialist society in which even tragedies receive the epithet "optimistic." I wrote a number of works reflecting my understanding of the question, and as it seems to me, they're not particularly optimistic works. The most important of them, I feel, is the Fourteenth Symphony; I have special feelings for it.

I think that work on these compositions had a positive effect, and I fear death less now; or rather, I'm used to the idea of an inevitable end and treat it as such. After all, it's the law of nature and no one has ever eluded it. I'm all for a rational approach toward death. We should think more about it and accustom ourselves to the thought of death. We can't allow the fear of death to creep up on us unexpectedly. We have to make the fear familiar, and one way is to write about it.

I don't feel that writing and thinking about death are symptomatic of illness and I don't think that writing about death is characteristic only of old men. I think that if people began thinking about death sooner they'd make fewer foolish mistakes. Somehow it's considered improper for young people to write about death. Why? When you ponder and write about death, you make some gains. First, you have time to think through things that are related to death and you lose the panicky fear. And second, you try to make fewer mistakes. That's why I'm not very concerned about what they'll say about the Fourteenth, even though I heard more attacks on the Fourteenth than on any of my other symphonies.

People might say, how can that be? What about *Lady Macbeth?* And the Eighth Symphony? And so many other works? I don't think I have any compositions that weren't criticized, but that was a different sort of criticism. Here the criticism came from people who claimed to be my friends. That's another matter entirely, that kind of criticism hurts.

They read this idea in the Fourteenth Symphony: "Death is all-powerful." They wanted the finale to be comforting, to say that death is only the beginning. But it's not a beginning, it's the real end, there will be nothing afterward, nothing.

I feel that you must look truth right in the eyes. Often composers haven't had the courage for that, even the greatest ones, like Tchaikovsky or Verdi. Just think of *The Queen of Spades*. Gherman dies and then comes music which was described by the old cynic Asafiev as "the image of a loving Liza hovering over the corpse." What is that? The corpse is just that, and Liza has nothing to do with it. It doesn't matter to the corpse whose image hovers over it.

Tchaikovsky gave in to the seduction of solace—you know, the best of everything in this best of all possible worlds. Something will hover over your corpse too. Liza's image or some banners. This was a cowardly act on Tchaikovsky's part.

And Verdi did exactly the same thing in *Otello*. Richard Strauss entitled one of his tone poems *Death and Transfiguration*. Even Mussorgsky, certainly a just and courageous man, was afraid to look truth in the face. After Boris's death in *Boris Godunov*, the music moves to such a major key that you can't be any more major.

To deny death and its power is useless. Deny it or not, you'll die anyway. But understanding that is not tantamount to bowing to death. I don't make a cult of death, I don't praise it. Mussorgsky didn't sing the praises of death either. Death in his song cycles looks horrible, and most important, it comes before it should.

It's stupid to protest death as such, but you can and must protest violent death. It's bad when people die before their time from disease or poverty, but it's worse when a man is killed by another man. I thought about all this when I orchestrated *Songs and Dances of Death,* and these thoughts also found reflection in the Fourteenth Symphony. I don't protest against death in it, I protest against those butchers who execute people.

That's why I chose Apollinaire's "The Zaporozhian Cossacks' Answer to the Turkish Sultan" for my Fourteenth. Everyone immediately thinks of Repin's famous painting* and smiles happily. But my music

*This painting by Ilya Efimovich Repin (1844–1930), which depicts a picturesque group of Zaporozhian Cossacks writing an insulting letter to Sultan Mahmud IV, is an "icon" of contemporary Russian mass culture. It is interesting to observe how Apollinaire (a French poet of Polish extraction) took his departure point from Repin's painting (as researchers suppose) and created his poem, which in turn inspired Shostakovich (a Russian composer of Polish extraction).

In 1949, under pressure from Stalin, Shostakovich came to
New York to attend the Cultural and Scientific Conference
for World Peace. He had very unpleasant memories of the
trip, especially the aggressiveness of American reporters.
From the left: the political head of the Soviet delegation, the
writer Alexander Fadeyev; Norman Mailer; Shostakovich;
Arthur Miller; Dr. William Olaf Stapledon of England.
(Wide World.)

December 15, 1949: Shostakovich and his wife Nina in a box at the Leningrad Philharmonic at the first performance of his oratorio *Song of the Forests*. Twenty-three years earlier, the triumphant première of the nineteen-year-old composer's First Symphony had taken place here. The conductor's wife, Mme. Mravinsky, is at the right.

With his mother, Sofiya Vasilyevna, in 1951. She died four years later, saying: "I have discharged my not-so-easy duties as a mother."

In the dressing room of his son, Maxim, a conductor, after a concert. Maxim remembered his father's words: "An artist on stage is a soldier in combat. No matter how hard it is, you can't retreat." Moscow, 1965.

Paul Robeson with Jewish
actor Solomon Mikhoels
in Moscow. Mikhoels,
killed on Stalin's orders in
1948, was an active defender
of Shostakovich's music.

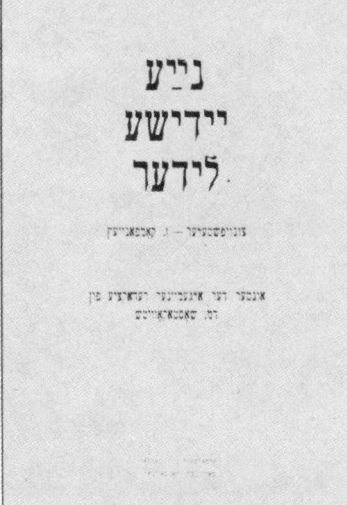

נייע
ייִדישע
לידער

זונויפֿגעשטעלט — ז. קאמפּאַניעץ

אונטער דער אינעווירער רעדאַקציע פֿון
ד. שאָסטאקאָוויטש

Title page of a collection of songs in
Yiddish, published in Moscow in 1970,
and edited and introduced by Shostakovich.
The introduction reflected
his delight in Jewish folk music.

Shostakovich
accompany-
ing a per-
formance
of his vocal
cycle *From
Jewish Folk
Poetry.*
Leningrad,
1956.

Shostakovich at work: he did not need any special conditions to compose music. Even noise did not distract him.

With his third wife, Irina. (His second marriage was unhappy and short-lived.)

Listening to folk musicians in the Kirghiz Republic in 1963. To the left of Shostakovich is the composer Vano Muradeli, whose claim to fame in Russian music is that in 1948 he was branded with Shostakovich as a formalist.

In 1959, the first visit to Moscow of the New York Philharmonic, under Leonard Bernstein. Shostakovich preferred Bernstein to all other American conductors. *(Wide World.)*

Aaron Copland presented a Certificate of Honorary Membership from the American Academy and Institute of Arts and Letters of the United States to Shostakovich at Tchaikovsky Hall in Moscow in 1960. Shostakovich treated such diplomas ironically but hung them neatly on his walls.

With Solomon Volkov.
Leningrad, 1965.

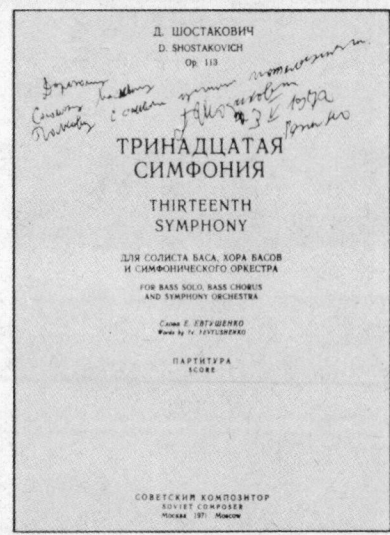

After work on this book had begun,
Shostakovich gave Volkov the score of his
Thirteenth Symphony ("Babi Yar") with the
inscription: "To dear Solomon Moiseyevich
Volkov with my very best wishes. D.
Shostakovich. 3 V 1972. Repino."

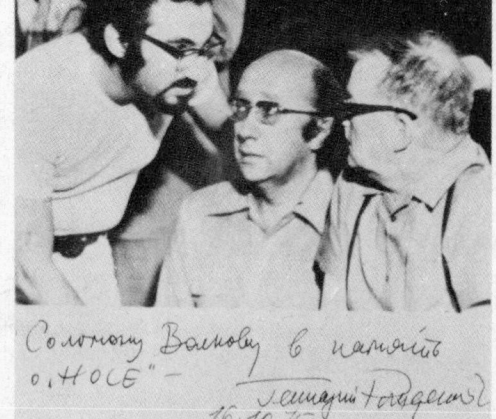

At a rehearsal of the opera *The
Nose,* revived in the Soviet Union
after a forty-four-year hiatus: an
exchange of opinions. From the
right: Shostakovich, conductor
of the production Gennady
Rozhdestvensky, Solomon
Volkov. The inscription reads:
"To Solomon Volkov as a
memento of *The Nose*—Gennady
Rozhdestvensky. 16 10 75."

At a performance of
his last quartet.
Leningrad, 1974.

At his dacha near Moscow
with his grandson.

Shostakovich
reading one
of his
many official
speeches. On
the left, then
Minister of
Culture of the
Soviet Union
Ekaterina
Furtseva.

Funeral of Shostakovich, August 14, 1975, at Novodevichy Cemetery in
Moscow. Aram Khachaturian is kissing the deceased's hand; next to him
is his wife, Nina Khachaturian. On the far left is Shostakovich's widow,
Irina; on the right, his son, Maxim, embracing his sister, Galya, and his
son. Solomon Volkov is seen between them.

bears little resemblance to Repin's painting. If I had Apollinaire's talent, I would address Stalin with a poem like that. I did it with music. Stalin is gone, but there are more than enough tyrants around. Another poem by Apollinaire also became part of the Fourteenth—"In the Santé Prison." I was thinking about prison cells, horrible holes, where people are buried alive, waiting for someone to come for them, listening to every sound. That's terrifying, you can go mad with fear. Many people couldn't stand the pressure and lost their minds. I know about that.

Awaiting execution is a theme that has tormented me all my life. Many pages of my music are devoted to it. Sometimes I wanted to explain that fact to the performers, I thought that they would have a greater understanding of the work's meaning. But then I thought better of it. You can't explain anything to a bad performer and a talented person should sense it himself. Yet in recent years I've become convinced that the word is more effective than music. Unfortunately, it's so. When I combine music with words, it becomes harder to misinterpret my intent.

I discovered to my astonishment that the man who considers himself its greatest interpreter does not understand my music.* He says that I wanted to write exultant finales for my Fifth and Seventh Symphonies but I couldn't manage it. It never occurred to this man that I never thought about any exultant finales, for what exultation could there be? I think that it is clear to everyone what happens in the Fifth. The rejoicing is forced, created under threat, as in *Boris Godunov*. It's as if someone were beating you with a stick and saying, "Your business is rejoicing, your business is rejoicing," and you rise, shaky, and go marching off, muttering, "Our business is rejoicing, our business is rejoicing."

What kind of apotheosis is that? You have to be a complete oaf not to hear that. Fadeyev† heard it, and he wrote in his diary, for his personal use, that the finale of the Fifth is irreparable tragedy. He must have felt it with his Russian alcoholic soul.

*Yevgeny Mravinsky.

†Alexander Alexandrovich Fadeyev (1901–1956), an author set up by Stalin as head of the Writers' Union. He signed many sanctions for the arrest of writers (as did the heads of the other "creative" unions to their members). After a shift in internal Soviet politics, he committed suicide.

People who came to the premiere of the Fifth in the best of moods wept. And it's ridiculous to speak of a triumphal finale in the Seventh. There's even less basis for that, but nevertheless, the interpretation does appear.

Words are some protection against absolute idiocy, any fool will understand when there are words. There's no total guarantee, but a text does make the music more accessible. The premiere of the Seventh is proof of that. I began writing it having been deeply moved by the Psalms of David; the symphony deals with more than that, but the Psalms were the impetus. I began writing. David has some marvelous words on blood, that God takes revenge for blood, He doesn't forget the cries of victims, and so on. When I think of the Psalms, I become agitated.

And if the Psalms were read before every performance of the Seventh, there might be fewer stupid things written about it. That's not a pleasant thought, but it's probably true. Listeners don't understand notes completely, but words make it easier.

This was confirmed at the final rehearsal of the Fourteenth. Even the fool Pavel Ivanovich Apostolov* understood what the symphony was about. During the war, Comrade Apostolov commanded a division, and after the war he commanded us, the composers. Everyone knew that you couldn't get through to that blockhead with anything, but Apollinaire was stronger. And Comrade Apostolov, right there at the rehearsal, dropped dead. I feel very guilty, I had no intention of killing him off, even though he was certainly not a harmless man. He rode in on a white horse and did away with all music.

It was after Apostolov's death that I was stunned by two facts. Fact number one: Comrade Apostolov (what a name!) had in his youth taken vocal music courses named after Stravinsky. Poor Stravinsky. It's like Ilf's joke: Ivanov decided to visit the king, who, hearing about it, abdicated. Fact number two: Comrade Apostolov was also a composer, the author of ten funeral epitaph pieces, including "Stars on the Obelisks," "A Minute of Silence," and "Heroes Are Immortal." And there was his life.

Death is simple, after all. It's as Zemlyanika says in Gogol: If a person is to die, he'll die anyway, and if he's going to survive, he'll

*Pavel Ivanovich Apostolov (1905–July 19, 1969), colonel, leader of the Party organization of the Moscow Composers' Union.

survive anyway. When you realize that, you see many things more simply and answer many questions more simply.

Now, I'm often asked why I do this and that and say this and that, or why I sign such-and-such articles. I answer different people differently, because different people deserve different answers. For instance, Yevtushenko once asked me a question of that kind, and I remembered it. I consider Yevtushenko a talented man. We did quite a lot of work together and perhaps we'll work together once again. I wrote my Thirteenth Symphony to his poetry, and another work, the symphonic poem *The Execution of Stepan Razin*. At one time Yevtushenko's poetry excited me more than it does now. But that's not the point. Yevtushenko is a worker, and I think he's worked hard. He had the right to ask me the question. And I answered as best I could.

Yevtushenko did a great deal for the people, for the reading public. His books had huge printings, all the Soviet copies must add up to millions, maybe more. Many of his very important poems were printed in the newspapers: for example, "Stalin's Heirs" in *Pravda,* "Babi Yar" in *Literaturnaya gazeta,* and they publish in the millions. I feel Yevtushenko's poems such as those mentioned are honest and truthful. It would do anyone good to read them, and I must point out this important circumstance. These important, truthful poems were available to almost everyone in the country. You could buy a book or a newspaper with Yevtushenko's poetry, or you could go to the library or any reading room and request the newspaper or magazine with a poem. It's important that you could do this peacefully, legally, without looking around, without fear.

People aren't used to reading poetry. They listen to the radio, read the papers, but not poetry, not often. Here you had poetry in the paper, and naturally you'll read it, especially if the poems are truthful. Such things have a powerful effect on the people. It's important that the work can be reread, savored, and thought over, and that it can be done in a quiet, normal atmosphere, and that you don't hear it over the radio, you read it with your own eyes.

You can't even hear well on the radio and the time might not be convenient, too early in the morning or too late at night.* You can't

---

*A reference to Western radio broadcasts in Russian, which—according to some sources—are regularly heard by a quarter of the urban population of the Soviet Union. These broadcasts are the main source of news for the intelligentsia of Moscow and Leningrad. Early morning or late night are best for good reception; there is less interference then.

think well then. You can't rush through an encounter with a work of art, it won't root itself in your soul then or have a real effect. Otherwise why was the work created? To tickle the artist's ego? Satisfy his own pride? To make him a bright figure on a dark background?

No, that I don't understand; if a work isn't created for your people, then for whom? As they say, love us when we're dirty, anyone will love us when we're clean—and even that is a moot point. But when I think about the people, all of them . . . But why all of them? You don't have to, just picture the lives of two or three real people, just two or three. Naturally, not politicians or artists but true workers, hardworking, honest people. There are hundreds of occupations that people never think about, a guard, for instance, or a train conductor, or a roofer.

So take a person like that. Do you think his biography will be so pure and clean? I doubt it. And does this person deserve scorn because of it? I doubt that too. He is the potential reader, listener, and viewer of every art form, great and not so great. These people should neither be turned into icons nor despised.

One man cannot teach or change all the other people in the world, no one has succeeded at that, even Jesus Christ couldn't say that He did. No one's made that world record, especially not in our troubled and rather nervous times. Experiments in saving all mankind at one fell swoop seem awfully dubious now.

But in my not so very long life I've come across sick people who were convinced that they were called to set mankind on the right path, and if not mankind in its entirety, at least, then, their own countrymen. I don't know, maybe I was lucky, because I personally saw two saviors of the world. Two such personages. These were, as they say, patented saviors; I also saw some five candidates for the job. Maybe four. I'm estimating now, and I can't remember exactly. I'll make a more accurate count another time.

All right, let's leave the candidates aside. The patented saviors had a lot in common. You couldn't contradict either and both were quick to vilify you in rather uncontrolled language if they were out of sorts. And most important, both had total contempt for the very people they were planning to save.

It's an astounding trait, this contempt. How can it be? Why, O great gardeners, wise teachers of all sciences, leaders and luminaries? All right, so you despise the ordinary people who have nothing special about them, who are dirty rather than clean. But then why declare yourselves prophets and saviors? That's very surprising.

Oh, yes, I forgot another trait common to these above-mentioned but not named leaders, their false religiosity. I know many will be surprised by that. All right, they'll say, one of the saviors, it goes without saying, called himself a religious man on every street corner and rebuked everyone else for lacking faith.* But what about the other one? The other one was an atheist, wasn't he?

I hope that it's clear that the other one is Stalin. And it's true he was considered a Marxist, a Communist, and so forth, and was the head of an atheistic state and put the squeeze on servitors of the cults.

But these are all externals. Who could seriously maintain now that Stalin had some idea of a general order of things? Or that he had some ideology? Stalin never had any ideology or convictions or ideas or principles. Stalin always held whatever opinions made it easier for him to tyrannize others, to keep them in fear and guilt. Today the teacher and leader may say one thing, tomorrow something else. He never cared what he said, as long as he held on to his power.

The most striking example is Stalin's relationship with Hitler. Stalin didn't care what Hitler's ideology was. He made friends with Hitler as soon as he decided that Hitler could help him keep and even expand his holdings. Tyrants and executioners have no ideology, they only have a fanatical lust for power. Yet it's that fanaticism that confuses people, for some reason. Stalin saw the church as a political enemy, a powerful rival, and that's the only reason he tried to do away with it. Of course, it would be hard to call Stalin a religious man, simply because he didn't believe in anything or anyone. But aren't there quite a few people just like him—believing in nothing, cruel, power-mad—who proclaim themselves to be deeply religious?

And Stalin could definitely be called superstitious. There are different kinds of superstitions, I know people who are afraid of black cats and the number thirteen, others fear Mondays, and so on. But there are superstitions that are connected to religion and I know people who have those too. Such a person thinks that he is a believer when what

*A reference to the writer Aleksandr Isayevich Solzhenitsyn (b. 1918).

he really is is superstitious. I personally don't care. It's rather funny, though sometimes quite sad.

For instance, I was saddened by Yudina. She was a marvelous musician, but we never became close friends, it wasn't possible. Yudina was a decent person, a kind one, but her kindness was hysterical, she was a religious hysteric. It's embarrassing to talk about, but it's true. Yudina dropped to her knees or kissed hands at the least provocation. We studied together with Nikolayev and sometimes it was very embarrassing. Nikolayev would make a remark and she would fall to her knees. I didn't like her clothes either, those monastic robes. She was a pianist, not a nun. Why walk around in a habit? It seemed immodest to me.

Yudina was always telling me, "You're far from God, you must be closer to God." Nevertheless, she behaved rather strangely. Take this story, for instance. Von Karajan came to Moscow, it was a siege, tickets were impossible to obtain. Police, mounted and on foot, surrounded the entrance. Yudina sat down in front of the theater and spread out her skirts. Naturally, a policeman came over to her. "You're disturbing the peace, citizeness, what's the problem?" And Yudina said, "I'm not getting up until I get into the concert."

Can a religious person behave that way? I was told that Yudina began reciting Pasternak's poetry from the stage at a concert in Leningrad. Of course, there was a scandal. And the upshot was that she was banned from performing in Leningrad. Now, why all the grandstanding? Was she a professional reader? No, she was an extraordinary pianist, and she should have gone on playing the pianoforte. Bringing happiness and solace to people.

I once ran into her in a cemetery, bowing to the ground. She said to me, "You're far from God, you must be closer to God." I waved her off and went on. Is that true faith? It's just superstition with a tangential connection to religion.

Stalin's superstition also touched on religion. This is apparent from many facts that are known to me and I'll tell a few. I know, for example, that Stalin had a predilection for people from the clergy. I think the reason is clear. Our teacher and leader had been a seminarian, and I think it's worth mentioning. He entered a religious school as a child, graduated, and went on to study in a Russian Orthodox seminary. Of course, Stalin's *Brief Biography** states that what they studied primarily in this seminary was Marxism. But I'll permit myself to doubt it. It was probably a seminary like any other.

And therefore, in his youth, when impressions are strongest, Stalin had all the religious stuff beaten into his head by his ignorant teachers. And the future teacher and leader of these teachers was afraid of them and respected them, as a student should, and Stalin carried this fear and respect for the clergy throughout his life.

Stalin deeply admired Alexander Konstantinovich Voronsky, a marvelous literary critic, a man who truly appreciated art and who created the best magazine of the twenties, *Krasnaya Nov'*. The most interesting works of literature that appeared were published in *Krasnaya Nov'*. It was the *Novy Mir* of those times, but probably more vivid and exciting. Zoshchenko was published in *Krasnaya Nov'*, for example.

Voronsky came from the clergy, his father was a priest. Stalin always took him along when he went to the theater, and particularly to the opera. He would call Voronsky and say, "Let's go to *Boris Godunov.*" Stalin tried to listen to what Voronsky had to say.

Voronsky was a Trotskyite, but that didn't bother Stalin. The seminarian respected the priest's son. But Voronsky didn't want to submit to Stalin, so Stalin had him exiled to Lipetsk, and then called him back to Moscow—an unheard-of occurrence.

"Well, now do you see that you can build socialism in one country? You see that I've built socialism in Russia?" Stalin said to Voronsky. All he had to do was nod his head and he would have been Stalin's adviser once more, but Voronsky replied thus: "Yes, I see that you've built socialism for yourself in the Kremlin." Stalin ordered, "Take him back."

Stalin tried a few more times to save Voronsky, but nothing worked. Voronsky was very ill in a prison hospital. Stalin came to see him, to convince him to repent before death. "Go to hell, priest," Voronsky rasped with his last few ounces of strength. Voronsky meant that he

---

**A Brief Biography of I. V. Stalin* was one of the two bedside books of every Soviet citizen in the postwar period (the other was *A Brief Course in Party History*). It is known that Stalin wrote such phrases into his own biography as "with a genius for perspicacity Comrade Stalin guessed the enemy's plans and thwarted them" and "the guiding power of the Party and the state was Comrade Stalin." These two books were quoted and referred to at every appropriate and inappropriate occasion.

refused to confess before Stalin, and he died in prison, unbroken. A man like that can probably be respected.

But sometimes I think that perhaps it would have been better if Voronsky had agreed with Stalin then about socialism. After all, the point was academic, Stalin just needed him to agree with him. It didn't change socialism in Russia in any way. And what if the leader and teacher had gone on listening to Voronsky's opinions, particularly in music? The life of many of us would have been quite different.

On the other hand, nothing can be predicted with any confidence in these matters. The leader and teacher had the psychology of an Oriental satrap: If I want to, I'll punish, if I don't, I'll show mercy—with an extra added dollop of madness.

As for music, he naturally didn't understand a damn thing about it, but did respect euphony, again as a result of his seminary training. Stalin was irritated by "muddle instead of music," and he was skeptical toward noneuphonious music like mine. And of course, the leader and teacher was a great lover of ensembles, for example, the Red Army Chorus. This is where our musical tastes diverge completely.

I want to remind you of Stalin's attitude toward fathers of the church. My good friend Yevgeny Shvarts told me this story. Everyone knows that you can't appear on radio if your text hasn't been passed by the censor. Not one, but almost ten censors, each of whom signs. If the papers aren't signed, no one will let you near a microphone. Who knows what you might say to the whole country?

And then it was decided that the Metropolitan of Moscow* should give a talk on radio. I think it had something to do with the struggle for peace. The Metropolitan was to speak to the faithful, a sermon calling on them to join the struggle. This interested the Great Gardener. The Metropolitan arrived at the radio station and walked straight up to the microphone. They grabbed him by the sleeve and pulled him away. "Your Eminence, where's the text of the speech?" The Metropolitan was taken aback. "What speech?" They began explaining that they meant the . . . well, not the speech, but the whatever-you-call-it. . . . In other words, if the Metropolitan was planning to speak now, where was the approved and signed text?

The Metropolitan, they say, took umbrage and stated that he never

*One of the highest ranks in the Russian Orthodox Church.

read his sermons from a piece of paper. This was a scandal; what to do? They asked the Metropolitan to wait a bit and rushed to call the bosses, but no one wanted the responsibility, only Stalin could resolve problems like this. And Stalin decided: let the Metropolitan say whatever he wanted, and they allowed the Metropolitan at the microphone. Funny? It's sad.

And what about the Leningrad *Ivan Susanin?* You know that Glinka's opera is called *A Life for the Tsar,* and I believe that it's performed abroad under that name. It's a totally monarchistic work and before the Revolution *A Life* played at the Maryinsky Theater on "tsar's days."

In the thirties, with the help of a miserable poet and great scoundrel, Sergei Gorodetsky,* the text of Glinka's opera was edited. (Stravinsky wrote two pleasant songs to poems by Gorodetsky. He says that Gorodetsky was a faithful friend of his wife's. Perhaps.) When with Gorodetsky's help *A Life for the Tsar* was changed to *Ivan Susanin,* they started editing the music. The opera was produced almost simultaneously in Moscow and Leningrad. In Moscow they threw out the prayer ensemble in the epilogue, but the musical director of the Leningrad production, stubborn Ari Pazovsky, refused. He insisted on keeping the prayer. Zhdanov was informed. You would think that all Zhdanov had to do was order them to take out the prayer. But he knew about Stalin's weakness, about his superstition. Zhdanov decided to let Stalin make the decision.

And the leader and teacher ordered, "Let them pray, the opera won't lose any of its patriotism." And so in Pazovsky's production they prayed, yet I don't think Pazovsky was baptized or anything.

Sometimes I have the feeling that Gogol wrote these stories. They seem funny but actually they're horrifying. Will they pray or not in the opera? Will the Metropolitan read his sermon from a paper or not? The leader, puffing on his pipe, decided these vital government problems. "Stalin thinks for us," as the popular poem went. He walked around his office at night and "pondered," mostly about such nonsense.

*Sergei Mitrofanovich Gorodetsky (1884–1967), a famous poet before the Revolution, who later wrote "ideologically correct" opera libretti and slavish poems "for occasions." Nadezhda Mandelstam once noted that there is one moral to be drawn from Gorodetsky's story: one should not let oneself be frightened to the point of losing one's human face.

Yes, I'll say it again: Stalin was a morbidly superstitious man. All the unforgiven fathers of their countries and saviors of humanity suffer from it, it's an inevitable trait, and that's why they have a certain respect for and fear of *yurodivye*. Some people think that the *yurodivye* who dared to tell the whole truth to tsars are a thing of the past. A part of literature, *Boris Godunov* and so on. "Pray for me, blessed one"—Mussorgsky is marvelous in that scene, he proves what a great operatic dramatist he is. He discards all effects for the sake of dramatic veracity, and it's so effective that it brings tears to the audience's eyes.

But the *yurodivye* aren't gone, and tyrants fear them as before. There are examples of it in our day.

Of course, Stalin was half mad. But there's nothing odd about that, there are lots of crazy rulers, we've had our share in Russia—Ivan the Terrible and Paul I. Nero was probably mad, and they say one of the Georges in Britain was crazy. So the fact itself should elicit no surprise.

What is amazing is this: Ivan the Terrible died in his bed, a fully empowered monarch. He had had some trouble, opposition, Prince Kurbsky and so on. But Ivan with the help of Malyuta Skuratov took care of his opponents. The next madman had a harder time. As you know, Paul I was killed; they were tired of him. That seemed like progress, enlightened people could believe in the progress of history, and Russian history specifically. It seemed that the future would go well, and that the next mad Russian leader could simply be invited to check into a sanatorium, relax from his work, and take a cure.

But nothing came of the rosy hopes of educated people. True, there was some small opposition to Nicholas I, but the most mad, most cruel of tyrants ruled without any opposition. Whether Stalin died in his bed or under it I don't know, but I do know that he caused more harm than all the abnormal kings and tsars of the past put together. And no one ever dared hint that Stalin was crazy.

They say that Vladimir Bekhterev, a prominent psychiatrist and a good friend of our family friend Dr. Grekov, a surgeon, dared to pronounce Stalin mad. Bekhterev was about seventy then, and he was world-famous. He was called to the Kremlin, he carefully probed Stalin's mental condition. He died soon afterward, and Grekov was certain that Bekhterev had been poisoned.

But that's just another horrible joke from the series on insane asylums and their inhabitants. The madman poisons his physician. Why? A wise man answered thus: "The point is that some madmen are allowed to start their own crazy kingdoms and others aren't." That's all.

In his final years, Stalin seemed more and more like a madman, and I think his superstitiousness grew. The leader and teacher sat locked up, in one of his many dachas, amusing himself in bizarre ways. They say he cut out pictures and photos from old magazines and newspapers, glued them onto paper, and hung them on the walls.

One of my friends (a musicologist, by the way) had the "luck" to live next door to one of Stalin's bodyguards. The man didn't crack right away, at first he denied it, but then they got drunk together and talked. The work paid well and, in the eyes of the bodyguard, was highly respectable and responsible. With his many co-workers, he patrolled Stalin's dacha outside Moscow. In winter on skis, in summer on bicycles. They circled the dacha without stopping, all day and all night, without a break. The guard complained that he got dizzy. The leader and teacher almost never went outside the dacha grounds, and when he did come outside he behaved like a real paranoiac. According to the guard, he kept looking around, checking, peering. The bodyguard was in awe. "He's looking for enemies. One look and he sees all," he explained delightedly over a bottle of vodka to my friend.

Stalin didn't let anyone in to see him for days at a time. He listened to the radio a lot. Once Stalin called the Radio Committee, where the administration was, and asked if they had a record of Mozart's Piano Concerto no. 23, which had been heard on the radio the day before. "Played by Yudina," he added. They told Stalin that of course they had. Actually, there was no record, the concert had been live. But they were afraid to say no to Stalin, no one ever knew what the consequences might be. A human life meant nothing to him. All you could do was agree, submit, be a yes man, a yes man to a madman.

Stalin demanded that they send the record with Yudina's performance of the Mozart to his dacha. The committee panicked, but they had to do something. They called in Yudina and an orchestra and recorded that night. Everyone was shaking with fright, except for Yudina, naturally. But she was a special case, that one, the ocean was only knee-deep for her.

Yudina later told me that they had to send the conductor home, he was so scared he couldn't think. They called another conductor, who trembled and got everything mixed up, confusing the orchestra. Only a third conductor was in any shape to finish the recording.

I think this is a unique event in the history of recording—I mean changing conductors three times in one night. Anyway, the record was ready by morning. They made one single copy and sent it to Stalin. Now, that was a record record. A record in yesing.

Soon after, Yudina received an envelope with twenty thousand rubles. She was told it came on the express orders of Stalin. Then she wrote him a letter. I know about this letter from her, and I know that the story seems improbable; Yudina had many quirks, but I can say this—she never lied. I'm certain that her story is true. Yudina wrote something like this in her letter: "I thank you, Iosif Vissarionovich, for your aid. I will pray for you day and night and ask the Lord to forgive your great sins before the people and the country. The Lord is merciful and He'll forgive you. I gave the money to the church that I attend."

And Yudina sent this suicidal letter to Stalin. He read it and didn't say a word, they expected at least a twitch of the eyebrow. Naturally, the order to arrest Yudina was prepared and the slightest grimace would have been enough to wipe away the last traces of her. But Stalin was silent and set the letter aside in silence. The anticipated movement of the eyebrows didn't come.

Nothing happened to Yudina. They say that her recording of the Mozart was on the record player when the leader and teacher was found dead in his dacha. It was the last thing he had listened to.

I'm telling this story with a specific aim, which I'm not hiding. I'm not a militant atheist, and I feel people can believe as they wish. But just because a person has a particular set of superstitions doesn't prove anything good about him. Just because a person is religious, say, he doesn't automatically become a better person.

Stalin was superstitious, that's all. Tyrants and *yurodivye* are the same in all eras. Read Shakespeare and Pushkin, read Gogol and Chekhov. Listen to Mussorgsky.

I recall that Yudina kept trying to read to me from the New Testament. I listened with interest and without any particular trepidation.

She read the New Testament to me and I read Chekhov to her: "Resolving everything through Bible texts is as arbitrary as dividing convicts into five groups." Chekhov went on to say, Why five and not ten groups? Why the Bible and not the Koran? And no fans of the Bible have ever been able to argue convincingly against Chekhov's healthy reasoning. Then why proselytize? Why all that pathos?

No, I have nothing to say to ambitious men, and I refuse to accept any comments from them on my behavior. All these luminaries were willing to get along with me on one condition: to wit, that I join their ranks, and join without a murmur, without a single thought. But I have my own opinion of what's right and wrong and I don't have to discuss my opinion with just anyone. I often hear just such demands and I often feel like saying, "And who are you?" But I control myself, because you can't ask everyone anyway, it would take too much time and they wouldn't understand.

But I would like to clear this up once and for all. I maintain that I can only have a serious conversation, a substantial one, so to speak, with a workingman. That is, with a man who has worked hard in his life and accomplished much. I won't bother with these citizens who flit about, whether they're curly-haired or bald, bearded or clean-shaven, who are without any specific profession and have a prosecutor's ambition.

And it's important to remember that there's work and there's work, and not every job gives a man the right to take on a prosecutor's role. For instance, if you've spent your entire life developing and perfecting the hydrogen bomb, you probably shouldn't be proud of the fact.* I would say that you would have a rather dirty work record. Rather dirty. And it's not too logical with such a record to strive to be a prosecutor, because you can kill one person with a cudgel but with a hydrogen bomb you can kill millions.

Participation in this astounding progress in the work of killing should frighten off decent people from the lectures of the participant. But as we see, it doesn't, and as we see, it even gives the lectures an additional popularity and piquancy. Which proves once more that things are not healthy in our criteria for nobility and decency. Things

*A reference to academician Andrei Dmitriyevich Sakharov (b. 1921).

are not right in that area. To put it bluntly, it's an insane asylum.

I refuse to speak seriously with lunatics, I refuse to talk to them about myself or others, I refuse to discuss questions about my proper or improper behavior.

I write music, it's performed. It can be heard, and whoever wants to hear it will. After all, my music says it all. It doesn't need historical and hysterical commentaries. In the long run, any words about music are less important than the music. Anyone who thinks otherwise is not worth talking to.

I am horrified by people who think the commentaries to a symphony are more important than the symphony. What counts with them is a large number of brave words—and the music itself can be pathetic and woebegone. This is real perversion. I don't need brave words on music and I don't think anyone does. We need brave music. I don't mean brave in the sense that there will be charts instead of notes, I mean brave because it is truthful. Music in which the composer expresses his thoughts truthfully, and does it in such a way that the greatest possible number of decent citizens in his country and other countries will recognize and accept that music, thereby understanding his country and people. That is the meaning of composing music, as I see it.

There's no point in talking to the deaf, and I'm addressing only those who can hear and it's only with them that I plan to converse, only with those people for whom music is more important than words.

They say that music is comprehensible without translation. I want to believe in that, but for now I see that music needs many accompanying words to make it understood in another country. I'm asked many stupid questions when I go abroad. That is one of the reasons why I don't like to go, perhaps the main reason.

Any obnoxious pest can say whatever comes into his head and ask you about anything. He didn't even know your name yesterday, the idiot, but today, since he has to earn a living, he manages to pronounce it. He has no idea of what you do—and he doesn't care. Of course, journalists aren't the only people in a country, but show me what newspapers you're reading and I'll tell you what's in your brain.

The typical Western journalist is an uneducated, obnoxious, and profoundly cynical person. He needs to make money and he doesn't give a damn about the rest. Every one of these pushy guys wants me to answer his stupid questions "daringly" and these gentlemen take offense when they don't hear what they want. Why do I have to answer? Who are they? Why do I have to risk my life? And risk it to satisfy the shallow curiosity of a man who doesn't give a damn about me! He didn't know anything about me yesterday and he'll forget my name by tomorrow. What right does he have to expect my frankness and my trust? I don't know anything about him, but I don't pester him with questions, do I? Even though he could answer my questions without endangering his hide.

It's all upsetting and insulting. The worst part is that these perversions have become commonplace, and no one stops to think how crazy it is. I'm judged on the basis of what I said or didn't say to Mr. Smith or Mr. Jones. Isn't that ridiculous? Newspaper articles should serve as means of judging Messrs. Smith and Jones! I have my music, and quite a bit of music it is, and let people judge me by my music. I have no intention of providing commentaries to it and I have no intention of telling how, where, and under what circumstances I was drenched by the "sweaty wave of inspiration."* Let poets confide such reminiscences to a trusting public; it's all lies anyway, and I'm not a poet.

I don't like talking about inspiration in general, it's got a suspicious ring. As I recall, I spoke of inspiration only once, and I was forced to do it. I was talking to Stalin. I was trying to explain how the process of composing music unfolds, with what speed. I could see that Stalin didn't understand, so I had to steer the conversation to inspiration. "You see," I said, "it's inspiration, of course. How fast you write depends on inspiration." And so on. I blamed it on inspiration. The only time it's not shameful to speak of inspiration is when you need to toss words around. The rest of the time it's best not to mention it at all.

And I have no intention of doing a measure-by-measure analysis of my scores either. That's certainly not very interesting in Stravinsky's memoirs. So what if I inform you that in my Eighth Symphony, in the fourth movement, in the fourth variation, in measures four through six, the theme is harmonized with seven descending minor triads? Who cares? Is it necessary to prove that you're erudite in the area of

*One of the ironic catch phrases of contemporary Russian life, borrowed from Ilf and Petrov's *The Golden Calf.*

your own work? Stravinsky's example doesn't convince me. He should have left the analysis of his works to musicologists. I would have preferred Stravinsky to tell more about the people he met and about his childhood.

Stravinsky describes his childhood well; as I said, I think those are the best pages of his memoirs. Usually it's revolting to read, "I was born into a musical family, Father played on a comb and Mother always whistled a tune." And so on and so forth. It's dreary.

Stravinsky was adept at answering journalists' questions—like a Cossack doing trick riding or chopping vines. But first of all, he didn't tell the truth. What he said was much too striking, and the truth is never that fascinating. (Sollertinsky once said that there is no rhyme for *pravda* [truth] in Russian. I don't know if that's so, but it's true that truth and advertising have little in common.) And second, Stravinsky and I are very different people. I found it difficult to talk to him. We were from different planets.

I still recall with horror my first trip to the U.S.A.* I wouldn't have gone at all if it hadn't been for intense pressure from administrative figures of all ranks and colors, from Stalin down. People sometimes say that it must have been an interesting trip, look at the way I'm smiling in the photographs. That was the smile of a condemned man. I felt like a dead man. I answered all the idiotic questions in a daze, and thought, When I get back it's over for me.

Stalin liked leading Americans by the nose that way. He would show them a man—here he is, alive and well—and then kill him. Well, why say lead by the nose? That's too strongly put. He only fooled those who wanted to be fooled. The Americans don't give a damn about us, and in order to live and sleep soundly, they'll believe anything.

Just then, in 1949, the Jewish poet Itsik Fefer was arrested on Stalin's orders. Paul Robeson was in Moscow and in the midst of all the banquets and balls, he remembered that he had a friend called Itsik. Where's Itsik? "You'll have your Itsik," Stalin decided, and pulled his usual base trick.

*Shostakovich made his first trip to the United States in March 1949 for the Cultural and Scientific Conference for World Peace, which took place at the Waldorf-Astoria Hotel in New York.

Itsik Fefer invited Paul Robeson to dine with him in Moscow's most chic restaurant. Robeson arrived and was led to a private chamber in the restaurant, where the table was set with drinks and lavish *zakuski*. Fefer was really sitting at the table, with several unknown men. Fefer was thin and pale and said little. But Robeson ate and drank well and saw his old friend.

After their friendly dinner, the men Robeson didn't know returned Fefer to prison, where he soon died. Robeson went back to America, where he told everyone that the rumors about Fefer's arrest and death were nonsense and slander. He had been drinking with Fefer personally.

And really, it's a lot easier living that way, it's more convenient to think that your friend is a rich and free man who can treat you to a luxurious dinner. Thinking that your friend is in prison is not pleasant. You have to get involved, you have to write letters and protests. And if you write a protest you won't be invited the next time and they'll ruin your good name. The radio and papers will smear you with dirt, they'll call you a reactionary.

No, it's much easier to believe what you see. And you always see what you want to see. The mentality of the chicken—when a chicken pecks, it sees only the one grain and nothing else. And so it pecks, grain by grain, until the farmer breaks its neck. Stalin understood this chicken mentality better than anyone, he knew how to deal with chickens. And they all ate out of his hand. As I understand it, they don't like to remember this in the West. For they're always right, the great Western humanists, lovers of truthful literature and art. It's we who are always at fault.

I'm the one who gets asked, "Why did you sign this and that?" But has anyone ever asked André Malraux why he glorified the construction of the White Sea Canal,* where thousands upon thousands of people perished? No, no one has. Too bad. They should ask more often. After all, no one can keep these gentlemen from answering, noth-

---

*A canal in northern Russia, constructed on Stalin's orders between September 1931 and April 1933 by penal labor. Hundreds of thousands of workers died during its construction. Stalin cleverly turned this "concentrated labor on gigantic objectives, stunning the imagination with their grandiose scope" (a quote from a contemporary Soviet source) to propaganda aims. The talents of hundreds of writers, artists, and composers were used to glorify the White Sea Canal. See Solzhenitsyn's *The Gulag Archipelago.*

ing threatened their lives then and nothing threatens them now.

And what about Lion Feuchtwanger, famous humanist? I read his little book *Moscow 1937* with revulsion. As soon as it saw the light of day, Stalin had it translated and printed in huge numbers. I read it with bitterness and contempt for the lauded humanist.

Feuchtwanger wrote that Stalin was a simple man, full of good will. There was a time when I thought that Feuchtwanger had the wool pulled over his eyes too. But then I reread the book and realized that the great humanist had lied.

"What I understood is wonderful," he announced. What he understood was that the political trials in Moscow were necessary—and wonderful. According to him, the trials favored the development of democratization. No, in order to write that, it's not enough to be a fool, you have to be a scoundrel as well. And a famed humanist.

And what about the no less famous humanist George Bernard Shaw? It was he who said, "You won't frighten me with the word 'dictator.'" Naturally, why should Shaw be frightened? There weren't any in England, where he lived. I think their last dictator had been Cromwell. Shaw just came to visit a dictator. It was Shaw who announced upon his return from the Soviet Union, "Hunger in Russia? Nonsense. I've never been fed as well anywhere as in Moscow." Millions were going hungry then and several million peasants died of starvation. And yet people are delighted by Shaw, by his wit and courage. I have my own opinion on that, even though I was forced to send him the score of my Seventh Symphony, since he was a famous humanist.

And what about Romain Rolland? It makes me sick to think about him. I get particularly nauseated because some of these famous humanists praised my music. Shaw, for one, and Romain Rolland. He really liked *Lady Macbeth*. I was supposed to meet this famous humanist from the glorious pleiad of lovers of truthful literature and just as truthful music. But I didn't go. I said I was ill.

Once I was tormented by the question: why? why? Why were these people lying to the entire world? Why don't these famous humanists give a damn about us, our lives, honor, and dignity? And then I suddenly calmed down. If they don't give a damn, then they don't. And to hell with them. Their cozy life as famous humanists is what they hold most dear. That means that they can't be taken seriously. They be-

200

came like children for me. Nasty children—a hell of a difference, as Pushkin used to say.

There were a lot of nasty children in Petrograd. You walk down Nevsky Prospect and you see a thirteen-year-old with a cigar in his mouth. His teeth are rotten, he has rings on his fingers, a British cap on his head, and brass knuckles in his pocket. He's tried all the prostitutes in the city and had his fill of cocaine. And he doesn't like life. It's scarier to run into a punk like that than any gangster. The little angel could playfully knock you off—anything can come into a child's head.

I have the same fears when I look at the famous humanists of our times. They have rotten teeth and I don't need their friendship. I just want my feet to carry me as far away as possible.

Once a young American woman was visiting me. Everything was going well, in a proper dignified way. We spoke of music and nature and other highfalutin subjects. It was nice. Suddenly she grew frightened and upset. Spots of color rose on her face. She began waving her arms and almost jumped on the table, shouting, "A fly, a fly!" A fly had got into the room and my highly educated guest was scared to death. I was in no shape to chase after the fly, so we said our good-byes.

For these people a fly is a mysterious animal from another world and I'm just an excavated dinosaur. All right, suppose that I am. Then, my honorable guests, do you take it upon yourselves to discuss dinosaurs? Their problems, rights, and duties? Ah, so you don't discuss dinosaurs? Then don't talk about me either. Because you know even less about my rights and duties than you do about the rights and duties of the dinosaur.

Once during the war they showed the Hollywood film *Mission to Moscow*. The makers must have thought that it was a drama, but we saw it as a comedy. I don't think I laughed as much during the war as I did at that film. A fly, a fly.

One day when he was in a good mood, Nemirovich-Danchenko told me about the Hollywood version of *Anna Karenina*. I think he was present when they shot the film, at least he read the screenplay when he was in America. In the American version Vronsky possessed Anna in an inn, taking advantage of the fact, you see, that his pajamas and slippers were in Anna's room. And the film had a happy ending (I think the great Garbo was Anna)—Karenin died and Vronsky and Anna got married.* Isn't that a fly? Of course it is.

I know, this is all silly, stupidly funny. Big deal: flies, mosquitoes, roaches. People just don't want to strain their minds. It's just not serious, just flitting around. A fly. All right, let them flit, but a creature born to crawl can't fly, as the stormy petrel of the Revolution Maxim Gorky said with great knowledge. And that holds in reverse.

But once you've got used to flitting, you don't feel like returning to our sinful soil. And everything looks marvelous and wonderful from above; even the White Sea Canal is marvelous and amazing.

Of course, I know that an entire brigade of respected Russian dullards wrote a collective book praising that White Sea Canal. If they have an excuse at all, it's that they were taken to the canal as tourists one day and the next day any one of them could have been shoveling dirt there. Then again, Ilf and Petrov got out of participating in that shameful "literary camp" anthology by saying that they "knew little" about the life of inmates. Ilf and Petrov were lucky, and they never did find out about that life, the way hundreds of other writers and poets did.

They did bring back one joke from the "recreational and familiarizing" trip to the canal. The writers and poets were greeted by a band whose members were all criminal (as opposed to political) convicts, imprisoned for crimes of passion. Ilf looked at the diligent musicians and remembered the famous Russian horn bands, and muttered, "This is a horned cuckold band."

Is that funny? I don't know. That was nervous laughter, you know, they were powerless and so they laughed. But it's not at all funny when you hear that Henry Wallace was touched by the Kolyma camps director's love for music. And he wanted to be President of the United States.

It wasn't funny when I was told how foreign visitors let down Akhmatova and Zoshchenko. Akhmatova had found herself on the brink of disaster many times. Gumilyov† was shot, her son was sent to the camps with a long sentence, and Punin died in the camps. She wasn't

---

*A reference to the 1927 M-G-M version, *Love*, in which Anna Karenina was played by Greta Garbo and Vronsky by John Gilbert. A later Hollywood version was called *Anna Karenina* and again starred Garbo as Anna, while Fredric March played Vronsky. In this version she did die.

†Nikolai Stepanovich Gumilyov (1886–1921), poet, Anna Akmatova's first husband. He was

published for many years, and what is published now is perhaps only a third of what she wrote. Zoshchenko and Akhmatova felt the first "Zhdanov blow"*—and there's no need to explain what might follow.

They were called out to meet with foreign tourists, some delegation of defenders of this or fighters for that. I've seen plenty of these delegations and they all have one thing on their minds—to eat as soon as possible. Yevtushenko has a pointed poem about these friendly delegations: "Meal coupons in the hand bring friends from all the continents." So Zoshchenko and Akhmatova were forced to meet with this delegation. The old trick, to prove that they were alive, healthy and happy with everything, and extremely grateful to the Party and the government.

The "friends" with meal vouchers in their hands couldn't think of anything cleverer to ask than what Zoshchenko and Akhmatova thought of the resolution of the Central Committee of the Party and Comrade Zhdanov's speech. This is the speech in which Akhmatova and Zoshchenko were used as examples. Zhdanov said that Zoshchenko was an unprincipled and conscienceless literary hooligan and that he had a rotten and decayed sociopolitical and literary mug. Not face. He said mug.

And Zhdanov said that Akhmatova was poisoning the consciousness of Soviet youth with the rotten and putrid spirit of her poetry. So how could they have felt about the resolution and speech? Isn't that sadistic—to ask about it? It's like asking a man into whose face a hooligan has just spat, "How do you feel about having spit on your face? Do you like it?" But there was more. They asked it in the presence of the hooligan and bandit who did the spitting, knowing full well that they would leave and the victim would have to stay and deal with the bandit.

Akhmatova rose and said that she considered both Comrade Zhdanov's speech and the resolution to be absolutely correct. Of course, she did the right thing, that was the only way to behave with those shame-

---

shot as a member of an antigovernment conspiracy (the so-called Professor Tagantsev Affair), despite Maxim Gorky's plea to Lenin to spare him. Nikolai Nikolayevich Punin (1888–1953), art historian, Commissar of the Hermitage after the Revolution, was Akhmatova's third husband. Arrested several times, he finally perished in Siberia.

*The postwar "tightening of the screws" began with Zhdanov's move against Zoshchenko and Akhmatova (1946). Both were expelled from the Writers' Union, stripped of all means of survival, and viciously badgered in the newspapers and at innumerable meetings.

less, heartless strangers. What could she have said? That she thinks she's living in an insane asylum of a country? That she despises and hates Zhdanov and Stalin? Yes, she could have said that, but then no one would have ever seen her again.

The "friends," of course, could have bragged about the sensation back at home, "among friends." Or even slipped a report about it into the papers. And we would have all suffered a loss, we would have lived without Akhmatova and her incomparable late poetry. The country would have lost its genius.

But Zoshchenko, a sweet and naïve man, thought that these people really did want to understand something. He naturally couldn't say everything he felt, that would have been suicide, but he embarked on an explanation. He said that at first he didn't understand either Zhdanov's speech or the resolution. They seemed unfair to him and he wrote a letter about it to Stalin. But then he started thinking and then many of the accusations seemed fair and just.

Poor Mikhail Mikhailovich, his nobility did not serve him well. He had thought that he was dealing with decent people. The "decent people" applauded and left. (They didn't think Akhmatova deserved applause.) And the already ill Zoshchenko was starved as punishment. He wasn't permitted to publish a single line. His feet were swelling, he was starving. He tried to make a living by repairing shoes.

The moral is clear. There can be no friendship with famous humanists. We are poles apart, they and I. I don't trust any of them and not one of them has ever done anything good for me. I do not acknowledge their right to question me. They do not have the moral right and they dare not lecture me.

I never answered their questions and I never will. I never took their lectures seriously and I never will. I am backed up by the bitter experience of my gray and miserable life. And I'm not happy in the least that my students have adopted my suspiciousness. They don't believe the famous humanists either and they're right.

It's too bad. I'd be very happy if they managed to find some famous humanist who could be trusted, with whom you could chat about flowers, brotherhood, equality and liberty, the European soccer championships, and other lofty topics. But no such humanist has been born. There are more than enough scoundrels, but I don't feel like talking to them: they'll sell you cheap for foreign currency or a jar of black caviar.

That's why I derive a sad satisfaction from the fact that my best students, seeing my sad example, refrain from friendship with humanists. I heartily recommend a dog to keep from being lonely.

Don't believe humanists, citizens, don't believe prophets, don't believe luminaries—they'll fool you for a penny. Do your own work, don't hurt people, try to help them. Don't try to save humanity all at once, try saving one person first. It's a lot harder. To help one person without harming another is very difficult. It's unbelievably difficult. That's where the temptation to save all of humanity comes from. And then, inevitably, along the way you discover that all humanity's happiness hinges on the destruction of a few hundred million people, that's all. A trifle.

Nothing but nonsense in the world, Nikolai Vasilyevich Gogol once said. It's that nonsense that I try to depict. World issues grab man by the collar; he's got plenty of problems of his own, and now there are world issues as well. You could lose your head—or your nose.

I'm often asked why I wrote the opera *The Nose*. Well, first of all, I love Gogol. I'm not bragging, but I know pages and pages by heart. And I have striking childhood memories of *The Nose*. Now when they write about *The Nose*, they harp on Meyerhold's influence: to wit, that his production of *The Inspector General* astounded me so that I took on *The Nose*. That's not correct.

When I moved to Moscow and into Meyerhold's apartment, I was already working on *The Nose*. It was all thought through, and not by Meyerhold. I was working on the libretto with two marvelous men, Sasa Preis and Georgi Ionin. It was a marvelous, magical time. We would get together in the morning, early. We didn't work at night, first of all because we were put off by the Bohemian style of work. You should work in the morning or afternoon, no need for midnight drama.

And secondly, Sasa Preis couldn't work at night. He was busy at night, working. His job had an important-sounding title, "agent in conserving nonliquid property," while what he really was was a watchman. He guarded a candy factory, formerly Landrin's. The owner, George Landrin, ran off abroad and his son did too. They left the property behind and Sasa guarded it to keep looters away.

It was a lot of fun. As Oleinikov said, "Truly, it was fun. Truly, it was funny." At first we approached Zamyatin, we wanted him to take charge of our libretto since he was a great master. But the great master didn't add to the fun and didn't stand out in any way from the rest of us.

Mayor Kovalyov needed a monologue. Everyone else backed away from doing it, but Zamyatin said, "Why not?" He sat down and wrote it. By the way, it's a bad monologue. That was the extent of the contribution by the great master of Russian prose. So Zamyatin got on the credits by accident, so to speak. He wasn't very much help, we managed on our own. So much for the influence of the great masters.

They were very special people, Preis and Ionin. Preis wrote Gogol's comedy *St. Vladimir Third Grade* for him. As you know, Gogol didn't finish the play, he only left rough sketches, and Sasa wrote the play. He didn't just write whatever came into his head, no, he put it together all from Gogol's own words. He didn't add a single word of his own, he got every line from Gogol's works. It's astonishing. The man worked scrupulously. I read the manuscript. After each bit of dialogue there's a reference for the source, the Gogol work from which it came. For example, if someone says, "Dinner is served," the footnote tells you the work and page number. Honestly. The play was staged in Leningrad and Sasa read a review in the papers titled "Slop it on, just as long as it's hot."

Later Sasa Preis was of great help with the libretto of *Lady Macbeth*. He also created a marvelous opera plot especially for me: the life of women who want to be emancipated. It was to be a serious opera. But nothing came of it, nothing. Alexander Germanovich Preis died, he died young. They killed him.

Ionin was also an outstanding figure in his way. He was once a street urchin and a criminal, and was brought up in the Dostoevsky Reform Colony for Handicapped Children. You couldn't make up a name like that. Ionin was an expert in Russian literature, I don't know where he learned all he knew. Literature teachers didn't stay long at the colony, Ionin drove them away. One lady came and read them "The Grasshopper and the Ant" out loud. Ionin said, "We know all that, why don't you tell us about the latest trends in literature instead?" She replied, "Don't talk dirty to me. What's a trend?"

Ionin also died young. He wanted to become a director. He caught typhus from someone and died. Two of his friends wrote a book in which Ionin is a protagonist. He's called The Jap in the book even though he was Jewish. But he was short and had slanted eyes. The book became very popular, you might say famous, and not so long ago it was made into a film. I understand they use the film for educational purposes. Think how strangely things turn out.

I'm surrounded by amazing subjects, perhaps because I'm surrounded by so many amazing people, even if they're not famous. And these people helped me much more than the famous ones. Famous people never have enough time. So much for Meyerhold.

And as for his *Inspector General*, well, of course I liked the production very much, but there's an inverse relation here: I liked it because I was already working on *The Nose* and saw that Meyerhold was resolving many things as I was, and not the reverse. I didn't like the music for *The Inspector General* at all. I'm not referring to the musical numbers that Gnessin wrote—no, they're excellent and quite appropriate. But Meyerhold threw all kinds of stuff into the play, and not all of it worked. For instance, I still don't understand why authentic folk songs (I think from the Kaluga region) were necessary for the characterization of Osip. Meyerhold thought that Osip was a healthy element in the play. I think that's a mistake. And I don't understand why they used Glinka's song "The fire of desire burns in my blood." There's nothing lustful in that song, but Meyerhold decided that it would express Anna Andreyevna's lust. Raikh played the role. I played the piano on stage, portraying one of the guests, and Raikh sang Glinka's romance, moving her voluptuous shoulders and glancing meaningfully at Khlestakov. Raikh played herself in *The Inspector General*—an obnoxious, pushy woman. God will forgive her, she died a horrible martyr's death.

I don't know, maybe Meyerhold did influence the production of my opera *The Nose* that Smolich directed at the Maly Theater. That's another matter, the composer has nothing to do with that. But as far as *The Nose* and myself are concerned, a greater influence was the production of *The Nose* at the famous Crooked Mirror.

This was before the Revolution, the war was raging, and I was just a kid. I remember my delight in the play, it was very cleverly staged. I remember that later, when I was looking for a subject for an opera, I immediately thought of the production of *The Nose,* and I thought that I would be able to write the libretto myself without much trouble.

And in general, that's what I did. I sketched the outline myself, basing it on memory, and then we developed it together. Sasa Preis set the pace. He was sleepy, coming straight from work, but he ignited us all, we set our course by him. And the three of us worked as one, merrily and well.

I didn't want to write a satirical opera; I'm not completely sure what that is. Some say that Prokofiev's *Love for Three Oranges* is a satirical opera. I just find it boring; you're constantly aware of the composer's attempts at being funny, and it's not funny at all. People find satire and grotesquerie in *The Nose,* but I wrote totally serious music, there's no parody or joking in it. It's rather hard to be witty in music—it's too easy to end up with something like *Three Oranges.* I tried not to make jokes in *The Nose,* and I think I succeeded.

Really, when you think about it, what's so funny about a man losing his nose? Why laugh at the poor monster? The man can't marry or go to work. I'd like to see any of my friends lose his nose. They'd all cry like babies. And that should be kept in mind by anyone who plans to produce the opera. You can read *The Nose* like a joke, but you can't stage it as one. It's too cruel, and most important, it won't fit the music.

The Nose is a horror story, not a joke. How can police oppression be funny? Wherever you go, there's a policeman, you can't take a step or drop a piece of paper. And the crowd in *The Nose* isn't funny either. Taken individually, they're not bad, just slightly eccentric. But together, they're a mob that wants blood.

And there's nothing funny in the image of *The Nose.* Without a nose you're not a man, but without you the nose can become a man, and even an important bureaucrat. And there's no exaggeration here, the story is believable. If Gogol had lived in our day, he would have seen stranger things than that. We have noses walking around such as to boggle the mind, and what's going on in our republics along those lines isn't funny at all.

A composer friend of mine told me a story that's extraordinary and ordinary at the same time. It's ordinary because it's true and extraordinary because it's about chicanery on an epochal level, worthy of the pen of Gogol or E. T. A. Hoffmann. This composer worked for decades in Kazakhstan. He's a good professional, a graduate of the Leningrad Conservatory, also in Steinberg's class but a year behind me. He really made it in Kazakhstan, becoming something like the court composer, and therefore he knew many things that are generally secret.

Everyone in the U.S.S.R. knows Dzhambul Dzhabayev, my son studied his poetry in school, and my grandsons study it too—in Russian, naturally, translated from the Kazakh. They're very touching little poems. You can imagine how it was during the war. "Leningraders, my children . . . " And this coming from a hundred-year-old wise man in a robe. All our foreign guests liked being photographed with him, the pictures were so exotic. A folk singer, the wisdom of the ages in his eyes, and so on. Even I fell for it, I confess, I wrote music for some lines of his. It happened.

And it turns out it was all made up. I mean, naturally Dzhambul Dzhabayev existed as a person, and the Russian texts of his poems existed too, the translations, that is. Only the originals never existed. Dzhambul Dzhabayev may have been a good man, but he was no poet. I suppose he might have been, but no one cared, because the so-called translations of the nonexistent poems were written by Russian poets and they didn't even ask our great folk singer for permission. And if they had wanted to ask they couldn't have, because these translators didn't know a word of Kazakh and Dzhambul didn't know a word of Russian.

No, that's not true. He knew one Russian word, the word for "fee." They explained it to Dzhambul: every time he signed his name (it goes without saying that Dzhambul was illiterate, but they taught him how to make a squiggle that represented his signature), he should say the magic word "Fee" and he would get money and he could buy many new sheep and camels.

Every time Dzhambul put his sign on a contract he got a fee, and he got richer and richer. He liked that. Once, though, there was a problem. They brought him to Moscow and as part of the itinerary of conferences, receptions, and banquets, they arranged for a meeting with children, a squad of Pioneers. The Pioneers surrounded Dzhambul and begged for his autograph. It was explained to him that he had to write his famous squiggle. He did, but kept saying, "Fee." He was sure that it was his signature that he was paid for, he didn't know anything about "his" poems. He was very disappointed when it was explained that there would be no fee this time and that his riches would not increase.

How sad that Gogol wasn't around to write about this—a great poet, known by the entire country, who doesn't exist. However, every grotesque story has its tragic side. Maybe this pathetic Dzhambul really was a great poet? After all, he plucked away at his *dombra* and sang something. But no one was interested. Magnificent odes to Stalin were needed, compliments in the Oriental style for any occasion—birthdays, the inauguration of the Stalin Constitution, then the elections, the Civil War in Spain, and so on. Dozens of reasons for rhyming, none of which the illiterate old man knew anything about. How could he have known, what did he care, about the "miners of Asturias"?

An entire brigade of Russian poetasters labored for Dzhambul, including some famous names, like Konstantin Simonov. And they knew the political situation well and wrote to please the leader and teacher, which meant writing mostly about Stalin himself. But they didn't forget his henchmen, Yezhov* for instance.

I remember that at the time the song about Yezhov was highly praised. It sang in pseudo folk style about the secret police and Yezhov, its glorious leader, and expressed the wish that "my song spread universal fame for our warrior around the world." Yezhov's fame was widespread, but not for the reasons they thought.

They wrote fast and prolifically, and when one of the "translators" dried up, he was replaced by a new, fresh one. That way production never halted, and the factory was closed down only on Dzhambul's death.

As usual, people will say that none of this is typical, and I'll reply: Why not, it's very typical. There's nothing here against the rules; on the contrary, everything followed the rules, everything was as it should be. The great leader of all the peoples needed inspired singers from all

*Nikolai Ivanovich Yezhov (1895–1939), major Party worker, and from 1936, Chief of Security Organs. In 1939, on Stalin's orders, Yezhov was apparently shot. Historians calculate that during the years of "Yezhovism," close to three million people were annihilated in the U.S.S.R.

the peoples, and it was the state's function to seek out these singers. If they couldn't find them, they created them, as they did Dzhambul. And the story of the appearance of the new great poet is also typical, as I see it, and educational. A Russian poet and journalist, working in the thirties on a Kazakh Party newspaper (published in Russian), brought in a few poems which he said he had written down from the words of some folk singer and translated. They liked the poems and printed them. Everyone was happy. Just then an exhibition of the accomplishments of Kazakh art was being planned in Moscow. The Party leader of Kazakhstan read the poems of the "unknown poet" in the paper and ordered him to be found and made to write a song in honor of Stalin immediately.

They approached the journalist—where's your poet? He hemmed and hawed and it became clear that he had lied. They had to get out of the fix and they needed a "native Kazakh poet" to praise Stalin anyway. Someone remembered that he had seen an appropriately colorful old man who sang and played the *dombra* and who would photograph well. The old man didn't know a word of Russian, there would be no problems. They would just have to find him a good "translator."

They found Dzhambul and a hurried song in his name praising Stalin was sent off to Moscow. Stalin liked the ode, that was the most important thing, and so Dzhambul Dzhabayev's new life began.

What is there atypical or unexpected in this story? Everything is as it should be. Everything develops smoothly, as planned. The story was so typical that it had even been predicted and captured in fiction, so to speak. My friend Yuri Tynyanov wrote a long story called *Lieutenant Kije,* based supposedly on historical material professedly from the reign of Tsar Paul. I have no idea what things were like in Paul's reign, but for our day this story was a reality. It tells how a nonexistent man becomes an existent one, and an existent one becomes nonexistent. No one is surprised by this—because it is usual and typical and could happen to anyone.

We read *Lieutenant Kije* with laughter—and fear. Every schoolboy knows the story now. A clerical error creates a mythical figure and that figure, Lieutenant Kije, goes through a long career, marrying, falling into disfavor, and then becoming the "emperor's favorite" and dying with a general's rank.

Fiction triumphed because a man has no significance in a totalitar-

211

ian state. The only thing that matters is the inexorable movement of the state mechanism. A mechanism needs only cogs. Stalin used to call all of us cogs. One cog does not differ from another, and cogs can easily replace one another. You can pick one out and say, "From this day you will be a genius cog," and everyone else will consider it a genius. It doesn't matter at all whether it is or not. Anyone can become a genius on the orders of the leader.

This mentality was reinforced fiercely. A popular song that was played on the radio several times a day insisted, "Anyone can become a hero here."

Mayakovsky, "the best, the most talented," often published his poems in *Komsomolskaya pravda*. Someone called up once and wanted to know why that day's paper didn't have a poem by Mayakovsky. "He's on vacation," they explained. "All right, but who's replacing him?" asked the caller.

I don't like Mayakovsky, but this is significant. The psychology is that every creative figure must have a replacement, and that replacement his own replacement. And they should always be ready, at any moment, to replace "the best, the most talented," as Stalin termed him. So remember, yesterday you were the best, the most talented, and today you're no one. Zero. Shit.

We're all familiar with that sensation—numerous nameless "replacements" standing behind your back, waiting for the signal to sit at your desk and write your novel, your symphony, your poem. Worthless composers were called "Red Beethovens" in the magazines. I don't compare myself to Beethoven, but it's impossible to forget that at any moment a new "Red Shostakovich" can appear and I'll disappear.

These thoughts pursued me quite frequently in connection with my Fourth Symphony. After all, for twenty-five years no one heard it and I had the manuscript. If I had disappeared, the authorities would have given it to someone for his "zeal." I even know who that person would have been and instead of being my Fourth, it would have become the Second Symphony of a different composer.*

*A reference to Tikhon Khrennikov. The years of terror and the shameless revision of history (including cultural history), coupled with an almost total absence of public outcry, created a good climate for officially sanctioned plagiarism. Historians think, for instance, that one of Stalin's fundamental theoretical works, "On the Bases of Leninism," was plagiarized (the real author, I. Ksenofontov, perished in 1937). A typical example from literature involves Nobel Prize–winning writer Mikhail Sholokhov: many people, among them Aleksandr Solzhenitsyn, think that Sholokhov's famous novel *The Quiet Don* was plagiarized.

You see, the atmosphere was conducive to the fabrication of geniuses on a mass scale and their equally massive disappearance. Meyerhold, with whom I worked and whom I dared to call my friend, is proof of this. It's impossible to imagine now how popular Meyerhold was. Everyone knew him, even those who had no interest in or connection with the theater or art. In the circus, clowns always made jokes about Meyerhold. They go for instant laughs in the circus, and they wouldn't sing ditties about people the audience wouldn't recognize immediately. They even used to sell combs called Meyerhold.

And then the man disappeared, he just disappeared and that was it. As though he had never existed. That went on for decades, no one mentioned Meyerhold. The silence was terrible, deathly. I met very well educated young people who had never heard anything at all about Meyerhold. He had been erased, like a tiny blot with a large ink eraser.

This was going on in Moscow, the capital of a major European power, with people who were known all over the world. You can imagine what was happening in the provinces, in our Asian republics. In the provinces this exchange in which a man became nothing, a zero, and the zeros and nonentities became important, was a usual occurrence, an everyday event. This spirit still reigns in the provinces.

It leads to sad consequences in music. An enormous number of operas, ballets, symphonies, oratorios, and so on produced in, say, Central Asia—Tashkent, Ashkhabad, Dushanbe, Alma-Ata, Frunze—are not written by the local composers credited on the published scores and the concert programs. The real authors will remain unknown to the public at large, and no one will ask, Who are these musical slaves?

I know many of them. They're different people with different destinies and there have been several generations of ghost composers by now. The oldest ones are dying off. They found themselves in the faraway provinces because they had been exiled there or because they ran away from Moscow and Leningrad, escaping possible arrest. Sometimes running to the sticks helped. A man changed his address and they left him alone. I know several such cases.

These composers made a life for themselves in the national republics. This was just when Moscow was interested in big showcases of native talent from the national republics. It was so shameful that I want to dwell on it separately, particularly since it is still thought that the cultural fests of the thirties were not only necessary but beneficial.

Actually, the first comparison that should spring to the mind of any sober (and not too stupid) person seeing all these jigs and dances is with Ancient Rome, because it was to Rome that the emperor had the natives brought from the conquered provinces, so that the new slaves could demonstrate their cultural accomplishments to the residents of the capital. As all can see, the idea is not new and we can be certain that Stalin borrowed more than his favorite architectural style from Rome. He also borrowed—to a certain degree—the style of cultural life, an imperial style. (I doubt that he was erudite, and it was probably an adapted version of Rome that impressed him, Mussolini's version.)

In short, the vanquished tribes sang and danced and composed hymns in honor of the great leader. But this shameful spectacle certainly had nothing to do with national art. This wasn't art. They simply needed fresh-baked odes to the greatest and the wisest.

Traditional national art and traditional—marvelous—music didn't fit. For many reasons. First of all, the art was too refined, too complex, too unfamiliar. Stalin wanted things simple, striking, quick. As pushcart *pirozhki* vendors used to say in Russia, "It'll be hot, but I can't vouch for the taste."

Second, national art was considered counterrevolutionary. Why? Because it was, like any ancient art, religious, cultic. If it's religious, then tear it out with its roots. I hope someone will write down the history of how our great native art was destroyed in the twenties and thirties. It was destroyed forever because it was oral. When they shoot a folk singer or a wandering storyteller, hundreds of great musical works die with him. Works that had never been written down. They die forever, irrevocably, because another singer represents other songs.

I'm not a historian. I could tell many tragic tales and cite many examples, but I won't do that. I will tell about one incident, only one. It's a horrible story and every time I think of it I grow frightened and I don't want to remember it. Since time immemorial, folk singers have wandered along the roads of the Ukraine. They're called *lirniki* and *banduristy* there. They were almost always blind men—why that is so is another question that I won't go into, but briefly, it's traditional.

214

The point is, they were always blind and defenseless people, but no one ever touched or hurt them. Hurting a blind man—what could be lower?

And then in the mid thirties the First All-Ukrainian Congress of Lirniki and Banduristy was announced, and all the folk singers had to gather and discuss what to do in the future. "Life is better, life is merrier," Stalin had said. The blind men believed it. They came to the congress from all over the Ukraine, from tiny, forgotten villages. There were several hundred of them at the congress, they say. It was a living museum, the country's living history. All its songs, all its music and poetry. And they were almost all shot, almost all those pathetic blind men killed.

Why was it done? Why the sadism—killing the blind? Just like that, so that they wouldn't get underfoot. Mighty deeds were being done there, complete collectivization was under way, they had destroyed kulaks as a class, and here were these blind men, walking around singing songs of dubious content. The songs weren't passed by the censors. And what kind of censorship can you have with blind men? You can't hand a blind man a corrected and approved text and you can't write him an order either. You have to tell everything to a blind man. That takes too long. And you can't file away a piece of paper, and there's no time anyway. Collectivization. Mechanization. It was easier to shoot them. And so they did.

And that's just one story out of many like it, but I've said that I'm not a historian. I just wanted to tell what I know well—too well. And I know that when all the necessary research is completed, when all the facts are gathered, and when they are confirmed by the necessary documents, the people who were responsible for these evil deeds will have to answer for them, if only before their descendants.

If I didn't believe in that completely, life wouldn't be worth living.

But let me return to where I began. I was talking about composers who left Moscow and Leningrad and moved to the boundaries of the country. They sat around in Godforsaken corners, living in fear, waiting for the knock on the door in the middle of the night, waiting to be taken away forever, like their friends or relatives. And then it turned out that they were needed. There was a crying need for triumphant songs and dances for festivities in Moscow, and for musical accusations of the past and musical praise for the new. They needed "folk" music that retained one or two reminiscent melodies from authentic folk art, something like the Georgian "Suliko," the leader and teacher's favorite song.

The real folk musicians had been almost completely eradicated, only individuals here and there were left alive. And even if they had been spared, they wouldn't have been able to switch over as fast as the authorities wanted them to, they wouldn't have been able to do it. The ability to switch over instantaneously is a quality of the professional of the new era. It's a quality of our intelligentsia. "Excellency, give the order and I'll switch over this instant," as one character said in Mayakovsky's play *The Baths*. (I'm sure that Mayakovsky wrote that about himself.)

It called for an "extraordinary nimbleness of thought," in Gogol's phrase, and a similar attitude toward the local national culture. The composers I'm talking about were strangers and professionals. And they were also very, very scared. Thus all the necessary prerequisites for a "lush burgeoning" (as they began calling it) of national art—a completely new socialist national art—were there. The fellows got to work and national operas, ballets, and cantatas poured forth in a mighty stream. Things weren't as good with symphonies, but there wasn't much of a demand for symphonies. They didn't need concertos or chamber music either. They needed loyal lyrics, an easy-to-understand plot. They took plots from the terrible past, usually about some uprising or other. It was easy to work out stereotyped conflicts within the plot and then add on a doomed love story to elicit a tear or two.

The central protagonist, naturally, was a hero without fear or reproach. But there always had to be a traitor, that was necessary, it called for increased vigilance. This corresponded to reality too. From a professional point of view, this was all rather sound, in the best traditions of the Rimsky-Korsakov school which I knew so well. It's disgusting to admit it, but it's true.

They took local folk melodies (the ones that were most accessible to the European ear) and developed them in a European style. Everything "superfluous" (from their point of view) was ruthlessly excised. It was just like the old joke: "What's a cane? A well-edited Christmas tree."

It was all harmonious and neat, but once the last note was written on the score and the ink had dried, the most difficult part began. They had to find an author for the concoction. An author whose name would be as euphonious as the music, but in the opposite direction, so to speak. While the music had to be maximally European, the author's name had to be maximally national. They glued a vivid exotic label onto a standard European product. In general, they managed well with this problem. They found some agreeable young, or some not so young but vain, *natsmen* (this derogatory contraction of *natsionalnoye men'shinstvo,* or national minority, became current at that time too), who, without the slightest tremor from his conscience, signed his name on the cover of a work he hadn't composed. The transaction was completed and the world gained one more rogue.

But our "professionals" didn't stay in the woodwork. First of all, their names sometimes appeared on the title pages of the scores or in the programs and posters, naturally only as co-authors, but that was a big honor for the homeless composers. Second, even if their names remained in the shadows, they were rewarded, and quite generously. They were given titles, decorations, and they were well paid. They ate well, slept on soft feather beds, and lived in their own little houses. Finally, and most importantly, they were less frightened, The fear hadn't disappeared completely, of course, it never does. The fear was in their blood forever, but they could breathe more easily. And for that they were eternally grateful to the national republics in which they had settled.

I have several friends among these workers and I can say that they were satisfied with the situation for decades. I was always amazed by that. I knew how poets suffered when need and extenuating circumstances (for instance, that same fear) drove them to translation. Poetic translation in connection with the "lush burgeoning" of the national cultures deserves special attention, but it's not my business. I will just say that the picture was the same. The poet was given a Russian "pony" of a poem that didn't exist at all in the national language. In other words, there was a bad prose Russian version of what the poem would have been had the national "author" been able to write it.

And so the Russian poet wrote a poem based on the plot summary and sometimes the poems were marvelous. The poet made candy from shit, as we say, forgive my vulgarity.

Pasternak and Akhmatova suffered when they did such work. They felt—and quite rightly—that they were committing a two-fold crime. The first was falsifying the true picture. For money and out of fear they pretended that something existed. The second crime was against their own talent. They were burying their own talent through this translation.

I'll admit that writing doesn't always come, but I'm totally against walking around looking at the sky when you're experiencing a block, waiting for inspiration to strike you. Tchaikovsky and Rimsky-Korsakov didn't like each other and agreed on very few things, but they were of one opinion on this: you had to write constantly. If you can't write a major work, write minor trifles. If you can't write at all, orchestrate something. I think Stravinsky felt the same way.

This seems to be the Russian composers' stand, and I feel it's thoroughly professional and differs greatly from what they apparently think about us in the West. I think that there they still believe that we write between bouts of drinking, dipping pen into vodka. Actually, interest in alcohol doesn't exclude professionalism and I'm not the exception to the rule of the Russian school of composition in this respect.

So you must constantly train your hand, and there's nothing bad about translations or reworkings per se, but you should work with material that is necessary or dear to you. I realize that you don't say to yourself: "This I need and this is dear to me," but you sense it in your gut. In the country, if a dog is sick it goes into the fields and seeks out the right herbs and grasses by instinct. It chews on them and gets well. I was saved that way by working "with" Mussorgsky several times and I could name a few other times when working with the composition of someone else refreshed and relaxed me. For instance, I did a new orchestration of the First Cello Concerto by the young and extraordinarily talented Boris Tishchenko* and gave the score to him on his birthday. I don't think he was terribly pleased, but the work gave me nothing but benefit and pleasure.

When Pasternak translated *Hamlet* or *Faust* it must have enriched him, but he also translated third-rate and completely unknown poets, a huge number of Georgian poets. This was a way—one way—to please Stalin. The same thing was happening to Akhmatova. They both suf-

---

*Boris Ivanovich Tishchenko (b. 1939), composer, Shostakovich's favorite student. He is extremely prolific and his works are widely performed in the Soviet Union.

fered, of course, and talked about it rather frequently. But my composer friends were always happy and satisfied. Things were going well for them, no one bothered them, and they feared less and less. It seemed that they would flourish for eternity. But alas, nothing is eternal on this earth, and even their strange happiness came to an end.

A new generation of national composers grew up. These young people were educated at our best conservatories and they were talented and ambitious—two elements that give the fastest chemical reaction. They had to make it themselves, and the sacred oaks, hung with orders and medals, were in their way. In most cases, there was no romance between the patriarchs and the young, the contrast in education was too great. At first the young composers from the national republics imitated Prokofiev, Khachaturian, me. Later, Bartók and Stravinsky. They studied whatever Western scores they could get their hands on. Not particularly avant-garde, but still . . . And as a result, they came to a conclusion: they had to seek their own paths, or they wouldn't get ahead. And then they remembered their own native music; not the songs that were always on the radio and television, but the real folk music—still not reworked, and unmutilated.

Until that time everyone used the anthologies of folk songs made by folklorists thirty, forty, and even fifty years earlier. They were considered the best and most literate recordings, and perhaps they were—for their time. But the young people were beginning to have doubts, so they started looking for real folk singers, and there weren't many left. But there were a few and those few had even secretly found students, young ones. I suppose it is true that folk culture can't be completely eradicated after all. It will go on living underground—or at least smoldering, like a weak flame, waiting for better times.

And the young composers saw an amazing picture, one they were seeing for the first time. They saw that what was passing as "folk" and "national" was sheer falsification. They tried to raise a hue and cry and in some places things reached the level of fights and even brawls. But they achieved only partial success. The sacred oaks stirred, the sacred rocks, covered with moss and medals, moved, and so did our old friends the professionals from Moscow and Leningrad, who had been living such a cozy life in their marvelous houses, planning on reaping the rich harvest forever.

Life in the fresh air, on the periphery, far from the worries and pollution of the capital, had been good for them. They were in wonderful health and were ready to work. They had no plans to stop putting out newer and newer "national" operas, ballets, and cantatas for all the holidays and festivities, which kept increasing in number. It was so good, and you could even creep into the history of music—not world music, but local music, and if not as a composer, then as co-composer. And suddenly their positions, their glorious historic past and future, were threatened. How unfair.

This was the first time that I saw my friends in a glum mood. They were very philosophical about it, they sighed and spoke of human ingratitude. They said that these savages would have remained savages if not for their enlightened help and support, and that the local bosses still ate lamb with their hands, which they wiped on their robes, and that they were scoundrels and polygamists.

But this period of pure unclouded reflection didn't last long, because their positions were crumbling on all fronts. Maybe this really wasn't so, maybe they just imagined it was. But the children of the Rimsky-Korsakov school, allied with the local sacred oaks, moved into counter-attack.

The oaks were pushed in front, moving awesomely and jangling their medals. It was an impressive sight, let me tell you. And in their hands they carried denunciations and complaints, written by the co-authors, of course. They were quite professional in that area too. Rimsky-Korsakov would spin in his grave from shame. The complaints held that a serious threat hung over our state, and that the threat was coming from the young *natsmen,* who were conspirators because their interest in folk music and art was only a cover. Actually, they were interested in a return of bourgeois nationalism, and hiding it under their interest in national art, those young people were planning to secede from our great and mighty lands. Such hostile actions must be stopped immediately and the rebels must be hit hard.

The complaints were sent to the most varying offices, from the Composers' Union on up. I don't know what was in the ones that went higher, but I did read some of those addressed to the Union. My advice wasn't sought, of course, but I did get to see the complaints. I did what I could to help the young people.

Of course, no one cared what I thought, but actually the whole business ended rather well, in that no one was shot or jailed or deprived of his means of support—as far as I know. I may be wrong about the last part, and then again, I'm speaking only of composers. Let someone else report on writers or cinematographers.

The decision made on these matters was indescribably, superhumanly wise. A decisive blow fell on bourgeois nationalism, with "discussions" and meetings in the appropriate offices. They discussed, they accused. The formula, as Ilf and Petrov joked, was a familiar one; just fill in the blanks: "In response to . . . we, Herculeans, as one . . . " In general, the young people were categorically forbidden "to make attempts on the life of sacred things." The sacred oaks could continue to grow in freedom from danger. The swamp was tranquil. Nothing floated up to the surface, not a single reputation suffered, and no dirty linen was aired.

The situation did change somewhat—every national culture divided into two parts. One was the old, in which everything was false, a fake: the names, the reputations, the list of works. The other part, whatever you might say about it, was authentic. The music might have been good or average or even very bad, but it was not false. It was written by the people whose names were on the title pages of the scores. And it was the real composer who came out for a bow after the performance, not a figurehead. So some progress was made.

But the false culture isn't giving up. I'm often invited to the republics for various gala performances of musical achievements, exhibits, plenums, and so on, and I often go. I act as the wedding guest and naturally praise everything in sight, or almost everything. But I see through it all, and my hosts see that I see. And both parties pretend that everything is fine.

These musical festivals always begin with the works of famous composers—and that is all baloney. And the opera house always has the premiere of another opera or ballet on the same theme—national uprising in the distant past. And that's all baloney too. I chuckle to myself when I see that the symphonies of various composers are written—or at the very least, orchestrated (and that's one and the same, as far as I'm concerned)—by one hand. And it's a game for me to guess who the composer really is. Most of the time I do guess, because the real composer (usually from Moscow or Leningrad) will also present a work under his own name.

I easily recognize individual styles in orchestration, even if the "style" is nothing more than good craftsmanship, and I'm almost never wrong. Sometimes I chastise myself for keeping quiet rather than talking, and not only talking but even publishing articles on these trumped-up musical festivals. But what can I do? Can I change anything? Earlier this was a tragedy, that's true. But now it's more of a comedy, things are changing somewhat, and without my participation. I can't do anything anyway.

The worst is behind us, and history can't be turned back. It's good that things are slowly changing. Who would listen to me? Everyone—or almost everyone—is interested in maintaining the status quo. I know for a fact that any attempt at a radical change would end badly, unsuccessfully. Several young Kazakh poets tried to expose the myth of Dzhambul Dzhabayev, and what happened? They were all ordered to keep quiet, and soon afterward they celebrated another anniversary of the long dead Dzhambul, with all pomp and glory—meetings, dramatic speeches, and a great amount of wine and vodka at the banquets.

The call for more Gogols and Saltykov-Shchedrins was probably prompted by these stories. This is a subject for Gogol and for a future composer who will write, perhaps, a marvelous opera called *Dzhambul's Nose*. But not I—no, not I.

And I'm not even sorry, the subject is no longer for me. I really understand Pushkin, who gave the plots of *The Inspector General* and *Dead Souls* to Gogol because they were no longer for him. Everything in its own time.

For instance, I have an unfinished opera, *The Gamblers*, lying around.* I began it during the war, after the Seventh. The fact speaks for itself. I wrote a lot, almost an hour's worth of music, and the score is written down. I had decided that I wouldn't throw away a single word of Gogol's. I didn't need a libretto, Gogol was the best librettist. I set the book in front of me and began writing, turning page after page in the book. And it went well.

But when I got past ten pages, I stopped. What was I doing? First

---

*In 1978, *The Gamblers* was first heard in Leningrad in a concert performance under the baton of Gennady Rozhdestvensky.

of all, the opera was becoming unmanageable, but that wasn't the important thing. The important thing was, who would put on this opera? The subject wasn't heroic or patriotic. Gogol was a classic, and they didn't perform his works anyway. And me, I was just dirt to them. They would say that Shostakovich was making fun, mocking art. How could you have an opera about playing cards? And then, *The Gamblers* had no moral, except perhaps to show how unenlightened people used to be—all they did was play cards and try to cheat one another. They wouldn't understand that humor was a great thing in itself and that it didn't need additional morals.

Humor is a manifestation of the divine impulse, but to whom was I going to explain that? They don't understand serious things like that in the opera houses and certainly not in the offices that run cultural affairs. So I abandoned *The Gamblers*. Sometimes now people suggest that I finish the opera, but I can't. I'm too old. You can't enter the same river twice, as the old saying goes.

I'm thinking about another subject for an opera now, and another writer, Chekhov. A different time and different songs. I'm definitely going to write the opera *The Black Monk*. I'm much more interested in *The Black Monk* than I am in *The Gamblers*. The subject has rubbed my soul full of calluses, you might say.

Chekhov was a very musical writer, but not in the sense that he wrote alliteratively, like *"chuzhdy charam chernyi chyoln."** That's bad poetry and there's nothing musical in it. Chekhov is musical in a deeper sense. He constructed his works the way musical ones are constructed. Naturally, this wasn't conscious, it's just that musical construction reflects more general laws. I am certain that Chekhov constructed *The Black Monk* in sonata form, that there is an introduction, an exposition with main and secondary themes, development, and so on.

One literary critic, to whom I confided my theory, even wrote a scholarly article on it, and quite naturally, got it all confused. Literary critics always get things wrong when they try to write about music, but the article was still printed in some scholarly collection. In general, literary men writing about music should follow the example of Count

*This line from a poem by Symbolist poet Konstantin Balmont is a textbook example of poor and primitive alliteration.

Alexei Tolstoy, who wrote two major articles about my symphonies—the Fifth and Seventh. Both articles are included in his collected works and there are few people who know that actually the articles were written for him by musicologists. They were summoned to Tolstoy's dacha and they helped him through the morass of violins and oboes and other confusing things that a count couldn't possibly fathom.

Braga's serenade, "A Maiden's Prayer," plays an important part in *The Black Monk*. Once upon a time it was very popular, but now the music is forgotten. I'll definitely use it in the opera. I even have a recording of it—I asked some young musicians to play it for me. When I listen to it, I can picture clearly what the opera must be like. I also think about this: What, in essence, is good music and bad music? I don't know, I can't answer definitively. Take that serenade, for instance. According to all the rules it should be bad music, but every time I listen to it, tears come to my eyes. And that music, that "Maiden's Prayer," must have affected Chekhov too, or he wouldn't have written about it as he did, with such insight. Probably there is no good or bad music, there is only music that excites you and music that leaves you indifferent. That's all.

And that, by the way, makes me sad. For example, my father liked gypsy songs and sang them, and I liked the music. But then those songs were humiliated so much, reduced to mud. They called it Nepman music,* bad taste, and so on. I remember how shocked Prokofiev was when I told him that I personally wasn't offended by gypsy music. He used every opportunity to point out that he felt above such things.

And what was the end result? The persecution was unsuccessful and gypsy music is flourishing. The audiences are breaking down the doors, I point out, disregarding the anger of the more advanced elements of musical opinion. And here's an opposite example, Hindemith's music. It's published and recorded but there's no great interest in listening to it. Yet once his works had a great impact on me. Hindemith is a true musician, a serious one, and a rather pleasant man. I knew him slightly, he played in Leningrad as part of a quartet. He

---

* "Nepman music" is one of the official pejorative definitions of pop music, an object of constant persecution in the Soviet Union. NEP (New Economic Policy, proclaimed by Lenin in 1921 in the face of economic problems) led to a renaissance of private enterprise and to the appearance of restaurants and nightclubs where, in addition to gypsy music, they played the tango, fox trot, Charleston, and so on—that is, "bourgeois" music. In 1928 Maxim Gorky in *Pravda* called jazz "music of the fat bourgeoisie," and for many years this was an official definition.

made a nice impression. And his music is like his personality; everything is in place, well put together, and it's not merely craft, it has feeling and meaning and content. It's just impossible to listen to. The music doesn't spark, it doesn't spark. But gypsy songs, damn them, do. Go figure it out.

I want to have time to write that opera based on Chekhov. I love Chekhov, I often reread "Ward Six." I like everything he wrote, including the early stories. And I feel sorry that I didn't do as much work on Chekhov as I had wanted to. Of course, my student Veniamin Fleishman wrote an opera based on Chekhov's "Rothschild's Violin." I suggested he do an opera on the subject. Fleishman was a sensitive spirit and he had a fine rapport with Chekhov. But he had a hard life. Fleishman had a tendency to write sad music rather than happy music, and naturally, he was abused for it. Fleishman sketched out the opera but then he volunteered for the army. He was killed. He went into the People's Volunteer Guard. They were all candidates for corpsehood. They were barely trained and poorly armed, and thrown into the most dangerous areas. A soldier could still entertain hopes of survival, but a volunteer guardsman, no. The guard of the Kuibyshev District, which was the one Fleishman joined, perished almost completely. Rest in peace.

I'm happy that I managed to complete *Rothschild's Violin* and orchestrate it. It's a marvelous opera—sensitive and sad. There are no cheap effects in it, it is wise and very Chekhovian. I'm sorry that our theaters pass over Fleishman's opera. It's certainly not the fault of the music, as far as I can see.

I would like to write more music on Chekhovian themes; it's a shame that composers seem to overlook Chekhov. I have a work based on motifs from Chekhov, the Fifteenth Symphony. It's not a sketch for *The Black Monk,* but variations on a theme. Much of the Fifteenth is related to *The Black Monk,* even though it is a thoroughly independent work.

I never did learn to live according to Chekhov's main tenet. For Chekhov all people are the same. He presented people and the reader had to decide for himself what was bad and what was good. Chekhov remained unprejudiced. Everything inside me churns when I read "Rothschild's Violin." Who's right, who's wrong? Who made life nothing but steady losses? Everything churns within me.

MUSSORGSKY and I have a "special relationship." He was an entire academy for me—of human relations, politics, and art. I didn't study him with only my eyes and ears, for that's not enough for a composer or any professional. (That holds for other arts as well. Think how many great painters spend years slaving over copies without seeing anything shameful in it.)

I revere Mussorgsky, I consider him one of the greatest Russian composers. Almost simultaneously with the creation of my piano quintet, I was busy on a new edition of his opera *Boris Godunov*. I had to look through the score, smooth out a few wrinkles in the harmonization and some unfortunate and pretentious bits of orchestration, and change a few discrete progressions. A number of instruments had been added to the orchestration that had never been used by either Mussorgsky or Rimsky-Korsakov, who edited *Boris*.

Mussorgsky had made many changes and corrections on the advice of Stasov, Rimsky-Korsakov, and others, and then Korsakov made quite a few changes on his own. Korsakov's edition of *Boris Godunov* reflects the ideology, ideas, and artistry of the last century. You can't

. help respecting the enormous amount of work done by him. But I wanted to edit the opera in a different way, I wanted a greater symphonic development, I wanted the orchestra to do more than simply accompany the singers.

Rimsky-Korsakov was despotic and tried to make the score submit to his own style, rewriting a lot and adding his own music. I changed only a few bars and rewrote very little. But certain things did have to be changed. The scene in the forest outside Kromy had to be given a worthy spot. Mussorgsky had orchestrated it like a student afraid of failing an exam. Falteringly and badly. I did it over.

This is how I worked. I placed Mussorgsky's piano arrangement in front of me and then two scores—Mussorgsky's and Rimsky-Korsakov's. I didn't look at the scores, and I rarely looked at the piano arrangement either. I orchestrated from memory, act by act. Then I compared my orchestration with those by Mussorgsky and Rimsky-Korsakov. If I saw that either had done it better, then I stayed with that. I didn't reinvent bicycles. I worked honestly, with ferocity, I might say.

Mussorgsky has marvelously orchestrated moments, but I see no sin in my work. I didn't touch the successful parts, but there are many unsuccessful parts because he lacked mastery of the craft, which comes only through time spent on your backside, no other way. For instance, the polonaise in the Polish act is abominable, yet it's an important moment. The same holds for Boris's coronation. And the bell—now, what kind of bell is that? It's just a pathetic parody. These are very important scenes and can't be tossed away.

Of course, there was one notable character, Boris Asafiev, who proposed that there was a theoretical basis for Mussorgsky's incompetence. This Boris was known for his ability to invent a theoretical basis for almost anything. He spun like a top. Anyway, Asafiev maintained that all the scenes I just mentioned were orchestrated wonderfully by Mussorgsky, that it was part of his plan. He intended the coronation scene to be lackluster to show that the people were against Boris's coronation. This was the people's form of protest—clumsy orchestration. And in the Polish act, Asafiev would have you believe, Mussorgsky was exposing the decadent gentry, and therefore let the Poles dance to poor instrumentation. That was his way of punishing them.

Only it's all nonsense. Glazunov told me that Mussorgsky himself played all these scenes for him on the piano—the bells and the coronation. And Glazunov said that they were brilliant and powerful—that was the way Mussorgsky wanted them to be, for he was a dramatist of great genius from whom I learn and learn. I'm not speaking of orchestration now. I'm talking about something else.

You don't enter by the front door in composition. You have to touch and feel everything with your own hand. Listening, enjoying, saying, "Ah, how wonderful," isn't enough. For a professional that's self-indulgence. Our work has always been manual, moreover—no machines, no technology can help. That is, if you work honestly, without any chicanery. You can always tape something and then let others arrange and orchestrate it for you. I know one such "talented" man* who behaves in just this ugly manner—he's lazy, I suppose. The Kirov put on an entire ballet written that way. In fact, things turned out quite mysteriously there; they wouldn't let the composer into the hall during rehearsal. The ushers at the Kirov tore the persistent "talented" composer's jacket when he insisted. The ushers are excellent bouncers; it's an official theater.

The funniest part was that the ballet was based on "the best, the most talented" Mayakovsky's *The Bedbug*. (The choreography by Yakobson,† however, was good.) *The Bedbug* on stage at the former Maryinsky Theater is grotesque enough to suit even Mussorgsky. Look how far it crawled, as they say. That bedbug didn't pass anyone by, including me.

Of course, composing by tape recorder is a special taste, like licking rubber boots, and I not only eschew such perversion, I don't even like composing at the piano. Now I really can't, even if I wanted to. I'm training my left hand to write, in case I lose ability in my right. That's gymnastics for the dying.

But composing at the piano was always a secondary way for me. That's for the deaf and those who have a poor sense of the orchestra, who need some small aural support for their work. Yet there are "great masters" who keep a staff of secretaries to orchestrate their epochal opuses.‡ I never could understand that way of increasing "productivity."

*A reference to Leningrad composer Oleg Karavaichuk.
†Leonid Veniaminovich Yakobson (1904–1974), avant-garde choreographer, one of the producers of Shostakovich's ballet *The Golden Age*.
‡A reference to Sergei Prokofiev.

As a rule, I hear the score and write it down in ink, finished copy—without rough drafts or studies—and I'm not saying this to brag. In the final analysis, everyone composes as best suits him, but I've always seriously warned my students against picking out tunes on the piano. I had a near-fatal case of this disease, improviser's itch, in childhood.

Mussorgsky is a tragic example of the dangers of piano composing. Very tragic—while he plinked away, so much great music was never written down! Of the many works about which only stories remain, I am most tormented by the opera *Biron*. What a piece of Russian history! It has villainy and a foreign martinet. He showed parts of it to friends, he did. They tried to talk him into writing it down, but he replied stubbornly, "I've got it firmly in my head." What you have in your head, put down on paper. The head is a fragile vessel.

People will say, What's this fellow doing teaching Mussorgsky? That's all we need, someone to teach the classics. But for me Mussorgsky is not a classic (incidentally, he wrote a marvelous musical lampoon, "The Classic," directed against critics; the subtitle reads: "Apropos the Musical Scribblings of Famintsyn") but a living man. Trite, but true. I would probably share several of my critical comments with Mussorgsky without fear of being laughed at. And I would not talk down, like the generals of the Mighty Five (I mean, above all, Cui,* a thoroughly average and self-reliant composer), or up, like Mussorgsky's boozy pals from the Maly Yaroslavets tavern, but as one professional to another. If I didn't feel that way about Mussorgsky, I wouldn't have taken on the orchestration of his works.

Doing the instrumentation of *Boris* was like a poultice for a wound. The times were difficult and mean, unbelievably mean and hard. There was the agreement with our "sworn friend,"† Europe was crumbling, and you know our hopes were dependent on Europe. Every day brought more bad news, and I felt so much pain, I was so lonely and afraid, that I wanted to distract myself somehow, to spend some

*Cesar Antonovich Cui (1835–1918), composer, general (military engineer), music critic, and member of the famous group of composers (Balakirev, Cui, Mussorgsky, Rimsky-Korsakov, and Borodin) called the "Mighty Five," or the "Mighty Bunch." The name, once used by critic Vladimir Stasov and entrenched in history, unites composers differing widely in tastes, temperaments, and levels of talent. Generally speaking, the common ideal of the Mighty Five might be termed "musical realism."

†The "sworn friend" was what wags called Nazi Germany, which signed a treaty of nonaggression with Stalin in August 1939, and in September of the same year a treaty of friendship. Any criticism of Hitler was strictly forbidden at the time and the word "fascism" disappeared from use. Instead the papers made daily attacks on England and France.

time with a musically like-minded man, tête-à-tête.

The Sixth Symphony was finished and I knew for sure what the next one would be about, so I sat down with the complete composer's piano reduction of *Boris,* published by Lamm (it included the St. Basil's and Kromy scenes). I put it on the desk and there it lay, for I didn't disturb it too often. After all, I do know the music rather well, in fact, quite well.

I should mention Lamm's role and work in the field. Whenever he acted alone, without Asafiev, his work was substantial and beautiful, you might say solid, in the St. Petersburg academic manner. But as soon as Asafiev involved himself, all kinds of unthinkable deviltry and nonsense crept in—for example, the so-called composer's score of *Boris,* published jointly by Asafiev and Lamm in the late twenties. I can suggest—with a strong sense of probability—that Asafiev's motivating impulse was for royalties for *Boris.* The old ring of the scorned metal. They slapped together the staging too, which was really shameful.

They turned a good idea—restoring the authentic *Boris*—into God knows what, some sort of self-serving enterprise with Marxist underpinnings. In order to put Rimsky-Korsakov's edition out of commission, our iconoclasts accused it of all the mortal "ideological" sins. And Glazunov, who came to Korsakov's defense—partly out of principle and partly out of conviction—was smeared in print by Asafiev, who used phrases like "shark of imperialism" or "the last imperialistic toady," I don't remember exactly which. But insults were used and Glazunov's feelings were badly hurt. I think it was the last straw—he was a patient man but this was too much. Soon after, Glazunov went "for a rest" in the West.

I was forced to consider this history while I was orchestrating *Boris.* I was entering into direct conflict with Asafiev and I think I later felt the repercussions. That's what Mussorgsky's music is like—it's always alive, too alive (if such a quality can ever be excessive)—and that means that an argument with citizens grabbing each other by the lapels is not far behind. Meyerhold told me that in his day and I've finally come to believe it.

Nothing compares with the feeling you get orchestrating a revered composer. I think it's the ideal method for studying a work, and I would recommend that all young composers make their own versions of the works of those masters from whom they want to learn. I had known *Boris* almost by heart since my Conservatory days, but it was only when I orchestrated it that I sensed and experienced it as if it were my own work.

I suppose I can spend some time talking about the "Mussorgsky orchestra." We must assume that his orchestral "intentions" were correct but he simply couldn't realize them. He wanted a sensitive and flexible orchestra. As far as I can tell, he imagined something like a singing line around the vocal parts, the way subvoices surround the main melodic line in Russian folk song. But Mussorgsky lacked the technique for that. What a shame! Obviously, he had a purely orchestral imagination, and purely orchestral imagery as well. The music strives for "new shores," as they say—musical dramaturgy, musical dynamics, language, imagery. But his orchestral technique drags him back to the old shores.

So, naturally, the Leningrad production of 1928 was a flop, and since then all attempts to stick to the composer's score have come to a shameful end. It's funny and it's sad that sometimes nowadays the basses with rather weak voices plump for the Mussorgsky score because they have to strain less. But the public isn't very concerned about that and therefore *Boris Godunov* is usually performed in either the Korsakov version or mine.

I kept thinking, Well, maybe I'll be able to do Mussorgsky a service, bringing his opera closer to the listener. Let them go and learn. There's plenty to learn here. I kept thinking that the parallels were so obvious, they'd have to notice, they wouldn't be able to miss them. Rimsky-Korsakov softened the point a bit, he muffled the eternal Russian problem of the upstart tsar versus the embittered people. Mussorgsky's concept is profoundly democratic. The people are the base of everything. The people are here and the rulers are there. The rule forced on the people is immoral and fundamentally anti-people. The best intentions of individuals don't count. That's Mussorgsky's position and I dare hope that it is also mine.

I was also caught up in Mussorgsky's certainty that the contradictions between the rulers and the oppressed people were insoluble, which meant that the people had to suffer cruelly without end, and become ever more embittered. The government, in its attempt to estab-

231

lish itself, was decaying, putrefying. Chaos and state collapse lay ahead, as prophesied by the last two scenes of the opera. I expected it to happen in 1939.

I always felt that the ethical basis of *Boris* was my own. The author uncompromisingly decries the amorality of an anti-people government, which is inevitably criminal, even inexorably criminal. It is rotten from within and it is particularly revolting that it hides under the name of the people. I always hope that the average listener in the audience will be moved by Boris's words, "Not I . . . it's the people . . . it's the will of the people." What familiar phraseology! The style of justifying villainy in Russia never changes, the stench of evil lingers. There are the same evocations of "legality." Boris is hypocritically incensed: ". . . Questioning tsars, legal tsars, tsars who were appointed, elected by the people, and crowned by the great Patriarch!" I shudder every time I hear it. The stench of evil lingers.

Strangely enough (and this may be a professional quirk), I don't see all that in the Pushkin—I mean, theoretically, I can understand it, but I don't feel it as much, I just don't. Pushkin puts it all much more elegantly. So for me, the abstract art—music—is more effective, even when it's a question of whether or not a man is a criminal. I was always very proud of music for that.

Music illuminates a person through and through, and it is also his last hope and final refuge. And even half-mad Stalin, a beast and a butcher, instinctively sensed that about music. That's why he feared and hated it. I've been told that he never missed a performance of *Boris* at the Bolshoi. He understood absolutely nothing in music, contrary to firmly rooted opinion. Now I'm observing a renaissance of the Stalin legend. I wouldn't be surprised if it turned out that his "brilliant works" were written by someone else. He was like Hoffmann's sweet Klein Zaches, but a million times more vicious and dangerous.

What bothered Stalin in *Boris*? That the blood of the innocent will sooner or later rise from the soil. That's the ethical center of the opera. It means that the ruler's crimes cannot be justified in the name of the people or hidden by the butcher's "legality." You will have to answer for your crimes someday.

However, Tsar Boris is much better than the "Leader of the Peoples." According to Pushkin and Mussorgsky, he worries about the well-being of those peoples and he is not completely lacking in kindness and fairness. Just take the scene with the *Yurodivy*. And finally, unlike Stalin, he's a loving, tender father. And what about his guilty conscience? That's not so little, is it? Of course, it's easy to feel guilty once you've committed evil. Sometimes that typically Russian trait sickens me. Our people are much too fond of making a mess and then pounding their chests and smearing tears all over their faces. They howl and howl, but how can howling help? That's a slave mentality, a treacherous habit.

Still, you can sometimes believe a repentant man, and here we have a repentant ruler, a truly rare sight. Yet the people hate Boris, because he forced himself on them, because he besmirched himself with murder.

I remember that I was very bothered by one other thought at the time. It was clear to everyone that war was coming, sooner or later it was coming. And I thought that it would follow the plot of *Boris Godunov*. A chasm had developed between the government and the people, and let's not forget that it was the breach with the people that caused Boris's armies to lose in the battle with the Pretender, and it was also the cause of the subsequent state collapse.

The time of troubles was ahead. "Dark darkness, impenetrable!" And "Sorrow, sorrow for Russia, weep, oh, weep, Russian people! Hungry people!" cries the *Yurodivy*. In those days it sounded like news from the papers—not the official brazen lies that paraded on the front pages, but the news that we read between the lines.

My score of *Boris* has several not bad, in fact rather nice spots, I'm pleased with them. It's easier for me to judge my work here because I'm not really dealing with my own music. After all, it is Mussorgsky's music. I just did the coloring, so to speak. But as I've said, I sometimes got so carried away that I considered the music mine, particularly since it came from within, like something I composed.

There was no mechanical work in that score for me. That's the way it is for me in any instrumentation. There are no "insignificant details," no "inessential episodes" or neutral phenomena when it comes to sound. Take the big monastery bell in the scene in the monk's cell. Mussorgsky (and Rimsky-Korsakov) used the gong. Rather elementary, too simplistic, too flat. I felt that the bell was very important here, I had to show the atmosphere of the monastery's estrangement, I had to cut Pimen off from the rest of the world. When the bell tolls, it's a reminder that there are powers mightier than man, that you can't escape the judgment of history. That's what I felt the bell was saying, so I depicted it by the simultaneous playing of seven instruments—bass clarinet, double bassoon, French horns, the gong, harps, piano, and double basses (at an octave)—and I think the sound was more like a large real bell.

In Rimsky-Korsakov's version, the orchestra often sounds more colorful than mine. He uses brighter timbres and chops up the melodic lines too much. I juxtapose the basic orchestral groups more often, and stress more sharply the dramatic "outbursts" and "splashes." Rimsky-Korsakov's orchestra sounds calmer and more balanced. I don't think that's appropriate to *Boris*. He should have followed the mood changes of the characters with more flexibility. And besides, I feel that the meaning of the choruses is more easily made clear by setting off the melody. In Rimsky-Korsakov's version the melody and the subvoices usually blend, which perhaps obliterates their meaning.

Meaning in music—that must sound very strange for most people. Particularly in the West. It's here in Russia that the question is usually posed: What was the composer trying to say, after all, with this musical work? What was he trying to make clear? The questions are naïve, of course, but despite their naïveté and crudity, they definitely merit being asked. And I would add to them, for instance: Can music attack evil? Can it make man stop and think? Can it cry out and thereby draw man's attention to various vile acts to which he has grown accustomed? to the things he passes without any interest?

All these questions began for me with Mussorgsky. And after him I must add the name of the little-known (despite all the reverence accorded him) Alexander Dargomyzhsky and his satiric songs "The Worm" and "Titular Counselor," and his dramatic "Old Corporal." Personally, I consider Dargomyzhsky's *Stone Guest* the best musical embodiment of the Don Juan legend. But Dargomyzhsky doesn't have Mussorgsky's scope. Both men brought bent backs and trampled lives into music and that's why they are dearer to me than so many other brilliant composers.

I've been berated all my life for pessimism, nihilism, and other socially dangerous traits. Once I came across a marvelous letter of the poet Nikolai Nekrasov, an answer to rebukes for excessive bile. I don't remember the exact words, but the point was that he had been told that one's attitude toward reality had to be "healthy." (Here's another opportunity to mention that aesthetic terminology does not change in Russia with the centuries.) Nekrasov answered this demand brilliantly: to wit, that a healthy attitude can be had only toward a healthy reality, and that he would get down on his knees to the Russian who would finally burst with anger, since there were so many reasons to do so in Russia. I think that's well said. Nekrasov ends, "And when we begin to get angry more, then we'll be able to love better, that is, more—and love not ourselves but our homeland." I would sign my name to those words. "Suddenly you could see far to the ends of the earth," as Gogol said in "The Terrible Vengeance."

It's become fashionable to talk about Mussorgsky over a glass or two, and I must confess that I, too, have had deep talks about him after a few rounds, but I think that I have two excuses. First, that I've always felt the same way about Mussorgsky, unaffected by fashion and "obligatory convictions," by what might please them "upstairs" or in Paris. And second, I have done something of a practical nature to popularize his music, though it didn't work that way. In fact, I think I lost and Rimsky-Korsakov's edition—rather crude, after all—is still ahead. My orchestral version of *Songs and Dances of Death* isn't performed too often either.

Really, we musicians do like to talk about Mussorgsky, in fact I think that it's the second favorite topic after Tchaikovsky's love life. There's much that is confused and unclear both in Mussorgsky's life and in the creation of his music. There's much that I like in his biography, above all its darkness—those entire chunks of his life about which we know nothing. There are many friends whom we know only by name, and probably we have the names wrong too. Unknown people, unknown ties: he cleverly escaped history's detectives. I like that a lot.

Mussorgsky was probably the most *yurodivy* of the Russian—and not only the Russian—composers. The style of his letters is horrible, simply horrible, yet he states astonishingly true and new ideas, though in very bizarre, unnatural, and tiring language. It's too pretentious.

You have to race through the letters to get their gist.

But there are a few gems, like: "The sky is dressed in a gendarme's blue-gray pants" (this is a typical Petersburg view). And I like the way Mussorgsky grumbles, " 'The world of sound is limitless.' But brains are limited!" Or take the expression "a well-hammered head." But you have to dig for such witty remarks, haul them out of the bathetic tirades. I'm very happy to say that he wasn't a boisterous bully or squabbler in life. As I understand it, he never took offense or fought over his works in public. When he was criticized, he kept quiet, nodded, almost agreed. But the agreement lasted only as far as the door; once he was outside, he took up his work again, like one of those dolls you can't knock down. I understand and like that very much!

Everyone who felt like it harangued and criticized him. His colleagues called him a lump of dough, even an idiot. Balakirev: "His brains are weak." Stasov: "He has nothing inside." Cui was right in line too, of course: "Naturally, I don't believe in his work." We can laugh now, dear comrades, everything's over, no one is hurt, art goes on. But how did Mussorgsky feel? I can imagine, based on my own reactions—you may understand it all, but you read a paper and your mood plummets.

Music that doesn't stir up arguments could be soothing and charming, but is more likely to be dreary. A hue and cry in itself doesn't prove a thing, naturally, and often is nothing but publicity. I remember that when I was young they used to lure people into side shows with loud patter, but once you got inside it was a total disappointment. But still I fear silence or concerted, nauseatingly saccharine praise much more. In the last few years my works have been praised more at home than abroad. Once it was just the reverse. But I didn't believe my "critics" then and I don't believe my bureaucratic praisers now. Quite often it's the same people, lackeys with brass faces. What do they want from my music? It's hard to guess. Maybe they're pleased that it's become soothing and toothless? Bringing on sweet dreams? I think that they don't understand it correctly, I think they're making an honest—as honest as they can—mistake. I seek my friends' opinions and get angry when they say stupid things. But I'm desperate to find out what audiences really think. It's impossible to tell from published reviews—whether here or abroad.

For the listener I'm a walking mummy, something like a resurrected pharaoh. I'm troubled by the thought that I'm appreciated only for the past. Troubled, but not tormented. Something else does torment me. I confess the hardest thing for me is to appear in public, to attend concerts or plays. I love the theater, and by nature I'm a gawker and an avid fan. I love all kinds of spontaneous cheerful gatherings, and my profoundly lowbrow devotion to soccer knows no bounds. And how can televised soccer compare with the fantastic impact of watching a match at the stadium? It's like distilled water and export Stolichnaya. But I've had to renounce that, like many other things. Doctors talk to me about my body's ills. They examine, prod, and poke me. But I'm sure that my problem is psychological, and that's what torments me. For some reason, I'm certain that everyone is staring at me, that they're all whispering and watching me behind my back, and that they're all waiting for me to fall, or at least trip. And that makes me feel that I will trip any second. When the lights go down and the play or music begins, I'm almost happy (if, of course, the play or music isn't rubbish), but as soon as the lights go back up, I'm miserable again, because I'm open to any stranger's gaze.

I'm drawn to people, "I don't think I could live a day without them,"* yet if I were to become invisible, I'd be happier. I think that this is a recent problem, once upon a time I derived more pleasure from appearing in public. Or am I mistaken?

I must note that I always felt bad when I read or heard something derogatory about myself. It was that way when, in Zoshchenko's words, I was young and strong, when my heart beat madly in my chest and all kinds of thoughts raced through my brain. It's that way now, when I've suffered what he called "a complete devaluation of the organism" and it's impossible to tell where my liver and bladder are any more. It doesn't matter, criticism upsets me even though I don't set much store by it, at least as it is represented by the majority of its practitioners.

Mussorgsky disregarded the critics and listened to his inner voice. (He was right to do so. This is an important example for me—what

---

*An ironic citation from Prince Eletsky's aria in Tchaikovsky's opera *The Queen of Spades*. Shostakovich sprinkled musical citations from this aria in his penultimate opus—the satiric vocal cycle to words from Dostoevsky's *The Possessed*.

Mussorgsky's friends said about his second Gogol opera. I heard something like it about *The Nose,* that's why I was so interested when I learned Mussorgsky's reaction.) But besides all that, Mussorgsky was truly an intellectually curious man, well educated in his own way. He read history and natural sciences, and astronomy, and literature, of course, both Russian and foreign. In general, as I go over Mussorgsky's character and personality, I'm amazed at how much we have in common. This despite the obvious, striking difference. Of course, it is rather impolite to say wonderful things about oneself (knowing that it will all be published one day), and a few bourgeois citizens are sure to reproach me for it.

But it interests me personally to continue drawing these parallels, and in this instance, I won't deny it, it's pleasant. I'm talking primarily about professional things but also about a few mundane traits, as well. For instance, musical memory. I can't complain about mine and Mussorgsky memorized Wagner's operas on first hearing. He could play Wotan's scene by heart after only one hearing of *Siegfried.* He was also an excellent pianist, which is not always remembered. In my opinion, that is indispensable for a composer. And it's not contradictory to my conviction that one must compose away from the piano. I think it's clear why. I've always told my students that only mastery of the piano can give you an opportunity to become acquainted with world literature in music. Perhaps that's not as obligatory now, since everyone can afford records and tapes. But still, a composer must master at least one instrument—piano, violin, viola, flute, trombone, it doesn't matter. Even the triangle.

As a pianist, Mussorgsky was compared with Rubinstein. His piano "bells" are often recalled, and even his enemies admitted that he excelled as an accompanist. He wasn't a purist about it either; he banged away as a young man, not because he needed the money as I did, but just "for company." When he was older, he did marvelous improvisations of humorous scenes—for instance, a young nun playing "A Maiden's Prayer" with great feeling on an untuned piano.

There are many other things I like about him. Mussorgsky understood children, he saw them as "people with their own little world, and not as amusing dolls"—his own words. He appreciated nature, and he was kind to animals, in general to everything living. He couldn't stand the idea of catching a fish on a hook. He suffered whenever any live creature was hurt. And finally there's the question of alcohol, which embarrasses most of our music historians in the Soviet Union. It truly is the dark side of the great composer's life, and they tastefully skirt it, so as not to insult the famous genius's memory. I will allow myself to make a heretical suggestion. If the colleagues and musicians around Mussorgsky had had greater respect for wine, he would have drunk less, or at least with greater benefit to himself. They, too, were what we call drinking citizens, but they were hypocritical about "lemonade," especially Balakirev with his "isn't it time to set our idiot straight?" and so on. That, of course, just depressed Mussorgsky more and he drank even harder. Incidentally, in a certain situation, drink doesn't hurt at all. I'm judging by my own experience. At a certain period of my life, I was greatly liberated by expanding my knowledge in that fascinating area. It did away with excessive reticence, which was almost a disease with me in my youth. My best friend,* who wasn't one to pass up a drink, realized it. I was acting more like an aesthete by then, bored by higher education. Actually, I was madly shy in front of strangers, probably mostly out of pride. So my friend started an intensive course of liberation, since he found great pleasure in a merry and liberated life himself, even though he worked very hard. For an extended period our drinking bouts were practically a daily occurrence. As they say, artists are probably meant to drink by the State Liquor Authority. It's very cozy drinking before lunch.

What hurts is that Mussorgsky died of it. Things were taking a turn for the better for him in the hospital, which makes me conclude that his organism was worthy of universal admiration and awe. The hospital guards were strictly forbidden to bring any wine into the ward, but he bribed one guard with an astounding sum. The wine brought on paralysis, he cried out loudly twice before dying, and that was all.

I'm also particularly moved by this death because the circumstances are rather similar to the ones surrounding the death of my best friend. This can't be passed over with complete silence.

I must say that I began thinking about these and other parallels

*Here and below, the reference is to Sollertinsky.

only very recently; probably it's a sign of advancing senility. I'm falling into my second childhood; in childhood you like to compare yourself with great men. In both cases (childhood and old age) a person is miserable because he doesn't live his own life, he lives other people's lives. You're happy when you live only in this life, and my unhappiness now lies in the fact that I live other lives more and more often. I exist in fantastic worlds and forget about our life, as though it were becoming unbearable for me.

I suppose the fact that I orchestrated *Songs and Dances of Death* as well as *Boris* and *Khovanshchina* proves that I am jealous of Rimsky-Korsakov—that is, that I wanted to surpass him when it came to Mussorgsky. Naturally, *Boris* came first, then *Khovanshchina*. Then for many years my favorite work was *Songs and Dances,* but now I think that I love *Without the Sun* most of all. I feel that this cycle has much in common with the opera I'm determined to write, *The Black Monk,* based on Chekhov.

Working with Mussorgsky clarifies something important for me in my own work. Work on *Boris* contributed greatly to my Seventh and Eighth Symphonies, and then was recalled in the Eleventh. (There was a time when I considered the Eleventh my most "Mussorgskian" composition.) Something from *Khovanshchina* was transferred to the Thirteenth Symphony and to *The Execution of Stepan Razin,* and I even wrote about the connection between *Songs and Dances of Death* and my Fourteenth Symphony.

Naturally, this is not an exhaustive list of possible parallels. With time, willing lovers of parallels can expand it greatly. Of course, in order to do that they would have to seriously dig around in my works—both those that have been given voice and those that are still hidden from the eyes of "musicological officials." But for a true musicologist, with a musical education and musical goals, this could be fruitful, albeit hard, work. That's all right, let them sweat a little.

Asafiev couldn't restrain himself and he orchestrated *Khovanshchina* too. This was in the early thirties, I think, when one could still count on the fact that anything done with Mussorgsky would be approved and praised, and bring an honorarium.

But things were developing swiftly in the direction of "good tsars," and *A Life for the Tsar* beckoned in the future, quickly renamed *Ivan*

Susanin. I love Glinka and I'm not embarrassed by the fact that Stalin "loved" him too, because I'm sure that the leader and teacher's attention was captured by the title alone—*A Life for the Tsar*—and by the plot, a Russian peasant sacrificing his life for the monarch, because Stalin was already anticipating how people would sacrifice their lives for him. So they did a quick job on the libretto, with some paint and some gilt, and it took on a fresh, topical look. Glinka's opera became quite acceptable for the day, not like the rather suspect work by Mussorgsky. Here the simple man was told clearly what was what and how to behave in a critical situation, and the instruction was accompanied by beautiful music.

Two other operas were updated then, *Prince Igor* and *Pskovitianka.* The powers that be really liked *Pskovitianka's* final chorus, in which the voices of the bandit *oprichniki* and the terrorized citizens of Pskov blend in touching harmony as they laud the autocratic rule of Ivan the Terrible. How freedom-loving Rimsky-Korsakov could have written that is beyond me. In Asafiev's words, this was "an all-healing feeling of the ultimate rightness of reality." That's it, word for word—I looked it up recently. That's an amazing little phrase, I can't think of a better example of the exalted pandering style. Asafiev's lackey spirit is served up on a tray.

Now, what kind of style is that? "The ultimate rightness of reality." And what's this "all-healing feeling"? Does it mean that we must have it for terror, purges, political trials, and torture? Does it mean that "ultimate rightness" is behind all that shame? No, I refuse to accept the ultimate rightness of the villains even if they're super-real. Obviously, Mussorgsky and I were in one camp on this issue and Asafiev in a completely different one. He was with the torturers and oppressors. He began finding flaws in *Prince Igor,* saying that Galitsky's personality was a rough spot and that several lines, not thought through, did not respond to the lofty patriotic concept of *The Lay of Prince Igor.*

According to Asafiev, Borodin is an optimist and Mussorgsky a pessimist. Asafiev also played at literature, and in one of his home-grown playlets he has Mussorgsky say to Borodin: "You are ruled by life and I by death." Now, what does that nonsense mean? As long as we're alive we are all, without exception, ruled by life, and when we die, again without exception, we will all be ruled by death. And it doesn't depend on the optimistic or pessimistic nature of our work. Whether that's fortunate or not, I don't know.

I've never completely understood what it means to say that a creative man is an optimist or a pessimist. Take me, for instance, which am I? It's hard for me to say. When I think about my neighbor* who lives a few floors above me I may be an optimist and in relation to my own life I may be a pessimist. Of course, there have been times when acute melancholy and irritation with people have brought me to the end of my tether, but sometimes it was just the reverse. I refuse to make the final judgment on my case.

In Russia we like to attack the defenseless composer and accuse him of darkest pessimism. I've been put down that way many times, but it doesn't hurt because all my favorites—Gogol, Saltykov-Shchedrin, Leskov, Chekhov, Zoshchenko—have been blackened with the same brush. But I am hurt for one of my works, I mean the Fourteenth Symphony. The point is that many of my other works, placed on the blacklist, were seen as pessimistic by citizens who were at a rather far remove from music. It would have been amazing if they had said anything else; that was their job. But in this case it was acquaintances and even friends who criticized the symphony harshly, upset that "death is all-powerful," saying that that was a crude calumny of mankind. And they used all kinds of high-flown words, like beauty and grandeur and, naturally, divinity.

One luminary† in particular pointed a finger at the glaring errors of this minor work. I said nothing and invited him to honor my living quarters with his overwhelming genius, as Zoshchenko would have put it, to have a cup of tea with me. But the luminary refused, saying he preferred tea for one to tea with such an irredeemable pessimist. Another, less hardened man would have been deeply wounded by that, but I survived. You see, I'm such an insensitive, almost criminal character. Besides, I don't quite understand the cause of the brouhaha. Apparently my critics have clarity and roses growing in their souls and that's why they see the symphony as a crude and boorish slander of the way the world is. I can't agree with that. Perhaps they feel that it's not so easy for a man to lose himself in our contemporary world. I feel

*Khachaturian.
†Solzhenitsyn.

that he's specially fitted out just for that. Too many people are applying their rather unusual talents to that end. Some major geniuses and future famous humanists are behaving extremely flippantly, to put it mildly. First they invent a powerful weapon and hand it over to the tyrants and then they write snide brochures.* But one doesn't balance out the other. There aren't any brochures that could balance the hydrogen bomb.

And I feel that it's the height of cynicism to besmirch yourself with ugly behavior and then speak beautiful words. I think that it would be better to speak ugly words and not commit any illegal acts. The guilt of a potential murderer of millions is so great that it can't be mitigated in any way. And there's certainly no reason to praise the man.

There are too many people around us who, as Mussorgsky used to say, are constantly raising questions of life and death with the solemnity of an Indian rooster. They are all conscientious citizens, who seriously think about life, fate, money, and art. Perhaps their seriousness and conscientiousness make them feel better. But not me.

Unpleasant factors are constantly taking place in the human body, and medical science is at a loss. Therefore the cessation of the organism is inevitable. There is no afterlife. Mussorgsky, who is seen by our official neo-Slavophiles as a deeply religious man, wasn't one at all, I think. That's the impression you get if you believe his letters, and what else is there to believe? In Mussorgsky's day, apparently, the reading of private correspondence by the secret police wasn't the art form it is now, nor was it as widespread. In a letter to Vladimir Stasov, Mussorgsky wrote about the death of Gartman,† quoting a ditty, "Dead man, sleep peacefully in your grave; take advantage of life, live man." And he added characteristically, "Foul, but sincere."

He grieved deeply over Gartman's death, but he didn't give in to the temptation of comforting thoughts; in fact, he may have gone overboard here. "There isn't and can't be any peace, there isn't and can't be solace—that's weakness." I sense his rightness with all my heart, but my mind keeps searching for loopholes, my mind keeps spinning various thoughts and dreams. My reason persists dully: What a man

*Sakharov.
†Victor Alexandrovich Gartman (1834–1873), architect and painter, whose drawings were the inspiration for Mussorgsky's piano cycle *Pictures at an Exhibition*.

has done lives on after him. And that unbearable Mussorgsky contradicts me again: "Another meatball (with horseradish to bring on a tear) made out of human pride."

Mussorgsky seems to be facing that sad process—dying—without any sugar coating, fancy dress, or drapery. Yet even he cuts himself off, as if to say enough of that. "Some things are better left unsaid." I'll leave them unsaid too.

I BECAME fascinated by Mayakovsky's poetry at an early age. There's a book called *Everything Written by Vladimir Mayakovsky*, printed on bad paper in 1919. That was my introduction to the poet. I was very young then, barely thirteen, but I had friends, young literary men, who were great fans of Mayakovsky, and they were happy to explain the more difficult parts of the book that I liked so much. In the years that followed, I tried never to miss a single one of his appearances in Leningrad. I went to his readings with my writer friends and we listened with great interest and enthusiasm.

My favorite poem of his was "Kindness to Horses," and I still like it and consider it one of his best works. In my youth, I was impressed by "A Cloud in Trousers" and I liked "Spine Flute" and many other poems. I tried to set some of his poems to music, but I couldn't do it. I must say that setting his poetry to music is very difficult, particularly for me, since even now I can hear his readings and I would want the music to reflect his intonations as he read his own work.

In early 1929, Vsevolod Emilyevich Meyerhold, who was producing

The Bedbug, asked me to write the music for the play. I took on the project with pleasure. I naïvely thought that Mayakovsky in real life would be just as he was in his poems. Naturally, I didn't expect him to be wearing his Futuristic yellow shirt and I didn't think that he would have a flower drawn on his cheek. That kind of foolishness in the new political climate could have done him only harm. But seeing a man who wore a new tie at every rehearsal of *The Bedbug* was also a shock, because in those days a tie was considered one of the most blatant attributes of a bourgeois.

Mayakovsky, as I understood it, really loved the good life, he dressed in the best imported clothing—a German suit, American ties, French shirts and shoes—and he bragged about it all. He publicized Soviet products in his poetry and his constant advertising was tiresome by then. But Mayakovsky despised the very products he hailed. I saw that for myself at the rehearsals. When Igor Ilyinsky, the actor who was playing Prisypkin, had to have an ugly suit, Mayakovsky said, "Go to the state store and buy the first suit you see. It'll be perfect." These were the suits that Mayakovsky praised in his inspired poems.

Well, it's just another example of the tragic discrepancy between romantic dreams and reality. The poetic ideal—in this case, a suit—is one thing and reality—in this case, the products of the state factories—is another. The difference between the two is the poet's honorarium. As they say, a tie doesn't bring happiness, and it doesn't prove a man's nobility either. When we were introduced to Mayakovsky at the rehearsal of *The Bedbug,* he offered me two fingers. I'm no fool and I responded with one, and our fingers collided. Mayakovsky was stunned. He was always impolite but here was a nobody, as low as the ground, asserting himself.

I remember that episode very well, and that's why I don't react when people try to convince me that it never happened, according to the old principle of "it can't be because it couldn't ever be," as the major once said upon seeing a giraffe. How could "the best, the most talented" be a boor?

Once I was asked to appear on a television program about "the best, the most talented." Apparently they felt that I would share my reminiscences about how sensitive, kind, and polite Mayakovsky was. I told the producers about my meeting with him. They seemed put out and said, "That's not typical." I replied, "Why not? It's very typical." So I didn't appear on the show.

If it hadn't been for Meyerhold, I wouldn't have written the music for *The Bedbug,* because Mayakovsky and I disagreed about it. Mayakovsky asked me what I had written, and I told him symphonies, an opera, and a ballet. Then he asked me whether I liked firemen's bands. I said that sometimes I did and sometimes I didn't. Then Mayakovsky said, "I like firemen's bands the best and I want the music for *The Bedbug* to be just like the kind they play. I don't need any symphonies." Naturally, I suggested that he get a band and fire me. Meyerhold broke up the argument.

Another time I almost quit when I heard what Mayakovksy was demanding from an actress. The point is, *The Bedbug* is a fairly lousy play, and Mayakovsky, naturally, was worried about its reception. He was afraid that the audience wouldn't laugh and he decided to guarantee laughs with a rather shabby trick. He demanded that the actress who played a speculator read all her lines with a pronounced Jewish accent. He thought that it would get a laugh. It was an unworthy trick and Meyerhold tried to explain that to Mayakovsky, but he wouldn't listen. Meyerhold resorted to trickery; he told the actress to do what Mayakovsky wanted at rehearsals and to drop the accent during the performance, since Mayakovsky would be too nervous to notice. And Mayakovsky didn't say anything.

The Theater of Meyerhold was poor, always struggling financially, yet Mayakovsky suddenly wrote on the cover of his play: "A Comedy in Six Acts," though it could just as easily have been in four. He did it to increase his royalties. I think that's ugly; after all, they were friends. Meyerhold complained to me, "How can you explain to an author that he should cut down those acts?"

I can readily say that Mayakovsky epitomized all the traits of character I detest: phoniness, love of self-advertisement, lust for the good life, and most important, contempt for the weak and servility before the strong. Power was the great moral law for Mayakovsky. He had mastered a line from one of Ivan Krylov's fables: "For the strong, it's always the weak who are wrong." Except that Krylov said it in condemnation, mockingly, but Mayakovsky took the truism seriously and acted accordingly.

It was Mayakovsky who first said that he wanted Comrade Stalin to give speeches on poetry at Party Congresses. Mayakovsky was a lead singer of the cult of personality, and Stalin didn't forget it, he rewarded Mayakovsky with the title "the best, the most talented." Mayakovsky compared himself with Pushkin, as you know, and even now many seriously rank him with Pushkin. I think that our comrades are mistaken. I'm not talking about talent now, talent is a moot point, I'm talking about position. In a cruel age Pushkin praised liberty in his writings and called for mercy for the fallen. Mayakovsky called for something completely different, he called on youth to model its life on Comrade Dzerzhinsky.* That would be like Pushkin asking his contemporaries to imitate Benkendorf or Dubelt.†

After all, you don't have to be a poet, but you do have to be a citizen. Well, Mayakovsky was not a citizen, he was a lackey, who served Stalin faithfully. He added his babble to the magnification of the immortal image of the leader and teacher. Of course, Mayakovsky wasn't alone in this unbecoming behavior, he was one of a glorious cohort. There were many Russian creative artists who were infatuated by the person of our leader and teacher and who rushed to create works of praise for him. Besides Mayakovsky, I could mention Eisenstein and his *Ivan the Terrible,* with music by Prokofiev.

For some reason I am included in this list—Mayakovsky, Eisenstein—as the representative from the composers' brotherhood. But I don't include myself in it and therefore I will decline the honor with great vehemence. Let them find another candidate. I don't care whom they pick—Prokofiev, Davidenko, the "Red Beethoven," or Khrennikov. Let them figure out which among them wrote the most joyous song about "our great friend and leader," as the line we sing goes.

Many, many men were drawn to the great gardener and master of the sciences. There are toadying stories about Stalin's special magic power, which manifested itself in personal contact. I heard a few of these stories myself. They're shameful, and the most shameful part is that people told them about themselves. One such story was told to me by a film director, I won't give his name. He's not a bad person and he's given me work many a time. Here's the story. Stalin loved the

*Felix Edmundovich Dzerzhinsky (1877–1926), creator of the Soviet secret police.
†Alexander Khristoforovich Benkendorf (1788–1844) and Leonti Vasilyevich Dubelt (1792–1862) were the highest-ranking police officers under Nicholas I.

movies and he saw *The Great Waltz,* about Johann Strauss, many times, dozens of times. (I might add that this fact has not altered my love of Strauss.) The waltz doesn't resemble the *lezghinka* greatly, and the director didn't have to fear Stalin's wrath. Stalin also liked Tarzan films, he saw all the episodes. He naturally saw all the Soviet films as well.

It didn't take long for Stalin to see every Soviet film made, because in the last years of his life there were very few pictures produced, just a few every year. Stalin had the following aesthetic theory. Of all the pictures produced, only a small fraction was any good, and even fewer were masterpieces, because only a few people were capable of making masterpieces. Stalin determined who could create a masterpiece and who couldn't, and then he decided that bad films weren't needed, nor were the good ones. He needed only masterpieces. If the production of cars and airplanes could be planned, then why not plan the production of masterpieces? It's no more complicated, particularly if you're dealing with film, since film is also an industry.

A poet can write poetry for himself, he doesn't even have to write it down, he can keep it in his head. A poet doesn't need very much money to write poetry. We've now found out that they wrote poetry in the camps. It's hard to keep an eye on poetry. And you can't keep watch over composers either, particularly if they don't write ballets or operas. You can write a little quartet and then play it at home with friends. It's a bit more difficult with music, of course, it's harder to keep out of range of the watchful eye. You need music paper and even special score paper for symphonies, and as you know, there's a shortage of score paper, which is sold only to members of the Composers' Union. But you can still make your own homemade variety and write your symphonies without the permission of the overseeing offices, getting around the regulations.

But what can a film maker do? It's a strange profession, something like being a conductor. The first impression one has is that the director—like the conductor—merely gets in the way of other people trying to do their work. The second impression is the same.

A lot of people are needed to make a movie, and a lot of money. Stalin could be in charge one hundred percent. If he ordered a film made, they'd make it. If he ordered them to stop shooting, they stopped shooting. That happened many times. If Stalin ordered a finished film destroyed, they'd destroy it. That happened more than once too. Eisenstein's *Bezhin Meadow* was destroyed on Stalin's command, and I for one am not unduly saddened by that because I can't understand how you can create a work of art from the plot of a boy denouncing his father. The film naturally glorified that marvelous child.

And so the great leader and teacher decided to organize the planned production of film masterpieces. He followed Ilf and Petrov's recipe. In one of their short stories they have a man walk into a publisher's office and inquire if they publish a certain percentage of dull, poorly selling books. They tell him that of course they do, and the man suggests that they commission him to produce that percentage of bad books.

Stalin's formula was that since only a few masterpieces came out each year, then only a few films should be made each year, and every one would be a masterpiece, especially if they were entrusted to the directors who had already, in Stalin's opinion, created masterpieces. Simple and brilliant. And so that's what they did. I remember that at Mosfilm, the country's major studio, they were shooting only three films, *Admiral Ushakov, The Composer Glinka,* and *Unforgettable 1919.* The directors were appointed because Stalin knew for sure that they would make masterpieces, naturally with his help and his personal direction. They were Mikhail Romm, Grigori Alexandrov, and Mikhail Edisherovich Chiaureli, one of the greatest scoundrels and bastards known to me. He was a great fan of my music, of which he understood absolutely nothing. Chiaureli couldn't tell a bassoon from a clarinet or a piano from a toilet bowl.

The planned masterpieces were under way, but it just so happened that all three guaranteed creators of masterpieces were put out of commission. Romm broke his leg, Alexandrov had trouble with his blood pressure, and Mikhail Edisherovich had too much to drink at somebody's wedding. There was a catastrophe—the Soviet film industry was at a standstill. All the sound stages at Mosfilm were shut down, the bats moved in. The only room with lights burning was the studio director's office, where he sat up at night and awaited Stalin's call, because Stalin liked calling at night.

The phone would ring and the trembling director would give the leader and teacher the lastest report on the condition of the master-piece makers. You might have thought that the man wasn't a studio head but the chief surgeon of a hospital. Stalin was angry, his theory wasn't being put into practice, and Stalin didn't like that. The fate not only of the studio head but of Mosfilm itself hung on the condition of Romm's leg. Stalin could have shut down the studio and let all the cinemas in the country show his favorite Tarzan and nothing else, except perhaps the newsreels.

Poor directors. Stalin watched each one like a hawk. They froze under his gaze like rabbits before a snake. And most shamefully, they were proud of it.

Stalin had his own projection room at the Kremlin, and he watched films at night. That was work for him and he worked, like all criminals, at night. He didn't like to watch alone and he made all the members of the Politburo, all the leaders of the country, so to speak, join him. Stalin sat behind them all, in his own row, he didn't let anyone sit in his row. I heard all these details more than once. Once, according to a director friend of mine, the leader and teacher had a brilliant new idea. Stalin was watching some Soviet film and when it was over he said, "Where's the director? Why isn't the director here? Why don't we invite the director? We'll invite the director. I think, comrades, that it will be beneficial to invite the director. If the director were here, we could have thanked him, and if necessary we could have given him our critical comments and wishes. Let's ask the directors to be present at our screenings. This will be beneficial for the directors and for their work."

It so happened that the first to be so honored—to watch his own film with Stalin—was my friend. He is a man who is well educated but not very brave, and he has a squeaky, high-pitched voice. He's no warrior, neither in spirit nor in body, but he did try to be a decent man, and whenever he found his film work too oppressive, he directed a play or two to give his unheroic body and spirit a rest. Stalin didn't keep such close tabs on the theater and one could breathe a little more freely there.

They brought the director to the Kremlin. He was searched fifteen times on the way to the screening room, where he was seated in the first row, next to Minister of Cinematography Bolshakov. An industry that was producing three films a year still had its own minister. I would give that minister three glasses of milk a day for the ulcers that his nerve-racking job had caused. They say the minister wrote his memoirs when he retired. I wonder what he called them—*Crime Without Punishment?*

The screening began. Stalin, as usual, sat in the back. Naturally, the director didn't watch his film and didn't listen to my sound track. He was listening to what was going on in the back row. He had turned into a giant receiver; every squeak that came from Stalin's seat seemed decisive, every cough seemed to toll his fate. That's how my director friend felt and how he later described it to me. This screening could carry my friend way up high—ah, how he wanted that—and it could spell his downfall.

During the screening, Poskrebyshev, Stalin's long-time secretary, came in. He was a faithful, experienced workhorse. Poskrebyshev went up to Stalin with some dispatch in his hand. The director was sitting with his back to Stalin, not daring to turn around. Therefore he didn't see any of this, but he could hear it. Stalin's angry voice proclaimed loudly, "What's this rubbish?" It was already dark in the screening room, but my friend saw black. There was a noise. My friend had fallen on the floor. The guards rushed up to him and took him out.

When the director came to, they explained his error to him and told him that Stalin had also said, "The film's not bad. We liked the film, but we won't invite directors; no, we won't. They're all so high-strung."

So my friend didn't fly way up high as he had hoped. And they didn't give him a new pair of trousers for the ones he soiled, either. But that's all right. As the poet Sasha Cherny said, "Instead of selling their souls on credit, they should let their souls go about without pants."

In this other story that I know, I will mention the hero's name, since he's named me once or twice in various articles and speeches, not to mention many reports to higher-ups. Posters in our stores exhort us: "Customer and clerk, be mutually polite." Inspired by these splendid posters, I will be polite. I'll be the customer and my hero can be the clerk. I'm talking about Tikhon Khrennikov, chairman of the Composers' Union, and therefore my chairman too. Then why am I the customer and he the clerk? Well, first of all, the clerk is always more important than the customer. You always hear him say, "There are lots of you and only one of me." That's the way it is with Khrennikov—there are lots of us composers and only one of him. You really have to look hard for the likes of him. And second, Khrennikov's father was a clerk, he found work in some rich merchant's store. That's why our immortal leader always put down in every application: son of a worker behind a counter. I think that circumstances played the decisive role when Stalin was looking for a "boy" to run the Composers' Union. First, as I was told, Stalin studied the applications of all the candidates for the post of administrator and then called for their photographs. He spread them out on the desk and after some thought, poked his finger at Khrennikov's face. "Him." And he was right. Stalin had a wonderful instinct for such people. "A fisherman sees another fisherman from afar," our old Russian proverb runs.

Once I saw a charming pronouncement by our leader and teacher. I even wrote it out, because it's such a perfect characterization of Khrennikov, I had the impression that Stalin was writing about him.

I apologize for the quote. "In the ranks of one part of the Communists there is still a condescending disdain for trade in general and for Soviet trade in particular. These Communists, if they can be called that, see Soviet trade as a second-rate, unimportant thing and workers in trade as lost people. . . . They don't understand that Soviet trade is our own, Bolshevik business and workers in trade, including workers behind a counter, if they work honestly, are champions of our revolutionary Bolshevik work."

And "our" hereditary worker behind the counter turned out to be a champion of "our" work (Stalin liked using the plural for himself).

The story about Khrennikov is this. As head of the Composers' Union, Khrennikov had to submit the composer candidates to Stalin for the annual Stalin Prize. Stalin had the final say and it was he who chose the names from the list. This took place in his office. Stalin was working, or pretending to work. In any case, he was writing. Khrennikov mumbled names from the list in an optimistic tone. Stalin didn't look up and went on writing. Khrennikov finished reading. Silence.

Suddenly Stalin raised his head and peered at Khrennikov. As the people say, "he put his eye on him." They say that Stalin had worked out this tactic very well. Anyway, the hereditary worker behind the counter felt a warm mass under him, which scared him even more. He jumped up and backed toward the door, muttering something. "Our" administrator backed all the way to the reception area, where he was grabbed by two hearty male nurses, who were specially trained and knew what to do. They dragged Khrennikov off to a special room, where they undressed him and cleaned him up and put him down on a cot to get his breath. They cleaned his trousers in the meantime. After all, he was an administrator. It was a routine operation. Stalin's opinion on the candidates for the Stalin Prize was conveyed to him later.

As we see, the heroes in both stories do not emerge very well. Both fouled their pants, yet both would seem to be grownups. Moreover, both men recounted their shame with rapture. To shit in your pants in front of the leader and teacher is not something that everyone achieves, it's a kind of honor, a higher delight, and a higher degree of adulation.

What vile, disgusting toadying. Stalin is made out to be some sort of superman in these stories. And I'm sure that both men tried very hard to make sure the stories got back to him so that he would appreciate their toadying zeal, their fear and loyalty.

Stalin liked hearing such things about himself, he liked to know that he inspired such fear in his intelligentsia, his artists. After all, they were directors, writers, composers, the builders of a new world, a new man. What did Stalin call them? Engineers of human souls.

You might say, Why are you discrediting worthy people with your unworthy petty complaints? We'd like to know how you, you old so-and-so, would behave with Stalin? You'd probably soil your pants with a big load.

I reply: I saw Stalin and I talked to him. I didn't soil my pants and I didn't see any magical force in him. He was an ordinary, shabby little man, short, fat, with reddish hair. His face was covered with pockmarks and his right hand was noticeably thinner than his left. He kept hiding his right hand. He didn't look anything like his numerous portraits.

You know that Stalin was very concerned with his appearance and wanted to look handsome. He liked watching *Unforgettable 1919*, where he rides by on the footboard of an armored train with a saber in his hand. This fantastic picture, naturally, had nothing to do with reality. But Stalin watched and exclaimed, "How young and handsome Stalin was. Ah, how handsome Stalin was." He talked about himself in the third person and gave an opinion on his looks. A positive one.

Stalin was very picky about portraits of himself. There's a marvelous Oriental parable about a khan who called for an artist to do his portrait. That seemed to be a simple enough order, but the problem was that the khan was lame and squinted in one eye. The artist depicted him that way and was immediately executed. The khan said, "I don't need slanderers."

They brought a second artist. He decided to be smart and depicted the khan in perfect shape: eagle eyes and matching feet. He was immediately executed too. The khan said, "I don't need sugar-coaters."

The wisest, as it should be in a parable, was the third artist. He painted the khan hunting. In the painting the khan was shooting a deer with a bow and arrow. His squinty eye was shut, and the lame foot rested on a rock. This artist was awarded a prize.

I have a suspicion that the parable doesn't come from the East, but was written somewhere closer to home, because this khan sounds just like Stalin. In *Unforgettable 1919* Stalin was played by the actor Gelovani, who had a personal make-up man who specialized in Stalin make-up and nothing else. And Stalin's famous field jacket that Gelovani wore was kept in a special safe at Mosfilm so that not one mote of dust should fall on it. Heaven forbid that someone should report that Comrade Stalin's field jacket was dusty. That was almost like saying that Comrade Stalin himself was ... you know, dusty.

Stalin had several painters shot. They were called to the Kremlin to capture the leader and teacher for eternity, and apparently they didn't please him. Stalin wanted to be tall, with powerful hands, and he wanted the hands to be the same. Nalbandian fooled them all. In his portrait Stalin is walking straight at the viewer, his hands folded over his stomach. The view is from below, an angle that would make a Lilliputian look like a giant. Nalbandian followed Mayakovsky's advice: the artist must look at his model as a duck looks at a balcony. And Nalbandian painted Stalin from the duck's point of view. Stalin was very pleased and reproductions of the painting hung in every office, even in barbershops and Turkish baths.

And Nalbandian used the money he received to build himself a luxurious dacha near Moscow. A huge place, with cupolas looking at once like a train station and St. Basil's Cathedral. One of my students dubbed it Savior-on-the-Mustache [*Spas-na-Usakh*, a pun on the church Spas-na-Peskakh, or Savior-on-the-Sands, in Moscow], referring to Stalin's mustache, which Akhmatova called "roach whiskers."

My meeting with Stalin took place under the following circumstances. During the war it was decided that the "Internationale" was not fit to be the Soviet anthem. The words were deemed inappropriate, and really, words like "no one will give us release—not God, not Tsar, not hero," were wrong. Stalin was both god and tsar, so the words were ideologically impure. They wrote new lyrics: "Stalin raised us"—you know he was a great gardener. And anyway the "Internationale" is a foreign composition, French. How could Russians have a French anthem? Couldn't we create our own? So they threw together new words and passed them out to composers: write a new national anthem. You had to participate in the contest whether you wanted to or not, otherwise they would make an issue of it, they'd say that you were shirking an important duty. Of course, this was the chance for many composers to stand out, to climb into history, so to speak, on all fours. Some composers tried hard. One of my friends* wrote seven anthems, that's how much he wanted to be the national composer. Actually, this world-famous composer wasn't particularly hard-working, but in this case he manifested wonders of diligence.

All right, I wrote an anthem too. Then began the endless auditions. Stalin appeared sometimes, and he listened and listened and then commanded that Khachaturian and I write an anthem together. The idea was extremely stupid; Khachaturian and I are very different composers, with different styles and different ways of working. Our temperaments are different too. And anyway, who ever wanted to work in a composers' kolkhoz? But we had to obey.

Naturally, we didn't work together, we didn't turn into Ilf and Petrov. Either I hindered him or he hindered me. I don't make any secrets out of my work. I don't need any special conditions and I don't pretend to be lost in another sphere. There was a time when I could

*Aram Khachaturian.

compose anywhere, with any amount of noise around me, with just a corner of a table to write on. Just as long as people didn't shove too much. But now it's much harder for me. And now I'm less eager to make broad announcements about my plans, for instance that I've thought of an opera on a contemporary theme—on mastering virgin lands and fallow ground—or a ballet on the struggle for peace, or a symphony about cosmonauts.

When I was younger, I did make such imprudent remarks, and people still ask me when I am going to complete my opera *The Quiet Don*. I'll never finish it because I never started it. It was just that, to my great regret, I had to say so to get out of a difficult situation. This is a special form of self-defense in the Soviet Union. You say that you're planning such-and-such a composition, something with a powerful, killing title. That's so that they don't stone you. And meanwhile you write a quartet or something for your own quiet satisfaction. But you tell the administration that you're working on the opera *Karl Marx* or *The Young Guards,* and they'll forgive you your quartet when it appears. They'll leave you alone. Under the powerful shield of such "creative plans" you can live a year or two in peace.

I think that every composer must answer for his own work. That doesn't mean that I'm opposed to collaboration in principle—it certainly works in literature—but I just don't know of any successful attempts in music. And Khachaturian and I did not become the exception to the rule, particularly since we were ordered to become co-authors. Therefore I certainly didn't treat the matter too seriously. Maybe I let him down as a result, I don't know.

Meeting Khachaturian means, first of all, eating a good, filling meal, drinking with pleasure, and chatting about this and that. That's why, if I have the time, I never turn down a meeting with him. So we got together. We ate and drank, discussed all the latest news. We didn't write a single note, we didn't even bring up the subject of work. And then it turned out that Khachaturian was really in the mood to work that day, but you see, I (O mysterious Slavic soul!) led him off the path of righteousness.

We set another date. This time I was full of the desire to work, it was like a sports competition. I thought, Let's create a huge canvas called the National Anthem. We got together, and it turned out that

Khachaturian (O mysterious Armenian soul!) was saddened by something. He didn't want to write, he felt philosophic and said that his youth was gone. In order to convince Khachaturian that it wasn't gone completely, we had to drink a bit. Next thing we knew, it was evening, time to go. And we still hadn't written a single note of our joint anthem.

We had to do something, so we made a decision worthy of Solomon. Each would write his own anthem and then we would get together and see who had done a better job. The best bits from mine and the best from Khachaturian's anthem would go into our joint one. Naturally, there was the chance that we would write two anthems that could not possibly be combined, so we showed each other our work as we went along.

Each wrote his sketch at home, then we met, compared, and went home again. But now we had each other's version in our minds, as well. It went quickly, even though there were some difficulties. We had to make some critical remarks to each other, and Khachaturian is a very touchy fellow. It's better not to criticize him.

When he wrote the Concerto Rhapsody for Cello for Mstislav Rostropovich,* the cellist handled the situation very well. He wanted Khachaturian to make some improvements, but how could he tell him that? He would be mortally offended. So this is what Rostropovich did. He said, "Aram Ilyich, you've written a marvelous work, a golden work. But some parts are silver, they need to be gilded." Khachaturian accepted criticism in that form, but I don't have Rostropovich's poetic gift.

In general, Rostropovich is a real Russian; he knows everything and he can do anything. Anything at all. I'm not even talking about music here, I mean that Rostropovich can do almost any manual or physical work and he understands technology.

I know a few things myself; for instance, I can still light a campfire with one match, in any wind. Well, at most, with two matches. I was taught the art in my youth and I'm proud of it. My favorite chore as a child was lighting the stove. I still can feel the coziness, the sense of

*Mstislav Leopoldovich Rostropovich (b. 1927), cellist and conductor. Shostakovich dedicated two cello concertos to him. Rostropovich has been living in the West since 1974. In 1978 he was deprived of his Soviet citizenship by special decree (see footnote p. 108). Rostropovich is the musical director of the National Symphony Orchestra in Washington, D.C.

safety and security it gave me. It was a long time ago. I was a nimble youngster, I had the Russian knack. But I have a long way to go to be like Rostropovich, and naturally I lack his poetic and diplomatic gifts, so I had a harder time with Khachaturian.

Nevertheless, we combined our anthems into a single wonder of art. The melody was mine, the refrain his. Let's not talk about the music; in fact, I wouldn't have dwelt on this at all if not for the tragicomic circumstances of its conception. But we almost got into an argument over its orchestration. It would have been silly trying to combine two orchestrations. It would have been faster to choose his or mine, and even faster to just have one of us do it and both of us sign it. But which? Neither of us wanted to do it, for our own reasons.

I settled the argument. I remembered a guessing game I played with my sisters to get out of unpleasant household chores. You had to guess which hand had the pebble. If you couldn't guess, you lost. I didn't have a pebble handy, so I asked Khachaturian to guess which hand held a matchstick. Khachaturian guessed and the loser, I, had to do the orchestration.

The auditions of the various anthems went on for a long time. Finally the leader and teacher announced that five anthems were in the finals. They were the ones written by Alexandrov, the Georgian composer Iona Tuskiya, Khachaturian, me, and Khachaturian and myself jointly. Now a more important round came up, held at the Bolshoi Theater. Each anthem was performed three times—without orchestra, orchestra without chorus, and chorus and orchestra. That way they could see how it would sound under different circumstances. They should have tried it under water, but no one thought of it. The performances, as I recall, weren't bad. Good enough for export. The chorus was the Red Army Chorus. The orchestra was the Bolshoi's. Too bad you couldn't dance the anthem, because then the Bolshoi Ballet would have done it. And they would have done a good job, since the orchestration was precise and parade-like, accessible to ballet folk.

Alexandrov, who directed his own chorus, bustled about madly, beside himself with excitement. His entry in the anthem race was a song now called "Anthem of the Bolshevik Party." Stalin liked the song. Alexandrov, choking with delight and the saliva of a faithful retainer, told me how Stalin had "singled out" the song among others. The Red

Army Chorus under the direction of Alexandrov sang it for the first time at an official concert. It was before the war. Alexandrov was called up to Stalin's box in the intermission and the leader and teacher ordered them to do the song once more at the end of the concert, for him personally. It was then called "Song About the Party," and Alexandrov and his ensemble performed it in the rhythm of a march. Stalin ordered them to sing it in a slower tempo—like an anthem. Having heard it, he called it "a battleship of a song," and gave it a new name, and it was called "Anthem of the Bolshevik Party" from that moment on.

The audition continued, the composers were anxious. Many came with their wives. Khachaturian brought his and I brought mine. Everyone peered cautiously over at the state box, trying to be inconspicuous about it. Finally the noise on the stage ended, and Khachaturian and I were taken to the box, to see Stalin. We were searched on the way. There was a small antechamber to the box and that's where we were brought. Stalin was in there. I've described him already. I'll be honest and tell you that I felt no fear upon seeing Stalin. I was nervous, of course, but not afraid.

You feel fear when you open the paper and it says that you're an enemy of the people, and there's no way you can clear yourself, no one wants to listen to you, and there's no one to say a word in your defense. You look around and everyone else has the same newspaper, and they're all looking at you in silence, and when you try to say something they turn away. They don't hear you. Now, that's really frightening. I've often had that dream. The most frightening thing of all is that everything has been said and decided, and you don't know why it's been decided that way, and it's useless to argue.

But here what was there to fear? Nothing had been decided, you could still say something. That's what I was thinking when I saw the chubby man. He was so short that he didn't allow anyone to stand next to him. For instance, next to that stormy petrel of a man Maxim Gorky, Stalin looked ridiculous, like Double Patte and Patachon.* That's why they were always photographed sitting down.

Stalin stood alone here, as well. Everyone else of high rank was

*Popular silent-film comedy actors, one very tall, one very short.

crowded together in the back. Besides Khachaturian and me, there were also the two conductors, Alexander Melik-Pashayev, who conducted the orchestra, and Alexandrov, who led the chorus. Why had we been called in? I still don't know. Probably Stalin suddenly felt like having a talk with me, but the conversation didn't flow.

First Stalin made a profound statement on what the national anthem should be like. A commonplace, the typical Stalin truism. It was so uninteresting that I don't even remember it. His intimates agreed, carefully and quietly. For some reason, everyone spoke softly. The atmosphere was appropriate to a sacred rite, and it seemed that a miracle was about to occur—for instance, Stalin would give birth. The expectation of a miracle was on every toady's face. But there was no miracle. If Stalin did give birth, it was only to some unintelligible snippets of thought. It was impossible to keep the "conversation" going. You could either say yes-yes or say nothing. I preferred to be silent. After all, I wasn't going to get into a theoretical discussion on writing anthems. I don't stick my nose into theoretical discussions. I'm no Stalin.

And suddenly the wan conversation took a dangerous turn. Stalin wanted to show that he was well versed in orchestration. Apparently he had been briefed that Alexandrov didn't orchestrate his own song. He had given it to a professional arranger, something many of the contestants had done. Several dozen anthems had been arranged by one very experienced hand. In that sense Khachaturian and I were in a glowing minority, for we did our own orchestration.

Stalin decided that he couldn't lose in bringing up orchestration with Alexandrov. It was better not to start with us, we were professionals after all, what if he made a mistake? But using Alexandrov as an example, the leader and teacher could demonstrate his wisdom and sagacity. That's the way Stalin always behaved, and in a sense the conversation on anthems was very typical. It proves that Stalin always prepared carefully for these talks, he prepared his wise pronouncements.

He wasn't too sure that they were adequately wise, these sickly pronouncements, and like a provincial theater director, he prepared an effective entrance for each of them. The provincial director knows his audience. He may confuse Isaak Babel with August Bebel, but he also knows that no one will catch him, because the audience is stupid and will buy anything. Stalin was surrounded by coarse, profoundly ignorant people, who read nothing, who were interested in nothing. It was easier for Stalin to make an impression against such a background. Particularly since he was the director and could determine the course of the conversation. He could change the topic at any moment, he could stop the conversation; in other words, all the cards were in his hands, the deck was stacked. And with that bunch of aces up his sleeve, Stalin still played a rotten game.

Stalin began asking Alexandrov why he had done such a poor arrangement of his song. Alexandrov had expected anything but this—a conversation with Stalin on orchestration. He was pulverized, confused, destroyed. You could see that he was bidding farewell not only to the anthem, but to his career and perhaps to something more. The composer of that "battleship of a song" turned purple and broke out in a sweat. He was a pitiful sight. And it's in moments like that that people reveal themselves. Alexandrov made a base move. In an attempt to defend himself, he blamed the arranger. That was unworthy and low. The arranger could have lost his head as the result of such a conversation.

I saw that things could end badly; Stalin was interested in Alexandrov's pathetic justifications. It was an unhealthy interest, the interest of a wolf in a lamb. Noticing the interest, Alexandrov began laying it on thicker. The poor arranger was being turned into a saboteur, who had purposely done a bad arrangement of Alexandrov's song.

I couldn't take any more. This vile spectacle could have meant a lot of trouble for the arranger, the man would have died for nothing. I couldn't allow that and said that the arranger in question was an excellent professional and added that it wasn't fair to take him to task.

Stalin was obviously surprised by the turn in conversation, but at least he didn't interrupt me. And I managed to lead the conversation out of dangerous straits. Now we were discussing whether a composer should do his own orchestrations or whether he was justified in turning to others for help. I expressed my deep conviction that a composer cannot entrust the orchestration of his works to anyone else. Strange, but Stalin agreed with me here too. I think he saw it from his point of view. He certainly didn't want to share his glory with anyone, and that's probably why he decided that Shostakovich was right.

Alexandrov's "battleship" was sinking. The arranger had been saved, I had cause to be happy. Finally Stalin began finding out from all of us which anthem we had liked best. He asked me too. I was prepared for the question. I had assumed that something like that would come up and I decided that I couldn't mention mine or the joint anthem, and I probably shouldn't mention Khachaturian's, because I would be accused of praising my co-author. I actively disliked Alexandrov's song. That left only one candidate out of five—the one by Iona Tuskiya. And I said it was the best, but added that it would be hard to remember. I think that Stalin agreed with me there too, even though Tuskiya was a Georgian.

From the ensuing conversation it became apparent that the greatest judge and expert of all time on anthems considered the one by Khachaturian and me the best. But according to Stalin, a few changes were necessary in the refrain. He asked how much time we would need, and I said five hours. Actually, we could have done it in five minutes, but I thought it might seem less than solid to say that we could have done it there and then while they waited. You can imagine my surprise when I saw that my answer angered Stalin greatly. He was obviously expecting something else.

Stalin spoke slowly and thought slowly, he did everything slowly. He must have thought, This is state business, the national anthem, you must measure seven times, cut once, and Shostakovich says he can do the corrections in five hours. This isn't serious. Such an unserious man cannot be the author of the national anthem.

This proves once more that Stalin didn't understand a thing about composing. If he had had the slightest idea of what it involved, he wouldn't have been surprised by my estimate, but it was clear that Stalin knew as much about music as he did about other subjects, and that he brought up the business of the orchestration just to show off, a gambit that hadn't worked.

Khachaturian and I weren't successful. Khachaturian later blamed me for frivolity; he said that if I had asked for at least a month, we would have won. I don't know, he may be right. In any case, Stalin lived up to his threat. Alexandrov's song was proclaimed the anthem. The battleship made it into port. But the composition wasn't lucky, and not because of the music, because of the words. As for the music, that's a tradition. A national anthem must have bad music, and Stalin didn't break with tradition, as was to be expected. He also liked the loyal text. But when the cult of personality was exposed, the text posed a problem. It was stupid to make people sing "Stalin raised us" when it had been officially announced that he hadn't raised anyone, that on the contrary, he had destroyed millions of people. People stopped singing the words, they just hummed the tune.

Khrushchev wanted to replace the anthem, but he wanted to do this and that and a hundred other things, and he did almost nothing. That was the story with the anthem. First they pursued it fervently; I was involved too, this time as an expert. And then it quieted down, and we were stuck with a hummed anthem. That's not so good.*

I might add that Alexandrov did manage to write one song that wasn't so bad, the famous "Holy War." It was sung everywhere during the war. Stalin called it a "cross-country vehicle of a song." One's a battleship, the other's a vehicle. What is this military transport lexicon? Boring, comrades, it's boring.

Actually, taking stock now, I can't call my behavior particularly heroic, there wasn't anything special about it, even though the little I did wasn't easy. And the times certainly weren't easy, not the best of all possible times. But as Zoshchenko said, citizens from future eras will hardly be able to appreciate the circumstances because they won't have enough information. If only Zoshchenko's works were studied in school! As required reading. Then the young people of the future would have some idea of our meager and unattractive life. Zoshchenko was our Nestor and our Pimen.†

I met Zoshchenko at Zamyatin's, in shameful circumstances, at the card table over a game of poker. I loved cards at that period of my life and gave in to that ugly vice. I spent days, and particularly nights, at cards. Once Beliayev managed to talk Liadov into going to the Caucasus, to enjoy the marvelous scenery, so to speak. The patron of the arts

*New words to the Soviet anthem were approved after Shostakovich's death, in 1977. The text is that of the same poets, and the changes are few—Stalin's name is replaced by Lenin's.

†Nestor was an ancient Russian chronicler; Pimen is the chronicler in *Boris Godunov*.

and the composer headed south. They moved into the best hotel they could find and played nonstop for three days. Neither Beliayev nor Liadov even remembered the scenery outside and they never left their rooms. Then they got back into the train and returned to Petersburg. So Liadov never did see the scenery, and he kept asking himself, "Why did I ever go to the Caucasus?" He became totally disillusioned by travel.

For the times, Zamyatin was well off and a man of substance. He had good tables and all kinds of chairs and armchairs, which were of course not the result of his literary success. Zamyatin was a famous engineer, a shipbuilder, and that's where the money came from. And the means to give small literary soirees. Young people came to them to eat something and to meet others.

Maître—now, that's the word for Zamyatin. He really liked to put people in the right pigeonhole, and he never missed an opportunity to lecture you. I didn't like that very much. But I will admit that Zamyatin was an educated man. A pity his index finger stuck out all the time. Zamyatin looked down on Zoshchenko, and it's true you couldn't call Zoshchenko a scholar. He did like Zoshchenko's stories, from a professional point of view, but he mocked him, never missing an opportunity to remind us that a bear had stepped on Zoshchenko's ear, and that he divided all music into two categories. One was the "Internationale" and the other, everything else. And Zoshchenko had a simple test to determine which category was being played. If they stood up, it was the "Internationale." If people stubbornly remained seated, it was something from category two.

This harsh appraisal of Zoshchenko's ear was absolutely accurate, and I had ample opportunity to prove it for myself. For instance, Zoshchenko was listening to Beethoven's Ninth, and during the finale, Zoshchenko decided that the music was over. There's that tricky spot in the finale. Zoshchenko applauded and headed proudly for the exit. Then he realized that he was alone, that the rest of the audience was seated, because the music was still on. He had to go back to his seat, his neighbors hissing him as he stepped all over their feet.

Another time Zoshchenko both touched me and distracted me from my worries. It was at the end of 1937. I came to the Philharmonic Hall for the first performance of my Fifth Symphony. The atmosphere at the premiere was highly charged, the hall was filled—as they say, all the best people were there, and all the worst too. It was definitely a critical situation, and not only for me. Which way would the wind blow? That's what was worrying members of the select audience—people in literature, culture, and physical culture. That's what had them in a feverish state. In the first part of the program, Mravinsky played Tchaikovsky's *Romeo and Juliet*. My Fifth was in the second half of the program. I felt like the gladiator in *Spartacus* or a fish in a frypan. I remembered Oleinikov's ditty "Tiny little fishie, fried little smelt, where's your smile from yesterday, remember how you felt?" *Romeo and Juliet* was over. Intermission, and Zoshchenko ran in all smiles, dressed nattily as usual. He headed over to me and congratulated me on the success of my composition.

It turned out that Zoshchenko liked my new work, it was melodious. "I just knew that you weren't capable of writing anti-people music," Zoshchenko praised me. I was flattered, of course, and had a good laugh, and even forgot about the second half and the fact that the Fifth was yet to come.

I was always drawn to Zoshchenko, I found him very simpatico. We were very different men, but we had the same point of view on many things. It sometimes seemed that Zoshchenko left all his anger on paper; he liked to appear gentle, he liked to pretend shyness. You see that sometimes, the humorist trying to be sad, a gentle person trying to be cruel. It's easier to live that way.

Zoshchenko tried to create a distance between himself and his works. Actually, he was very good at being mean and ruthless in life, just as in his stories. He was cruel to women, there were many around him, and why not: he was nationally famous, he had money, and he was handsome in a way that women liked.

His good looks always seemed suspect to me. They were too pretty, I guess. If he had behaved more obnoxiously, he could have passed for a pimp. But he was quiet and modest, and he told his passionate and persistent lovers horrible, vile things in a quiet and modest voice. Zoshchenko didn't have a drop of sentimentality, luckily. We agreed on that. He once told me laughingly that he had to write a paper in high school on "Liza Kalitina as the Ideal Russian Woman." What could be more nauseating than Turgenev? Particularly when on the subject of women? I was happy to hear that Zoshchenko got a 1 [F] for the composition. I told him that Chekhov didn't like Turgenev's maidens either. He said that all those Lizas and Elenas were intolerably false, and that they weren't Russian girls at all, but unnatural pythonesses with pretensions above their station.

Zoshchenko wrote marvelously about himself and his relations with women and women in general. This is the final truth, the way he wrote. It's hard to imagine that one could write more truthfully. It is very crude prose. Pornography is often sugary, but there isn't any sugariness here. It's crystalline Zoshchenko. Some pages of *Before Sunrise* are hard to read, they're so cruel. And most important, there's no fanfare, no cynicism, no pose. Zoshchenko treats women with detachment.

Zoshchenko published *Before Sunrise* during the war and his self-analysis drove Stalin mad. He felt that it was wartime and we should be crying "Hurrah!," "Go to hell!," and "Long live!," and here people were publishing God knows what. So the pronouncement was made: Zoshchenko was a vile, lustful animal, just like that, word for word. Zoshchenko had no shame or conscience.

That's how incensed our leader and teacher was by Zoshchenko's incorrect attitude toward women. And he rushed to women's defense. It was a topic that interested Stalin deeply. For instance, it was decreed from on high that my *Lady Macbeth* praised lust among the merchants, which naturally had no place in music. Out with lust. Now, why would I want to praise merchant lust? But the leader and teacher knew better than we did. "Does Stalin know?" and "Stalin knows" were the two favorite sentences of the Soviet intelligentsia in that period. And I must stress that this wasn't from the lectern, and not at meetings, but at home, with the wife, in the bosom of the Soviet family.

Stalin placed great hopes in the family. At first Stalin tried to destroy it with every means available to him. Son denounced father, wife informed on husband. The papers were full of announcements like "I, So-and-so, announce that I have nothing to do with my father, enemy of the people So-and-so. I broke off with him ten years ago." Everyone had grown accustomed to such announcements, they didn't even pay attention. So you broke off with him. It was like reading "Selling my furniture" or "French lessons, also manicure, pedicure, and electrolysis."

The hero of the era was little Pavlik Morozov, who informed on his father. Pavlik was sung in poetry, prose, and music. Eisenstein took part in the praises, working long and hard on a great art film that glorified the little snitch.

In *Lady Macbeth* I depicted a quiet Russian family. The members of the family beat and poison one another. If you looked around, you'd see I wasn't exaggerating in the least. It was just a modest picture drawn from nature. The exceptions were rare; one was Tukhachevsky's mother, Mavra Petrovna. She refused to brand her son an enemy of the people, she was adamant. And she shared his fate.

Having destroyed the family unit, Stalin began resurrecting it, that was his standard pattern. It's called dialectics. He destroyed barbarically, and he resurrected barbarically too. Everyone knows the shameful laws on family and marriage promulgated by Stalin. And it got worse. A ban on marrying foreigners, even Poles and Czechs, who were our own people, after all. Then the law on sexual segregation in schools. Boys and girls separated, in order to maintain morality, and so that they wouldn't ask teachers stupid questions about "things" and "holes."

We still haven't shaken ourselves free of that struggle for a healthy Soviet family. I was on a suburban train once and my neighbor, a buxom woman, was telling her girlfriend about a film she had seen, *Lady with the Dog,* based on the Chekhov story. She was incensed. He has a wife, she said, and she has a husband, and you should see what they do. It's too shameful to tell you, she said. It's propaganda of moral decay through films, and they teach Chekhov in the schools, too! Stalin is dead, but his work lives on. When the Dresden Museum exhibit was in Moscow, schoolchildren didn't see it, because it was restricted to those over sixteen to protect that Soviet family. Otherwise the children might see some naked women, by Veronese or Titian. And then they would become incorrigible and move on to really dangerous behavior.

One thing leads to the next. They cover plaster figures with bathing suits and cut out kissing scenes from movies, and watch out, artist, if you plan to exhibit a nude. You'll be showered with threatening letters, and not all of them from above. The simple folk will be incensed, saying that the depiction of naked women is offensive to our simple Soviet worker-peasant point of view.

One simple man wrote a really wonderful put-down of such shamelessness in the representational arts. He said, "Such depictions arouse extraordinary lust and lead to the destruction of united family life." He ended with, "The artist should be put on trial for such moral decay!" This isn't something that Zoshchenko or I invented, it actually happened.

All art is under suspicion, all literature. Not only Chekhov, but Tolstoy and Dostoevsky. That chapter from *The Possessed* will never be published,* they are worried about its effect on the Soviet citizen. Soviet man has withstood everything: hunger, and destruction, and wars—one worse than the other—and Stalin's camps. But he won't be able to take that chapter from *The Possessed,* he'll crack.

And so Stalin suspected Zoshchenko of wanting to undermine the Soviet family. They hit him, but not fatally. They decided to give him the final blow later, and for the same reason that they hit me. The Allies set us up.

Actually, to be accurate, there are three versions. When you think of it, it's amazing—why did they pick Zoshchenko and Akhmatova, why those two as the main target? They put them out naked and threw stones at them. One version goes like this: Akhmatova and Zoshchenko were the victims of a struggle between two of Stalin's toadies, that is, between Malenkov† and Zhdanov. Allegedly Malenkov wanted to become Stalin's main ideological adviser, a rather important position, right below Stalin's top executioner, Beria. He would be the executioner on the cultural front. Malenkov and Zhdanov fought to prove themselves worthy of that honored position. The war with Hitler was won and Malenkov decided to stress public relations and to glorify the homeland, so that the entire enlightened world would gasp and see that Russia was the "homeland of elephants."

Malenkov worked out grandiose plans, one of which was a series of

---

*A refe..nce to the chapter "At Tikhon's" (also known as "Stavrogin's Confession"), deleted by Dostoevsky under pressure from the censors from the edition of *The Possessed* published in his lifetime. In the Soviet Union, "Stavrogin's Confession" was not printed for over fifty years, although it was known that Dostoevsky valued the chapter highly.

†Georgi Maximilianovich Malenkov (b. 1902), a Communist Party leader who was chairman of the Council of Ministers after Stalin's death. In 1957 Khrushchev removed Malenkov from power as a member of an "anti-Party group."

deluxe editions of Russian literature from antiquity to the present. I think the series began with *The Lay of Prince Igor* and ended, believe it or not, with Akhmatova and Zoshchenko. But Malenkov's idea didn't work and Zhdanov outguessed him. He knew Stalin better and considered that laudatory editions were fine, but steadfast struggle with the enemy—vigilance, so to speak—was more important.

With the aim of getting rid of Malenkov, Zhdanov attacked Malenkov's ideas and proved to Stalin, like two plus two, that it was vigilance that Malenkov had lost. Zhdanov, unfortunately, knew what and how Akhmatova and Zoshchenko wrote, since Leningrad was Zhdanov's own turf.

This was Zhdanov's argument: The Soviet Army is victorious, we are advancing on Europe, and Soviet literature must be an aid in this, it must attack bourgeois culture, which is in a state of confusion and decay. And do Akhmatova and Zoshchenko attack? Akhmatova writes lyric poetry and Zoshchenko writes derogatory prose. Zhdanov won, Stalin took his side and Malenkov was removed from leading the cultural front. Zhdanov was empowered to strike a blow at harmful influences, at "the spirit of negative criticism, despair, and nonbelief."

Zhdanov later announced, "What would have happened if we had brought up our young people in the spirit of despair and nonbelief in our work? What would have happened was that we would not have won the Great Patriotic War." Now, that scared them. Just think, one short story by Zoshchenko, and the Soviet regime might have toppled. Another symphony by Shostakovich, and the country would fall into the slavery of American imperialism.

The second version is that Stalin pointed out Zoshchenko personally and for personal reasons. You see, the leader and teacher was hurt. Years ago Zoshchenko had written a few stories about Lenin to make some money, and one of the stories depicted Lenin as a gentle and kind man, a luminary. For contrast, Zoshchenko described a crude Party official, as an exception, just for contrast. The crude man, naturally, was not given a name, but the story made it clear that the boor worked in the Kremlin. In Zoshchenko's story the boor had a beard and the censor said that the beard had to go because people might think he was Mikhail Kalinin, our president. And in their hurry, they made a horrendous mistake. Zoshchenko removed the beard, but left the mustache. The crude Party official had a mustache in Zoshchenko's story. Stalin read it and took offense. He decided that it was about him. That's how Stalin read fiction.

Neither the censor, nor certainly Zoshchenko, could have foreseen or imagined such a turn of events and so they didn't think about the fatal consequences of removing the beard.

I think that both versions have some truth in them, that is, both did take place. But I still think that the main cause, for both Zoshchenko and me, was the Allies. As a result of the war, Zoshchenko's popularity in the West grew considerably. He was published frequently and discussed readily. Zoshchenko wrote many short stories that were perfect for newspapers, and they didn't even have to pay, since Soviet authors weren't protected by copyright law. It was cheap and satisfying for the Western press. And it turned out to have tragic consequences for Zoshchenko.

Stalin kept a close eye on the foreign press. Naturally, he didn't know any foreign languages, but his flunkies reported to him. Stalin weighed other people's fame carefully and as soon as it seemed to be getting a little too heavy, he threw them off the scales.

So they let Zoshchenko have it, they used every four-letter word they could think of about him. Zoshchenko's morals were disgusting, and he was rotten and putrid through and through. Zhdanov called him an unprincipled, conscienceless literary hooligan. Criticism in the Soviet Union is a wondrous thing. It's construed along the famous principle: they beat you and don't let you cry. In antediluvian times it wasn't like that in Russia. If you were insulted in the press you answered in another literary forum, or your friends took your part. Or if worst came to worst, you vented your spleen in your circle of friends. But that was before the flood. Now things are different, more progressive.

If you are smeared with mud from head to toe on the orders of the leader and teacher, don't even think of wiping it off. You bow and say thanks, say thanks and bow. No one will pay any attention to any of your hostile rejoinders anyway, and no one will come to your defense, and most sadly of all, you won't be able to let off steam among friends. Because there are no friends in these pitiable circumstances.

People shied away from Zoshchenko on the street, just the way they had from me. They crossed the street, so that they wouldn't have to say hello. And they smeared Zoshchenko even more at hurriedly arranged meetings, and it was his former friends who did it the most, the ones who yesterday had praised him the loudest. Zoshchenko seemed surprised by it all, but I wasn't. I had gone through it at a younger age and the subsequent storms and bad weather had hardened me.

Akhmatova was undercut by Stalin for the same reason: envy of her fame, black envy. Sheer madness. There are many losses and blows in Akhmatova's life: "my husband is in the grave, my son in prison." And yet the Zhdanov episode was her hardest trial.

We all had different destinies, yet we shared some common traits. Strangely enough, for Akhmatova, as for me, it was easiest during the war. During the war everyone heard about Akhmatova, even people who had never read poetry in their lives. While Zoshchenko had been read by everyone always. It's interesting that Akhmatova was afraid to write prose and considered Zoshchenko the highest authority in the field. Zoshchenko told me about that later, with a laugh but with some pride.

After the war an evening of readings by Leningrad poets was given in Moscow. When Akhmatova came out, the audience rose. That was enough. Stalin asked, "Who organized the standing up?"

I had met Akhmatova a long time before, in 1919, that "unforgettable year," or perhaps in 1918, at the home of Dr. Grekov, the surgeon, a famous man and a friend of our family. He ran the Obykhovskaya Hospital. Grekov is worth telling about; he did many things for us, for my father and for me. When Father was dying, Grekov spent the night at our house, trying to save him. It was Grekov who removed my appendix, even though he often said, "It's not much fun cutting up someone you know." Grekov was a large man and he smelled of tobacco. Like all surgeons, he was gruff—that's a professional trait.

I hated Grekov. Every time I left his house, I found food for my parents in my coat pocket. I choked with anger—was I a beggar, were we beggars? But I couldn't refuse. We really did need the food, desperately. But I hate handouts, and I don't like to borrow money. I always wait until it's urgent and then I pay it back at the first opportunity. That's one of my major faults.

Grekov liked to boast, of course. I remember one famous operation of his. He had to do something with a girl who wasn't growing. Grekov decided that if he widened her hips, everything would proceed normally. He moved her hipbones and the girl grew broader and taller, and even had a child.

Grekov's wife, Elena Afanasyevna, dabbled in literature. She was a talentless scribbler who would probably have died from her unrequited love for literature. But from time to time, Grekov, who had money to burn, published some work of his wife's at his expense, and thereby prolonged her life. The Grekovs also had a sort of literary salon. They gave receptions, the table groaned with food. Writers and musicians came to eat. I saw Akhmatova at their house. She grazed there periodically. She came to the salon for the spread, of course. It was a hungry time.

The Grekovs had a grand piano, and I was part of the entertainment, working off the food in my pockets. But I don't think that Akhmatova was too interested in music then. She created a field of majesty about herself, and you had to freeze within two yards of her. Her behavior was worked out to the smallest detail. She was very beautiful, very.

Once my friend Lenya Arnshtam and I dropped in at a writers' bookshop. Akhmatova came in and asked the clerk for one of her books. I don't remember which, either *White Flock* or *Anno Domini*. The clerk sold her a copy, but Akmatova wanted to buy ten copies. The clerk grew angry and said, "No, that's unheard of. The book is selling very well, and there might be a request for it at any moment. I have to satisfy my customers and I won't sell ten copies to just anyone. What will I say to my other customers? Hah?"

He was rather impolite and Akhmatova looked at him in amazement, but she didn't seem to want to speak up. Arnshtam spoke up. Don't you know this is Akhmatova herself? Why be impolite to the famous poetess? Especially since it's her own book you're talking about? Akhmatova gave us a dirty look, meaning that we were sticking our nose in her business, destroying her majesty, blowing her regal incognito, and she immediately left the bookstore.

Later on, Akhmatova attended the premieres of my works and she must have liked them, since she wrote poems about them. Basically I can't bear having poetry written about my music. I also know that

Akhmatova expressed her displeasure over the "weak words" I used for the vocal cycle *From Jewish Folk Poetry*. I don't want to argue with the famous poetess, but I think she didn't understand the music in this instance, or rather, she didn't understand how the music was connected to the word.

I was always put off by conversation with Akhmatova, because we were such different people. Yet we both lived in the same city and were equally devoted to it, we had the same world view, and common acquaintances, she seemed to respect my music, and I esteemed her work highly, both her early poems and her late ones, and of course, the *Requiem*. Particularly the *Requiem*; I honor it as a memorial to all the victims of the years of terror. It's so simply written, without any melodrama. Melodrama would have ruined it.

I would greatly love to set it to music, but the music exists already. It was written by Boris Tishchenko, and I think that it's a marvelous work. Tishchenko brought to the *Requiem* what I think it lacked: protest. In Akhmatova, you feel a kind of submission to fate. Perhaps it's a matter of generations.

And so, despite our mutual likes, I had trouble talking with Akhmatova. I bring this up apropos of "historic meetings." A special historic meeting with Akhmatova was arranged for me in Komarovo, near Leningrad, and it turned out to be quite embarrassing. We were all tieless out there—it's the country, after all. They tried to talk me into dressing more appropriately for a meeting with the celebrated poetess, and I just said, "Come off it. A fat old woman is coming, that's all." I was very light-hearted about the whole thing. I didn't put on a good suit or a tie. When I saw Akhmatova, I felt nervous. She was a grande dame, quite regal. The celebrated poetess, dressed with great thought. You could tell that she had paid attention to her clothes, prepared for the historic meeting, and behaved in a manner commensurate with the occasion. And there I was, tieless. I felt naked.

We sat in silence. I was silent and Akhmatova was silent. We said nothing for a while and then parted. I heard that she later said, "Shostakovich came to see me. We had such a good talk, we talked about everything."

That's how most historic meetings go, and then the rest comes in the memoirs. I said to him, and he said to me, and then I said . . . It's all lies. I wonder if the public knows how historic photographs are taken. When two "celebrities" are seated next to each other and they don't know what to talk about. The traditional method is to say to each other with a smile, "What do we talk about, when we have nothing to say?" Flash. The other method, which I myself invented, is to say, "Eighty-eight, eighty-eight." You don't even have to smile, because the words stretch your lips into a smile and you give the impression of having a lively conversation. The photographers are happy and leave quickly.

No, I can't go on describing my unhappy life, and I'm sure that no one can doubt now that it is unhappy. There were no particularly happy moments in my life, no great joys. It was gray and dull and it makes me sad to think about it. It saddens me to admit it, but it's the truth, the unhappy truth.

Man feels joy when he's healthy and happy. I was often sick. I'm sick now, and my illness deprives me of the opportunity to take pleasure in ordinary things. It's hard for me to walk. I'm teaching myself to write with my left hand in case my right one gives out completely. I am completely in the hands of the doctors, and I obey their orders with extreme submissiveness. I take all the medicine they prescribe, even if it nauseates me. But there is no diagnosis, they won't make one. Some American doctors came and said, We're amazed by your courage. And nothing else. They can't do a thing. Before, they bragged that they would cure me without question, they had made such great progress in the field, etc. And now all they talk about is courage.

But I don't feel like a superman yet, supercourageous. I'm a weak man. Or are things so bad with me?

They've come up with a tentative diagnosis: something like chronic poliomyelitis. Not infantile polio, of course. There are a few other people in the Soviet Union with the same mysterious illness. One film director walks around, they say, dragging his leg. And no regimen, no treatment seems to help. When I'm in Moscow, I feel worst of all. I keep thinking that I'll fall and break a leg. At home I can even play the piano. But I'm afraid to go out. I'm terrified to be seen, I feel fragile, breakable.

No, every new day of my life brings me no joy. I thought I would find distraction reminiscing about my friends and acquaintances.

Many of them were famous and talented people, who told me interesting things, instructive stories. I thought that telling about my outstanding contemporaries would also be interesting and instructive. Some of these people played an important role in my life and I felt it was my duty to tell what I still remembered about them.

But even this undertaking has turned out to be a sad one.

I have thought that my life was replete with sorrow and that it would be hard to find a more miserable man. But when I started going over the life stories of my friends and acquaintances, I was horrified. Not one of them had an easy or a happy life. Some came to a terrible end, some died in terrible suffering, and the lives of many of them could easily be called more miserable than mine.

And that made me even sadder. I was remembering my friends and all I saw was corpses, mountains of corpses. I'm not exaggerating, I mean mountains. And the picture filled me with a horrible depression. I'm sad, I'm grieving all the time. I tried to drop this unhappy undertaking several times and stop remembering things from my past, since I saw nothing good in it. I didn't want to remember at all.

But for many reasons I went on. I forced myself and went on remembering, even though some of the memories were difficult for me. I decided that if this exercise helped me to see anew certain events and the destinies of certain people, then perhaps it wasn't completely futile and perhaps others would find something instructive in these simple tales.

And besides, I reasoned this way: I've described many unpleasant and even tragic events, as well as several sinister and repulsive figures. My relations with them brought me much sorrow and suffering. And I thought perhaps my experience in this regard could also be of some use to people younger than I. Perhaps they wouldn't have the horrible disillusionment that I had to face, and would go through life better prepared, more hardened, than I was. And perhaps their lives would be free of the bitterness that has colored my life gray.

DMITRI SHOSTAKOVICH
1906–1975
MAJOR COMPOSITIONS, TITLES, AND AWARDS

1924–25	First Symphony, opus 10
1926	Piano Sonata no. 1, opus 12
1927	Ten Aphorisms for Piano, opus 13
	Second Symphony ("Dedication to October"), for orchestra and chorus, to poem by Alexander Bezymensky, opus 14
1927–28	*The Nose*, an opera based on Gogol, opus 15
1928	Orchestral transcription of "Tea for Two" by Vincent Youmans, opus 16
1928–29	Score for film *New Babylon* (directors, Grigori Kozintsev and Leonid Trauberg), opus 18
1928–32	Six Romances for Tenor and Orchestra, to poems by Japanese poets, opus 21
1929	Music for Vladimir Mayakovsky's comedy *The Bedbug* (directed by Vsevolod Meyerhold), opus 19
	Third Symphony ("May First"), for orchestra and chorus, to poem by Semyon Kirsanov, opus 20
1929–30	*The Golden Age* (ballet), opus 22
1930–31	*Bolt* (ballet), opus 27
1930–32	*Lady Macbeth of Mtsensk District,* an opera based on Nikolai Leskov, opus 29
1931–32	Music for *Hamlet* (directed by Nikolai Akimov), opus 32
1932–33	Twenty-Four Preludes for Piano, opus 34
1933	Concerto for Piano and Orchestra, opus 35
1934	Sonata for Cello and Piano, opus 40

1934–35	*Bright Stream* (ballet), opus 39
1934–38	Scores for films *Maxim's Youth, Maxim's Return,* and *The Vyborg Side* (directors, G. Kozintsev and L. Trauberg), opuses 41, 45, 50; film trilogy received Stalin Prize First Grade, 1941
1935	Five Fragments for Orchestra, opus 42
1935–36	Fourth Symphony, opus 43
1936	Four Romances for Voice and Piano, to poems by Alexander Pushkin, opus 46
1937	Fifth Symphony, opus 47.
1938	First String Quartet, opus 49
1938–39	Score for film *The Great Citizen,* two parts (director, Fridrikh Ermler), opuses 52, 55; film received Stalin Prize First Grade, 1941
1939	Sixth Symphony, opus 54
1940	Piano Quintet, opus 57; Stalin Prize First Grade, 1941
	Orchestration of Modest Mussorgsky's opera *Boris Godunov,* opus 58
	Music for *King Lear* (director, G. Kozintsev), opus 58a
	Order of the Red Banner of Labor
1941	Seventh Symphony, opus 60; Stalin Prize First Grade, 1942
1942	Piano Sonata no. 2, opus 61
	Six Romances for Bass and Piano, to poems by Walter Raleigh, Robert Burns, and William Shakespeare, translated by Samuel Marshak and Boris Pasternak, opus 62 (version for bass and chamber orchestra, 1970, opus 140)
	Honored Artist of the R.S.F.S.R.
1943	Eighth Symphony, opus 65
	Honorary Member of the American Academy and Institute of Arts and Letters
1944	Score for film *Zoya* (director, Leo Arnshtam), opus 64; film received Stalin Prize First Grade, 1946
	Piano Trio, opus 67; Stalin Prize Second Grade, 1946
	Second String Quartet, opus 68
1945	Ninth Symphony, opus 70
1946	Third String Quartet, opus 73
	Order of Lenin
1947	Score for film *Pirogov* (director, G. Kozintsev), opus 76; film received Stalin Prize Second Grade, 1948
1947–48	Score for film *Young Guards,* two parts (director, Sergei Gerasimov), opus 75; film received Stalin Prize First Grade, 1949
	First Violin Concerto, opus 77

1948	Score for film *Michurin* (director, Alexander Dovzhenko), opus 78; film received Stalin Prize Second Grade, 1949
	From Jewish Folk Poetry, vocal cycle for soprano, contralto, tenor, and piano, opus 79
	Score for film *Meeting at Elba* (director, Grigori Alexandrov), opus 80; film received Stalin Prize First Grade, 1950
	People's Artist of the R.S.F.S.R.
1949	*Song of the Forests,* oratorio to poems by Yevgeny Dolmatovsky, opus 81; Stalin Prize First Grade, 1949
	Score for film *The Fall of Berlin,* two parts (director, Mikhail Chiaureli), opus 82; film received Stalin Prize First Grade, 1950
	Fourth String Quartet, opus 83
1950–51	Twenty-Four Preludes and Fugues for Piano, opus 87
1951	Ten Choral Poems by Revolutionary Poets, opus 88; Stalin Prize Second Grade, 1952
	Score for film *Unforgettable 1919* (director, M. Chiaureli), opus 89
1952	Four Monologues for Bass and Piano, to poems by Alexander Pushkin, opus 91
	Fifth String Quartet, opus 92
1953	Tenth Symphony, opus 93
1954	*Festive Overture,* opus 96
	People's Artist of the U.S.S.R.
	International Peace Prize
	Honorary Member of the Swedish Royal Academy of Music
1955	Corresponding Member of the Academy of Arts of the German Democratic Republic
1956	Sixth String Quartet, opus 101
	Order of Lenin
	Honorary Member of the St. Cecilia Academy of Arts, Italy
1957	Second Piano Concerto, opus 102
	Eleventh Symphony, opus 103; Lenin Prize, 1958
1958	*Moscow, Cheryomushki,* operetta, opus 105
	Member of the British Royal Academy of Music
	Honorary Doctorate, Oxford University
	Chevalier des Arts et Lettres, France
	International Jan Sibelius Prize
1959	Orchestration of Mussorgsky's opera *Khovanshchina,* opus 106
	First Cello Concerto, opus 107
	Silver Medal, World Peace Council

1960	Seventh String Quartet, opus 108
	Satires, cycle for voice and piano, to poems by Sasha Cherny, opus 109
	Eighth String Quartet, opus 110
1961	Twelfth Symphony, opus 112
1962	Thirteenth Symphony, for bass, bass choir, and orchestra, to poems by Yevgeny Yevtushenko, opus 113
	Orchestration of Mussorgsky's vocal cycle *Songs and Dances of Death*
1962–75	Deputy of the Supreme Soviet of the U.S.S.R.
1963	*Katerina Izmailova* (new edition of *Lady Macbeth of Mtsensk District*), opus 114
	Overture on Russian and Kirkhiz Folk Themes, opus 115
	Honorary Member of International Music Council of UNESCO
1963–64	Score for film *Hamlet* (director, G. Kozintsev), opus 116
1964	Ninth String Quartet, opus 117
	Tenth String Quartet, opus 118
	The Execution of Stepan Razin, for bass, choir, and orchestra, to poem by Yevgeny Yevtushenko, opus 119; State Prize of the U.S.S.R., 1968
1965	Five Romances for Voice and Piano, to texts from the satirical magazine *Krokodil,* opus 121
	Honorary Doctorate in Music, U.S.S.R.
	Honorary Member of Serbian Academy of Arts
1966	Eleventh String Quartet, opus 122
	"Preface to the Complete Collection of My Works and a Brief Meditation on This Preface," for bass and piano, opus 123
	Second Cello Concerto, opus 126
	Order of Lenin
	Hero of Socialist Labor
	Member of International Music Council of UNESCO
	Gold Medal of the British Royal Philharmonic Society
1967	Seven Romances for Soprano, Violin, Cello, and Piano, to poems by Alexander Blok, opus 127
	Second Violin Concerto, opus 129
	Grand Decoration of Honor in Silver for Services to the Republic of Austria
1968	Twelfth String Quartet, opus 133
	Sonata for Violin and Piano, opus 134
	Corresponding Member of the Bavarian Academy of Fine Arts

1969	Fourteenth Symphony, for soprano, bass, and chamber orchestra, to poems by Federico Garcia Lorca, Guillaume Apollinaire, Vilgelm Kukhelbecker, and Rainer Maria Rilke, opus 135
	Mozart Memorial Medal of the Mozart Society in Vienna
1970	*Fidelity*, cycle for male chorus, to poems by Yevgeny Dolmatovsky, opus 136; State Prize of the R.S.F.S.R., 1974
	Score for film *King Lear* (director, G. Kozintsev), opus 137
	Thirteenth String Quartet, opus 138
	March of the Soviet Police, for band, opus 139
	Honorary Member of the Society of Composers of Finland
1971	Fifteenth Symphony, opus 141
	Order of the October Revolution
1972	"Great Star of the Friendship Among People" in gold (German Democratic Republic)
	Honorary Doctorate in Music, Holy Trinity College (Dublin)
1973	Fourteenth String Quartet, opus 142; State Prize of the R.S.F.S.R., 1974
	Six Poems by Marina Tsvetayeva for Contralto and Piano, opus 143 (version for contralto and chamber orchestra, 1974, opus 143a)
	The Sonning Prize (Denmark)
	Honorary Doctorate of Fine Arts, Northwestern University (Evanston, Ill.)
1974	Fifteenth String Quartet, opus 144
	Suite for Bass and Piano, to poems by Michelangelo Buonarotti, opus 145 (version for bass and symphony orchestra, same year, opus 145a)
1975	Four Poems of Captain Lebyadkin (from Dostoevsky's novel *The Possessed*), for bass and piano, opus 146
	Sonata for Viola and Piano, opus 147
	Honorary Member of the French Academy of Fine Arts

INDEX

In subentries the name of Shostakovich is abbreviated as S.

Abendroth, Hermann, 71
Akhmatova, Anna Andreyevna, xvi, xxxvi, 56, 136, 137, 152n, 202-204, 217-218, 256; persecuted, 269-270, 272-273
Akimov, Nikolai Pavlovich, *Hamlet* production, 84-90
Alexandrov, Grigori, 250, 259-264
Andersen, Hans Christian, xxiv
Andronikov, Irakli Luarsabovich, 38
anti-Semitism, xxxv, xxxviin, 128, 131, 157-158, 166-167
Apollinaire, Guillaume, 182-184
Apostolov, Pavel Ivanovich, 184
Arkhangelsk, 113
Arnshtam, Leo Oskarovich (Lenya), 80, 273
Asafiev, Boris Vladimirovich, xxvi, 41-42 *and n,* 45, 61, 121n, 146, 182, 227, 230, 240, 241
Ashrafi, Mukhtar, 175

Babi Yar, 158-159; *see also* Yevtushenko
Bach, Johann Sebastian, xxii, 5, 54, 60, 125
Balakirev, Mili Alexeevich, 164, 229n, 236, 238
Balmont, Konstantin, 223n
Bartók, Bela, xxiv, 53, 219
Beethoven, Ludwig van, xxxii, 52, 71, 126-128, 141
Bekhterev, Vladimir, 192
Beliayev, Mitrofan Petrovich, 165, 264-265
Belinkov, Arkady, 76n
Benkendorf, Alexander Kristoforovich, 248n
Berg, Alban, 42-45; *Wozzeck,* 35, 42-44, 108

Beria, Lavrenti Pavlovich, 141, 151, 269
Bezymensk, Alexander, xxiv
Bizet, Georges, *Carmen,* 108
Bolshakov, Minister of Cinematography, 251-252
Boris Godunov, see Mussorgsky
Borodin, Alexander Porfirievich, 121n, 160-162, 229n; *Prince Igor,* 162, 241
Braga, Gaetano, "A Maiden's Prayer," 224
Brahms, Johannes, xxxii, 20, 173
Brecht, Bertolt, 109n
Brezhnev, Leonid, xx
Britten, Benjamin, xxx
Bruckner, Anton, 173
Budyonny, Semyon Mikhailovich, 100
Bukharin, Nikolai Ivanovich, 80n
Bulgakov, Mikhail Afanasievich, xvii, 83
Burns, Robert, 14

Chaliapin, Feodor Ivanovich, portrait of, 18
Chekhov, Anton Pavlovich, xiii, 10, 35, 43, 46, 82, 110, 149, 178-180, 194, 195, 223-225, 240, 242, 267-269
Chekhov, Mikhail, 85
Cherny, Sasha (Alexander Mikhailovich Glikberg), 78, 171, 252
Chiaureli, Mikhail Edisherovich, 151, 250
China, People's Republic of, 153
Chukhovsky, author, 75
Chulaki, Mikhail, 142
Churchill, Winston, 133n
Communist International of Youth (KIM), 150-151
Communist Party, S in, xxxix

283

Composers' Union, xxxix, 57, 115, 120n, 114, 150, 172–175, 220, 249, 253
Cui, Cesar Antonovich, 229n, 236
Czechoslovakia, Soviet invasion, xxxx

Dadaists, xxvi
Daniel, Yuli, xxxix–xxxx
Danilyevich, Lev Vasilyevich, 122n
Dargomyzhsky, Alexander, 234
Davidenko, Alexander, 112n, 248
Debussy, Claude, 62–63
Delson, Viktor Yulyevich, 122n
Diaghilev, Sergei Pavlovich, 129–130
Dmitriev, Vladimir, 19
Dostoevsky, Feodor Mikhailovich, xvii, xxviii; The Possessed, xlin, 237n, 269
Dostoevsky Reform Colony for Handicapped Children, 206
Dovzhenko, Alexander, 141
Dranishnikov, Vladimir, 44
Dubelt, Leonti Vasilyevich, 248n
Durov, clown, 15
Dzerzhinsky, Felix Edmundovich, 248n, 248
Dzerzhinsky, Ivan, 60, 139
Dzhabayev, Dzhambul, 209–211, 222

Ehrenburg, Ilya, xxxiv
Eisenstein, Sergei Mikhailovich, xxvii, 30n, 124n, 152n, 248, 250; and The Valkyrie, 131–133
England: Glazunov in, 74–75; S's music in, xxxiv
Experimental Studio of Chamber Opera, Leningrad, xiii

Fadeyev, Alexander Alexandrovich, 183n
family life and morality, 267–269
Fefer, Itsik, 198–199
Feuchtwanger, Lion, 200
Fiddler on the Roof, 158
films: as propaganda, 148–151; Stalin's authority over, 149, 248–252; Unforgettable 1919, Stalin portrayed in, 254–255
Fleishman, Veniamin, 31n, 225; Rothschild's Violin, xiii–xiv, 225
folk music, 219; imitations of, 216–217; Jewish, 156–157; Ukrainian singers shot, 214–215
food distribution, 92–93
formalism, xxix–xxx, xxxvi, xxxvii, xxxviii, 36n, 115, 139, 142, 144, 152; as conspiracy, 145–147; definition of, 83n
Frunze, Commissar, 102

Gabrieli, Andrea, 60
Gachev, Dina, 122
Garbo, Greta, 202

Gauk, Alexander Vasilyevich, 38n, 39
Gelovani, actor, 255
Gerdt, Elizaveta, 39
Germany, pact with Soviet Union, 128, 131, 229n
Gladkovsky, Arseny, 102
Glazunov, Alexander Konstantinovich, 20–22, 27–30, 40, 67–75, 120, 227–228, 230; character, 162–171; compositions, 163–164; drinking problem, 47–50, 59, 162; Raymonda (ballet), 45–46, 163; relationship with S, 45–51, 164; Suite from the Middle Ages, 163; as teacher, 58–63, 65
Glazunova, Elena Pavlovna, mother of the preceding, 70, 163, 165
Glebov, Igor, see Asafiev
Gliasser, Ignatiy Albertovich, 5
Gliasser, O. F., 5
Glière, Reinhold Moritzovich, The Red Poppy, 42
Glinka, Mikhail Ivanovich, 67, 129, 174, 207; A Life for the Tsar (Ivan Susanin), 134, 191, 240–241
Gnessin, Mikhail Fabianovich, 165, 207
Godowsky, Leopold, 73
Gogol, Nikolai Vasilyevich, xvii, xix, xxiv, 66, 180, 184, 191, 194, 205, 206, 210, 216, 222–223, 235, 242; grave, 16; The Inspector General, 205, 207, 222; The Nose, xxvii, 207–208
Gorky, Maxim, 106, 202, 203n, 224n, 260
Gorodetsky, Serge Mitrofanovich, 191
Great Friendship, The, see Muradeli
Grekov, Dr., 192, 272–273
Grekova, Elena Afanasyevna, 273
Griboyedov, Alexander, 81n
Gulag Archipelago, xxix, xxx
Gumilyov, Nikolai Stepanovich, 202–203n
gypsy music, 5–6, 224–225

Haydn, Franz Joseph, xxxii, 5, 60
Hindemith, Paul, xxiv, 42, 53, 72, 224–225
Hitler, Adolf, 99, 103, 155, 156; relations with Soviet Union, 128, 131, 187, 229n
Hoffmann, E. T. A., 232
housing arrangements, 90–92

Ilf, Ilya (Ilya Arnoldovich Fainsilberg) and Petrov, Yevgeny (Yevgeny Petrovich Kataev), xvii, 35n, 83, 94, 142, 197n, 202, 221, 250
Ilyinsky, Igor, 246
"Internationale," 256, 265
Ionin, Georgi, 205–207
Israel, 158
Ivan the Terrible, Tsar, 124, 192

284

Jewish folk music, 156–157
Jews, 156–158, 166; persecution of, 157; *see also* anti-Semitism
Josquin des Prés, 60

Kabalevsky, Dmitri Borisovich, 146*n*
Kaganovich, Lazar Moiseyevich, 81
Kalinin, Mikhail Ivanovich, 270
Kalmykov, Betal, 151
Karajan, Herbert von, 188
Karavaichuk, Oleg, 228
Karapetian, singer, 41
Karms, Daniil Ivanovich (Yuvachev), 9*n*
Kemal Ataturk, 112
Khachaturian, Aram, xxxvi, 148, 219, 242*n*; and national anthem, 256–261, 263
Khrennikov, Tikhon Nikolayevich, 120*n*, 138–139, 142, 146, 149–150, 153, 212*n*, 248–254; *Into the Storm,* 138–139, 142*n*
Khrushchev, Nikita, xxxvii, xxxviii, 33*n*, 152, 153, 264, 269*n*
Khubov, Georgi Nikitich, 153*n*
Kirov, Sergei Mironovich, 95, 151
Klemperer, Otto, xxiii
Klimov, choirmaster, 32
Komsomolskaya pravda, 212
Korneichuk, Alexander, 152–153
Koussevitsky, Serge, xxxiv
Koval, Marian Viktorovich (Kovalev), 142*n*, 153
Kozintsev, Grigori Mikhailovich, 84*n*
Krasnaya Nov', 189
Křenek, Ernst, xxiv, 42, 53, 95
Kronstadt Uprising, 15*n*, 97
Krylov, Ivan, 247
Ksenofontov, I., 212*n*
Kubatsky, Viktor, 113
Kurbsky, Prince Andrei Mikhailovich, 192
Kustodiev, Boris Mikhailovich, 16*n*, 17–20, 110; portrait of S, xxiii, 16–17

Lamm, Pavel Alexandrovich, 121*n*, 230
Landrin, George, 205
Lasso, Orlando di, 60
Lenin, Vladimir Ilich, xxii, 7, 24, 37, 49, 104, 113*n*, 149, 270; as character in operas, 142*n*; musical tastes, 94–95; "political will," 23*n*, 80*n*
Leningrad, xx–xxi; Bolshoi Dramatic Theater, 19; Bolshoi Theater, xxix, 36–37, 111, 114, 119, 128, 131, 132, 142, 145, 259; Bright Reel Theater, 9–11; Conservatory, xxii, xxiii, 6, 20*n*, 28–30, 50–51, 55–61, 65, 67, 69–70, 165–167, 169; festival of S's music xii–xiii; Finland Station, march to, xxii, 7; Kirov Theater, 32, 42, 95*n*, 228; Maryinsky Theater, 18, 44, 95*n*, 128, 129,

Leningrad (Continued)
191; Shidlovskaya Gymnasium, 5, 7, 9; Theater of Young Workers (TRAM), 31*n*, 109, 112; in World War II, xxxiii, 103
Lermontov, Mikhail Yuryevich, 46*n*, 83, 164
Leskov, Nikolai Semyonovich, xxvii, 18*n*, 19, 37, 242; *Lady Macbeth of Mtsensk District,* 18–19, 106, 107, 110
lezghinka, 143–145
Liadov, Anatol, 50, 264–265
Liszt, Franz, 51–52, 71, 129
Literaturnaya gazeta, 185
Litvinov, Maksim Maksimovich, 128
Lopukhov, Fyodor Vasilyevich, 42*n*
Lunacharsky, Anatoly Vasilyevich, 95, 110*n*, 167

Mahler, Gustav, xxxii, 38, 42, 69, 173
Malashkin, Sergei, *Moon from the Right,* 109
Malenkov, Georgi Maximilianovich, 269–270
Malko, Nikolai Andreyevich, 53
Malraux, André, 199
Mandelstam, Nadezhda, 191*n*
Mandelstam, Osip, xxii, 131*n*
Mayakovsky, Vladimir Vladimirovich, xxvii, 30*n*, 44, 82, 212, 216, 245–248, 255; *The Bedbug,* 3*n*, 82, 228, 246–247; monument, 30
Melik-Pashayev, Alexander, 261
Mendeleyev, Dmitri, xxi
Mendelson-Prokofieva, Mira Alexandrovna, 37
Meyerbeer, Giacomo, 129
Meyerhold, Vsevolod Emilyevich, xxvii, xxix, 3–4 *and n,* 17, 30*n*, 57, 88, 97, 105, 109, 115, 137, 156, 205, 207, 213, 230, 245–247; conflict with Nemirovich-Danchenko, 63–65; last work in theater, 132–133; productions, 81–83; relationship with S, 77–84
Meyerhold, Zinada, *see* Raikh
Miaskovsky, Nikolai Yakovlevich, xxxvi, 31, 148; correspondence with Prokofiev, 37–38
Mighty Five (composers), 229*n*
Mikhoels, Solomon Mikhailovich, 87*n*
Milhaud, Darius, 42
Mission to Moscow, film, 201
Molotov, Vyacheslav Mikhailovich, 128, 147*n*
Moscow: Conservatory, 31*n*, 121, 172, 173; Stanislavsky Opera Theater, 132; Theater of Meyerhold, 64–65, 77–79, 81, 83, 247
Moscow Art Theater, 19*n*, 64, 87, 90, 92
Mosfilm, 250–251, 255
Moskvin, actor, 64
Mozart, Wolfgang Amadeus, xxxii, 5, 60, 125, 126; Jupiter Symphony, 62

Mravinsky, Yevgeny Alexandrovich, xi, xxxiii–xxxiv, 22n, 183n, 266

Muradeli, Vano Ilyich, 142–145; *The Great Friendship,* 24n, 142–145; resolution against, xxxvi, 142–144, 151, 152; second resolution on, 152–153

music: composers exiled to provinces, 213, 215–217; contemporary Russian attitudes on, 173–177, 219–222; folk, *see* folk music; government supervision of, 138–147; gypsy, 5–6, 224–225; Mighty Five (composers), 229n; and national culture, 214, 216, 219–222; Nepman (pop), 224n; plagiarism, 172–175; taste of Soviet leaders, 125–134; *see also* Stalin; Western, prejudice against, 173

musicians persecuted by government, 120–123

Mussolini, Benito, 214

Mussorgsky, Modest Petrovich, xxv, xxvi, xl, 8, 54, 121n, 129, 130, 156, 167, 194, 218, 226–244; *Biron,* 229; *Boris Godunov,* 182, 183, 192, 226–227, 229–234, 240; death, 239; Khovanshchina, 110, 240; *Songs and Dances of Death,* orchestration by S, 108n, 182, 235, 240; *Without the Sun,* 240

Nalbandian, painter, 255–256

Narodniki, 7n

national anthem, Soviet, planned, 256–264

nationalistic campaign, inventions made in Russia, 173n

Nekrasov, Nikolai, 235

Nemirovich-Danchenko, Vladimir Ivanovich, 19n, 63–65, 111, 201

Nepman music, 224n

New Babylon, film, 149n, 150–151

New Economic Policy (NEP), xxiv, 224n

Nicholas I, Tsar, 153, 192

Nikolayev, Leonid, xxii, 51, 52, 57, 58, 188

Novy mir, xxxix

Oberiu Circle, xxvi

Oborin, Lev, 113

Oistrakh, David, 113

Oleinikov, Nikolai Makarovich, 128n, 266

Olesha, Yuri Karlovich, 76

oprichniki, 124n

Ordzhonikidze, Grigo (Sergo) Konstantinovich, 24n, 102, 142–143

Ormandy, Eugene, xxxiv

Ostrovsky, Alexander Nikolaevich, 83

Palestrina, Giovanni, 60

Pasternak, Boris Leonidovich, xl, 30n, 54, 87, 113n, 188, 217–218

Paul I, Tsar, 192

Pazovsky, Ari, 191

Pechkovsky, Nikolai, 115–116

Petersburg (Petrograd), *see* Leningrad

Petipa, Marius, 45–46

Petri, Egon, 71

Petrov, Yevgeny (Yevgeny Petrovich Kataev), *see* Ilf

Plutarch, 27

Pogrebov, musician, 37

Poland, S's background in, xxi, 34

Popov, Gavril Nikolayevich, xxxvi, 146n, 148

Popov, Sergei, 121

Poskrebyshev, Stalin's secretary, 252

Potsdam conference, 57

Pravda, xxix, 99, 151, 185; "Balletic Falsity," 119; "Muddle Instead of Music," xxviii–xxix, 36, 65, 76n, 98, 113–114, 119; second article against S, 114–115

Preis, Alexander Germanovich, 106, 111, 205–206, 208

Prokofiev, Sergei Sergeevich, xxiv, xxxii, xxxvi, 6, 7, 27–28, 34–38, 66, 72, 120n, 121n, 130, 142n, 144, 148, 153, 219, 224, 228n, 248; correspondence with Miaskovsky, 37–38; as formalist, 146, 147; *Love for Three Oranges,* 208; *Scythian Suite,* 27; *Semyon Kotko,* 132–133

Psalms of David, 184

Pshibyshevsky, Boleslav, 121–122

Punin, Nikolai Nikolayevich, 202, 203n

Pushkin, Alexander Sergeevich, xx, xxiv, xxvii, 30–31, 34, 45, 46, 66, 151, 194, 201, 222, 232, 248

Pushkin, Natalya Nikolayevna, 40

Radek, Karl Berngardovich, 80n

Raikh, Zinaida Nikolayevna, wife of Meyerhold, 78–80, 85, 88–89, 207

Red Army chorus, 23, 190, 259–260

Repin, Ilya Efimovich, 182–183

revisionism, 153

Ribbentrop, Joachim von, 128

Rimsky-Korsakov, Nikolai Andreevich, xxiii, 28, 34, 60, 61, 63, 65, 68, 159, 160, 162, 163, 169, 172, 216, 220, 229n, 240; *Boris Godunov* edited by, 226–227, 231, 233–235; hostility to Tchaikovsky, 66–67, 218; *Pskovitianka,* 241; *Sadko,* 129–130; *Tale of the City of Kitezh,* 110n

Robeson, Paul, 198–199

Rodzinski, Artur, xxviii, xxxiv

Rolland, Romain, 122, 200

Romm, Mikhail, 250, 251

Rostropovich, Mstislav Leopoldovich, 108n, 258, 259

Rozanova, music teacher, 6

Rubinstein, Anton, 71, 238

Russian Association of Proletarian Musicians (RAPM), 112

Russian Association of Proletarian Writers (RAPP), 112
Russian Revolution of 1905, 8

Sabinsky, Cheslav, 110
Sakharov, Andrei Dmitriyevich, xl, 243n
Shchedrin, N. (Mikhail Evgrafovich Saltykov), 242
Schnabel, Artur, 71
Schreker, composer, 63
Schubert, Franz, 125
Schuman, William, 173
Schumann, Robert, 57, 173
Scriabin, Alexander Nikolaevich, 40, 45, 61–62
Serebriakov, Pavel Alexeyevich, 55–56
Shakespeare, William, 86–87, 194; *Hamlet*, Russian productions, 83–90; *King Lear*, 84–87, 131n; *Macbeth*, 86
Shaporin, Yuri Alexandrovich, 44n
Shaw, George Bernard, 200
Shcherbachev, composer, 35
Shchukin, Boris, 89–90
Shebalin, Vissarion Yakovlevich (Ronya), xxxvi, 31, 112, 121, 148
Shneyerson, Grigori Mikhailovich, 34n
Sholokhov, Mikhail Aleksandrovich, 60, 212n
Sholom Aleichem (Solomon Rabinowitz), 72
Shostakovich, Boleslav, grandfather of Dmitri, xxi
Shostakovich, Dmitri:
    Biography: birth, xx; childhood and early life, xxi–xxiii, 4–11, 13–16; composing techniques in old age, 228; death, xviii, xli; end of his life, xl–xli; family, xxi, 5–8; and films, 148–151; as formalist conspirator, 145–147; later years, xxxvii–xli; marriages, xxx, xxxvii, xl; meets Stalin, 254, 256, 260–263; and national anthem, 256–264; obituaries, xix–xx, xli; *Pravda* attacks him, 113–115, 119; see also *Pravda;* Stalin's relationship with him, xxviii–xxxi, xxxiii, xxxvi, xxxvii, 140–142, 147–150, 197, 198, 256; in Turkey, 112–113, 147–148; in United States, xxxvii–xxxviii, 147–148, 169, 198
    Ideas and Opinions: childhood, 6, 8–9, 240; communal apartments, 91–92; composers asking for help, 170–171; death, 14–16, 180–182, 241, 243; depression and anxiety, 116–119; eternity, 159–160; fear, 14–16, 116–119; Jews, 156–158; new life style in music, 93–94; old age, 240, 275–276; pessimism, 241–243; plagiarism, 172–175, 212n; praise and criticism, 236–238; public appearances, 237; religion and superstition, 187–188; rudeness, 23–27; saviors of mankind, 186–187; talking about

Shostakovich, Dmitri (Continued)
    music, 196–198; torture, 123–125; tyranny, 134–137, 155–156; tyrants as patrons of arts, 123, 125, 128; Western humanists, 199–205; Western journalists, 196–197; women's movement, 161–162; work, 20, 195
    Works: The Bedbug, music for Mayakovsky's play, 3n, 82, 246–247; *The Black Monk,* unwritten, 223–225, 240; *Bolt* (ballet), 42n, 85n, 111; *Bright Stream* (ballet), 114; *The Golden Age* (ballet), 111; Eighth Quartet, xi, xii, 156; Eighth Symphony, xxxiii–xxxv, 22n, 136, 138–140, 155, 181, 197, 240; Eleventh Symphony, xi–xii, xxxii, 8, 240; *The Execution of Stepan Razin,* 152, 155, 185, 240; Fifteenth Symphony, 225; Fifth Symphony, xxxi–xxxiii, xxxvii, 22n, 39, 135, 136, 148, 156, 183–184, 224, 265–266; First Piano Sonata, xii; First Symphony, xxiii–xxiv, 11–12, 45, 53n, 75, 80, 156; First Violin Concerto, xxxvii, 157; "Four Poems of Captain Lebyadkin," 237n; Fourteenth Symphony, xxx, xli, 152, 181–184, 240, 242; Fourth Quartet, 157; Fourth Symphony, xxx, xxxix, 23, 39, 119, 155, 158, 212; *From Jewish Folk Poetry* (Jewish Cycle), xi, xxxvii, 157, 274; "Funeral March in Memory of the Victims of the Revolution," xxii, 7; *The Gamblers,* 222–223; *The Golden Age* (ballet), 228n; *The Gypsies,* 66; *Hamlet,* music for, 83; *Katerina Izmailova* (second version of *Lady Macbeth*), xxviii, xxxix, 19, 43, 107, 111, 154; *King Lear,* music for, 84n; *Lady Macbeth of Mtsensk District,* xii, xxvii–xxix, 16n, 18–19, 36, 82, 85n, 98, 106–108, 110–112, 114, 119, 156, 181, 200, 206, 267–268; "Luminary," xxxixn; "March of the Soviet Police," xxxixn, 179; "McPherson Before Execution," 14; Mussorgsky's *Boris Godunov* edited, 226–227, 229–234, 240; Mussorgsky's *Songs and Dances of Death,* orchestration, 108n, 182, 235, 240; Ninth Symphony, xxxv, 22n, 140–142, 146, 153; *The Nose,* xxvii–xxviii, 18, 19, 43, 78, 82, 95, 111, 205–208, 238; "Preface to the Complete Collection of My Works and a Brief Meditation on This Preface," xxxix; *Rothschild's Violin,* Fleishman's work, finished, xiii–xiv, 225; *Satires,* 108n, Second Piano Sonata, 53; Second Symphony, 7, 53n; Seventh (Leningrad) Symphony, xxxii–xxxv, 25, 66, 136–137, 139–140, 154–156, 183, 184, 200, 224, 240; Sixth Symphony, 22n, 39n, 119, 230; *The Story of the Priest and His Worker Balda,* 19;

Shostakovich, Dmitri (Continued)
  The Story of the Silly Mouse, 19; "A Symphonic Dedication to October," xxiv–xxv; "Tea for Two," transcription from Youmans, 53*n*; Tenth Symphony, xxxviii, 22*n*, 141; Thirteenth Symphony, xxxviii*n*, 151–152, 155, 185, 240; Twelfth Symphony, 7, 141; vocal suite on poems of Michelangelo, xxxxi*n*
Shostakovich, Dmitri Boleslavovich, father of Dmitri, xxi, xxii, 5–6, 48–49, 224, 272
Shostakovich, Galya, daughter of Dmitri, xxx
Shostakovich, Irina Supinskaya, wife of Dmitri, xl
Shostakovich, Margarita Kainova, wife of Dmitri, xxxvii
Shostakovich, Maria, sister of Dmitri, xxii, 20
Shostakovich, Maxim, son of Dmitri, xii, xxx, xxxiv*n*
Shostakovich, Nina Varzar, wife of Dmitri, xxx, xxxvii, 85*n*, 108
Shostakovich, Pyotr, great-grandfather of Dmitri, xxi
Shostakovich, Sofia Vasilyevna, mother of Dmitri, xxi–xxii, 5, 6
Shostakovich, Zoya, sister of Dmitri, xxii
Shvarts, Yevgeny, 190
Simeonov, Konstantin, 107
Simonov, Konstantin, 210
Sinyavsky, Andrei, xxxix–xxxx
Six, Les, xxiv
Skuratov, Malyuta, 124, 192
Smolich, Nikola Vasilyevich, 111*n*, 207
Sofronitsky, Vladimir Vladimirovich, 44*n*, 57, 72
Sokolovsky, Mikhail Vladimirovich, 31
Sollertinsky, Ivan Ivanovich, xxxii, 25*n*, 25–26, 38–42, 69, 108, 198, 239*n*
Sologub, Fyodor Kuzmich, 12–14
Solzhenitsyn, Aleksandr Isayevich, xxxix, xli, 187*n*, 199*n*, 212*n*, 242*n*
Sovetskaya muzyka, xvii, 56, 142*n*, 153
Stalin, Joseph, 15*n*, 18*n*, 24*n*, 30*n*, 37, 56*n*, 57, 64, 67, 80*n*, 81*n*, 95*n*, 98, 100, 112*n*, 152, 153, 155, 156, 204, 212; and *Boris Godunov,* 232–233; *Brief Biography,* 189; censorship of writers, 270–272; character and temperament, 137–138, 187–194, 198, 199; control of culture and creative arts, xxx–xxxi, xxxv–xxxvi, 36*n*, 95–96, 113–114, 120*n*, 139, 146, 147; death, xxxviii, 192, 194; dislikes Shakespeare, 86–87; and family relations, 267–268; in film, *Unforgettable 1919,* 254–255; films controlled, 149, 248–252; hatred of Allies, 138, 142; "historical resolutions" after World War II, xxxv–xxxvi; Khrushchev denounces,

Stalin, Joseph (Continued)
  xxxviii; mental condition, 192–193; and Muradeli, 142–143, 145; musical taste, 100, 126–128, 134, 143, 190, 232, 241; and national anthem, 256–264; "On the Bases of Leninism," 212*n*; portraits of, 254–255; praise and flattery of, 210–211, 214, 218, 248, 253–254; public reaction against, 134–135; relationship with Hitler, 128, 131, 133–134, 187, 229*n*; relationship with S, xxviii–xxxi, xxxiii, xxxvi, xxxvii, 140–142, 147–150, 197, 198, 256, 260–263; Rome as influence on, 214; rudeness, 23–24; and Tukhachevsky, 98, 99, 102–104; Western impressions of, 200
Stanislavski, Konstantin, 90, 92, 126
Stasov, Vladimir Vasilievich, 226, 236, 243
Steinberg, Maximilian Oseyevich, xxiii, 28*n*, 29, 66–68, 121
Steinberg, Nadezhda Nikolayevna, 66
Stiedry, Fritz, 120
Stokowski, Leopold, xxiii, xxxiv
Stolypin, Peter Arkadyevich, 166
Strauss, Johann, 63
Strauss, Richard: *Death and Transfiguration,* 182; *Salome,* 63
Stravinsky, Igor Fyodorivich, xxiv, xxxii, 6, 8, 32–34, 36, 42, 52, 130, 184, 191, 197–198, 218, 219; life, 33*n*; works, S's opinion of, 32–33, 62
Strelnikov, Nikolai, 43
"Suliko," 143*n*, 216
Szigeti, Joseph, 71

Taneyev, Sergei Ivanovich, 68
Tarkovsky, Andrei Arsenyevich, 15*n*
Tchaikovsky, Peter Ilich, xxxii, 5, 108, 235; *1812 Overture,* 140; *Eugene Onegin,* 41, 129; *The Queen of Spades,* 57, 81, 88, 115, 182, 237*n*; Rimsky-Korsakov's hostility to him, 66–67, 218; *Romeo and Juliet,* 266; *Voyevode,* 121
Tinyakov, poet, 176–177
Tishchenko, Boris Ivanovich, 218, 274
Tolstoi, Alexei, 136, 224
Tolstoy, Leo, 10, 269; *Anna Karenina,* American film version, 201–202; *War and Peace,* 8
torture, 123–125
Toscanini, Arturo, xxiv, xxviii, xxxv, 24–25
Tretyakov, Sergei Mikhailovich, 109*n*
Trotsky, Leon, 80
Truman, Harry S, 57
Tsekhanovsky, Mikhail, 19
Tukhachevsky, Mikhail Nikolayevich, xxix, 15*n*, 17, 121, 137, 156; death, 116; mother of, 268; relationship with S, 96–105; in World War II, 103–104

Turgenev, Ivan Sergeevich, 266–267
Turkey, S in 112–113, 147–148
Tuskiya, Iona, 259, 263
Tynyanov, Yuri, *Lieutenant Kije,* 211
Tyshler, Alexander Grigoryevich, 131

Ukraine, blind folk singers, 214–215
United States, 151; radio broadcasts in Russian, 185n; S in, xxxvii–xxxviii, 147–148, 169, 198; S's attitude toward, xxxviii; S's music in, xxxiv–xxxv

Vasilyeva, Raya, 151
Verdi, Giuseppe, *Otello,* 115, 182
Vishinsky, Andrei Yanuaryevich, 133–134
Vishnevskaya, Galina Pavlovna, 108n
Volkov, Solomon, associated with S, xii–xviii
Volynsky, Akim Lvovich (Flekser), 10–11; memorial service for, 11–14
Voronsky, Alexander Konstantinovich, 189–190
Voroshilov, Kliment Efremovich, 100
Vygodsky, Nikolai, 121

Wagner, Richard, 130–131, 173, 238; popularity in Soviet Union, 128–129, 134; *Rienzi,* 129; *The Ring of the Nibelung,* 128; *The Valkyrie,* 63, 128, 131–134
Wallace, Henry, 202
Walter, Bruno, xxiii
Warsaw, 104
Weingartner, Felix, 71

White Sea Canal, 199, 202
Willkie, Wendell, 137
Wood, Sir Henry Joseph, xxxiv
World War II, 103–104, 134–136, 155, 156, 229; Stalin's hatred of Allies, 138, 142

Yagodkin, Vladimir, xx
Yakobson, Leonid Veniaminovich, 228n
Yarustovsky, Boris Mikhailovich, 34n
Yevtushenko, Yevgeny, xxxviin, xxxviii, 152, 185, 203; "Babi Yar," 151n, 158–159, 185
Yezhov, Nikolai Ivanovich, 210
Yudina, Maria Veniaminovna, 44n, 51–58, 72, 188, 193–195
yurodivy, xxv–xxvii, xxxvi, xxxviii, xxxx, 22, 55, 192, 194, 233, 235
Yuvachev, *see* Karms

Zamyatin, Yevgeny Ivanovich, 18n, 19, 179, 206, 264–265
Zaslavsky, David Iosifovich, 113–114
Zhdanov, Andrei Alexandrovich, 56, 100, 145–147, 159, 191, 203, 204, 269–272
Zhilayev, Nikolai Sergeevich, 17n, 121
Zhukovsky, Vasili Andreevich, 46
Zinoviev, Grigori Evseyevich, 80n, 95
Zoshchenko, Mikhail Mikhailovich, xvii, xxvi, xxxvi, xxxixn, 9n, 13–14, 48, 91, 94, 180, 202–204, 237, 242, 264–267, 269; character and ideas, 14, 116–118, 266–267; persecuted, 269–272

SOLOMON VOLKOV

Solomon Volkov was born in Leninabad, Central Asia, in 1944, received his diploma with honors from the Rimsky-Korsakov State Conservatory in 1967, and continued graduate work in musicology at the Conservatory until 1971. His principal research has been in the history and aesthetics of Russian and Soviet music, and in the psychology of musical perception and performance. He published numerous articles in scholarly and popular journals, wrote a well-received book, *Young Composers of Leningrad,* in 1971, was a senior editor of *Sovetskaya muzyka,* the journal of the Composers' Union and the Ministry of Culture of the U.S.S.R., and was the artistic director of the Experimental Studio of Chamber Opera. He became a member of the Composers' Union in 1972.

Mr. Volkov came to the United States in June 1976. Since then he has been a Research Associate at the Russian Institute of Columbia University in New York City. In addition to preparing *Testimony* for publication, he has published articles on various musical subjects in *The New York Times, The New Republic, Musical America, The Musical Quarterly,* and other periodicals in the United States and Europe. He has presented papers at La Biennale in Venice and at the Twelfth Congress of the International Musicological Society in Berkeley, California. He and his wife, Marianna Volkov, a pianist and photographer, live in New York.